D0892309

Sociology of Work

THE PINE FORGE PRESS SOCIAL SCIENCE LIBRARY

The McDonaldization of Society: An Investigation Into the Changing Character of Contemporary Social Life *by George Ritzer*

Sociological Snapshots: Seeing Social Structure and Change in Everyday Life *by Jack Levin*

What Is Society? Reflections on Freedom, Order, and Change *by Earl Babbie*

The Production of Reality: Essays and Readings in Social Psychology *by Peter Kollock and Jodi O'Brien*

Adventures in Social Research: Data Analysis Using SPSS® *by Earl Babbie and Fred Halley*

Crime and Everyday Life: Insights and Implications for Society *by Marcus Felson*

Sociology of Work: Perspectives, Analyses, Issues *by Richard H. Hall*

Aging: Concepts and Controversies *by Harry R. Moody, Jr.*

Worlds of Difference: Inequality in the Aging Experience *by Eleanor Palo Stoller and Rose Campbell Gibson*

Forthcoming

Sociology for a New Century *A Pine Forge Press Series edited by Charles Ragin, Wendy Griswold, and Larry Griffin*

- **Social Psychology and Social Institutions** *by Denise D. and William T. Bielby*
- **The Social Ecology of Natural Resources and Development** *by Stephen G. Bunker*
- **How Societies Change** *by Daniel Chirot*
- **Ethnic Dynamics in the Modern World: Continuity and Transformation** *by Stephen Cornell*
- **Sociology of Childhood** *by William A. Corsaro*
- **Cultures and Societies in a Changing World** *by Wendy Griswold*
- **Crime and Disrepute: Comparative Perspectives** *by John Hagan*
- **Racism and the Modern World: Sociological Perspectives** *by Wilmot James*
- **Religion in the Global Village** *by Lester Kurtz*
- **Waves of Democracy** *by John Markoff*
- **Organizations in a World Economy** *by Walter W. Powell*
- **Constructing Social Research** *by Charles C. Ragin*
- **Women, Men, and Work** *by Barbara Reskin and Irene Padavic*
- **Cities in a World Economy** *by Saskia Sassen*

Sociology of Work

PERSPECTIVES, ANALYSES, AND ISSUES

Richard H. Hall
STATE UNIVERSITY OF NEW YORK, ALBANY

With contributions by Robert T. Buttram
A. B. FREEMAN SCHOOL OF BUSINESS,
TULANE UNIVERSITY

PINE FORGE PRESS
Thousand Oaks • London • New Delhi

For information, address:

 PINE FORGE PRESS
A Sage Publications Company
2455 Teller Road
Thousand Oaks, California 91320

Copy Editor: Steve Summerlight
Production Editor: Megan M. McCue
Designer: Lisa S. Mirski
Typesetter: Danielle Dillahunt
Cover: Paula Shuhert

Printed in the United States of America

Library of Congress Cataloging-in-Publication Data

Hall, Richard H., 1934-

    Sociology of work: perspectives, analyses, and issues/ Richard
H. Hall; with contributions by Robert T. Buttram.
      p. cm. — (Pine Forge Press social science library)
    Includes bibliographical references and index.
    ISBN 0-8039-9003-0 (pb : acid-free paper)
    1. Industrial sociology. I. Buttram, Robert T. II. Title.
III. Series.
HD6955.H3 1994
306.3'6—dc20   93-27788
                                        CIP

 This book is printed on acid-free paper that meets
Environmental Protection Agency standards for recycled
paper.

94 95 96 97 10 9 8 7 6 5 4 3 2 1

This book is dedicated to my students

ABOUT THE AUTHORS

Richard H. Hall is Distinguished Service Professor of Sociology and former Dean, College of Social and Behavioral Sciences, at the State University of New York at Albany. Former editor of *Work and Occupations* and a respected scholar in the field of organizations, his other works include *Organizations: Structures, Processes, and Outcomes* (5th ed.).

Robert T. Buttram currently studies organizational behavior at the A. B. Freeman School of Business, Tulane University, New Orleans, where he serves as instructor and research assistant. He holds a master's degree in social psychology from Purdue University and a bachelor's of science in psychology from Ball State University.

ABOUT THE PUBLISHER

Pine Forge Press is a new educational publisher, dedicated to publishing innovative books and software throughout the social sciences. On this and any other of our publications, we welcome your comments and suggestions.

Please call or write us at:

Pine Forge Press
A Sage Publications Company
2455 Teller Road
Thousand Oaks, CA 91320
(805) 499-0721
Internet: sdr@pfp.sagepub.com

Contents

Preface

In the United States and in other post-industrial societies (as sociologist Daniel Bell named them), few realms of human activity are more central to human existence than the work we, and others, do. Not only do most of us spend the majority of our time first preparing for work and then working, but the very meaning of our existences as well as the identities that we attach to ourselves are inextricably linked to our work. How many of us, for example, after meeting someone for the first time, seek to establish an identity for that person by asking "what do you do?" or "what's your major?" or some other work-related question? And how do our impressions of others change once we know their occupations and we interpret them through our own socially constructed view of the world?

The work of others is equally important to our lives. Even for the most independent among us, the way we live is dependent on the labor of thousands, even millions of others, not just in the workforce of our own society, but from many quarters of the globe. To cite one common example, think about the considerable workforce and the complex, interconnected tasks that are involved in bringing us a television program that we turn on and ordinarily take for granted. Actors, actresses, and stand-ins; directors and producers; camera crews and sound technicians; writers and editors; make-up artists and drama coaches; publicists and agents; lawyers and financiers all comprise a mere fraction of the complex labor network involved. Beyond the people creating and marketing the program, consider the other groups involved in bringing it to our attention. Who manufactured the various parts of our television set and where were the parts made? (Probably several countries). Where were the components of our television assembled and by whom? (Perhaps a different workforce in another country). Who was involved in shipping the television to its location of purchase? What people and organizations were involved in getting the program's electronic signal delivered to the set? Regardless of our stations or inclinations in life, our lives are inextricably bound to the activities and roles of the world's labor force.

The Sociological Perspective

Sociology assumes a constantly changing, reciprocal relationship between individuals and the society we have created. Sociological research into the nature of work, therefore, addresses a number of fundamental questions related to the ways in which individuals view and shape their labor and how the institution of work, in turn, shapes us and other aspects of our social lives. A random selection of a few of those questions include: Why do some organizations (be they schools, offices, or factories) create more value with less material resources at their disposal than others? Why are most physicians and dentists in Russia today women, whereas these medical professions are occupied primarily by men in the United States? Why, contrary to the principles of economics, do women earn less than men for the same work in almost all of the world's societies? Why does a high school or college diploma get a person a better job than someone with the same amount of education but no diploma? Why is the work in a society unequally distributed among its members along boundaries marked by gender, race, and social class? Are these inequalities changing and if so, how and in what directions? Under what conditions (if any) does the division of household work within a family become equally shared between couples? Are jobs becoming more routinized and less satisfying for the people who perform them or is the opposite taking place in our society? The process of finding reliable answers to these and other such questions is what makes the sociology of work so fascinating.

Problems in Teaching the Undergraduate Course

Research into such questions (produced by sociologists as well as labor economists, industrial psychologists, historians, anthropologists, and others) produces a vast and disparate literature and therein lies a dilemma in teaching the subject effectively to undergraduate students. On the one hand, most sociologists would like to teach a first course that fairly represents and introduces the field as a whole. But because the sociology of work is so broad and the types of questions asked are at such different levels of analysis, the textbooks currently available to support such an approach tend to be descriptive surveys of the various subfields and therefore have an unfortunate tendency to leave students with a forgettable assortment of facts about seemingly random topics. At the other end of the teaching spectrum, undergraduate students can get more explanatory power and acquaintance with theory from a sociology of work course by reading a variety of excellent research monographs such as Rosabeth Kanter's *Men and Women of the Corporation*, Arlie Hoschild's *The Managed Heart* or Robert Jackall's *Moral Mazes*. But this approach has its limitations as well. Undergraduates often have a difficult time mastering such works thoroughly and relating the ideas to the course as a whole. My own teaching experience suggests that assigning one or two of these monographs is highly worthwhile, but I still feel the need to accompany them with a text that provides my students with an effective foundation for the course as a whole. I want my students to have a view of the entire field (vast and jumbled though it may be), what the important perspectives are, and how these various "lenses" can often be profitably used in combination with one another to analyze and interpret.

Rationale for This Text

The content of this book is rooted in an earlier book, *Dimensions of Work,* that I wrote a number of years ago, but has been entirely rewritten with the needs of the undergraduate sociology of work course in mind. I have specifically written this text so that instructors can adopt flexibly its use and steer their course in the direction of their choice. The book provides a current, clear, and representative account of the many important studies comprising the sociology of work field. At the same time, the book is sufficiently short and economically priced so that it can be used in addition to a variety of other monographs in the field. Moreover, the text is not merely descriptive; the various chapters of the book provide different dimensions or "lenses" that students can use to interpret and analyze the work issues that interest them most.

Chapter 3, for example, looks at work from the individual's perspective: how do people create meaning in their work and derive satisfaction from their jobs? Chapter 4 looks at the classic relationship between social status and work, and the various explanations for this relationship. Chapter 5 provides another interesting way to see how society values different forms of work by looking at job content and labor market perspectives. The next three chapters study age, gender, race, ethnicity, and religion and ways in which these socially constructed variables shape the structure of work and how we experience it. The final group of chapters on the organizational dimension of work, power, and work and family issues provide additional lenses at the macroscopic level that examine how work is structured and experienced. A concluding chapter explores the relationship between the book's various perspectives on work and the global, social forces that affect it as well as the workplaces and work issues that students are likely to experience early in our next century.

Sociological Interpretations of Work and Workplace Issues

In my experience, one of the most difficult teaching assignments in an undergraduate course is making the literature of the field (which is highly abstract and dry) meaningful to students.

Throughout this book, I have tried to do this in the same way I do in my teaching, by turning the literature back onto students' personal experience of work and the concerns they have about their futures. To amplify this quality in my text, Robert T. Buttram from the A. B. Freeman School of Business at Tulane University has written special application essays at the end of each chapter. These are excellent extended examples illustrating how the dimensions or "lenses" in each of the chapters can be used to enrich our understanding of a work or workplace issue that concerns us all.

Acknowledgments

I want to thank a group of people who have made major contributions to this project. As noted, the applications at the end of each chapter were written by Robert T. Buttram of the A. B. Freeman School of Business, Tulane University. I thank him sincerely for his work. In addition, I hope that you find simple and direct writing in these chapters. My manuscript editor Becky Smith has gone over each page and clarified matters or forced me to clarify them. She has been completely helpful and supportive. Susan McKie and Chiara Huddleston of Pine Forge Press have been particularly helpful in the evolution of this book from first draft to finished chapters. I also owe particular thanks to Michelle "Missy" Tillapaugh for her willingness to pitch in at a moment's notice on some project that had nothing to do with her role as Secretary to the Dean. She has been great. Steve Rutter of Pine Forge Press has been the rudder for this entire operation. He has pushed and prodded and nudged and shoved toward revision and completion. He has always done it in a gracious and supportive way. I am grateful to him.

Finally, I want to thank my wife Sherry for her good cheer and support. I try very hard not to take my work home, but she can tell when I am worried and frustrated. She makes me the opposite.

Richard H. Hall

1   The Nature of Work

Why study work? To me the answer is easy: It is what I do. It takes up more time in my life than anything else. I get a lot of enjoyment out of my work (granted, some days more than others). Work is vital to the way I think about myself.

If I move away from myself and think about its broader consequences, I see that work affects *who* one marries or even *if* one marries. The kind of work people do even affects whether they stay married. Work also affects the number of children people have. I have known situations in which work has affected abortion decisions.

Work has policy implications as well. Certainly, work-related issues such as welfare and unemployment, sexual harassment in the workplace, child-care and elder-care benefits, and pension plans are part of the social fabric and political discourse in the United States.

At an even broader level, work-related issues have global implications. They were at the core of the breakup of the former Soviet Russian system and Eastern European socialism. Work relationships have been key to the startling rise of such Pacific Rim nations as Singapore, Hong Kong, Taiwan, South Korea, and Japan. And they are central to comparisons between U.S. and Japanese workers.

It is vital to note that work has personal, microlevel implications, as well as broader, macrolevel implications. In this book, we will deal with both levels of analysis.

Definitions of Work

The purpose of this first chapter is to consider what work is and is not. As you will see very shortly, work involves many things that we do not consider in our casual, contemporary, everyday conceptualizations of work.

I begin with a personal example that involves an activity that most people would find antithetical to work: downhill or alpine skiing. Skiing would appear to be a form of recreation, whether thought of in terms of fun, danger, hedonism, invigoration, après-ski partying, or whatever.

I love to ski. I am a proud member of the National Ski Patrol System, Incorporated, of the United States. Ski patrollers are the people who help injured skiers and try to prevent such injuries. When I am ski patrolling, I am not paid, although there are paid "professional" ski patrollers, particularly at larger ski areas.

During ski season, I am on duty every Saturday during the day and every Tuesday night. I wear a uniform, to set me apart from so-called civilians who are not on the ski patrol. Being a ski patroller provides me with a certain status and prestige among skiers. And although I am a volunteer, I do get some slight financial remuneration: a lift ticket for the next ski season for every time I patrol. This ticket can be used by anyone whom I invite to ski. There are other financial incentives, such as being able to buy equipment at discounted prices.

Some aspects of patrolling are completely enjoyable, but others are less so. On the infrequent occasions that I help to bring an accident victim down the mountain on a cold and icy day, skiing feels like work. On the other hand, I feel good about using my skills for a worthwhile cause. Some days I just do not feel like going to the mountain, and other days I am eager to get there. Some co-workers are delightful, others are bores.

Other aspects of ski patrolling resemble the more typical examples of work that would come to mind. One of the most obvious is the rather complex division of labor at even the relatively small mountain where I work. We have a ski-area management team, fellow workers who are ski instructors (it is an interesting phenomenon, but most ski areas see friction between instructors and patrollers), lift attendants, snow makers, groomers, cafeteria help, bartenders, ski-shop sales personnel, and other workers.

As in "regular" work, ski patrolling contains anomalies that are part of the culture of the work. We are constantly reminded that we are to act professionally in carrying out our duties, but no one has really defined "professionally" for us. The hierarchy of authority is sometimes vague and confusing, because some patrollers have more skills than some who hold positions as officers. There are also those who move up through the ranks very quickly and who are on some sort of fast track to the top.

After I wrote the paragraphs above about the ski patrol, my mind went off and I thought about skiing—not about this book and not about sociology. Other times, such as when I am driving to my work at the university, I am thinking about this book and about sociology. Frequently, while I am relaxing at home and reading the *New York Times*, I come across an article that would be very good for an upcoming class or writing project. I physically get out of my chair and cut out and then file the article. While "at work," I similarly do things that are of a strictly nonwork nature. For example, I just put down the phone after calling a friend about setting up a handball game for noon. On other days I may devote "work" time to family activities or personal projects, such as getting a haircut. As you can see, distinguishing between work and nonwork is not always easy.

These examples should give you an idea of how slippery the concept of work is. Yet we all use the term *work*. We see it all the time in newspapers and magazines and hear it on news and talk shows. We all have a hazy but seldom questioned idea of what people do when they go to work.

For sociologists, such vague and general definitions are worthless. It is very important for sociologists to be specific in what they are talking about and studying so that they can measure phenomena precisely and produce legitimate comparisons.

Work in the United States and Beyond

Many people and organizations have struggled to explain exactly what work is, including the U.S. government. In 1973 it published a report titled *Work in America* (O'Toole, 1973). One goal was to define work precisely so that statistics could be gathered and compared and the health of our system could be measured. The report's authors got at the heart of the problem:

> We measure that which we can measure, and this often means that a rich and complex phenomenon is reduced to one dimension, which then becomes prominent and eclipses the other dimensions. This is particularly true of "work," which is often defined as "paid employment." The definition conforms with one readily measurable aspect of work but utterly ignores its profound personal and social aspects and often leads to a distorted view of society.
>
> Using housework as an example, we can see the absurdity of defining work as "paid employment." A housewife, according to this definition, does not work. But if a husband must replace her services—with a housekeeper, cook, baby sitter—these replacements become workers, and the husband has added to the Gross National Product the many thousands of dollars the replacements are paid. It is, therefore, an inconsistency of our definition of work that leads us to say that a woman who cares for her own children is not working, but if she takes a job looking after the children of others, she is working. (pp. 2-3)

The authors further note that equating work with pay also has the unfortunate consequence of implying something about the individual's worth based on the amount of pay received for work. To get around these problems, *Work in America* finally defines work as "an activity that produces something of value for other people" (O'Toole, 1973, p. 3).

Now we have a definition of work that we can use to distinguish between activities—right? Well, not quite. What about those activities that do not produce goods, that provide services of value to other people? Are we saying that the accountant, the auto mechanic, or the teacher is not working? Of course not. Thus, the following definition is perhaps more useful: Work is "any activity, or expenditure of energy, that produces services and products of value to other people" (Fox & Hesse-Biber, 1984, p. 2).

This definition has the advantage of introducing the concept of *services*. As you will see in detail later in this chapter, the provision of services, rather than the production of goods, has become a central component of contemporary work.

Work also involves more than the activities of providing goods or services; it may include, for example, work-related time, such as that spent grooming oneself for work or traveling to and from work (Parker & Smith, 1976). And some activities fall between the cracks of work and leisure, such as daydreaming about skiing while at work or thinking about work while reading the newspaper at home.

Other issues also must be taken into account. A strong tradition within sociology is concerned with the meanings that people attach to their activities (Miller, 1981). What people define as *reality* is based on continuing personal negotiation and social interactions. For example, if I define my skiing as work, then it *is* work for me. A complete definition of work thus requires a consideration of the fact that work is what we define as work. Work is thus a "socially constructed" phenomenon, as well as an objective activity.

Considering all of these issues, we can now formulate a definition of work that will be the basis for the rest of this book: *Work is the effort or activity of an individual that is undertaken for the purpose of providing goods or services of value to others and that is considered by the individual to be work.*

This is a rather cumbersome definition, but it does contain those elements identified as important components of work from several different perspectives. This definition of work also focuses on workers, which answers the concern of those who worry that the sociology of work is coming to resemble the field of economics too much (Simpson, 1989). Our definition is grounded nicely in sociology while allowing us to examine the economics of work when doing so is relevant.

Occupation, Job, and Career

We have now defined work, but we are only part of the way toward pinning down the concept. My students often ask, "Will I ever get a job with a degree in sociology?" I recently had parents ask, "What are the career possibilities in the social sciences?" Whenever I fill out a federal or state income-tax form, I have to list my occupation. All of these terms fall within the broader concept of work.

One of the most common questions people ask one another when they first meet is "What do you do?" Anyone who has grown up in our society knows that this question is really about occupation and not about personal habits. Instead of saying, "I carefully add up numbers" or even "I keep track of the company's accounts payable," a person is likely to say, "I am a bookkeeper." Similarly, instead of saying, "I prepare food in a restaurant," a person will say, "I am a chef." Occupation provides an identity in contexts where people do not know one another very well. In fact, for most of us, occupation is our prime identifying characteristic.

One reason we rely on information about occupation to identify people is because it says a good deal about their social position (Salz, 1944). We tend automatically to assume that someone identified as a doctor has higher status than someone who is identified as a bartender. We also make assumptions about where the two individuals live, what kinds of cars they drive, how many years of education they have, who has the wealthiest and most powerful friends, and myriad other indications of status in our society.

The idea of occupation also implies a set of social relationships (Hughes, 1945). For instance, my occupation as a professor implies that students are part of my set of relationships. Relationships with other professors, deans, department secretaries, and publishers' representatives are also part of the set of social relationships for a professor.

Finally, occupations are typically linked to the work of adults (Roe, 1956, p. 3). As you will see in Chapter 7, the work carried out by teenagers is seldom considered an occupation, because it does not make up a major part of their identities as individuals.

Taking into account all of these considerations, I define *occupation* as "the social role performed by adult members of society

that directly and/or indirectly yields social and financial consequences and that constitutes a major focus in the life of an adult"
(Hall, 1975, p. 6). The key aspect of the concept of occupation,
then, is that it is an identifiable social role with meanings both
for the individual and for others in interaction with the role. This
is a more limited definition than the one developed for work—
namely, occupation has more to do with adults' social identity than
work does.

The focus of this book quite obviously must include the notion
of occupation, but it will also include work that is not commonly
thought of as occupation: for example, "hustling" and "chores"
such as mowing the lawn or doing the dishes. However, most of
the analysis in this book will involve work in occupations.

Although the concept of occupation is useful, we must note that
many workers shift their occupational category over time. For
example, Abbott (1989) writes:

> Electrical and chemical engineers, operations researchers,
> accountants, clergy, and college teachers all face probabilities
> of more than 50% of leaving by age 40 the census categories
> in which they began their careers. If this is the case among
> professionals, how much greater is it among other workers!
> (p. 280)

The point is a simple one. For example, I began my career in the
occupational category of professor. As luck would have it, my
occupational category at the moment is dean. Perhaps someday I
will tire of the academic world and decide to become a professional
ski patroller. The point is that people can move out of one category
of occupation into another in the normal course of a career.

I have now informally introduced the idea of career. It is
easiest to understand the idea of career if we start with the basic
idea of job. A *job* is a person's occupation at one point in time. A
career is the unfolding sequence of jobs that a person has over the
life course.

Unfortunately for conceptual clarity, sociologists have not always neatly distinguished work, occupation, job, and career. For
example, Chapter 3 will discuss studies of job satisfaction, while
Chapter 4 will consider careers in terms of their relationship to

changes in social status. Quite obviously, there is overlap in the meaning of these terms.

For me, it is easiest to think of *job* as the simplest concept: the person in an occupation at a point in time. A *career* is the set of jobs that a person has over time; it can be planned or unplanned. The *occupation* is the category of work that the person fills on the job. *Work* encompasses all of these ideas.

Work Activities

When people work, what do they do? The answer seems simple at first: Work is defined in terms of the activity undertaken in the provision of goods and services. Thus, the typist types, the teacher teaches, the truck driver drives, the administrator administrates.

Unfortunately, delineating work activities for a given occupation is not so simple. First, few occupations require a single activity; most involve a variety. For example, the typist surely types but also consults with a supervisor about which tasks to perform when, asks the writers of documents to explain ambiguous marks, looks up words in the dictionary when they do not seem to be spelled right, and perhaps even arranges birthday parties for fellow office workers.

A second complicating factor is that the central work activity is not always easy to define. Consider, for example, school administrators. We can say that their main work activity is administering a school. But what do they do when they administer? You might be surprised to learn that they spend much of their time talking, which they do to control the activities of those whom they administer (Gronn, 1983). Similarly, chief executive officers (CEOs) of business firms spend most of their time talking with others and very little time in direct supervision (Kurke & Aldrich, 1979; Mintzberg, 1979). Talk is thus a key work activity for both school administrators and CEOs, although we might not think so at first glance.

Sometimes work activities spill over or seep over into what might be considered the leisure or social sphere. Many managers are expected to participate in community affairs (Christensen, Hougland, Ilvento, & Shepard, 1988); membership in the Kiwanis or the Rotary Club is thus a work activity for some people. Sales representatives may be expected to develop skills, such as playing golf, that will allow them to interact on a social basis with potential customers.

Another feature of work activities is that most occupational roles involve complex social, political, and economic networks that create widely varying activities for individual workers. For instance, a retail clerk at a big department store may rarely do anything but wait on customers and straighten clothes on the racks. A retail clerk in a small boutique might do those things and more: set up displays, answer the phone for the proprietor, and empty the trash. Furthermore, two retail clerks in the same department store, even in the same department, may have quite different work activities. Perhaps the one with more political skills is the one allowed to help the department manager create displays.

In short, then, work activities for any individual are usually varied, hard to define, and not confined to work time, and they may be different from those of others with the same job.

The Labor Force

If I ask my sociology of work students if they are working, almost all say yes. One common form of work for my students is working in a pizza shop—most for only 10 or so hours per week. Some earn money by typing papers for other students or selling magazine subscriptions in the dorm. Those who are about to graduate are often actively involved in a job search, sending applications to companies in which they are interested and taking interviews. The lucky ones will begin a career within a few weeks, as soon as school ends.

As different as these students are, they are all members of the labor force. The *labor force* includes people 16 years of age and older who:

- are employed or self-employed and receiving pay for full- or part-time work or who work at least 15 hours as unpaid workers in a family business;

- had jobs from which they were absent because of illness, vacation, or strikes;
- are unemployed and looked for work during the last four weeks by answering advertisements, checking with friends, or writing letters of application; and
- are waiting to be called back to jobs when business picks up or to start a new job within 30 days.

This rather precise definition of who is in the labor force comes to us courtesy of the U.S. Department of Labor. It is used in monthly counts of labor-force participation and once every 10 years when the census is taken. It also is common worldwide.

Labor Force Statistics

Data collected by the U.S. Department of Labor provide us with a great deal of useful information. For example, look at Table 1.1. It shows that the U.S. labor force is growing in both numbers of people available to work and proportion of employed adult population. Two factors contribute to this growth. The first is simply the growth in population. The second and more interesting factor is women's greater labor-force participation rate. The reasons for this increased participation rate will be discussed in detail in Chapter 6, but we note here that the rate has increased for both married and single women. Also note that the participation rate among married women with children has increased dramatically, as Table 1.2 indicates.

"Official" measurements of the labor force and labor-force participation are useful, but they are not benign. Definitions of who is and is not employed have a great deal to do with government policies about workers and the unemployed (Burawoy, 1983).

In fact, in some ways, the labor force is a creation of government measures of labor-force participation. The labor force is whatever the government defines it to be. In the United States, for instance, the definition includes only people over 16 years of age. Clearly, 16-year-old workers at fast-food restaurants have a different relationship to their work than do 40-year-old workers who have similar jobs and are the sole source of support for

TABLE 1.1   Labor-Force Participation Rates (%), 1960-1993

	Total noninstitutional population 16+ years (1,000)	Total participation rate	Men	Women
1880	36,762	47	79	15
1900	47,950	50	80	19
1920	82,739	50	78	21
1940	100,147	53	79	25
1960	119,106	56	83	37
1970	139,203	58	80	43
1980	169,349	64	77	51
1982	173,939	64	77	52
1988	186,322	66	76	56
1993	193,142	67	75	58

Notes: Alaska and Hawaii added in 1960. Lower age limit for official statistics on labor force, employment, and unemployment raised from 14 to 16 years in July 1967. New figures are revisions.
Source: U.S. Department of Labor (1989, August). *Handbook of Labor Statistics.* Bureau of Labor Statistics, Bulletin 2340 (1993 data from U.S. Bureau of Census, 1993) *Employment and Earnings, 40*(3), 1993.

TABLE 1.2   Married Women's Labor-Force Participation and Children (%), 1960-1988

Presence and age of children	Wives' labor-force participation rates				
	1960	1970	1972	1980	1988
Children under 3 years				41	55
Children 3 to 5 years				52	61
Children under 6 years	19	30	30	45	57
Children 6 to 18 years	39	49	50	62	73
No children under 8 years	35	42	43	46	49
All Wives	31	41	42	50	57

Source: U.S. Department of Labor. (1989, August). *Handbook of Labor Statistics.* Bureau of Labor Statistics, Bulletin 2340.

themselves or their families. Still, 16-year-olds work, according to our definition.

The labor-force definitions used by government agencies also have the potential of underestimating the participation of some social groups. For example, women are seriously undercounted as part of the agricultural labor force. Studies of farm wives have found that the vast majority are engaged in activities such as driving tractors, caring for a kitchen garden, bookkeeping, and feeding cattle. Although they are not counted as part of the labor force, farm wives obviously play an important role in agricultural work (Boulding, 1980; Rosenfeld, 1986).

Labor-force statistics contain important nuances and distinctions that can actually mask important worker characteristics. For example, the growth in home-based telephone-sales work shows up in labor-force statistics in the sales category. However, just looking at the statistics, we might miss the fact that many of those who work in home-based telephone sales are disabled and elderly workers, mothers of small children, and rural residents— all of whom require flexibility in their employment. We also need to be aware that these workers usually receive lower wages than do others in the sales category (Kraut & Grambsch, 1987).

In other ways, too, the statistics can often hide important realities about the labor force.

Nontraditional Workers. I have known quite a few students and nonstudents who do not engage in work activities that are measured by government labor statistics. I have known gamblers, drug dealers, and probably some prostitutes. I have known others who completely devote themselves to a cause such as a religious quest or to a cult such as that surrounding the Grateful Dead. Their work activities—hustling and so-called countercultural work—do not fit within traditional conceptualizations of work and thus are not measured.

Hustling is often relegated to the "nonwork" category in official statistics, especially when the activity is considered immoral. Women prostitutes (who refer to themselves as "working girls"), drug dealers, racketeers, strippers, thieves, and others engaged in crime and deviance work as we have defined it, but moralistic evaluations of the *forms* of their activities often hide that fact (Miller, 1981, p. 133).

However, hustling can also include more acceptable work activities. For example, construction workers often turn to self-employment during hard economic times (Linder, 1983), attempting to find whatever work they can. Yet another example of hustling is part-time farming (Wimberley, 1983), which may be a way into or out of full-time farming. But for the part-timer, the work supplements other employment.

So how shall we think of hustling?

> The most basic feature of workers who hustle for a living is that they do not have full-time conventional jobs; rather they seek their livings in other ways. Sometimes they may work at low-paying, temporary jobs, but at other times they may do any number of other things to earn income. . . . They must be alert at all times to opportunities for making a living [as] found in their environments. As a result, their histories reflect frequent job changes, and outsiders often describe them as unstable. (Miller, 1981, pp. 134-135)

Thus whether hustlers engage in acceptable or unacceptable activities, what they do constitutes work. It might not be counted in official statistics, but it is real work for the participants as long as they consider it work and provide something of value to others.

The second form of nontraditional work is countercultural work (Miller, 1981), or that performed within groups that reject contemporary values and practices and adopt an alternative perspective. Examples of countercultural groups are the Israeli kibbutzim and the Hare Krishna movement. Those who are involved in countercultural work tend to believe in equality of rewards, the fusion of work and leisure activities, and the rejection of traditional notions of career. Again, although they definitely engage in work activities, they are often not counted in labor statistics.

Labor Markets

Why do some workers have satisfying, well-paid jobs while others work at the fringes of society or are lucky to find any work at all? Sociologists often rely on an economic concept—labor markets—to explain the discrepancy. In fact, sociologists have taken the idea of labor markets much farther than economists have.

The labor market idea is at once very simple and very complex. But it is easy to grasp when you compare it to other types of markets: stock markets, produce markets, flea markets, and so on. In all of these markets, something is traded for a sum of money that reflects the value of the thing being sold. In labor markets, the thing being traded is human labor power. People exchange their effort and ability for a wage or salary. Just as vendors at a flea market try to get the best possible price for their wares, job seekers hope to sell their labor power to the highest bidder. To increase the value of their "product," they enhance it with education or experience.

Labor markets also resemble other types of markets by often being subject to the laws of supply and demand. A hard freeze in Florida ruins the orange harvest; as a result, diehard orange juice lovers have to pay a higher price. The same dynamics operate in the labor market. A critical shortage of registered nurses may drive up wages and salaries. On the other hand, an employer who seeks to fill a position for which qualified applicants are in great supply has the luxury of paying lower wages—and of being highly selective in the hiring process.

This concept of labor markets comes from neoclassical economic theory. The basic principle is that the labor market is shaped by economic motivation, with people rationally pursuing their own interests in a competitive and fluid market (Montagna, 1977, pp. 65-66). Workers make investments in their "human capital" through education, training, and experience. Employers adjust their recruitment patterns and wages to achieve maximum productivity. This approach is based on an assumption of perfect competition: a single labor market in which all workers and all employers interact, with the laws of supply and demand governing wages and productivity. But this picture is much too simple.

Complexity of Labor Markets

In some respects, the labor market is quite complex. For one thing, people do not all compete for jobs in a single market. Instead, multiple markets exist, distinct arenas where different types of workers compete for different types of jobs. For instance, most of my students take part-time jobs with the knowledge that the work is not lifetime employment. When they graduate from college, they will enter a different labor market—that for full-time, permanent workers. My graduate students will enter yet another labor market once they earn their doctorates. Now think about all of the people who are looking for work—old and young, male and female, well and poorly educated—and all of the employers who are looking for employees—small firms and large, high-technology and low-technology, rural and urban, and so on.

Even more complexity is added when we consider the job changes that take place *within* employing organizations. We can thus distinguish between internal and external labor markets (Doeringer & Piore, 1971). An *internal labor market* exists within an individual organization, which has its own personnel policies. The *external labor market* comprises all of the workers who are not in that particular organization. The typical college student enters the external labor market on graduation. Once a person is hired, he or she is then a part of an organization's internal labor market. Promotion to higher-level jobs is possible only for those already in the organization. However, organizational rules can be used to limit the promotion opportunities for members of certain groups, such as minorities, women, or workers over a certain age. Thus, internal labor markets cannot operate on the basis of perfect competition.

A second important distinction is between the core or primary labor market and the peripheral or secondary labor market. The *core labor market* is characterized by stable employment, relatively high wages and salaries, and rules that protect tenure or seniority. For the most part, college graduates who find employment in big companies have passed into the core market. In the *peripheral labor market*, on the other hand,

> jobs tend to be low-paying, with poorer working conditions, little chance for advancement, a highly personalized relationship between workers and supervisors [that] leaves wide latitude for favoritism and is conducive to harsh and

capricious discipline; and with considerable instability in jobs and a high turnover among the labor force. (Piore, 1972, p. 3)

Most of the jobs held by college students are in the periphery. So, too, are the jobs of former auto workers who are forced to find work in fast-food restaurants. In addition, according to Simpson and Simpson (1983, p. ix), peripheral work includes:

- part-time, seasonal, and moonlighting work;
- work that is outside the main economy, such as hustling, gambling, and that found in sweatshops;
- and work done by those considered outside the normal labor force, including children, the elderly, and undocumented aliens.

In terms of finances, status, and fulfillment, peripheral workers tend to fall behind workers employed in the core labor market.

A final point about the complexity of labor markets: They cannot be viewed as static. For example, former industrial giants General Electric and USX (formerly U.S. Steel) have intensively "deindustrialized" by transforming themselves into service-based organizations that deal largely in the financial industry. As such deindustrialization occurs, there is a spinoff effect on suppliers and other small firms, undoubtedly sending some into bankruptcy and others into the peripheral regions of the labor market (Wallace & Rothschild, 1988). At the same time, a significant and robust rise in self-employment has taken place since 1970 (Steinmetz & Wright, 1989). When self-employment is successful and a small business turns into a large business, a different type of labor market is created. Labor markets are thus complex and always changing.

Work in Historical Context

We will now broaden our perspective and put labor markets in a historical context. There have been many analyses of the history of work, most of them Eurocentric. Here I follow Tausky (1984). (For excellent summaries, see Berg, 1979; Hodson & Sullivan, 1990; Ritzer & Walczak, 1986).

It is hard to know when people started to consider their productive labor as work, but certainly hunting-and-gathering nomads produced goods and services of value to others. Extensive trade networks indicate that to be true. Gradually, as people began to plant crops, towns and villages developed near sources of water, and work began to be more specialized. Approximately 5,000 years ago, cities arose in Egypt and Sumeria with kings, nobles, and priests forming a privileged class. There were also professional armies and tax-paying peasants. The basic division between ruler and ruled now developed. The division between peasants and the wealthy and powerful continued through the Greek and Roman eras, the Middle Ages, and into the Industrial Revolution.

The Industrial Revolution truly was a revolution. It coincided roughly with the development of both capitalism and colonialism. This was a period of massive change not only in Europe, but also around the world. England was the homeland of the revolution. There the centralized factory grew to become the dominant means of producing goods. Previously, production was accomplished by individuals and families making goods on contract in their own homes or shops. The factory could produce many more goods much more cheaply. Railroads, along with canals and improved roads, permitted food and other supplies to be shipped long distances, which in turn facilitated the growth of cities. Although the cities offered factory work to people who could no longer support themselves by farming, the early industrial cities were harsh places, full of filth and danger. Child labor and worker exploitation were common. In just 100 years, industrial work became the dominant form of work in England (Tausky, 1984).

Patterns in the United States were quite similar, with the Civil War providing an impetus for increased industrial (war) production and better rail systems. Another important development was the growth of organizations through mergers, acquisitions, and the development of subsidiaries that supplied the organization and sold its goods. These patterns of growth led to the large monopolies that characterized the United States in the late 19th and early 20th centuries.

In both England and the United States, another phenomenon—the development of a middle class—was taking place around the turn of the century. This class emerged as factory pay began to increase and workers were permitted to form labor unions. Union power developed late in the United States because unions received no government recognition and approval until the 1930s. The middle class also grew as increasing organizational size and scope created a need for administrators and clerks.

We have now moved into what some analysts call the *postindustrial era* (Bell, 1973; Touraine, 1971). Today, the provision of services is a more important part of the U.S. economy than the production of goods. The professional-technical class is gaining strength. But whether or not we are in a postindustrial era remains an unresolved and hotly debated issue.

Other analysts focus on changes such as growth in transnational ventures and global corporations, deindustrialization, decentralization, and rapid technological innovation. Because work is constantly changing, workers continually need to be trained in new skills. Unfortunately, there is compelling evidence that many people entering the labor force lack the basic reading and mathematics skills required for this new economy (Fiske, 1989). At the same time, many workers are acquiring more responsibility—and hence more pressure to perform. New work hazards are linked to high technology and new work pressures are associated with the presence of beepers, facsimile (fax) machines, and cellular telephones. And the lines between work, family, and leisure are increasingly blurred. An example of this was evident to me when I was on a ski vacation with my wife. Every day at breakfast, we ended up next to "Laptop Larry" and his family. They were all dressed to ski, but Larry continued to work with his laptop computer, jumping through invisible work hoops.

The new forms of work are "added onto" existing forms. Agricultural work did not disappear with industrialization. Industrial work still exists, although its place is being usurped by service work. Materially, these changes have left the vast majority of workers far better off. Simultaneously, of course, conditions for some workers are little different than they were in the more dismal past.

Unemployment

Since the beginning of the Industrial Revolution, displaced workers have flocked to cities. Those in the United States were the destination of waves of European immigrants, Southern whites and African-Americans, and rural Northerners, all of whom were being displaced by changes in the agricultural system. Despite prejudice and difficult working conditions, these new arrivals succeeded in finding employment:

> Our cities offered growing numbers of jobs. Moreover, well into this century, the gap between skill requirements for urban employment and skills possessed by disadvantaged migrants was minimal. This afforded immigrants access into the mainstream economy (albeit to the bottom rungs of the socioeconomic ladder), while overall growth in city economics created numerous opportunities for social mobility. (Kasarda, 1983, p. 22)

Over the past four decades, dramatic social and technological changes have created serious deficits in the number of entry-level jobs available in U.S. cities. The figures that document this trend are quite startling. New York City, for example, gained more than 650,000 jobs in such information-processing industries as banking and insurance between 1953 and 1980. In the same period, the city lost some 525,000 jobs in manufacturing and construction. The same pattern has been documented for Philadelphia and Boston. In the decade between 1970 and 1980, employment in the information-processing industries continued to expand, while employment in such blue-collar service industries as car washes and domestic-cleaning services declined considerably. The result has been unprecedented levels of unemployment among unskilled workers living in cities. Sociologists look at a phenomenon such as this and wonder who the unemployed are and what social forces have contributed to their unemployment.

Frictional and Structural Unemployment

To answer these questions, we must understand the differences between frictional and structural unemployment. *Frictional unemployment* exists when people are temporarily out of work while changing jobs or seeking new jobs. Such unemployment results from "layoff" decisions made within employing organizations. An economic explanation would stress that individuals have value to employers in proportion to their training and experience. More highly trained individuals are harder to replace and are, theoretically, the least likely to be laid off. Thus there is the supposition that layoffs will take place in a reverse order of seniority—that is, last hired, first fired.

However, we also could say that organizational decision making really involves jobs, not individuals (Cornfield, 1983). When demand for a product decreases, jobs that deal directly with production of a good are the most vulnerable. The repetitive manual jobs that require little expertise are even more vulnerable. These are the jobs most likely to be subject to layoff and technological change.

At the same time, organizational change can place another category of jobs at high risk: Those that are redundant because of reorganization, including clerical work, some professional staff positions, and some managerial and administrative positions. Mergers, buyouts, and takeovers put still other categories of workers at risk.

Frictional unemployment is thus the consequence of decisions made within employing organizations. Exactly who will be laid off depends on the source of pressure on the organization. However, the disadvantaged are most at risk in the vast majority of layoffs. As Table 1.3 clearly shows, minority group members, the less educated, the young, and women who head families bear the brunt of unemployment. Chapters 6, 7, and 8 offer detailed examinations of the problems faced by these groups.

Economists believe that an unemployment rate of approximately 3% is unavoidable and normal, because of the natural turnover in jobs. In recent years, however, the unemployment rate has been double or triple the 3% figure. The increase results from, in general terms, *structural unemployment*: long-term or perma-

TABLE 1.3 Unemployment Rates and Selected Characteristics, 1988

	Percentage unemployed
Race, sex, and age	
White, total	5
Men: 20 years and over	4
16 to 19 years	15
Women: 20 years and over	4
16 to 19 years	12
Black, total	12
Men: 20 years and over	10
16 to 19 years	33
Women: 20 years and over	10
16 to 19 years	32
Education	
Less than high school	9
High school completed	5
College: 1 to 3 years	4
4 or more years	2
Family status	
Married men, spouse present	4
Married women, spouse present	4
Women who head families	8
Type of workers	
Full-time workers	5
Part-time workers	8

Source: U.S. Department of Labor. (1989, August). *Handbook of Labor Statistics.* Bureau of Labor Statistics, Bulletin 2340. Note: Beginning January 1983, 1980 census occupational system evolved from the Standard Occupational Classification System, which was radically different from systems used January 1971 to December 1982.

nent unemployment brought about by technological change or the decline of an entire industry. For example, the U.S. auto and steel industries have been sources of structural unemployment over the past 10 or 15 years as entire plants have shut down (Tausky, 1984). These industries have undergone major change because of technological advances that make production less labor-intensive and long-term changes in demand for their products.

The decline of an industry and technological change are not the only factors in structural unemployment. In fact, structural unemployment can be disguised as frictional unemployment. Consider the U.S. firm that decides to seek cheaper or less organized labor in a country such as Taiwan or Mexico or in one of the so-called Sunbelt states. The decision of that individual firm may create frictional unemployment, but more serious and ominous structural unemployment results when many such companies make the same decision.

Another example of how an organization's decisions—or non-decisions—contribute to structural unemployment is the case of U.S. automobile manufacturers. They have lost a great deal of their market share to foreign auto makers. Part of this has resulted from higher U.S. labor costs. Another part of this loss, however, came because domestic companies did not respond in a timely fashion to the threat of foreign imports. They were using a short-term accounting system, with a heavy emphasis on cost control and immediate financial return on sales, service, and warranty work (McNeil & Miller, 1980). These companies were blind to customers' desires for better quality and reliability.

A final source of structural unemployment is consumer preferences. U.S. automobile manufacturers continued to churn out big, complicated cars long after the phenomenal success of the simple Volkswagen "bug" in the 1960s. A form of reverse snob appeal took U.S. manufacturers by surprise. Not until the 1980s did they finally start producing attractive small cars.

As you can see, structural unemployment has many sources. But the dominant ones come from moves by organizations to reduce costs through less expensive labor and such technological changes as mechanization, automation, computerization, and robotization.

Consequences of Unemployment

Unemployment has always had severe social consequences, especially for members of racial and ethnic minorities and the underclass. They are often last hired and first fired. Without jobs, they drift farther from the social and economic mainstream. They end up with less and fall even farther behind. Their frustration and rage have often ignited social conflagrations.

Although education and training have been identified as a solution to structural unemployment, our society has been notably inept in delivering appropriate education to those who most need it. Central-city minority group members are especially unlikely to have the educational background necessary for entry-level positions, particularly in areas outside of the Western states (Kasarda, 1983, p. 30). The result is a large difference between the percentages of whites and blacks who are unemployed and not in the labor force.

The human costs of structural unemployment are also high. Many so-called Rustbelt factories have closed in the last decade. The closing of an RCA plant in Indiana was quite typical (Perrucci, Perrucci, Targ, & Targ, 1988). Most of the laid-off workers found blue-collar or service jobs that required less skill and did not pay the bills, even when the workers cut way back on household expenditures. The former RCA employees also experienced higher levels of physical and mental illness when compared with employed counterparts.

Structural unemployment is a major social problem, one exacerbated by technological change and development. But the most striking aspect of structural unemployment is that it appears to be inevitable and irreversible. Enterprises seek cheaper labor. Technological developments continue apace. And although massive changes in the educational system might remove the inequities between social groups, increased education could also contribute to the phenomenon of underemployment.

Underemployment

I recently asked my students, "What are you going to do when you graduate?" A very bright young woman said, "I want to go into retailing, but I don't want to be stacking jeans for the rest of my life!" She did not want to experience underemployment or work in a position in which she could not use all of her skills. What she wanted was retailing management. As luck would have it, a month later she told me she had a job with a major New York retail firm.

Sociologists are concerned also with underemployment. Educational levels have increased steadily since World War II. Fortunately, jobs requiring the resulting skills and developed talents have become more numerous. But if work that requires well-educated workers is not available, then underemployment can become a massive problem. People who do not feel that their skills are being used or appreciated are more likely to be dissatisfied with their work. When many workers become discontented, society may become more volatile.

The Deskilling Argument

Some theorists would say that underemployment is not just a matter of increasing levels of education in our society. They also point to *deskilling*, or the systematic reconstruction of jobs so that they require fewer skills and so management can have more control over workers. The issue is whether all levels and all forms of work are becoming ever more deskilled. The ideological left would say that the combined forces of capitalism and technology lead to increasingly deskilled work, particularly for the disadvantaged. The ideological right would say just the opposite, that capitalism and technological change bring enhanced working conditions and prosperity to all classes of workers. A rapidly accumulating body of evidence supports neither position.

The debate over deskilling provides an intriguing picture of how sociologists go about defining and studying a problem. In 1974, Harry Braverman, probably the best known proponent of the deskilling argument, attempted to show how the capitalist class and management increase their control over workers by altering production systems. (For additional arguments from this perspective, see Burawoy, 1979; Clawson, 1980; Heydebrand, 1977; Marglin, 1974.) Braverman believed that management was purposely seeking to develop machinery that would carry out the production functions performed by skilled (hence higher paid and more powerful) workers. Work was being divided and subdivided into ever simpler and more routine tasks as a way to control workers. According to Braverman, deskilling was part of the capitalist approach to production.

Edwards (1979) approached this issue in a slightly different manner. He traced the development of technical and bureaucratic control of the workplace and based his analysis on the idea that management decisions are driven by the desire for ever greater profits. In these enlightened times, exhortation and threats are no longer used to control workers. Instead, management relies on *technical control* (in the form of the assembly line and other technical developments) and *bureaucratic control* (in the form of job requirements, promotion policies, and compensation). These are more subtle but more effective forms of control. In his analysis of work at the Polaroid Corporation, Edwards (1979) noted the following:

> The positive incentives, the relief from capricious supervision, the right to appeal grievances and bid for better jobs, the additional job security of seniority—all these make the day-to-day worklife of Polaroid employees more pleasant. They function as an elaborate system of bribes, and like all successful bribes, they are attractive. But, they are also corrupting. They push workers to pursue their self-interest in a narrow way as individuals, and they stifle the impulse to struggle collectively for those same self-interests. (p. 145)

The major focus of both the Braverman and Edwards arguments is factory work. Other sociologists and economists have argued that deskilling also is an important feature of office work (Benet, 1972; Form & McMillen, 1983; Glenn & Feldberg, 1977). Today offices are larger and more automated than in the past, and office work is increasingly routinized and repetitive.

Evidence of Deskilling

Braverman, Edwards, and other early proponents of the deskilling hypothesis supported their arguments largely from historical evidence or limited observations in the form of case studies. Their arguments have been powerful enough to attract the interest of many sociologists, but their evidence has not been sufficiently convincing. Thus, several researchers have been investigating the deskilling hypothesis more rigorously.

Essentially, sociologists have begun to investigate if, where, how, and why deskilling has taken place. One of the main researchers has been William Form, who began by analyzing the actual proportions of skilled and unskilled workers over a 100-year period (Form, 1981):

> I attempted to reconstruct the skill distributions of U.S. manual workers for 1870-1970. The most striking trend is the slow rise in male skilled workers since 1900 and the rapid decline of unskilled labor. For women, the percentages remained stable, but service occupations have increased as domestic workers declined. We can conclude that, contrary to received wisdom, skilled work has not declined for over seventy years. (p. 149)

Form then examined office work and concluded that it now is actually more complex than in the past. He concluded his analysis by noting that a study of the ways in which people respond to their machines (Mueller et al., 1969) was additional evidence against deskilling:

> The large majority of people working with machines, even those who have little control over them, like their machines and are satisfied with their work. This finding suggests that the alleged link between the spread of machine technology, work routinization, and worker alienation may be a myth waiting to be exposed. (Form, 1981, p. 155)

Another approach to this issue was taken by Kenneth Spenner (1979, 1983, 1990; see also Attewell, 1987, 1990; Vallas, 1990). In his studies, Spenner posited three hypotheses about deskilling and the content of work. The *downgrading hypothesis* was just discussed: the idea that technology is an instrument of capitalist production that lowers skills. The *upgrading hypothesis*, on the other hand, suggests that work is becoming more complex, with looser supervision and greater independence for workers, and that it requires more education. Finally, the *no-change hypothesis* suggests that some work has been downgraded and other work has been upgraded, with the balance yielding no change.

In 1979, Spenner concluded that, in general, work had become slightly more complex during the previous 10 to 15 years. He also concluded that the number of upgraded jobs had exceeded those that had been downgraded. But he noted that the evidence was not strong. Spenner used U.S. Department of Labor statistics in his research. These data contain information on skill distributions and change that can be analyzed over time.

Spenner's 1983 analysis was more complicated and involved a detailed analysis of the labor force's composition. His analysis revealed some anomalies. For example, he noted that the occupation of engineer had been somewhat downgraded over time but that there were many more engineers than in the past. In other words, the occupation itself was downgraded, but the labor force as a whole was upgraded as more people moved into this more complex kind of work.

Spenner's research led him to a couple of interesting conclusions. First, the focus in the upgrading-downgrading controversy must be the jobs that people actually have, not their personal qualifications. Improving public education is not the same as upgrading the labor force, unless the actual jobs that people have also are upgraded. Second, although Spenner did not find evidence of massive upgrading or downgrading, he did find hints of some downgrading in terms of autonomy and control.

Other researchers have found similarly mixed results in a wide range of occupations. A study of dock workers on the West Coast found that the shift to containerized cargo ships required the operators of the huge cranes to upgrade their skills (Finlay, 1988). Although the work of other dock workers became more routinized, they could retain some control of their work through union contract negotiations. The dock-worker study also found that management would support increased worker control if it contributed to increased productivity. A study of retail meatcutters found that skills both increased and decreased as technological change was introduced (Walsh, 1989). Telephone workers had their skills upgraded in the 1950-1980 period, but more recently automation has led to less autonomy and less demand for thinking skills (Vallas, 1988). Skilled machinists faced with the introduction of numerical control devices were called on to do more troubleshooting and to monitor more machines (Zicklin, 1987). Federal office workers such as head secretaries who were once at the top of the clerical work ladder had their work redefined as *lower management* (DiPrete, 1988). Technology opened an array of new possibilities to them.

When ideological rhetoric is stripped away, the results of the research on deskilling resulting from technological change must be viewed as indeterminate (Vallas & Yarrow, 1987). But the evidence about deskilling does lead to one firm conclusion: It is *not* an inevitable consequence of technological change.

If technological change by itself does not determine whether jobs are upgraded or downgraded, then what does? Management controls decisions about the complexity of jobs, but it is bound by the way work is already organized and by economic circumstances (Kelley, 1990). Another important variable is the local economy in which the technological change is introduced (Colclough & Tolbert, 1990). In poor local economies, where few alternative jobs are available, the introduction of advanced technologies can put workers at a disadvantage. But in more affluent local economies, the introduction of advanced technology tends to produce upgraded jobs. An example is the introduction of the Saturn automobile factory in rural Tennessee, which has led to higher skill and wage levels. Managerial attitudes and competence are another key factor (Hodson, 1988). Managers who fall back on old solutions to new problems often promote deskilling. The final variable is the workers themselves (Vallas & Yarrow, 1987). One worker might perceive a change in the content of work as upgrading, while another sees it as downgrading.

There is an irony here that should not be overlooked. Analyses of deskilling and underemployment typically focus on lower-level workers, not management or professionals. Sociologists and economists, the predominant researchers in this area (and themselves professionals), have not yet examined the extent of deskilling in their own form of work.

The Many Aspects of Work

From our original efforts to define work, we have moved through considerations of the nature of the labor force, the nature of labor markets, the history of work, and forms of unemployment and underemployment. As you can see, the sociology of work is highly complex. The rest of the book tries to bring order to this complexity by analyzing work on three levels.

The next two chapters extend the definition of work introduced here. Chapter 2 provides an overview of the types of work that are traditionally identified in books that deal with work and occupations, including white-collar, blue-collar, unskilled, and housework. Chapter 3 is concerned with the individual aspect of work, including work motivation and the meanings that people attach to work.

The second level of analysis concerns the differentiations among occupations and workers. The work itself can be analyzed from vertical and horizontal perspectives, and workers can be classified by gender, age, race, and ethnicity. To be specific, Chapter 4 deals with status, or the vertical dimension of occupations. This is a topic that has dominated research on the sociology of work—and sociology itself—in recent years. Chapter 5 deals with job content and labor markets, or the horizontal dimension of occupations. Chapter 6 focuses on the gender of workers, particularly its relationship to status and income. The chapter also includes analyses of the role conflicts faced by single parents and married women and the issues faced by dual-career families. The focus shifts to age in Chapter 7 and how work changes throughout the life cycle. Chapter 8 deals with racial, religious, and ethnic factors that affect work, such as discrimination and segregation. The material presented in Chapters 6, 7, and 8 is the foundation for additional notes about gender, age, race, and ethnicity throughout the book.

The final four chapters of the book deal with the context of work. Work obviously does not take place in a vacuum. Chapter 9 considers how organizations affect workers' status and income attainment and how they affect the nature of work. Chapter 10 examines the power context—namely, worker control and the labor movement. Chapter 11 deals with the links among family, health, and mental health. Chapter 12 ends the book with an analysis of the trends that appear to be crucial for the future of work.

As a matter of fact, all of these topics intersect. My reactions to my work are based on my age and gender and my employer. My reactions are also based on my family relationships, which are in turn shaped by my wife's work and my own. Similarly, my social status is based on how much my employer pays me and on the fact that I work in what is typically thought of as a profession.

For you, as a worker now and in the future, these topics also interact. If you are a "typical" college student, your youth may be a problem as you move into the labor force, and you may be frightened by the size and scope of your potential employer. If you are not a "typical" college student, then you are probably older and thus affected by that fact in the workplace. You also have work experiences that have shaped your expectations about future work and may have family relationships that affect your school and your work.

The rest of this book is designed to analyze work both as sociologists do and in ways that will help you understand how you fit in. The sociology of work does not tell people how to get jobs or get ahead in their careers. But it should increase your understanding of what work involves and how it affects all aspects of your adult life.

■■■ **APPLICATION**

What the Unemployed Know About Work

This chapter opens with the question "Why study work?" One way to answer it is to examine the experiences of the unemployed, particularly those who have been unemployed for a long time.

> Long term unemployment is defined . . . as being out of work for three months, while very long term unemployment carries a six month cutoff. Although these stretches may not seem long, . . . they often mark a time beyond which no steady

> employment will ever again be found or sought. Equally
> important, after six months, because of the termination of
> benefit payments, organizations and governmental agencies
> normally lose touch with the unemployed. And as they fall off
> the lists in the unemployment offices, so do they appear to
> fall off the ends of the earth—sometimes in their own minds,
> sometimes in the most literal ways. (Cottle, 1992, p. 43)

What impact does long-term, or structural, unemployment have on people's lives? Some victims of structural unemployment fare better than others. Many displaced workers eventually find new jobs, although some must settle for underemployment in jobs that do not fully use their skills and abilities. Other displaced workers are not so lucky. After a lengthy and unsuccessful job search, they become discouraged.

These "discouraged workers" would like to work but quit actively looking for a job because they believe that no jobs exist or that they are not qualified for the jobs that do (Rothman, 1987). The exact number of discouraged workers is hard to estimate. Official unemployment rates include only those who are "available for work" and who have made specific attempts to locate a job within the preceding month. As a result, government data often grossly underestimate the true extent of joblessness.

What happens to discouraged workers? The following are some of the effects of long-term unemployment, as compiled by Rothman (1987, pp. 207-208).

- *Financial effects* include interrupted or reduced income; reduced or eliminated spending on entertainment and such "luxuries" as clothing; the use of savings accounts and the cash values of insurance policies to meet living expenses; the sale of televisions, cars, and other property; and trading residences for cheaper housing.

- *Social relationships* are affected by the ending of relationships with all or most former co-workers, the ending of social activities that require spending money, and the disruption of family roles if a spouse seeks paid work.

- *Self-esteem* is affected by an individual's uncertainties about his or her role in being dismissed and a loss of personal pride that results from the frustrations and humiliations of job hunting.
- *Physical and mental health* suffer from the effects of "nervousness, tension, fear, boredom, headaches, stomach upsets, and sleep problems"; increased drinking; high cholesterol and blood-pressure levels, which increase the risk of heart disease; possible psychiatric problems; and an increased possibility of suicide.

Clearly, the costs of long-term unemployment are sometimes high.

These findings give us some perspective on the important role that work plays in people's lives. Work not only is a source of financial gain, but also shapes interpersonal relationships, acts as a source of self-esteem, and appears to be a necessary ingredient for good mental and physical health.

We also have other reasons to study work. Work-related issues have implications not only for individuals, but also for communities, social groups, and even entire societies. As you can see, work is an important topic of study. To help you understand the connection between the sociological study of work and real life, the remaining chapters also are followed by Applications.

■ SUGGESTED READINGS

A complete bibliographical entry for each work cited here can be found in the reference section at the back of this book.

Bell, *The Coming of Post-Industrial Society* (1973), is now 20 years old, but it is still useful in its description and prediction of work and life after the industrial era fades.

Clawson, *Bureaucracy and the Labor Process* (1980), is a careful and well reasoned analysis of the factors associated with deskilling in U.S. industry.

The other major text in the sociology of work is Hodson and Sullivan, *The Social Organization of Work* (1990), which can be consulted for alternative explanations and discussions of the topics discussed here. The basic perspective is really quite similar to this one.

Tausky, *Work and Society* (1984), is an excellent source of definitions of employment, labor force, and unemployment, among other key terms.

2 Varieties of Work

Imagine yourself at a party with a lot of people you don't know. You decide to try starting a conversation. You say something about the weather or the food or the music. If the other person is responsive at all, you will probably soon ask, "What kind of work do you do?" This question opens many doors: It tells you about the person's education, status, and interests. It will help you decide how—even whether—to interact any further.

People tend to answer questions about the type of work they do in one of three ways. If you asked me, I could say, "I work for the State University of New York," which specifies my organizational affiliation. Or I could say, "I work in education," which specifies the labor-market sector in which I work. Or I could say, "I'm a college professor," which would tell you my occupation.

This chapter deals with the third type of response. An occupation as "college professor" implies many things about the work I do and how I do it. And it implies certain similarities to other types of workers. Not only do such generalizations help strangers understand one another better, but grouping people by occupation is also common practice for social scientists and policy makers.

The occupational categories examined in this chapter are based on distinctions made in the sociology of work and in government statistics. The analysis begins with the professions and management, which are at the top of the social status hierarchy, and then moves "down" this hierarchy to white-collar work and blue-collar work. (The linkage between work and status is examined in detail in Chapter 4.) These categories are very close to those developed half a century ago for the U.S. Bureau of the Census (hereafter simply census bureau) as a way to delineate segments of society (Edwards, 1943). Events since then have blurred some of the distinctions, and the U.S. Department of Labor has also revised the categories. But the status hierarchy remains. This chapter also analyzes four types of work that do not fit neatly into the hierarchy: service work, farm work, housework, and work in the so-called underground economy.

Figure 2.1 lists occupations very similar to those used by the census bureau. Some will be familiar to you, others will not. The critical factor here is *variety*. Work comes in many sizes and shapes.

Most forms of work are found in organizations large and small. Although some sociologists believe that modern work is increasingly free of administrative authority (see Freidson, 1973), this chapter has been written on the assumption that organizations are the dominant shapers of the form and content of work. Some work, including housework and some artistic and creative work, is carried out virtually free of direct organizational constraints. Most work, however, is carried out in an organizational setting.

Professional Work

Of all the varieties of work, professional work is the most prestigious and perhaps the most visible. On his TV show, Bill Cosby was Dr. Huxtable, a physician. In an earlier era, M*A*S*H was a show about doctors and nurses. Supreme Court cases are argued and decided by lawyers. Students are taught by professors. The term *professional* also includes accountants, air-traffic controllers, and many other work roles. In addition, people are judged in terms of whether they behave "professionally" in many other settings (Haga, Graen, & Dansereau, 1974).

Professional work has been a growing segment of the labor force in our society. Only 4% of the labor force was classified as "professional and technical" in 1900; by 1990 the figure had risen to 17%. Furthermore, the development of what we consider "established" professions is quite recent. For example, medicine did not achieve its high status (and recognition as a profession) until the beginning of the 20th century (Starr, 1982, pp. 81-82).

Text continued on page 42

FIGURE 2.1 Varieties of Work

Professional, technical, and kindred workers
Accountants
Architects
Computer specialists
Engineers
Lawyers and judges
Librarians, archivists, and curators
Mathematical specialists
Life and physical scientists
Physicians, dentists, and related practitioners
Nurses, dietitians, and therapists
Health technologists and technicians
Religious workers
Social scientists
Social and recreation workers
Teachers, college and university
Engineering and science technicians
Technicians, except health, engineering, and science
Writers, artists, and entertainers

Managers and administrators, except farm
Assessors, controllers, and treasurers,
  local public administration
Bank officers and financial managers
Buyers and shippers, farm products
Buyers, wholesale and retail trade
Credit managers
Funeral directors
Health administrators
Construction inspectors, public administration
Inspectors, except construction, public administration
Managers and superintendents, building
Office managers, n.e.c. (not elsewhere classified)
Officers, pilots, and pursers; ship
Officials and administrators; public administration, n.e.c.
Officials of lodges, societies, and unions
Postal officials

FIGURE **2.1** Continued

Purchasing agents and buyers, n.e.c.
Railroad conductors
Restaurant, cafeteria, and bar managers
Sales managers and department heads, retail trade
Sales managers, except retail trade
School administrators, college
School administrators, elementary and secondary
Managers and administrators, n.e.c.
Advertising agents and salespeople
Auctioneers
Demonstrators
Hucksters and peddlers
Insurance agents, brokers, and underwriters
Newspaper carriers
Real estate agents and brokers
Stock and bond salespeople
Sales workers and sales clerks, n.e.c.

Clerical and kindred workers
Bank tellers
Billing clerks
Bookkeepers
Cashiers
Clerical assistants, social welfare
Clerical supervisors, n.e.c.
Collectors, bill and account
Counter clerks, except food
Dispatchers and starters, vehicle
Enumerators and interviewers
Estimators and investigators, n.e.c.
Expediters and production controllers
File clerks
Insurance adjusters, examiners, and investigators
Library attendants and assistants
Mail carriers, post office
Mail handlers, except post office
Messenger and office assistants

FIGURE 2.1 Continued

Meter readers, utilities
Office machine operators
Payroll and timekeeping clerks
Postal clerks
Proofreaders
Real estate appraisers
Receptionists
Secretaries
Shipping and receiving clerks
Statistical clerks
Stenographers
Stock clerks and storekeepers
Teacher aides, except school monitors
Telegraph messengers
Telegraph operators
Telephone operators
Ticket, station, and express agents
Typists
Weighers
Miscellaneous clerical workers
Not specified clerical workers

Craftspeople and kindred workers
Automobile accessories installers
Bakers
Blacksmiths
Boilermakers
Bookbinders
Brick masons and stone masons
Brick masons and stone masons, apprentices
Cabinetmakers
Carpenters
Carpenter apprentices
Carpet installers
Cement and concrete finishers
Compositors and typesetters
Printing trades apprentices, except press operators

FIGURE 2.1 Continued

Crane operators, derrick operators, and hoist operators
Decorators and window dressers
Dental laboratory technicians
Electricians
Electrician apprentices
Electric power line workers and cable workers
Electrotypers and stereotypers
Engravers, except photoengravers
Excavating, grading, and road machine operators
Floor layers, except tile setters
Foremen, n.e.c.
Forge operator and hammer operator
Furniture and wood finishers
Furriers
Glaziers
Heat treaters, annealers, and temperers
Inspectors, scalers, and graders; log and lumber
Inspectors, n.e.c.
Jewelers and watchmakers
Job and die setters, metal
Locomotive engineers
Machinists
Machinist apprentices
Mechanics and repairpeople
Millers; grain, flour, and feed
Millwrights
Molders, metal
Molder apprentices
Motion picture projectionists
Opticians; lens grinders and polishers
Painters, construction and maintenance
Painter apprentices
Paperhangers
Pattern and model makers, except paper
Photoengravers and lithographers
Piano and organ tuners and repairpeople
Plasterers

FIGURE 2.1 Continued

Plasterer apprentices
Plumber and pipe fitters
Plumber and pipe fitter apprentices
Power station operators
Press operators and plate printers, printing
Press operators apprentices
Rollers and finishers, metal
Roofers and slaters
Sheetmetal workers and tinsmiths
Sheetmetal apprentices
Shipfitters
Shoe repairpeople
Sign painters and letterers
Stationary engineers
Stone cutters and stone carvers
Structural metal craftspeople
Tailors
Telephone installers and repairpeople
Telephone line workers and splicers
Tile setters
Tool and die makers
Tool and die maker apprentices
Upholsterers
Specified craft apprentices, n.e.c.
Not specified apprentices
Craftspeople and kindred workers, n.e.c.
Former members of the Armed Forces
Craftspeople and kindred workers—allocated
Current members of the Armed Forces

Operatives, except transport
Asbestos and insulation workers
Assemblers
Blasters and powder worker
Bottling and canning operatives
Chainmen, rodmen, and axemen; surveying
Checkers, examiners, and inspectors; manufacturing

FIGURE 2.1 Continued

Clothing ironers and pressers
Cutting operatives, n.e.c.
Dressmakers and seamsters, except factory
Drillers, earth
Drywall installers and lathers
Dyers
Filers, polishers, sanders, and buffers
Garage workers and gas station attendants
Graders and sorters, manufacturing
Produce graders and packers
Heaters, metal
Laundry and dry cleaning operatives, n.e.c.
Meat cutters and butchers, except manufacturing
Meat cutters and butchers, manufacturing
Heat wrappers, retail trade
Metal platers
Milliners
Mine operatives
Oilers and greasers, except auto
Packers and wrappers, n.e.c.
Painters, manufactured articles
Photographic process workers
Precision machine operatives
Punch and stamping press operatives
Riveters and fasteners
Sailors and deckhands
Sawyers
Sewers and stitchers
Shoemaking machine operatives
Solderers
Stationary firepersons
Textile operatives
Welders and flame cutters
Winding operatives, n.e.c.
Machine operatives, miscellaneous specified
Machine operatives, not specified
Miscellaneous operatives

FIGURE 2.1 Continued

Not specified operatives

Transport equipment operatives
Boat workers and canal workers
Bus driver
Conductors and motor operators, urban rail transit
Deliveryperson and routeperson
Fork lift and tow motor operatives
Motor operators; mine, factory, logging camp, etc.
Parking attendants
Railroad brake and switch operators
Taxicab drivers and chauffeurs
Truck drivers

Laborers, except farm
Animal caretakers, except farm
Carpenters' helpers
Construction laborers, except carpenters' helpers
Fishermen and oystermen
Freight and material handlers
Garbage collectors
Gardeners and groundskeepers, except farm
Longshorepersons and stevedores
Lumber workers, rafts workers, and woodchoppers
Stockhandlers
Teamsters
Vehicle washers and equipment cleaners
Warehouse workers, n.e.c.

As might be expected, sociologists have a strong interest in the professions. In fact, until quite recently, articles on the professions have dominated the research literature on the sociology of work in the United States; they still dominate in Great Britain.

The study of professional work can be divided into two phases. In the first, sociologists were concerned primarily with spelling

FIGURE 2.1 Continued

Miscellaneous laborers
Not specified laborers

Farmers and farm managers
Farmers (owners and tenants)
Farm managers
Farmers and farm managers—allocated
Farm foremen
Farm laborers, wage workers
Farm laborers, unpaid family workers
Farm service laborers, self-employed

Service workers, except private household
Cleaning service workers
Food service workers
Health service workers
Personal service workers
Protective service workers

Private household workers
Child care workers, private household
Cooks, private household
Launderers, private household
Housekeepers and servants, private household
Private household workers—allocated

Source: Adapted from U.S. Bureau of the Census. (1971). *1970 Census of Population: Alphabetical Index of Industries and Occupations.* Washington, DC: Government Printing Office.

out the attributes of the professions. Various "models" of the professions were presented, criticized, and sometimes tested empirically.

The second phase, which began in the 1970s, approaches professional work from the perspective of power. Sociologists who take this view study how occupational groups obtain power and maintain it in the face of threats from other occupational groups, the government, and employing organizations. The current definitive study of the professions defines them as "exclusive occupational groups applying somewhat abstract knowledge to particular cases" (Abbott, 1988, p. 8). But the key to understanding the professions is to notice that they constantly struggle with other professions over the "ground" they occupy. They struggle to gain and maintain the exclusive right to do a particular type of work.

Professional Attributes

Although the power perspective is currently dominant, the attribute approach is still somewhat useful. Many authors have tried to capture the essence of professional work by developing definitions, lists of characteristics, or models that separate professional work from other varieties. These authors typically started by identifying types of work that everyone already thought of as professional, such as medicine or law. Then they listed the similarities among these professions and their differences from nonprofessional occupations.

Some sociologists have considered the major criterion for professional status to be an intellectual technique that performs a service for society, that is acquired by special training, and that is unavailable to those outside the profession (Carr-Saunders & Wilson, 1944, p. 547) Each profession has its own basic body of knowledge (Parsons, 1959). Students go to medical schools, law schools, and graduate schools to learn this knowledge. Then they can either apply it in practice or use it for future theoretical development in the laboratory or the library. Increasingly, many occupational groups that aspire to be known as professions—such as nurses, teachers, and social workers—demand that people in these fields attend graduate school to acquire a specialized knowledge base.

The most frequently cited list of professional attributes may be that of Greenwood (1957), who proposed the following five key professional attributes.

1. A profession must have research-based, systematic theory.

2. A profession's practitioners must have authority over clients. "Doctor's orders" is a familiar term that exemplifies this form of authority. Unfortunately, this criterion seems to imply that clients have neither the knowledge nor ability to make judgments that affect their own lives. Naturally, many clients are offended by such an assumption. Furthermore, some forms of professional work have trouble identifying clients. For instance, it is difficult to name the true clients of the scientist at a laboratory bench.

3. The profession must have formal and informal community sanction. Many professions are licensed or certified by state agencies. For example, most states require that veterinarians undertake specific professional studies, follow specific procedures (including personal conduct while taking their exams) to get a state license, and advertise in limited ways. Similar regulations govern chiropractic, social work, architecture, public accountancy, medicine, and nursing. Law is regulated through the court system. In addition, powerful professions such as law and medicine have a strong say about regulations concerned with their practice. Weaker professions have not been so fortunate. Often the regulations that govern them are shaped by a more powerful profession. Nursing and pharmacy, for example, follow many rules dictated by physician groups (Freidson, 1972). Another aspect of community sanction is professional confidence. The information that a client gives to a professional is viewed as privileged, which protects the rights of the client and reaffirms the authority of the professional.

4. The profession must have a code of ethics. The profession itself is charged with ensuring that ethical standards are followed in interactions with clients and fellow professionals.

5. There must be a *professional culture*: norms governing membership in professional associations, the appropriate sites for practice, and standards and locations of professional training. Professional culture also involves the language and symbols associated with a particular kind of professional work, which serve to separate professionals from outsiders.

Other scholars concerned with the professions added other attributes, but the attempt to develop more and more refined lists of professional attributes was largely abandoned after an article appeared that turned Greenwood's list upside down. Roth (1972) claimed that the theoretic base of a profession often serves the faculty of professional or graduate schools more than it serves the clients and that little or no relationship can be found between advanced knowledge and higher-quality service. He also pointed out that the knowledge base is inconsistent. In fields such as medicine, for example, new theories replace old, and treatments come and go. Professional authority is meaningless because clients are free, after all, to fire professionals. Community sanction is a political matter. Codes of ethics are devices for curbing competition within the profession, not for ensuring that all clients receive equal service. And many occupational groups, not just the professions, have a unique culture.

The Power Perspective

Roth's (1972) direct attack on the attribute approach to the professions was developed during the same period that the power approach was being developed. The attempt to define what a profession was through lists of attributes was virtually abandoned. The new thrust became defining how an occupation becomes a profession.

The work of Eliot Freidson, a major proponent of the power perspective, has been very important in the switch. His 1972 study showed how physicians dominate the entire health-care industry, even in the face of aggressive attempts by other professions to gain power (see also Abbott, 1988). For example, Freidson (1972) claimed that the bulk of what nurses learn is "ultimately specified by physicians" (p. 78). Some 20 years after this study, physicians are still dominant, although their power has been eroded somewhat by outside forces. The key point here is that professional status is based on power rather than on the possession of some set of attributes.

Freidson examined specific aspects of the attribute approach from a power perspective. For example, instead of taking the existence of a specialized training program as proof of professional status, Freidson (1972, p. 79) argued that the key question is *who* controls that training? Similarly, he concluded that many nonprofessional occupations also have codes of ethics and a "service orientation"—as do social workers, for instance. What makes the professions different is that they have successfully persuaded the public and state legislatures that they are devoted to public service (p. 82).

It is instructive to note that nursing, one of the medical occupations Freidson analyzed, appears to be fully aware of the importance of the power issue. The American Nurses' Association, the largest professional nursing organization, published *Professionalism and the Empowerment of Nursing* (1982). The very title indicates awareness of the power issue.

Development and Maintenance of Power

The process by which occupations gain power and autonomy seems clear enough. Members of the occupation convince legislators and regulators that they should have the right to self-determination, and legislation or regulations are passed that permit the group to exclude nonmembers from practice and to set fees or rates of payment—in short, to have a monopoly in their area of activity.

The process is not so simple, however. It is not clear why one occupation can gain more power than another. Why, for instance, is a teacher of history in college (the *professor* of history) considered more professional than the teacher of history in high school (the history teacher)? Why does medicine have more power than chiropractics? Why do lawyers have more power than realtors in real-estate transactions, and why do members of the clergy have more power to explain life and death than lay people do? The answers we have are tentative and will undoubtedly remain that way, because it is impossible to reconstruct the history of the professions except by noting that power was gained. We do have some clues, however, about how power is generally gained and maintained.

One set of clues involves the manner in which occupations deal with the public. Well-organized occupational groups take vigorous steps to inform the public and the government of their principles. Occupations that cannot convince the general public or key segments of the public that they actually possess professional features fail to achieve full professional status (Grimm & Kronus, 1973). A key component in gaining public and political acceptance is the ability to use mass media (Stein, 1981). If media begin to treat an occupation as if it were a profession, then the battle for professional status is being won.

There is an interesting paradox here: Professional specialties that have high public recognition and status, such as criminal law, often have low status within the profession itself (Abbott, 1981). Perhaps the public has higher regard than do professionals for occupations that effectively deal with disorder or the lack of order. If so, then we can understand the difference in the professional status of the history professor and the history teacher. The professor can develop a new order by publishing a book showing, for example, a new understanding of the colonial United States. The history teacher can do the same thing but is much less likely to because of the demands of the high-school teaching job. But the professor is expected to publish, and thus the occupation of professor is accorded greater professional status by the public.

Knowledge and power also go hand-in-hand (Cullen, 1978). An organized occupation that has gained power through public recognition of the value and importance of its knowledge is considered a profession. Incidentally, individuals gain and maintain power within specific work settings in much the same way. Thus, at both the macrolevel and the microlevel, knowledge is the basis for the power that is the basis for professional status. The public must perceive this knowledge as important, and media and policy makers must go along with this perception.

Internal Threats to Professional Power

So far, we have been thinking of professional work as if it were all of one kind within a given profession. Obviously, it is not. Wide variations exist in professional practice based on location of work (whether urban or rural), organizational affiliation (whether self-employment as a solo practitioner or employment as a salaried staffmember of a large corporation), and type or degree of specialization (whether a general practice or a highly esoteric specialty).

Consider the variations in the legal profession. Heinz and Laumann's (1983) comprehensive analysis of lawyers in Chicago vividly depicts the diversity. Chicago lawyers can be grouped by type of practice:

- large corporate (for example, antitrust defense or securities),
- regulatory,
- general corporate (for example, banking or commercial),
- political (criminal prosecution),
- personal business (for example, tax or real estate), and
- personal plight (for example, divorce or personal injury).

This level of differentiation is not universal, however. The work of rural lawyers is very homogeneous (Landon, 1990). But the legal profession is politically and numerically dominated by urban lawyers.

Heinz and Laumann (1983) also found major differences in the type of client served: corporate versus individual. The type of client served is in turn linked to the lawyers' social origins. Heinz and Laumann (1983) concluded that, especially in large cities, there are "two legal professions, one recruited from more privileged social origins and the other from less prestigious backgrounds. . . . The first kind of lawyer serves corporate clients that are quite wealthy and powerful, and the other serves individuals and small businesses that are far less powerful" (p. 385). In a separate study, Erlanger (1977) found that lawyers with experience in a federal program aimed at providing legal services for minorities and the poor also had less prestigious private practice, less corporate counsel work, and a stronger orientation to social reform in their later practices.

Despite such diversity in the legal profession, lawyers continue to be perceived as powerful. But diversity becomes an internal threat to professional power when it leads to the creation of separate organizations for each professional subgroup. Nursing, for example, is a highly fragmented occupation. Nurses are differentiated by level of education: diploma, associate degree, baccalaureate degree, and graduate degree. There are also several national associations for nurses, plus state associations and labor unions that represent nurses. In addition, there are strong associations of nurses who are engaged in specialized practices, such as operating room nurses, oncology nurses, nurse midwives—a total of 52 such specialty groups. There are also professional associations for men in nursing and associations based on the ethnic background of their members, such as African-Americans and Latinos. Such internal differentiation is viewed by many as the main barrier to nurses achieving full professional status (Styles, 1982).

Extreme internal differentiation can rip a profession apart. In the field of psychology, for instance, academic psychologists recently split from practitioner psychologists and formed their own professional association (the American Psychological Society, as opposed to the American Psychological Association). New professional associations are more homogeneous, they also are less wealthy and powerful than the old ones. The psychologists are thus victims of internal threats to professional power.

External Threats to Professional Power

The threats to professional power are not all internal. Professional work also faces a variety of external threats, some from the organizations that employ professionals, some from social and political trends, and some from allied professions.

Organizations threaten the power of professions in two ways. First, they threaten individuals when the organizational goals, control, supervision, incentives, and decision making conflict with professional norms and standards. For the military psychiatrist, for example, good psychiatric practice might conflict directly with military needs, because a diagnosis of battle fatigue could keep a soldier out of combat. The key factor is the autonomy of the individual professional in the face of organizational demands. In one interesting study, engineers were found to have a great deal of autonomy in their day-to-day work but less autonomy in choosing projects and controlling resources and time (Meiksine & Watson, 1989). The engineer who had an idea about an interesting and potentially cost-saving new project could be overruled by an organizational superior, which lessened the engineer's autonomy and hence professional status.

Second, organizations threaten professional power in a more general way. Because the organization is the employer and the professional is the employee, the organization wins when organizational norms run counter to those of a profession. The result, in some cases, is that the organization absorbs some professionals (Evans & Laumann, 1983). A surprisingly large number of people move out of the professions in which they began their career. Such movement is common in the engineering professions, where people are often promoted out of the ranks of engineers into the ranks of managers and administrators (Perrucci, 1973; Perrucci & Gerstl, 1969). This fluidity limits the engineering profession's ability to control its own destiny. On the other hand, movement from the legal profession into organizational management, which is also rather common, has hardly been a threat to the already entrenched legal profession.

Organizations are a special threat to those occupations known as *semiprofessions* (Etzioni, 1969) such as nursing, teaching, social work, and librarianship; these have never attained full professional power and status. Instead of having autonomy in their work, semiprofessionals are subordinate to a large administrative system, such as a school board or a set of public-welfare regulations. Power eludes them because there are multiple sources of power within the system.

Broad social and political trends also may threaten professional power. One such trend has been called the *information explosion*. With the advent of do-it-yourself publications on divorces and wills, the public has become more knowledgeable and thus less dependent on lawyers (Rothman, 1984). In addition, computer-based information storage and retrieval have made it possible to routinize a great deal of legal research (Haug, 1977). Computers can generate legal documents and assist in the preliminary screening of jury lists. Consider also computer programming, which began as an occupational offspring of electrical engineering. With the development of high-level computer languages and more sophisticated software, engineers could be replaced by less expensive nonprofessionals (Kraft, 1979).

New employment patterns can also threaten professional power. For example, the growing employment of lawyers within organizations contributes to their deprofessionalization, in part by reducing professional autonomy (Rothman, 1984). A study of U.S. Department of Justice attorneys found that both political and organizational pressures dictated a good part of the attorneys' work (Eisenstein, 1978). In medicine, too, the invasion of large corporations, such as private health-insurance firms and hospital conglomerates, is eroding physicians' professional power (Starr, 1982). Similar trends are affecting professionals in education and social welfare.

Yet another social or political threat comes from consumers and clients. Individual consumers, consumer groups, and state and federal governmental bodies have begun to scrutinize and challenge the professions. For instance, in *Bates v. State of Arizona* (1977) the U.S. Supreme Court outlawed Arizona's ban on advertising by lawyers, opening the door for "unprofessional" competition. Similar threats to other forms of professional work have also been identified. For example, it is not uncommon to find students challenging curricular decisions made by faculty.

Another social or political threat is the general state of the economy. Some forms of professional work are particularly vulnerable to economic upturns and downturns. Scientists and engineers, for example, are quite likely to be laid off or fired during downturns in the business cycle (Leventman, 1981; Schervish, 1983a). A profession whose members are in and out of the labor force and who must sometimes seek alternative forms of employment would appear to be weakened. People who leave their professional work tend to drop their professional identities and their memberships in professional organizations.

The final type of external threat to professional power comes from allied professions. For example, several other professions have been attempting to take over part of the work of lawyers:

accountants, bankers, title insurers, tax consultants, realtors, and underwriters (Rothman, 1984). These other occupational groups, themselves organized as professions, seek to expand their power—in this case, at the expense of lawyers. But lawyers also try to encroach on other professions.

Gender and Professional Power

Aside from the threats to power we have already reviewed, the professions face the uncertain effects of growing numbers of female professionals. Sociologists have been fascinated by the idea of a gender threat to professional power.

Apparently, the influx of women into certain professions has actually lowered autonomy and hence deprofessionalized those occupations (Simpson & Simpson, 1969). According to this argument, women enter the semiprofessions of nursing, teaching, and social work with less autonomy than men, and this lowered autonomy itself plagues the occupation. Furthermore, in the established professions of medicine, law, and academia, women tend to be found in the less prestigious specialties and are greatly disadvantaged in terms of salary (Fox & Hesse-Biber, 1984). Even in female-dominated semiprofessions such as librarianship, social work, nursing, and teaching, men who are in the field are disproportionately in administrative positions (Grimm & Stern, 1974; Parelius & Parelius, 1978).

The tide of women moving into the well-established professions is unlikely to stop. The semiprofessions will probably continue to be dominated by women. The consequence cannot be predicted with certainty, but it would appear to be deprofessionalization. It is also quite possible that as professions become more feminized, they will also become less elite and more egalitarian as the values expressed by most feminists are put into place.

Managerial Work

Another high-status, high-power occupational group consists of executives, managers, officials, and administrators. Of interest is that managers share many values with members of the professions, which is not unexpected given the generally high social position of both groups (Wuthnow & Shrumm, 1983). In an industrial society, however, the key group is management (Campbell, Dunnette, Lawler, & Weick, 1970). This group comprises people who decide how to use society's resources to produce the necessary goods and services.

Above all, managerial work is organizational. It is carried out at the very top of organizations, in the case of executives, or throughout what is known as the *managerial hierarchy*. Both public and private organizations—entities as diverse as Procter & Gamble, the State University of New York system, the Minnesota Vikings, the American Red Cross, the U.S. Department of Labor, Apple Computer, and Ben & Jerry's Ice Cream—rely on people engaged in this form of work. In general, management is the term used in the private sector. The not-for-profit sector, such as hospitals and museums, uses administrators; governmental agencies employ officials. The term *executive* is used across sectors to refer to management people at or near the organization's top. Executives include the *chief executive officer* (CEO) and those people (frequently, *vice presidents*) who report directly to the top executive.

Surprisingly little sociological research has been done on managerial work. However, a vast literature does prescribe *how* to manage. Business schools at such prestigious universities as Harvard and Stanford, as well as myriad less well-known institutions, are specifically in the business of turning out managerial personnel. They have carefully devised curricula that deal with management.

What Managers Do

To understand the nature of managerial work, we will begin with one of the few sociological studies of managers. Caplow (1983, p. 4) noted that all managers must deal with the same issues, because all human organizations are similar. In addition, every organization, except the smallest, has subunits—divisions, departments, branches—with the same characteristics as the total organization. According to Caplow, all managers must establish their authority, engage in continuous communication with people in and out of the organization, maintain both productivity and employee morale (no easy task, because productivity and morale have been shown to be independent of each other), and react to changes in the external environment.

Managers' day-to-day activities revolve around communication. In her analysis of a large industrial firm, Rosabeth Kanter (1977a) described the work of a typical manager:

> One typical day, a Monday in March in the Midwest, began at
> 7:30 when the manager arrived at the office. From 7:30 to
> 9:00 he finished reading his mail, wrote letters, and called
> headquarters. From 9:00 to 10:30 he met informally with
> sales people and customer service people to discuss current
> problems and offer help. From 10:30 to 11:30 he interviewed a
> job candidate. From 11:30 to 12:00 he returned phone
> messages, and from 12:00 to 1:00 he had lunch with a sales
> person in order to conduct an informal performance appraisal
> before the formal meeting. From 1:00 to 2:00, he read more
> mail, and from 2:00 to 2:30 he answered phone messages,
> again from the headquarters office. At 2:30 he received a wire
> on the state of the business, which he was expected to
> communicate to the field and receive a response to. He began
> on this and continued until 3:30. From 3:30 to 4:30 he worked
> on his quarterly review and at 4:30 left for home. Tuesday
> and Wednesday were spent out of town visiting another
> office. Thursday and Friday he returned to his own office, and
> Friday evening he attended a senior executive dinner from
> 7:00 to 11:00 p.m. (p. 57)

The organization that Kanter (1977a) studied was large, complex, and geographically dispersed. Communication had to be rapid and accurate. Given the organization's size and complexity, communication also had to pass through a variety of channels. Kanter concluded that this communication structure generated a desire for smooth social relationships and hence the selection of managers with whom communication would be easiest—in this case, white men. Each manager could trust that other managers would have the same experiences and values and understand communication in a common way. Strong pressures for social conformity in this organization further increased the homogeneity among managers.

An important finding of the Kanter (1977a) study was that there were no objective criteria for the evaluation of managerial performance. Instead, managers in this organization were evaluated on their perceived loyalty, which was taken to mean putting the company first, spending long hours at work, being willing to be transferred, and demonstrating total devotion to the work.

A major motivation of the managers Kanter studied was advancement within the firm. Advancement indicated that the person was doing a good job. (Remember, doing a good job could not be measured concretely.) These managers also wanted to gain power within the organization. *Power* here means more than official position. Individuals whose careers were seen as being on the "fast track" had more power than those at equivalent levels who were not moving as quickly. Still, managerial power is at least partly a function of the manager's position within the organization.

Management Classifications

Unlike professionals, who are classified primarily on the basis of industry, managers tend to be classified primarily on the basis of their position within an organization. The two dimensions of classification are line versus staff work and level of management.

Line Versus Staff Work

Managers are often classified as doing line or staff work (Dalton, 1950, 1959). *Line work* involves direct management of whatever it is the organization does: production, sales management, or management of such activities as transportation, communication, and purchasing. Hospital or museum administrators would also be considered line managers.

Staff work involves some kind of expertise, such as human-resource management, public-relations management, accounting, or law (Smigel, 1964). In high-technology industries, however, what is typically thought of as staff work, such as engineering or systems design work, is actually line work. In some ways, staff management could be considered professional work. The key point is that staff managers provide expertise for other managers (Montagna, 1977). Staff work has grown in importance as organizations have become more reliant on specialized expertise.

Indeed, although line management was once considered the route to CEO positions, it is now staff positions that lead to the top. A legal background has been found to be a major route to the executive suite: More top corporate officers hold legal degrees than advanced business degrees (Priest & Rothman, 1985). This development is not surprising, because legal problems are among the most pressing issues facing modern corporations.

Management Levels

The line-staff distinction tends to mask the other major way of classifying managerial work, which is based on the level in the organization at which the individual is working. These levels are called *upper* (or *top), middle,* and *lower management—*or *institutional, managerial,* and *technical* levels (Parsons, 1960).

The institutional or top level of management is concerned with how the organization relates to its external world. Executives at this level must ensure that the organization continues to receive support from its constituency and from other organizations. Very commonly, top-level executives maintain relationships with important outsiders through interlocking directorates, in which officers of one firm sit on the board of directors of another firm (Burt, 1980; Pennings, 1980; Useem, 1979). Of the 797 largest U.S. firms, only 62 had no such relationships (Pennings, 1980). Interlocking directorates are most common in concentrated industries where near monopolies exist; financial firms are disproportionately represented. Those who serve on corporate boards also tend to be members of government advisory boards, directors of philanthropic organizations, trustees of colleges and universities, and directors of other major power groups within the social system (Useem, 1979).

Top executives do not actually "execute." Instead, the managerial or middle level is concerned with the internal administration of the organization, and the technical or lower level deals with specifics, such as productivity, a particular legal issue, or a single operating unit. Thus, the higher the level in the managerial hierarchy, the more general the work.

Proprietors

Another type of managerial work should be noted here. *Proprietors* are people who own and manage their own businesses. Farms, motels, gas stations, grocery stores, barber and beauty shops—all of these can be proprietorships. We will consider proprietors only briefly here; this form of work will come up again in Chapter 8, where we consider the racial and ethnic aspects of work, for it is among minorities that proprietorships assume particular importance.

The types of operations that proprietors typically own and operate are subject to three pressures that make this form of work less viable than it may have been in the past. The first pressure is competition. The very high failure rate of small businesses makes this a very unstable form of work. If a proprietor is successful, then the enterprise will probably do one of two things—which accounts for the other two pressures. The first option is to grow, in which case the proprietor becomes the executive of at least a moderate-sized organization. The second option is to be purchased by a larger firm, in which case the proprietor may be retained as a manager or executive. Small, family-run farms remain proprietorships, but the pressures in other spheres are such that proprietorship is becoming an impossible dream.

A relatively new form of work, which gives the illusion of proprietorship, is performed by people who hold franchises from large organizations. Franchises are common in the fast-food industry and its thousands of McDonald's, Burger Kings, and the like. They are also found in other retail areas, such as records and tapes, computers, hardware, and dry cleaning. Like proprietors, franchise holders make a financial investment and hire and fire employees. But to the extent that portions and prices are predetermined by the parent organization, franchise holders are more lower-level managers than proprietors.

Top Management and Social Class

Sociological studies of the relationship between management and the larger society have focused on top management: its orientations toward profit, public good, and personal gain. In reviewing the literature, James and Soref (1981) found that top executives have more control over corporations than do owners (stockholders). One result is the growth of a class of technically competent managers and professionals at the expense of "the capitalist class," which in another era derived power from the ownership of productive property. Today, according to James and Soref (1981), "positions in organizations determine wealth, rather than the reverse" (p. 1). The researchers further noted that top corporate managers, unlike owners, are more inclined to pursue goals other than profit maximization, such as social responsibility. Managers can also pursue strategies that benefit management rather than owners.

James and Soref (1981) tested their ideas in a study of 286 of the largest 300 industrial firms in the United States. They found that at least 5% of the firms had dismissed the CEO in 1965. Poor profit performance was the major reason for such firings. James and Soref concluded that profit remains the major criterion by which performance is measured and that social responsibility is subordinate to profit.

Although other sociologists have written about the capitalist class as though it were unified and united in self-protection (Useem, 1979; Zeitlin, 1974), James and Soref found that CEOs who were related to the owners—and hence of the same social class—were as likely to be fired in much the same way as nonfamily members. However, the class argument is supported by a study of the pathways taken to top corporate-management positions (Useem & Karabel, 1986). Movement into these positions is apparently facilitated by an undergraduate degree from an elite school or by a Master's of Business Administration (MBA) or law degree from a prominent school. All other things being equal, upper-class background helps people move into top-management positions. Class factors also play a role in people's ability to move into formal and informal intercorporate networks.

White-Collar Work

Thus far, we have examined forms of work that are characterized by both power in the work setting and high status. We now turn to forms of work that have less power and status.

White-collar work is clerical and sales work. It is a very rapidly growing segment of the labor force. In 1900, white-collar workers made up only 7% of the labor force; in 1990, the figure was 28% (U.S. Department of Labor, 1990). Like managerial work, white-collar work is organizational work, but it has much lower status and much less power.

A major distinguishing characteristic of white-collar work is its high concentration of women. The "typical female worker" is likely to hold a white-collar job. The majority of women do clerical work (the so-called pink-collar occupations) or work in retail sales (Fox & Hesse-Biber, 1984). It is interesting to note that department store salespeople for "big ticket" items such as television sets and appliances usually are men, even though women may be the predominant users of these items. Similarly, most car salespeople are men. These products are the ones that have the highest potential commissions. A fascinating exception is real-estate sales work, where women are particularly evident.

Clerical Work

In a caricature reminiscent of Charles Dickens, C. Wright Mills (1956) portrayed an early office worker as

> [an] old-young man, slightly stoop shouldered, with a sallow complexion, usually dyspeptic-looking, with black sleeves and a green eye-shade. . . . Regardless of the kind of business, regardless of their ages, they all looked alike. . . . He seemed tired and he was never quite happy, because . . . his face betrayed the strain of working toward the climax of his month's labors. He was usually a neat penman, but his real pride was in his ability to add a column of figures rapidly and accurately. In spite of this accomplishment, however, he seldom, if ever, left his ledger for a more promising position. His mind was atrophied by that destroying, hopeless

influence of drudgery and routine work. He was little more than a figuring machine with an endless number of figure combinations learned by heart. His feat was a feat of memory. (p. 191)

Office work has changed dramatically for two reasons. First, the demand for office workers is rising as a result of important organizational developments. Organizations have grown larger and more complex, requiring more administrative or coordinating activities (Blau & Schoenherr, 1971). There has also been an explosive growth of information-handling organizations such as banks, insurance companies, financial institutions, government agencies, and communications firms. This growth, combined with the decline in goods-producing industries, has resulted in a shift in demand from unskilled or semiskilled laborers to clerical employees who are capable of working with symbols rather than things.

Second, office work has changed because of technological development, which has occurred in four stages (Shepard, 1971). The first stage was characterized by "craft accurate work," which includes the fast and accurate shorthand of the secretary, the precise accounts of the bookkeeper, and the penmanship of Mill's ledger clerk. In the second stage, "early mechanization," typewriters, adding machines, and dictating machines were introduced. These required skills, but not the highly developed craft of the earlier era. The third stage was "punched-card data processing." The IBM card became universal, and people were employed as keypunchers, verifiers, and business machine operators. At this point, office work began to resemble factory work. The fourth and current stage is "electronic data processing." Not only data, but also words are electronically processed. Note that new stages did not completely replace earlier ones. Some secretaries still take shorthand, some firms still use typing pools (Kanter, 1977a), and data are still entered at a keyboard, whether onto cards, tapes, or disks.

The Feminization of Clerical Work. As these changes were occurring, white-collar work was also becoming *feminized,* or dominated by female workers. The introduction of the typewriter was the key reason. The Remington Company hired women to demonstrate the new machines (Fox & Hesse-Biber, 1984). Typing became a "feminine specialty" (Glenn & Feldberg, 1979). Typing did not take over men's work, because the work simply had not existed before. Women were also far more likely to be hired as telephone operators, because they were viewed as "more dexterous and 'chatty' than men" (Fox & Hesse-Biber, 1984). This work was attractive to women: It had higher pay and status than other work available to women at the time.

With these developments, clerical work became increasingly dominated by women, who were willing to work for less pay, which led companies to lower their costs by hiring women rather than men. As organizations grew and developed, so did the number of women in clerical positions. The typing job of the past is the word-processing job of the present. It is still likely to be held by a woman.

Telephone operator is another highly feminized position, although today it is one of the less desirable white-collar jobs (Montagna, 1977, p. 317). Because switchboards must be open 7 days a week, 24 hours a day, telephone work is shift work, which is relatively uncommon in the white-collar world. There is also close, direct supervision and little freedom of movement. Even with the technological changes that are occurring in the telecommunications industry, it appears that the telephone operator will remain tied to a switchboard.

Clerical jobs are usually dead-end jobs, because clerical workers are not usually linked to other areas of the organization in ways that would permit advancement (Seidman, 1978). Banks and telephone companies have systematically excluded their female clerical workers from advancement (Fox & Hesse-Biber, 1984). But this situation is changing. For example, those who work in U.S. government agencies can move from the top word-processing job to the lowest-level administrative job and then up the management ladder (DiPrete & Soule, 1988). This pattern will open up many opportunities for women.

The Deskilling of Clerical Work. Clerical work has been the focus of heated debates about *deskilling.* Some say that technological changes in the office have neither "deskilled" work nor decreased the numbers of clerical workers, that they have instead enhanced productivity (Smith, 1988). Others have found evidence of the restructuring of clerical work.

In the communication industry, clerical work has been restruc-tured to provide more managerial control and less conceptual content; the result has been clerical workers who feel more alien-ated from their work (Vallas, 1987). A study of female workers in Chicago found that low-level clerical and sales positions lack complexity (Lopata, Znaniecki, Norr, Barnewolt, & Miller, 1985). However, the social relationships the women formed on the job apparently made up for the lack of complexity in their tasks, because the workers reported their jobs as being complex.

Rosabeth Kanter (1977a) analyzed white-collar workers as well as managers, and her findings are consistent with the points made here. The secretaries brought flowers and bright colors to their work areas, remembered birthdays, and chatted with one another and their bosses. "In many ways—visually, socially, and organizationally—the presence of secretaries represented a re-serve of the human inside of the bureaucratic" (p. 70). Clerical workers in this setting were able to create their own world, a counterweight to any deskilling that had taken place.

Another form of clerical work that adds an interesting wrinkle to the picture is *temporary* clerical work. "Temp" workers are employed by service firms and then placed in other organizations for some length of time. In effect, these workers are controlled by two firms—the employer and the client firm (Gottfried, 1991). Temporary service firms such as Kelly and Manpower have developed elabo-rate systems to control their workers and maintain their loyalty. Temporary clerical work has the potential to make major changes in the shape of white-collar work in the future, because organiza-tions may no longer need large, stable cadres of clerical workers.

Sales Work

The other form of white-collar work to be considered here is sales work. We are not considering sales executives here: Such workers are in the managerial hierarchy and are able to use their own discretion to decide such issues as cost per unit and estimated time of delivery. The white-collar salesperson does not have that sort of discretion. Like clerical work, the nature of sales work is determined by the employing organization. Product characteristics and prices are set in advance by others in the organization. Product demand is created through marketing and advertising strategies.

Sales work is not completely routinized, of course. By controlling the customer, sales workers enhance their chances of making the sale and also are able to protect their own self-concept. Automobile salespeople, for example, prefer to have customers that they have recruited rather than people who walk in off the street (Miller, 1964). The person who just wanders in is an unknown, while the sale worker's own "prospects" have some certainty about them. In a similar fashion, the travel agent—a seller of a service— tries to develop regular clients. Still, although travel agents can exercise some discretion by suggesting routes or accommodations, they are ultimately bound by published timetables, fares, and regulations.

In contrast, the retail sales worker, as exemplified by the department store clerk, has very limited discretion on the job. Consider the major discrepancy in status between sales clerks and their customers. Sales clerks must "wait on" customers, which in itself connotes negative status (Mills, 1956). They have no discretion about the products offered and cannot dicker over price. Nonetheless, retail clerks can choose from a variety of techniques to sell their products and can sometimes earn commissions. They can suggest which shirt, perfume, or stove would best suit a particular customer. In addition, retailing is one of the few industries that allows a person to move from the white-collar level into management. Sales clerks can become buyers, although the tendency among larger retail establishments is to hire college graduates and have them work as clerks as part of their management training. Still, the potential for advancement in retail sales is greater than in most other white-collar work.

Sales work also is one of the major bastions of entrepreneurship. Most automobile dealerships have been developed by former auto salespeople, for example. The same phenomenon would appear to be operative with appliances and men's and women's clothing. For most sales workers, of course, such moves are not likely.

Another form of sales work takes place outside of an organization: home-based direct-sales work for companies such as Amway,

Mary Kay Cosmetics, and Tupperware. Four out of five direct sellers are women (Biggart, 1989). This form of work allows flexibility in timing and control over the extent of one's own effort. However, direct-sales workers cannot control the products they sell (Kraut & Grambsch, 1987). In addition, direct-sales workers are only marginal participants in the labor force.

The final form of sales work is one that many of my students have tried: telemarketing. This is typically very tightly controlled, high-pressure work, with banks of telephones in operation at the same time and a continually repeated message. Most of my students have reacted to this form of work with intense displeasure.

Blue-Collar Work

Blue-collar workers share one major distinguishing characteristic: In one way or another, they are involved in goods, not services. They can be employed in the:

- extraction of a raw material, as are miners, oil-rig workers, and lumberjacks;
- physical assembling of a product, as are auto workers, carpenters, and garment workers;
- repair of a product, as are airplane mechanics, telephone repair persons, and shoe repair persons; and
- distribution of a product, as are truck drivers, railroad engineers, and gas-pipeline workers.

In other words, blue-collar work is industrial work.

Industrial work has been the subject of a great deal of scholarly and literary analysis. Marxian theory is based on a particular view of the industrial worker. The fields of industrial sociology and industrial psychology began with a focus on this form of work.

In later chapters we will deal with many of the important issues regarding industrial work, such as alienation, the extent to which there is a working class, unequal pay between genders and racial and ethnic groups, possible empowerment through unionization, and class identification. The purpose here is to show that blue-collar work involves a wide range of activities and surprising differentiation in such important variables as pay, status, and power.

Foremen and First-Line Supervisors

The term *foreman* is generally accurate, because the overwhelming number of *first-line* production supervisors are men. Indeed, even where there are both men and women workers, there is a strong tendency for men to be promoted into the supervisory positions. (For analyses of this pattern, see South, Bonjean, Corder, & Markham, 1982; Wolf & Fligstein, 1979a). Still, female first-line supervisors face the same dilemma as their male counterparts.

The first-line supervisor's role is not an easy one. Writing some four decades ago, Roethlisberger (1945) noted that, in theory at least, the foreman "has to be a manager, a cost accountant, an engineer, a lawyer, a teacher, a leader, an inspector, a disciplinarian, a counselor, a friend, and, above all, an example" (p. 283). Quite obviously, no one could have all of these skills or possess all of the knowledge required. And more important, staff experts at the managerial level have taken over most of these duties (Miller & Form, 1964, p. 211). Thus, the primary duty of today's foreman is direct supervision.

This supervisory role is complicated first by the origins of the supervisors. Traditionally, foremen have been promoted from the ranks of the workers. There is mixed evidence in regard to the extent to which members of the rank-and-file desire promotion to foreman. One study of automobile workers found that they viewed promotion to foreman as desirable (Walker, Guest, & Turner, 1952), but another study found that less than 10% of auto workers wanted to take such a position (Chinoy, 1955). A British study found mixed but mostly negative attitudes toward the possible promotion to foreman (Goldthorpe, Lockwood, Bechhofer, & Platt, 1970). The other route to the position is from outside the immediate work group. When the foreman is brought in from outside, it is typically as part of the training for later movement up the managerial ladder. The new foreman, typically a college graduate, has not been "one of the boys."

We can begin to see one aspect of the dilemma that foremen face. Are they managers or are they workers? As first-line supervisors, they are really neither.

Second, their position's awkwardness is exacerbated by the necessity for them to implement decisions made at higher levels in the organization (Wray, 1949). Furthermore, foremen are expected to focus on the task at hand and on the relationships among subordinates (Etzioni, 1961, 1965). It is next to impossible to act in both ways at the same time. A task-oriented foreman is likely to behave in ways that threaten socioemotional ties with workers, and an overemphasis on work relationships impedes productivity. The whole situation is made even more difficult if the workplace is unionized. The union structure further erodes the foreman's authority (Halpern, 1961).

There are four ways to adapt to this sort of role conflict (Miller & Form, 1964). First, the foreman can identify with management, which is most likely in the case of the outside person who has been brought in and who expects to move into higher management. Second, the foreman can identify with workers, which is the most likely adaptation made by those who have been promoted from the ranks. These first two forms of identification are the most common adaptations. Third, the foreman can attempt a dual orientation, identifying equally with both management and workers. This orientation is most likely to occur among those who have been recently promoted. It is also likely to last only until a crisis forces the individual to take a stand with one group or the other. Fourth, the foreman can identify with other foremen through a foremen's union or association. In essence, though, this approach is a recognition of the foreman's marginal status.

The orientation trend among foremen appears to be in the direction of management (Grimm & Dunn, 1986). Changes in manufacturing technology are producing more complex sociotechnical systems, and the old "boss-worker" split is becoming less severe. As a result, the role conflicts experienced by foremen are lessening. If the trend continues, of course, foremen will no longer be blue-collar workers.

Skilled Workers

Skilled workers, the "aristocracy of labor" (Mackenzie, 1973), are often called *craftsmen*. As with "foremen," the gender designation is accurate, because the overwhelming majority of workers in this category are men—usually, white men. Skilled workers and foremen are generally assumed to be of relatively equal status. "Craftsmen" and "foremen," in fact, are grouped together by the U.S. Department of Labor. They have composed a surprisingly stable component of the labor force, moving from 10% in 1900 to 14% in 1950 to 12% in 1990 (Tausky, 1984; U.S. Department of Labor, 1990).

Many forms of skilled work are found in the building trades: carpenter, plumber, painter, steamfitter, mason, welder. Others, such as the tool-and-die maker, work in traditional industrial settings. Still others, such as the long-distance truck driver or railroad engineer, are engaged in transporting raw materials and finished products. Some forms of skilled work border on the provision of services, as with the auto mechanic, the television repair person, or the computer technician. However, inasmuch as the service is performed on an object, it is reasonable to classify these occupations as blue-collar work.

Technological change is a major factor in skilled work. For example, the older craft of printing is dying, but automated printing and the repair of automated typesetting equipment are emerging as new crafts (Hull, Friedman, & Rogers, 1982). This is not to suggest that the percentage of skilled workers in the labor force remains in equilibrium. Nor is it to suggest that employing organizations would not like to reduce their dependence on skilled workers (they cost more than semiskilled or unskilled workers). What it does suggest is that the production and maintenance of goods has always required skilled workers and skilled work. This pattern is likely to continue.

Crafts share many characteristics of the professions (Caplow, 1954, pp. 102-198). For example, the occupation (through the union) controls recruitment, training, and advancement, which can create a monopoly and hence increase rewards for its members. It can, has, and does exclude such "undesirables" as women and minority group members. Membership in a craft also usually involves a lifelong commitment, as it does in the professions. The craft is responsible for evaluating individual workers as they move through the stages of apprentice, journeyman, and master. Craft control is exercised outside the employing organization at the local community level; professional control is at the local, state, and national levels. Furthermore, skilled workers can have a strong occupational community (Blauner, 1964). Employing organizations (such as construction firms) recognize this and are organized very much like professional organizations (Stinchcombe, 1959).

The profession-craft analogy can be carried too far, of course. There are major differences in the content and length of training programs, with the professions emphasizing theory and the crafts emphasizing hands-on experience. There are obvious differences in status and power between the groups. There is also the subtle but important distinction between "clean" and "dirty" work (Hughes, 1958). Craft workers get dirty, which has negative consequences for their status (Reiss, 1961, p. 11). One could argue that surgeons and surgical nurses also get dirty, but their hands and bodies are encased in sanitary clothing.

The point is that skilled craft work has characteristics that are quite different from those of other blue-collar workers. In addition, craft workers have a far greater potential for becoming entrepreneurs. For example, the painter can become a painting contractor. If the operation succeeds, the skilled worker becomes a proprietor and joins the ranks of management. When skilled workers do become self-employed, they tend to make more money and have different identities than do employed workers (Form, 1982).

Semiskilled Workers

Semiskilled work is somewhat specialized but is designed to be learned in a relatively short time. The most obvious examples of semiskilled work are found in factories (Montagna, 1977):

> The large majority of factory workers are semiskilled
> workers, persons who operate a multitude of different
> machines. There are filers, polishers, sanders, buffers, punch
> and stamp press operatives, welders, drill press operatives,
> lathe and milling machine operatives, textile operatives,
> grinders and winders, automobile assembly line workers,

rubber, chemical, and paper plant workers, shoe factory
workers, and many hundreds more. (p. 345)

Individual factory workers do only a small portion of the assembly.
They are expected to meet certain production goals and are closely
supervised.

Factory work has declined in the United States, which has
been described as being in the throes of "deindustrialization."
Semiskilled workers composed 20% of the labor force in 1950, but
only 11% in 1990 (U.S. Department of Labor, 1990). Several
factors are contributing to this decline. First, U.S. employers seek
the lowest costs for their production processes. Many are going
"offshore," placing manufacturing operations in other countries or
buying components made overseas. The second factor is very
strong competition from well-run organizations in other countries. Japanese electronics and automotive firms have demonstrated innovative ways to design and process products, many of
which reduce the need for semiskilled workers. Finally, automation and robotics are having a profound effect on the availability
of semiskilled work.

There are several myths about semiskilled work. The first is
that anyone can do it. This myth was inadvertently exposed by
Linhart (1981), who took a job on the assembly line of a French
automobile factory. His express purpose was to politicize and
organize the workers. But his experiences were also an unintended
demonstration that not everyone can do semiskilled work, because
he found that he could not because he lacked the requisite strength
and dexterity. He was also unsuccessful in his organizing efforts.

Linhart's study also vividly demonstrates the invalidity of
another myth: that semiskilled work has become relatively safe
and easy. The work that Linhart and his co-workers were asked
to perform involved noxious fumes, sharp pieces of metal, and the
inexorable movement of the assembly line, which threatened the
workers' mental and physical well-being.

The biggest myth about semiskilled work is that it is always
alienating to the worker. We will examine alienation in detail in
Chapter 3. For now, it is enough to understand two important

meanings of alienation (see Allardt, 1976, for an interpretation of Marx & Engels, 1939). The first meaning arises from the private ownership of the means of production and the division of labor. Semiskilled workers are clearly alienated or divorced from decisions in these matters, except in cases of employee ownership (see Chapter 10). The second meaning of alienation is psychological and involves the ways in which people react to the objective conditions of their work. Here the issue is much more confusing. The key factor seems to be the expectations that people bring to their semiskilled work. For some workers, routine and repetitive work is alienating; for others, it is a source of satisfaction (Walker & Guest, 1962).

Not all semiskilled work is work in factories. Transportation is another important industry for semiskilled workers. The work of the cabdriver, for instance, is semiskilled but much less structured than that of the factory worker (Davis, 1959). The driver's success depends on finding fares. Although these are most likely found in such locations as airports, hotels, and entertainment areas, there is almost no predictability of where the fare might want to be taken or how much the fare will tip the driver. There are few steady customers and thus a great deal of uncertainty. In addition, the skills involved in driving a cab are usually possessed by the fares themselves. They frequently know exactly where they are going and how to get there. The cabdriver is thus an appendage to the vehicle. Finally, the cabdriver's opportunities for developing close relationships with fares is extremely limited, and developing relationships with other cabdrivers is counterproductive, because time spent talking is time not spent earning money.

To some extent, labeling work as skilled or semiskilled is arbitrary. The long-distance truck driver is considered a skilled worker, but the local truck driver is considered semiskilled. The distinction seems to be based on the length of time it takes to learn the job and the job's earning potential.

Another basic characteristics of most semiskilled work is that workers have their work defined for them by the employing organization. Potential employees apply for work but not for specific jobs. Training times are brief, and so employers assume that the workers themselves are quite interchangeable.

Semiskilled workers are not entirely controlled by their employers. In one perceptive study, workers were observed deliberately slowing down the pace of their work so that their rates for piecework (a system in which workers are paid by the unit produced) remained high (Roy, 1952, 1954, 1959-60). Collusion between work groups, as well as with foremen, was also found. "Games" were developed to relieve the monotony of the work. There were special times each day or every few days for breaks. In a related study, the work group actually increased its productivity by using an illegal technique to make its production quotas (Bensman & Gerver, 1963). The illegal technique had the unfortunate potential for making the product—airplanes—less safe.

The point here is that, as in all work, informal work groups humanize and personalize the work itself. The development of such work groups, of course, is more difficult when there is a great deal of noise, as in a noisy factory, or when workers are spatially separated, such as delivery-service drivers. Work groups cannot form if people cannot interact.

Unskilled Workers

Aside from farm work, *unskilled work* is the category that has declined most rapidly in the United States. In 1900, some 13% of the labor force was in unskilled work; by 1990, this figure had declined to only 4% (U.S. Department of Labor, 1990). The nature of unskilled work and technological change explain this phenomenon.

Unskilled work involves physical labor, such as digging ditches, unloading trucks or railroad cars, and hauling lumber and other materials at a construction site. The basic criterion for unskilled work is the appearance of having enough strength to accomplish the work. People who engage in unskilled work are called *laborers*, a term with strong negative connotations, especially when it is combined with a modifier to become "common laborers."

The impact of technological change is always in the direction of reducing the need for human labor, so the tendency for less and less unskilled work to be available is almost inevitable. A more subtle form of technological change also affects unskilled work.

The building janitor, for example, is frequently viewed as an unskilled worker. However, janitorial work has increased in its skill requirements as the materials used in buildings have become more varied and their cleaning more complex. Janitors must be able to read labels, for example, to distinguish between cleaning agents designed for asphalt tile as opposed to marble floors. Thus, what was once rather simple labor has become more complex and no longer a form of unskilled work.

Another aspect of unskilled work is the regularity of employment. People in unskilled work are employed irregularly (Caplow, 1954). Hiring is often by the day, with workers showing up at hiring or union halls hoping for work. The demand for such jobs varies and is affected by such variables as the weather; snow-removal jobs are available only when and where there are snow storms. In any case, the availability of work is out of the hands of the potential workers.

An interesting anomaly in unskilled work should be noted. In New York City, sanitation workers are very well paid, although much of the work is unskilled. In emptying trash and garbage into a truck, the workers are simply using physical labor. But the high pay is a consequence of a strong union. This form of unskilled work is also much more regular than is typical of most unskilled work.

Other Work

The neat hierarchy of occupations used by the U.S. Bureau of the Census does not adequately account for four significant types of work: service work, farm work, housework, and work in the underground economy.

Service Work

Statistically, a major form of work that has not yet been discussed is *service work*. Official government statistics indicate an increase in service work from 4% of the 1900 labor force to 13% of the 1990 labor force (U.S. Department of Labor, 1990). Not entirely by coincidence, these are exactly the opposite of the percentages of unskilled workers.

In a general sense, such professionals as accountants and lawyers do service work, because they provide services instead of making goods. But technically, service work includes far lower levels of occupation (Tausky, 1984), many of them paying only the minimum wage:

> For instance, in food services, counter workers, waiters, waitresses, and dishwashers are included, as are cooks, but bakers are counted as skilled workers, and food service supervisors are classified as managers. In health services, practical nurses and attendants are counted as service workers while registered nurses appear in the professional, technical category. Also among service workers we find guards, doorkeepers, watchmen, porters, janitors, bootblacks, as well as barbers and beauticians, midwives, firefighters, police, and detectives. (pp. 59-60)

The labor department's classification of service workers contains some interesting anomalies. In food services, for example, the server in an exclusive restaurant has a very different job and a very different status than that of the food-service worker in a local pizzeria or the counter person at a fast-food franchise—yet both fall into the same occupational category. Similarly, cooks and chefs are classified alike despite significant differences in their jobs and status.

Many women are employed in service work (Fox & Hesse-Biber, 1984, p. 98), mostly in food services and health and personal services (orderlies, hairdressers, cosmetologists, and the like). Private household work and cleaning are also common forms of service work for women. As might be expected, minority group members are also heavily concentrated in lower-level service-work occupations (Tausky, 1984, p. 61).

Most forms of service work involve direct interactions with customers or clients. These interactions can be demeaning and demoralizing unless the worker gains some control. Waitresses attempt to control their interactions with customers in several ways, but such control is next to impossible in some situations (Hearn & Stoll, 1975):

> In a dimly lighted, escapist atmosphere (i.e., The Shangri-La Club) the function of the waitress is to sell drinks with as much ingenuity, speed, and grace as possible. At the end of the evening she turns in money received from customers according to the reading on the cash register. Money over and above the reading is hers—her tips. The waitress is dependent on tips for her livelihood since in this city, as in many others, weak unionization allows management to pay usually no more than [$1] per hour for her services. Since the waitresses feel they must make a total of at least [$35] to have had a "good" night, it is imperative that the waitress please the customer, which shapes the interaction to the advantage of the customer. In addition, she must please the management or lose her job. A less than cordial relationship with her bartender can also lead to slow service and fewer tips, a situation which highlights her lack of control over the work setting. (pp. 106-107)

The cocktail waitress's control of her situation is made even more difficult by the fact that her customers are mostly men who are drinking. Such customers can become drunk, obnoxious, and engage in sexual harassment.

All service workers who depend on tips or other discretionary payment (barbers, beauticians, shoe shiners, and the like) attempt to exert control within the limits of their interactions with customers. Barbers and beauticians try to build a clientele, which increases the potential for control. These forms of personal service also have the potential for leading to entrepreneurship, because the capital costs for starting one's own shop are quite low. Entrepreneurship usually raises an individual's status and perhaps income.

The issue of control takes a different and more ominous form when another type of service work is considered. A study of airline flight attendants found that attendants are trained to behave in their occupational role and to feel the emotion being expressed (Hochschild, 1983). Emotions are managed for the sake of the employer. The attendants are taught to control interactions but are themselves controlled in doing so.

The airline flight attendant has relatively high status. Police work is another high-status form of service work and is probably the most visible, given all of the news-related and fictional treatment of police in media. For the most part, however, service work is low in visibility, low in power, and low in status. The nature of the job—serving other people—in and of itself lowers the status of the work.

Farm Work

Farm work is in obvious decline as a form of work in the United States. In 1900, some 38% of the labor force was in farming; by 1990, this figure had dropped to 3%. This is not the case worldwide, however. Farm work is the major form of work in Third World countries, and 70% of the Third World's female population is involved in agriculture (Boulding, 1980). In the United States and elsewhere, technological change, industrialization, and greatly increased farm productivity have led to rapid decreases in farm work.

There are two basic forms of farm work. The family farm is most typical in the U.S. East and Midwest. In the far South (e.g., Florida), Southwest (Texas and Arizona), and West (especially California), however, the norm is increasingly a form of "agribusiness," which is characterized by factory-like production and large-scale farms (Friedland, 1981).

In large farm operations, much farm work is like the unskilled type of labor. Contrary to popular belief, much of this labor is not migratory. Grape and citrus workers, for example, migrate very little if at all (Friedland, 1981).

Family farm work is different from almost every other form of work we have considered. The work, after all, is carried out "at home." Except for very large farms or ranches, which are absentee-owned, the farmer and his wife run the operation from home. For farm women, housework and farm work are intimately intertwined (Boulding, 1980; Rosenfeld, 1986). Farm women regularly keep the books and maintain records, run farm errands, take care of animals, and help with harvesting. They are less likely than farm men to work with heavy farm equipment. Farm men are most involved in the use of fertilizers, herbicides, and insecticides—work that is considered hazardous. The more that farm women are involved in farm work, the greater their role in decision making about the farm.

Many farm men and women have off-farm jobs. When the men have such jobs, their wives handle more tasks and make more decisions about the farm; when the women have off-farm jobs, their farm roles are diminished. Thus in farm work there is an interplay of farm roles, off-farm work roles, and family roles.

Family farm work is clearly different from the industrialized and postindustrialized forms of work that will occupy most of our attention in the balance of this book. A small survey of farm women (Boulding, 1980) captured the differences well:

> We asked them what they liked best, and what they liked least, about farming. Togetherness with husband, having the husband around to father the children and be companion and work-partner to the wife, and experiencing family togetherness are the most valued things about farm life. Love of nature and love of independence, not being bossed around by others, are also highly valued, as is the sense of creating something for the future that will endure. Even harvest time, the time when women have to be three places at once for 18 to 20 hour workdays, is chosen by three as what they love best about farming. They love the excitement, the bustle. Work with animals is intrinsically enjoyable for many.
>
> The list of what farm wives like least is much shorter. A few mention specific chores, such as cleaning milking utensils, or heavy lifting jobs, but the majority complain that they cannot get away. Cows have to be milked twice a day, all animals have to be fed daily, and emergencies like sick animals tend to occur whenever a family trip (rare enough at that) is planned. Planning is risky. Some are embarrassed that they always arrive at gatherings late and have to leave early because of chores. Others worry about getting rid of the barn smell in a hurry when they need to go to meetings or out

> on errands. Two of the women give housework as their
> least-liked task—one can be sure they spend most of their
> time in the fields. The dislike of winter is an understandable
> choice for the two who give it, in that the interviews took
> place just after the worst winter in decades. Keeping cattle
> alive through blizzards is a physically awesome task, and one
> in which the women were strenuously involved. (pp. 284-85)

The dislike of winter is a seasonal matter, but the dislike of
housework is not. And farm wives are not the only ones who
complain about housework.

Housework

This type of work can be controversial. Feminist authors argue
that housework is inherently oppressive for women (Hartmann,
1981; Oakley, 1974, 1980). Marxists view housework as the by-
product of a larger social conflict (Berk & Berk, 1979; Berk & Shih,
1980). Spokespersons from the far right such as Phyllis Schlafly
would view housework as the most rewarding and moral activity
for a woman (see Eisenstein, 1982). We can perhaps steer a course
through these political reefs by first describing the nature of
housework and then analyzing who does it and under what circumstances. Issues such as the dual-career family and other
aspects of the marital relationship will be discussed in Chapters
6 and 11. The focus here is on housework as a form of work activity.

The nature of housework varies with the circumstances of the
individuals doing it. The single person living in a small apartment
has a set of activities that is very different from that of the family
with young children, a house, and a yard. Housework may include
cooking meals, washing and putting away dishes, making beds,
housecleaning, laundry and clothing care, shopping for food, caring for children, taking care of finances, gardening, heavy cleaning,
chauffeuring, lawnmowing, painting and wallpapering, working in
the yard, and maintaining household equipment.

In her analysis of housework, Lopata (1971, pp. 32-44) identified several stages in the life cycle of the housewife role. When a
woman becomes a housewife, she has little formal training for the

role, but the role itself has relatively few demands. In the second stage of the role, demands increase as child-rearing activities become dominant. In the next stage, the full-house plateau, all of the children have been born but none have yet left home. Child-care duties are heavy during this period but decrease as the next stage is entered and the children leave home. The final stage is widowhood; here the demands of the housewife are further reduced. These stages are relevant for houseworkers whether they are housewives, househusbands, or hired housekeepers.

However, except for single men, housework is largely women's work, whether or not they work in the labor market. Analysis of a national sample of husbands and wives found that wives who are employed in the labor force spend less time with housework than do wives who are not employed outside the home. The husbands of employed wives spend little more time in housework than do the husbands of wives not employed (Huber & Spitze, 1983). But because the employed wives spend less time, the relative contribution of the husbands with employed wives is greater (Pleck, 1977; Vanek, 1974).

Many women are very comfortable in the housewife role and find that it provides them with opportunities to develop and demonstrate their competencies (Lopata, 1971). For other women, however, housework is boring and monotonous, and this is one reason they seek employment outside the home. But when both husband and wife work outside the home, it is the wife who is the primary provider of housework. In this regard, women are disadvantaged.

Various attempts have been made to boost the prestige of housework and thus the status of housewives. One such effort has focused on specifying the exact economic value of each housework activity if it were to be purchased in the market (see Montagna, 1977, pp. 131-133). The "new home economists" have attempted to explain why wives tend to do most of the housework in terms of men's and women's relative productivity in each market (Becker, 1976, 1981). Men can earn more than women in the outside labor force, so the family receives maximum benefit when the wife does the housework. Critics of this theory have noted that we still do not know how families reach these decisions: "It is just as plausible to suppose that women's prior assignment to household work makes them less able to compete with men in wage work as it is to conclude that women do housework because their wages are lower than men's" (Huber & Spitze, 1983, p. 77). Furthermore, it is impossible to calculate the value of housework in the marketplace, despite efforts to do so. The most powerful explanation for the phenomenon of women and housework is simply tradition.

Housework, like all work, has been affected by technological change. However, contrary to popular opinion, technological change has not reduced the amount of time devoted to housework (Bose, 1979; Bose & Bereano, 1983). True, hot and cold running water eliminated the need to pump, carry, and heat water; and electricity and gas reduced the need for coal or wood stoves and hence wood chopping, coal carrying, and the stoking and cleaning of stoves. However, the time saved was apparently shifted to other household tasks. New small appliances, such as food processors and microwave ovens, require more elaborate cleaning, create storage problems, and increase the likelihood of maintenance problems. Similarly, the increase in eating out may well be offset by the preparation of more elaborate gourmet-type meals at home (Bose, 1979). The quantity of tasks performed may have decreased, but the new emphasis on quality has not allowed a reduction in the time expended in housework.

In addition, although technological change has altered the composition of housework, it has not really altered who does it. Instead, the greatest impacts on housework have come from nontechnological changes—increased labor demand for women, reduced household size, home monotony, aspects of contemporary feminist thought, and the pressures of inflation drawing women to paid work. These in turn have decreased the time available for housework. Technology has fostered the redefinition of housework away from production and toward consumption, transportation, and child care. This redefinition may have facilitated, but not caused, the current distribution of women's time and effort between paid and unpaid labor. Technology allowed individual women's labor to substitute for the loss of servants and other primarily female family members' aid, raise the standard of living, and reduce the necessary hours of housework. But its goal was never to decrease male power in the home (Bose & Bereano, 1983, p. 92).

Housework has changed, to be sure, but it will not go away. It remains a category of work with high value and low prestige.

Work in the Underground Economy

The final form of work we will consider was touched on in Chapter 1, when we looked at hustling as a work activity. Here we consider work that does not show up in official statistics. Most of it is illegal. This is not the defining characteristic, however. The defining characteristic is that income is not reported and taxes are not paid.

The underground economy involves many forms of work. It includes growing marijuana in rural New York state and selling drugs on the streets of New York City. It can be fencing stolen property anywhere. It can be transporting toxic waste and dumping it undetected in a rural area of Ohio.

All of the occupations we have considered can take place in a wide variety of settings with quite varied outcomes for the people involved. Such is also the case with work in the underground economy. Consider prostitution. This form of work encompasses the independent and usually poor streetwalker and the glamorous call girl, who may become quite wealthy (Miller, 1978). Prostitutes can be men or women, young or old. Prostitution also involves a whole array of other people, ranging from customers, pimps, and massage-parlor owners to police officers, lawyers, physicians, and sex researchers (Gagnon, 1977).

Not all underground work is illegal. There is now a rich research literature on ethnic enclaves and the nontraditional work systems that have evolved in them, such as Cuban immigrants in Miami (Portes & Jensen, 1989). Employment in such enclaves frequently takes the form of a husband becoming an entrepreneur, with a spouse and other family members as the primary employees. As the firms grow, other Cuban women are hired. The firms provide goods and services for fellow Cuban immigrants. Much of the income earned in enclave economies is not reported. A good deal of part-time work also falls into the category of underground work. For instance, the off-duty police officer who works as a bouncer in the local bar and who is paid in cash is working in the underground economy.

We do not know the number of people in the underground economy. We all know it exists, and all of us probably know people who are active in it. Some of us are in it ourselves. It is crucial to remember that the classification of work as *underground* is a creation of official government decisions. It is still work.

Conclusions

We have explored a variety of work forms in this chapter, beginning with the professions. At one time, sociologists attempted to define professional work in terms of attributes. This effort was largely abandoned when it was realized that gaining and maintaining power was the essence of turning an occupation into a profession. The task is not easy, given all of the ongoing threats to the professional status of occupations.

Another set of high-status occupations includes executives, managers, officials, and proprietors. Except for proprietors, managers are organizational creations and guardians. These occupations are in all segments of society: government, business, the arts, sports, and leisure.

Clerical and sales work, which are next on the hierarchy, constitute white-collar work. These tend to have gender segregation, with women in the lower-paying jobs with less autonomy and control.

Blue-collar work has a lot of variety. First-line supervisors and skilled craft workers are at the top of the hierarchy, followed by semiskilled operatives and unskilled workers. Technological change and offshore manufacturing, however, are reducing the options for blue-collar workers.

These four categories of work are those of the official statistics. Other forms of work exist, although they do not fit conveniently into the hierarchy. Service work is the most prominent in terms of numbers of people involved. Service jobs are increasing rapidly as the service sector grows and manufacturing fades. The other types of work to be considered are farm work, housework, and work in the underground economy.

When we return to these forms of work in subsequent chapters, we will have a common set of meanings. But now we can focus on basic questions about us as individuals: Why do we work? How do we learn our work roles? What do we get out of our work?

■■■ APPLICATION

Growing Pains in the Service Sector

One of the most dramatic employment trends in the United States over the past 30 years has been the increasing number of service jobs. More than three times as many people were employed in service jobs in 1990 as were employed in similar jobs at the turn of the century. Recent data from the U.S. Bureau of Labor Statistics show that growth in the service sector accounted for the majority of new jobs during the 1980s. By 1989, more than twice as many people were employed in the service sector (including government) than were employed in goods-producing industries (Plunkert, 1990).

It seems that if a client is willing to pay for it, a service is designed to do it. For example, Manhattan residents need not concern themselves with getting home in time to walk the dog. For $10 an hour, a personal "dog walker" will do the job. And if the dog develops a personality disorder, see the dog psychologist. Planning on getting married but dread the hassle? A New Jersey firm will arrange everything, including honeymoon reservations, for a mere $4,000. For those of us whose lives are in disarray, there are even people willing to organize our closets for a fee (Machan, 1988; Solo, 1990).

Unusual services such as these cannot account for all of the growth in the service sector. Employment has also grown in more traditional service industries, such as the food-service industry, legal services, financial services, and health services for the elderly

(Plunkert, 1990). The demand for day-care services has also risen in recent years as the number of working mothers has increased. Finally, advances in communications and data-handling technologies have caused an explosion of information-related services. As we enter the 21st century, information has taken on the status of a commodity. The result is a dramatic upsurge in job opportunities for those who have the ability to process and provide valued information.

In some ways, the expansion of the service sector is a positive development. Service jobs are a valuable form of employment for people living where goods-producing industries are in decline—most notably, inner-city residents. However, the service sector has experienced its share of growing pains.

One problem is that many service industries have trouble recruiting workers to fill entry-level positions. In the fast-food industry, "Help Wanted" signs have become commonplace. In fact, the problem has become so acute that several unorthodox recruiting techniques have been tried. For example, managers are attempting to fill vacant positions by appealing to groups they ignored in the past, including retirees and the disabled. Mothers of school-aged children are being enticed with offers of flexible working hours and free day-care programs (Amante, 1989). Employees are being paid hefty referral fees for bringing in new applicants (Sellers, 1990). Employers are raising wages and encouraging workers to remain in their jobs by offering school scholarships to long-term employees. Finally, businesses located in suburban areas have even "bused in" workers from the inner city.

Why have service jobs become so hard to fill? There are several contributing factors. One major factor is demographics: Young workers are and will continue to be in short supply. Many entry-level service jobs, such as those in fast-food restaurants, have traditionally been filled by teenagers. However, these jobs go begging even when unemployment is high among young workers (Nasar, 1986). They apparently find the prospect of a low-skill, low-paying job unappealing and opt for extended education instead of the job market. It is also possible that inner-city youths are more attracted to financial opportunities in the underground economy than those in the service sector.

Not all service-sector jobs are low-skill, low-pay jobs. In fact, the service sector offers many good opportunities to those who have good communication and information-handling skills. The U.S. Bureau of Labor Statistics reports that business services and computer- and data-processing services enjoyed above-average growth from 1979 to 1989 (Plunkert, 1990).

Thus it would seem that business and information-related services provide an alternative for those who are disenchanted with the prospect of "flipping burgers." However, one crucial problem remains: low skill levels in the labor force. According to the U.S. Department of Education (cited in Milkovich & Boudreau, 1991), "17 million to 21 million adults cannot read well enough to cope with everyday life . . . and . . . while many of these are recent immigrants unable to understand or speak English, illiteracy is a problem even among high school graduates" (p. 35).

Service-sector industries are already encountering a mismatch between employee qualifications and the skill requirements for many jobs. For example, corporate training programs often teach basic reading, math, and computer literacy. Writing in *Fortune* magazine, Louis Richman (1988) issued the following lament: "Occupations requiring post-secondary education will account for 30% of the growth in new service sector employment. . . . But a dishearteningly large number of workers lack the basic skills the job market increasingly requires" (p. 44).

There is little question that service work is becoming increasingly prevalent. However, there is some question about whether jobs in the service sector will fulfill the aspirations and accommodate the qualifications of all types of job seekers. These are issues that will be of keen interest to sociologists and society at large in the coming years.

■■ SUGGESTED READINGS

A complete bibliographical entry for each work cited here can be found in the reference section at the back of this book.

Terkel, *Working* (1974), is the best description of a wide array of work. Terkel lets people describe their own work in their own terms. In the same genre but more critical is Garson, *All the Livelong Day* (1975).

Kanter, *Men and Women of the Corporation* (1977a), provides rich descriptions and analyses of the work of executives, managers, and clerical workers in a large corporation.

Abbott, *The System of Professions* (1988), is a state-of-the-art analysis of the rise and sometimes fall of professions.

Shaiken, *Work Transformed* (1985), looks at the impact of computers and robots on the jobs of skilled workers.

Chinoy, *Automobile Workers and the American Dream* (1955), remains the classic study of assembly-line work.

Gale Miller has two useful books: *Odd Jobs* (1978), which focuses on work in the underground economy, and *It's a Living*, which covers some of the same ground and has a good section on housework.

3 The Individual Experience of Work

Why do people work? This chapter tries to answer that question. The focus is on individuals: you and me. We will look at why we work, how we learn our work, and how we react to our work. We will also see if there are ways to improve the work experience.

Four assumptions guide the analysis. First, an individual's orientation toward work changes all the time—hour to hour, day to day, year to year. On some days, I am highly motivated to get work done. On others, I would rather be skiing or golfing. On some days I am happy with my work, while on others I am frustrated or bored. Moreover, what motivated me when I was young is really quite different from what motivates me now that I am older. Most analyses of work cited in this chapter do not consider this sort of variation; instead, they treat individuals as if they have a constant orientation toward their work.

The second assumption is closely related to the first: Work itself varies widely in what it provides the individual. Some facets of my work are very enjoyable, such as teaching a good class and writing a good chapter. I also like getting my paycheck. Other facets of my work are dreadful, such as grading exams and answering administrative memos. Here again, many analyses treat work as if it were all of one kind, although there is a growing awareness that various facets of work should be the basis for study, rather than work as a whole.

The third assumption is that all motivations for working are equally valid. Extrinsic motivations, such as money, are neither less moral nor of a "lower order" than more intrinsic motivations, such as fully using one's talents. Some analysts believe there are higher- and lower-order motivations. I disagree.

The fourth and final assumption is that the way individuals relate to their work is important for both them and the wider society. The links between satisfying human relationships in the workplace and national prosperity are increasingly being recognized (Lincoln & Kalleberg, 1990). For example, many theorists believe that worker productivity is greater in Japan because of that nation's system for motivating workers and encouraging their commitment to their jobs. Some U.S. firms, such as the Saturn branch of General Motors, have directly borrowed some of the Japanese techniques with the idea that they will motivate workers to turn out quality products. It is to motivation—or why people work—that we now turn.

Motivations for Work

I have deliberately used a plural title for this section, because I believe that one person may have many motivations, or reasons, for working. These motivations are both intrinsic and extrinsic. As I write this chapter, I am motivated by my own inner desire for self-expression: I want to say what I mean as clearly as possible; this is an *intrinsic* motivation. I would also like to have this work be recognized as high quality by my students and peers, which is an *extrinsic* motivation, or one that comes from outside. I would also like this book to sell well, because authors do get financial gain from their work; this is also an extrinsic motivation. I intrinsically like to write. I also intrinsically like the subject matter.

These motivations vary over time in their meaningfulness, but none stands out as better or of a "higher order" than the others. This conclusion is at direct variance with the best known theories of motivation, which I label "misplaced humanism."

"Humanistic" Theories of Motivation

You may have heard of one "humanistic" theory of motivation: Maslow's (1954) famous *hierarchy of needs*. Maslow believed that people's needs can be ranked, beginning with basic subsistence, then moving up through safety, belongingness and love, esteem, and finally self-actualization. Once one need is satisfied, it no longer motivates. The person is then motivated by the next higher order of need.

Herzberg (1966) took a slightly different approach. He divided the factors associated with work motivation into two categories based on their relationship with work satisfaction and dissatisfaction. The first category, called *satisfiers*, are a part of the job—achievement, recognition, the work itself, responsibility, advancement, and growth. The second category, labeled *hygiene factors*, relate to the work context—company policy and administration, salary, supervision, working conditions, status, job security, and personal life. According to Herzberg, only the first category, the satisfiers, motivate people to work. Their presence contributes to satisfaction. In their absence, there is less or no satisfaction. Presence of the hygiene factors, on the other hand, serves only to keep workers from being dissatisfied. The absence of hygiene factors creates dissatisfaction.

McGregor (1960) believed that worker satisfaction is related to the assumptions of the managers and the resulting work environment. One set of assumptions, called *Theory X*, is the rather authoritarian view that workers respond only to the exercise of power and financial concerns—in other words, extrinsic motivations. The alternative is *Theory Y*, which involves the idea of self-actualization and posits that workers are more intrinsically motivated.

Although these theories have a nice humanistic ring to them, they have not stood up well under the test of empirical research. The importance of intrinsic and extrinsic motivators has been shown to vary with age, gender, and race (Hall, 1975; Shapiro, 1977). In fact, these humanistic theories appear to "apply only to an elite minority of workers" (Fein, 1976, p. 500). For those few, the chance to get involved with their work is important. But for the majority, factors such as pay and job security are the real motivators.

Expectancy Theory

Instead of looking for one simple explanation of work motivation that applies to everyone, it seems more reasonable to assume that people work for a variety of reasons. These reasons change with time and with an individual's life situation. For the high-school student, work may be primarily a vehicle for establishing social contacts outside of school. For the newlywed, work may be viewed as an important source of the income needed to begin and support a family. Still other people may be motivated to work because of the personal challenge or the intellectual stimulation that work provides. Thus what people expect from work and how they react to it is a function not only of the work itself, but also of their own characteristics and preferences. And the differences in people's backgrounds interact with the differences in the characteristics of the job to yield a continually changing set of motivations.

This approach to motivation has been captured in what is known as *expectancy theory* (Lawler, 1973; Vroom, 1964). Lawler (1973, p. 49) offers the following basic premises for the theory:

- People have certain preferences among the various potential outcomes.
- They have expectations about how an action or effort on their part will lead to an intended result, behavior, or performance.
- They have expectations that certain outcomes will follow from their behavior.
- In any situation, the actions a person chooses to take are determined by the expectancies and preferences that he or she has at the time.

Expectancy, then, is our understanding of the rewards for doing certain things and our estimate of the probability that we can achieve the rewards that we want. As workers, we have expectancies about the outcomes that will be produced by our job performance. Our work behavior is therefore shaped by the expectancy that our actions will accomplish what we believe they can.

Consider the behavior of students. Presumably, all students prefer good grades to bad ones. But would you be motivated to study if you thought your work would not be reflected in a higher grade? You might conclude that the course material is so difficult that no amount of studying will get you a good grade on the final exam. Or you might consider it possible to score well on the final exam but still not get a good overall grade for the course. Whatever the reason, this pattern of expectancies may be enough to undermine your motivation to work hard in the class. Expectancies can have similar implications for people pursuing all kinds of outcomes, including those derived from paid employment.

A great advantage of expectancy theory is that it allows for the fact that people often want several different outcomes at the same time. People can seek both intrinsic and extrinsic rewards; I can thus hope to write a good book that sells well.

Expectancy theory also explains why some people are not involved with their work. If people are oriented toward advancement, but their work does not contain that possibility, then they are likely to become disengaged.

Remember that people come to their work with a variety of background experiences that teach them to prefer different outcomes or rewards. They also have all kinds of other entanglements—with spouses, children, relatives, and friends. Furthermore, people have differing capabilities in performing the kinds of work that are likely to yield the outcomes they prefer. Thus they define their work situation on their own basis (Goldthorpe, Lockwood, Bechhofer, & Platt, 1970).

Scholars, managers, and political analysts from the left and right all too typically look at work and work motivation from their own perspective and ignore the reality that workers themselves construct for their work. What they fail to recognize is that both high-status and low-status workers can be highly motivated to work. Auto workers and office clerks can feel as good about their work performance as higher-status workers, even if the work itself is not given high status. The truth is that work motivations are learned, just as work roles are learned.

Learning About Work

The topic of learning about work is a vast one that occupies the full attention of both sociologically and psychologically based social psychologists. I will not attempt to summarize and integrate all of this literature, because it would fill several volumes in its own right. Instead, the purpose here is to provide an overview of the ways in which people learn their work roles.

Socialization has been defined as "a process of learning to participate in social life" (Mortimer & Simmons, 1978, p. 422). The focus here is on work-related, adult socialization, which takes place as people prepare to and actually enter the work force. Our focus is thus on learning to work. However, preadult socialization affects individuals and their work. As a result, individuals arrive for their work roles with widely different skills and values.

Socialization of Work Values and Roles

Before a person learns about a particular job, he or she learns how to feel or think about work. In other words, the person first develops work values. As you might guess, work values are usually transmitted from parent to child. For example, if a father likes working with people—or data or things—his son will probably learn the same work values (Mortimer, 1974). This would particularly be the case when there are close and empathetic relationships between parent and child (Mortimer & Kumka, 1982).

Another great influence on work values is the person's colleagues. Much of what is known about this type of socialization comes from research in professional schools, particularly medical schools. Some of these studies are quite old but are sociological classics, such as *The Student Physician* (Merton, Reader, & Kendall, 1957) and *Boys in White* (Becker, Geer, Hughes, & Strauss, 1961). These and other studies of professional schools have come to two main conclusions: (1) Students learn from both faculty and peers and (2) socialization is both formal (intentional) and informal (coincidental). Students learning the role of the practicing professional often experience "reality shocks." They find that their ideals about their intended profession are not consistent with the actual nature of the work. Most studies of professional schools have found that students suffer a great deal of anxiety as they confront the large amounts of information to be learned, continual evaluation from faculty, and uncertainty about how to apply their limited knowledge in dealing with clients or patients. As students move through the anxiety-laden socialization process in these schools, cohesion with fellow students and the profession itself increases.

The alternative approaches to defining what a profession is (discussed in Chapter 2) provide additional insight into socialization for work. In terms of the attribute approach, professional schools are the settings in which the theoretical backgrounds of professional practice are learned, as well as where students learn the components of professional culture. From the power perspective, professional schools are the settings where solidarity among members of the profession develops. This solidarity will enhance the ability of a profession to obtain and maintain power over other occupations and in the larger political arena.

Although studies of professionals in training are interesting, they are concerned with only a limited segment of the labor force and only a small slice of the socialization process. Socialization for work continues to take place on the job through interaction with the individuals, ideas, and ideologies associated with particular forms of work. For example, although it is conventional to think of artists as among the most solitary of workers, they in fact learn their roles in interaction with other artists, support personnel, and the prevailing artistic conventions (Becker, 1974, 1982). Even artists who are mavericks learn their maverick roles in interaction with artistic conventions, other artists, art critics, and the public. Research carried out in a social services office found much the same thing: Workers were in continual interaction with other staffmembers, clients, and supervisors (Miller, 1991). Organizational practices and procedures were a key component of work-role definitions.

This research provides strong evidence that the development of work values is not some neutral and placid activity. Instead, values are hammered out of interactions with real people in real organizations and throughout a person's work life.

Reciprocity

In looking at how work values and roles develop, you may have formed the mistaken impression that the relationship between the work and the person is entirely one-sided. Nothing could be farther from the truth. Not only does a person's work affect his or her orientation toward work, but also a person's orientation affects his or her work. The link between individuals and their work settings is one of reciprocity.

A longitudinal study of American men found that the person who must deal with complex matters on the job and who is allowed to be more self-directed tends to be more flexible and tolerant off the job; jobs that are repetitive and not challenging are linked to a conformist orientation (Kohn & Schooler, 1973, 1978, 1982, 1983). At the same time, people who are flexible and tolerant tend to seek more complex jobs, and those who are conformists tend to seek less challenging jobs.

People tend to either find work that matches their orientation or try to change the content of their work so that it more closely matches their personality. For instance, a worker valuing autonomy might take steps to increase his or her freedom from direct supervision. The worker might even wish to "telecommute" rather than work in an office where he or she is subject to direct scrutiny. If all else fails, the worker might seek another job in a setting that offers more autonomy.

Some evidence suggests that the reciprocity between work orientation and job complexity applies to everyone, not just American men. For instance, the same basic relationship has been found in a sample of employed women (Miller, Schooler, Kohn, & Miller, 1979). And a comparison of men in Poland and the United States revealed strong similarities between these two countries (Slomczynski, Miller, & Kohn, 1981), although with interesting differences. In Poland, the lower-level, less-challenging jobs were associated with greater self-confidence and less anxiety, while in the United States, higher-level jobs that allowed more self-direction were associated with a more favorable self-conception.

Additional research on the linkages between people's orientations and their work relates back to the earlier discussion of work values. A 10-year longitudinal study of University of Michigan graduates found that rewarding occupational experiences reinforce the values that served as the basis for choosing a job or type of work (Mortimer & Lorence, 1979). The researchers found, for instance, that a person who valued extrinsic rewards and who received a good income had his or her extrinsic work values reinforced. An analogy is that of a novice shutterbug choosing to take a photography class, only to find his or her interest in photography growing dramatically as a result of this classroom experiences. Thus a person's values both affect and are affected by work experiences.

The reciprocal relationship has implications for a person's whole career. People who have developed interest and enthusiasm (with regard to work) before actually entering the labor force have work values that promote stability early in their careers (Lorence & Mortimer, 1981). This stability in turn facilitates higher income and increased work autonomy. Finally, these work experiences, especially work autonomy, stimulate still greater involvement with work. In other words, the links between work experiences and work values go both ways, and the nature of those links has great implications for a person's career.

Career Stages

The assumption that work values and interactions with co-workers change as the person gains experience leads directly to the approach to socialization and work that analyzes career stages. Typical of this approach is the *three-stage socialization model*: anticipatory socialization, encounter, and change and acquisition (Feldman, 1976, 1981).

Anticipatory socialization involves forming expectations about an employer organization from job interviews and other information from potential employers. The individual may or may not form a realistic picture of a potential job but nonetheless goes into the work situation with a distinct set of expectations about what the job will involve, what the work environment will be like, and what rewards are possible.

The next stage is the actual *encounter* with the organization. Here the individual must deal with the processes of managing outside conflicts, such as scheduling, demands from family, and demands on family—as well as work-related conflicts: management of intergroup role conflicts, role definition (that is, knowing one's own role within the work group), initiation to work tasks, and initiation to the work group. These processes are strongly interrelated. For example, until people are integrated into the work group, they may not be able to perform work tasks well because information is withheld from them (Becker & Strauss, 1956).

The final stage, *change and acquisition*, is associated with the resolution of role demands, task mastery, and adjustment to group norms and values. This is an ongoing and continuous stage throughout a person's career.

Other researchers have proposed alternatives to this three-stage model, including some with four or six stages, but the process is basically the same (Porter, Lawler, & Hackman, 1975; Schein, 1971; Wanous, 1980). One important point to remember is that people pass through these stages whenever they change jobs. Even if one is promoted within an organization, there is anticipation, encounter, and change.

A different approach to career stages and socialization was taken in an analysis of professionals in a variety of organizational settings (Dalton, Thompson, & Price, 1977). The first stage is apprenticeship, in which the new professional engages in routine duties under the supervision of an established person or mentor in the field. This can be a frustrating experience, because routine work is not emphasized in professional schools. The second stage occurs when the individual begins to work independently and has developed a reputation as a competent performer. Most of the social ties here are with colleagues. The individual begins to develop independence from the mentor of the first stage. In the third stage, the individual becomes a mentor and begins to take care of and supervise new professionals entering the first stage. In this stage, the individual is learning managerial skills, while also maintaining technical competence in the professional field. In the final stage, the individual is removed from day-to-day details and becomes a sponsor of other key people in the organization. Not all professionals will move into the fourth stage; not doing so does not imply failure. At the same time, those who do move into the fourth stage have more power in the organization.

A very different view of career stages is reported in a study of correctional officers (Regoli, Poole, & Schrink, 1979). Here the focus is on the development and decline of cynicism among the officers. Correctional workers come into the system with lofty goals, then pass through a cynical stage, before moving to a stage of acceptance of conditions as they are.

This sort of evidence strongly suggests that the content of career stages will vary widely, according to the form of work involved. Still, the idea of career stage is useful in that it sensitizes us to the fact that the socialization process is different at different times in people's lives.

The findings on socialization of work values and career stages together suggest this sequence of learning about work: Parental Occupation → Parental Occupational Values → Preadult Socialization → Preadult Values and Work Expectations → Work Setting → Ongoing and Continuing Socialization and Reactions to Work.

The implication is that this pattern would be recycled across generations.

Reactions to Work

So far we have learned that people's motivations for work are many and complex, as is the process of learning about work. In the same way, our reactions to work vary. We can love it or hate it; look forward to it or dread it; have our best of times or our worst of times. Work is not a neutral activity.

Both psychologists and sociologists study reactions to work. Psychologists tend to examine individual responses, whereas sociologists tend to look more at the setting and the ways people interact and respond in those settings. We will first look briefly at forms of response that take the form of direct, overt actions. We will then turn to more subjective reactions, such as job satisfaction and alienation.

Overt Responses to Work

Overt responses to work are the things we might observe from the boss's chair or the human-relations department in an organization. They are not the private, personal reactions known only to the worker. Overt responses are the obvious signs that workers are happy or unhappy with their jobs.

One overt response that can be measured and observed is *turnover*, or the percentage of an organization's work force that voluntarily leaves within a certain period and must be replaced. Turnover is most likely to take place when people are dissatisfied with their work and other employment opportunities are available. Levels of pay, integration into work groups, and communications quality are important determinants of turnover (O'Reilly, Caldwell, & Barnett, 1989; Price, 1977, 1989). There are also consequences of high levels of turnover for the employing organization, among them financial costs and poor morale among those who remain, who are themselves susceptible to turnover (Price, 1977, 1989). Turnover can also have a negative effect on the person who leaves. Frequent job changes turn out to be a distinct disadvantage when a person is seeking subsequent employment (Bills, 1990).

Of course, turnover is not the only possible overt response to dissatisfaction on the job. Hirschman (1971) suggested two others in his well-known analysis of the ways people respond to their work. He used the term *exit* to mean turnover when one is dissatisfied. *Voice*, on the other hand, refers to speaking out about conditions that people find uncomfortable or displeasing. *Loyalty* refers to people who stay on at work and continue to be loyal to the employer, regardless of conditions. Others have added to Hirschman's list the option of *neglect*, which refers to those circumstances where workers stay in an unpleasant situation but reduce their level of effort and involvement (Withey & Cooper, 1989). Neglect may follow an extended period of loyalty.

An interesting new categorization of responses to work defines people as being *good soldiers* (those who subscribe to organizational goals), *smooth operators* (those who are having their own needs met whether or not the organization is being served), or *saboteurs* (those who are trying to get even with the organization because they feel overconstrained by rules or supervisors or that they are underpaid) (Hodson, 1991).

Focusing on overt responses to work has some advantages for sociologists. It is easier to observe overt responses than to elicit information about subjective responses. Nevertheless, it is important to know how people feel about their work.

Job Satisfaction

A subjective response to work, *job satisfaction* has been studied exhaustively. A 1976 study found that literally thousands of books, articles, and dissertations had been produced in the preceding 20 years (Locke, 1976). There are three basic reasons for all of this attention.

First, patterns of change in job satisfaction over time can be taken as a sort of social indicator. Between 80% and 90% of the people surveyed in the United States report that they are "satisfied" or "very satisfied" with their work, and this figure does not change much over time (Tausky, 1984, p. 97). Of course, some people are reluctant to say that their jobs are bad or boring, because that would be almost an admission of failure in life.

Second, job satisfaction is commonly believed to be linked to worker productivity. There is such a linkage, but in the direction of productivity contributing to satisfaction, rather than the reverse (Lawler & Porter, 1967; Mortimer, 1979; Sheridan & Slocum, 1975). Evidence has also linked satisfaction to lowered turnover and lower absenteeism (Martin & Miller, 1986; Price, 1977). However, job satisfaction is not the major predictor of these phenomena.

Third, job satisfaction has been said to "spill over" into other spheres of life. Although there is limited evidence that this might be the case, the evidence seems fairly strong that it is the quality of the nonwork activities that predicts satisfaction with them. Thus the quality of family life is a better predictor of satisfaction with family life than is job satisfaction (Bergermaier, Borg, & Champoux, 1984).

Job satisfaction is thus not a strong predictor of other work and nonwork phenomena. Why then study it? The answer is deceptively simple: Job satisfaction is important in its own right. If work is the major activity of adult life for most people, then whether they are satisfied with what they are doing is important. People's well-being on the job is just as important as their well-being off the job.

One other point about job satisfaction: It is an overall emotional response that people have to their jobs. When we talk about job satisfaction, we are not talking about satisfaction with specific aspects of the job (e.g., pay, working conditions, opportunity to use one's skills, etc.). Rather, we are referring to a general attitude toward the job as a whole. This definition of job satisfaction is consistent with Kalleberg's (1977) definition of job satisfaction as a unitary concept. Kalleberg allows that overall job satisfaction may be based on multiple dimensions in real work situations and that people have specific satisfactions and dissatisfactions with various aspects of their work. However, he argues that people can combine their assessments of these multiple dimensions into a composite satisfaction with the job as a whole.

We will follow Kalleberg's usage and think of job satisfaction as a unitary concept, while recognizing that it is legitimate to examine facets of satisfaction within this broader concept. One could examine satisfaction with financial rewards across a variety of work settings or examine satisfaction with the degree to which work is experienced as interesting across different age groups. The advantage to using the unitary concept is that this recognizes the fact that work is multifaceted and yet experienced as a whole.

Determinants of Job Satisfaction. Having defined job satisfaction, it is appropriate to begin seeking an answer to this question: What determines whether a person is satisfied? We can make a basic differentiation between job characteristics or external factors and individual influences on satisfaction (Loscocco & Rochelle, 1991). Individual attributes include social characteristics (such as age, education, and stage in the life cycle), values (such as variations in the values placed on intrinsic and extrinsic rewards), and needs (such as for personal growth, safety, or social affiliations).

Those who stress external determinants of satisfaction have found high satisfaction to be strongly related to such factors as autonomy, freedom from close supervision, good pay and other economic or fringe benefits, job security, promotional opportunities, use of valued skills and abilities, and interesting work. There is also a positive relationship between satisfaction and the job's socioeconomic status (Quinn, Staines, & McCullough, 1974). The astute reader will recognize that these external characteristics are most readily found in the core, rather than the peripheral, part of the labor market. Also note that we can easily find people in high-paying and autonomous jobs who are stressed out and hate their work. The general relationships just described, however, do operate.

Instead of distinguishing between external and individual determinants, some writers draw a distinction between extrinsic and intrinsic features of work (Fein, 1976; Herzberg, Mausner, & Snyderman, 1959). *Extrinsic factors* include pay and fringe benefits and security. *Intrinsic* factors are more psychological, such as work that is interesting, provides the capacity to use one's abilities, and provides the ability to grow and develop on the job.

Some theorists—notably those with humanistic ideas of work motivation, such as Maslow—see a hierarchy, with intrinsic features somehow more worthy or lofty than extrinsic features. Support for the importance of intrinsic features can be seen in several studies (see Kahn, 1972; Locke, 1976; Seashore & Taber, 1975; Shepard, 1973; Stone, 1976; Tannenbaum, Kavcic, Rosner, Vianello, & Wieser, 1974). For example, one study found that male workers who were generally satisfied with their work were most likely to mention such intrinsic features as interest, variety, responsibility, and competence (Gurin, Veroff, & Feld, 1960). Another study identified *occupational self-direction* (relating to the autonomy and scope of the job) as having the most important influence on job satisfaction (Kohn & Schooler, 1973).

There is also strong evidence that supports the importance of extrinsic features of the job (see Bacharach & Aiken, 1979; Fein, 1976; Locke, 1976; Oldham & Rotchford, 1983; Strauss, 1974; Tannenbaum et al., 1974; Voydanoff, 1978). These studies examined extrinsic features such as the presence of explicit rules (some workers prefer such rules), merit systems for advancement, and the physical surroundings in office spaces.

With evidence supporting the importance of both extrinsic and intrinsic job characteristics, how is the controversy resolved? We may approach an answer by examining the nature of the "fit" between the individual and the job.

The Fit Hypothesis. The fit hypothesis places major emphasis on the compatibility of "external" work features and "internal" attributes brought by the individual to the work situation (Mortimer, 1979, p. 4) The idea is actually very simple. Imagine that a supervisor undertakes a new program of increasing positive feedback and giving employees more autonomy on the job. This program will increase the satisfaction of those who have a strong need for personal growth more than it will increase the satisfaction of those who need a greater feeling of security and stability. The worker must "fit" with the environment and vice versa for job satisfaction to result.

There are interesting pieces of evidence in regard to the fit hypothesis—most notably about the fit between satisfaction and worker expectations, education, age, and gender. Let us start with expectations. For example, a researcher found that workers in economically depressed communities expressed satisfaction with their work; the same sort of work was less satisfying for workers in other communities (Hulin, 1966). Apparently, individuals bring a different set of expectations to their work when work is hard to find and there are few job alternatives. Likewise, some workers in the peripheral sector of the labor market reported higher satisfaction levels than workers in the core sector, presumably because their expectations were a better fit with job conditions (Hanson, Martin, & Tuck, 1987).

Mixed evidence has been reported in regard to the relationship between education and satisfaction. On the one hand, some writers suggest that higher levels of education raise expectations that, if unmet, lead to lower levels of satisfaction (Quinn, Staines, & McCullough, 1974; Seybolt, 1976; Tannenbaum et al., 1974). A common assumption is that overeducated individuals will be dissatisfied and either politically left or politically alienated. The evidence indicates little such relationship, except among the very highly overeducated, who do have slight dissatisfaction and lean toward leftist or Marxist ideology (Burris, 1983). In general, however, the overeducation argument has been overstated. Others report, with much greater support, a generally positive relationship between education and satisfaction (Burris, 1983; Glenn & Weaver, 1982; Hamilton & Wright, 1981; Wright & Hamilton,

1979). Overall, those who have more education are likely to be more satisfied with their work.

Age has also been shown to be related to satisfaction. Younger workers are consistently less satisfied with their work than are older workers (Mottaz, 1987a; Quinn et al., 1974; Wright & Hamilton, 1978). This is attributed to the fact that younger workers, in the early stages of their careers, have objectively poorer jobs than their older counterparts. But there is some debate here. Some theorists argue that the performance of older workers is not necessarily better, it is just that older workers have lower expectations (Janson & Martin, 1982).

Gender is another individual characteristic that has been linked to satisfaction, but again with mixed results. Differences between men and women appear to be based on the specific work conditions. Women's satisfaction is affected by the complexity of the work, the hours worked, the dirtiness of the work, and income levels. Men are affected by the closeness of the supervision they experience, their job protection, and organizational characteristics (Miller, 1980). Women with more education and an urban background also tend to be less satisfied. Other studies found that women were more satisfied with their work than were men, despite their objectively poorer jobs and greater conflicts with family responsibilities (Hodson, 1989; Loscocco, 1989). These findings may seem confusing, but they are actually consistent with the fit hypothesis. Men and women bring different expectations to work and therefore derive satisfaction from different job conditions (Bokemeier & Lacy, 1987; Martin & Sheehan, 1989).

In essence, our analysis of the determinants of job satisfaction has come full circle. Although some evidence supports the fit hypothesis—that workers bring expectations with them to the job and that these will vary by education, age, and gender—the evidence appears stronger in support of the idea that the characteristics of the work itself are the key determinants of satisfaction. That brings us back to one very important job characteristic: autonomy.

Job Satisfaction and Autonomy. Most people want to have some autonomy in their work, some control over the work situation, which determines the extent to which rewards can be obtained. Autonomy, then, can be linked to job satisfaction. But there is a continuum between having complete discretion and being completely controlled. In some occupations, such as outside sales, individuals have great control; in others, such as assembly work, the job can be specified in exacting detail, giving individuals literally no leeway in when, where, or how to perform their work (Stewart & Cantor, 1982). To some extent, however, any job offers opportunities to exercise autonomy and control. The individual is not a passive bystander (Miller, 1991; Rothman, 1979).

One classic study of the manner in which workers attempt to control their work is Whyte's (1946) analysis of waitresses. The waitress (the term then in use) is under pressure from customers who want food and drink to their individual specifications. The waitress is dependent on these customers for tips—a major source of income. At the same time, the waitress must also interact with the rest of the organization, such as the pantry staff, cooks, bartenders, and other waitresses. These other workers have a great deal of power over the waitress. If they dawdle in providing beverages or produce a tasteless soup, it is the waitress who suffers the customer's wrath. The real problem for the waitress, however, is the customers. A waitress who wants some measure of control over her work environment must gain the initiative over them. Whyte describes how the waitresses in his study manipulated customers to get the upper hand. The customers were led to believe that they were dependent on the waitress. This way, the waitresses could move at the pace they set, serve more customers, and earn more tips. In other words, they could control their work situation to produce the rewards they valued.

Although all workers have some influence over their work situation, external or exogenous factors tend to be more influential. Class or socioeconomic status is one such factor. People in higher-status positions have more autonomy and are better able to obtain the rewards that yield job satisfaction. Working-class jobs offer fewer rewards and fewer opportunities to obtain those rewards (Kalleberg & Griffin, 1978). This does not suggest that working-class people work in misery; people adapt to their circumstances because they have to work (Gruenberg, 1980). It is also incorrect to assume that because a form of work has low status, workers will never experience autonomy and the capacity for control.

Another external factor that influences autonomy is the degree to which the work is bureaucratized—that is, bound by organizational rules. Bureaucracies typically offer job protections, income, and substantially complex work (Kohn, 1971). Job protection leads to accepting personal responsibility and to the use of intellectual talents, which gives workers a feeling of control. Then, because modern work is increasingly bureaucratized, we would expect workers to be increasingly self-directed. Unfortunately, the matter is not that simple.

An interesting and rather offbeat study examined job satisfaction among samples of professors, garbage collectors, park workers, bartenders, mail carriers, barbers, and teachers (Walsh, 1982). It is not surprising that college professors were least dissatisfied with their work. But what was quite interesting was that garbage collectors were not significantly different than professors in their level of dissatisfaction. The results are not so surprising, however, if you think about the relative autonomy that garbage collectors experience in their jobs. Another surprising finding from this study is that relatively high-status teachers and mail carriers reported more dissatisfaction than did garbage collectors. Why? Perhaps bureaucratization was increasing for mail carriers and teachers, thus leading to discomfort and dissatisfaction.

Job satisfaction, then, is a complex mixture of work characteristics, the characteristics and experiences of the individuals involved, the expectations and values of those individuals, and their ability to obtain the rewards associated with those values (Faunce, 1989; Schwalbe, 1988). Some aspects of satisfaction can be manipulated by the worker, some by the employer, and others perhaps through mechanisms of public policy. Others appear to be quite incapable of being changed.

Work Commitment and Centrality

We turn now to a consideration of a concept that is closely related to job satisfaction: the extent to which individuals are committed to or involved with their work. For some people, work is their "central life interest" (Dubin, 1956, 1992) or the core of their identity (Lawler & Hall, 1970), while for others their major life interests and involvements are away from the job, such as with their family or in leisure activities.

When carried to its extreme, high involvement in work leads to *workaholism* (Machlowitz, 1981). Here an individual is unable to engage effectively in roles outside the workplace. The opposite extreme of low involvement manifests itself in extreme apathy and alienation—a topic we will consider in the next section.

As you might expect, there is a positive correlation between job satisfaction and work commitment and centrality (Glisson & Durick, 1988; Kraut, 1975; Mottaz, 1987b). Although the concepts of satisfaction and commitment are correlated, it is useful and necessary to keep them distinct. People can be really satisfied with their work but have their major commitments elsewhere. In a similar manner, people could be heavily involved with their work but be quite dissatisfied with it. Revolutions and insurrections, after all, are caused by highly committed but dissatisfied people.

Work commitment can be oriented toward occupations or organizations. This distinction is particularly relevant for professional workers. Such a person can experience conflict between orientations toward profession and employer (Patchen, 1970; Sheldon, 1971). I have friends who are strongly involved in the profession and discipline of sociology but do not really care at all about their colleges or universities. I have other friends who are completely uninvolved with sociology but live and die for their college or university. Still others are committed to neither or to both.

There are several correlates of high levels of commitment (Mortimer, 1979). One is that more-committed workers are less likely to voluntarily terminate or quit their work. They may also be more ambitious in terms of seeking promotions. Evidence also suggests that highly involved workers are more likely to perform better. An interesting study of blue-collar workers in a telephone company found that job-oriented workers were rated highest in terms of initiative and application, cooperation, and quantity of work; the same workers, however, rated quite low in terms of their adaptability (Dubin & Champoux, 1974). Low adaptability may be one cost of high commitment. A highly committed labor force, of course, can bring great benefits to an organization or even a nation, such as is the case with Japan (Lincoln & Kalleberg, 1990).

Development of Work Commitment

There have been several attempts to explain the development of work commitment. One of the most interesting is the idea of *side bets* (Becker, 1960). The basic idea is that certain costs and investments (the side bets) develop over time that make it difficult for a person to disengage from work. Side bets lock a person into a position. When a person gets married, the spouse is now part of the "bet," because leaving a job would threaten more than just the worker involved. Health insurance and pension plans also can be viewed as additional contributions to the "pot" in the poker game of work. If you leave, you lose access to the pot.

Side bets are a factor when workers agree to be relocated or transferred (Sell, 1982). Corporate policies have contributed to the growth of the Sunbelt in the United States as workers are relocated to new installations. Such relocation or migration may not be desired by the people involved, but they move because of the commitments brought about by side bets. IBM is frequently called "I've Been Moved" by its employees. The company has been able to develop many side bets.

Individual Influences

Although the idea of side bets is intriguing, a more straightforward approach deals with individual and organizational influences on involvement and commitment. Among the individual influences on work commitment are age, gender, and educational level (Loscocco & Rochelle, 1991). Gender and educational level play essentially the same role for commitment as they did in the case of satisfaction. The gender factor is complicated by the fact that women are expected to play a dominant role in families in our society. As we will see in Chapters 6 and 11, this can create severe problems for women.

However, a strong and positive relationship is seen between age and involvement (Lorence, 1987; Loscocco & Kalleberg, 1988; Shoemaker, Snizek, & Bryant, 1977). Involvement is quite volatile at younger ages but becomes stable with time. There may be some tailing off of occupational commitment among older workers, but the general relationship holds (Alutto & Belasco, 1974). Note that involvement and commitment at middle age have important implications for career achievement (Lorence & Mortimer, 1985). If people remain committed at middle age and opportunities for advancement are present, then continued career advancement is possible.

Organizational Characteristics

In recent years, considerable attention has been paid to the characteristics of employing organizations in regard to commitment. Crucial to this attention has been the realization that the organizational forms adopted by Japanese industries appear to be strongly related to high levels of worker commitment—and to the high quality of Japanese manufacturing.

The major research on this topic has been carried out by Lincoln and Kalleberg (1985, 1990), who depict Japanese firms as models of what Dore (1973) calls "welfare corporatism." According to Lincoln and Kalleberg (1990), this involves:

> permanent employment guarantees that reduce turnover and increase workers' investment in [the] firm. . . ;
>
> organizational structures such as tall job hierarchies and proliferating work units [that] break up class and occupational loyalties while encouraging organization-wide cohesive bonds. . . ;
>
> programs for relieving the fragmentation and monotony of jobs and tasks through rotation and enlargement that increase the intrinsic rewards of working and build identification with the organization as a whole. . . ;
>
> mechanisms for fostering employee participation in decision making without the formal guarantees or high level access that might threaten management control. . . ;

> a legal structure of formalized rights and obligations that confer corporate citizenship on employees and avert reliance on alienating personal forms of supervisory domination. . . ;
>
> and the trappings of strong organizational culture—ritual, ceremony, symbolism and the like—along with a potpourri of tangible welfare benefits including family subsidies, educational programs, housing, and health benefits. (pp. 248-249)

Lincoln and Kalleberg do not claim that Japanese workers have higher commitment levels than U.S. workers. Indeed, they note (1985) that workers in the core sector in both countries report high commitment. A member of their research team has found lower levels of commitment among Japanese workers who are not exposed to the organizational forms noted above (Near, 1989). Another member of the same research team used U.S. data and found high employee commitment in firms that provided opportunities for advancement (Loscocco, 1990b).

The major conclusion here is that some organizations are able to provide structures and practices that enhance worker commitment. These same structures and practices appear to lead to high performance levels in terms of quality and quantity. Unfortunately, not all organizations can provide the characteristics that have been identified. They may be in the peripheral sector or they may have ownership or management that feels threatened by such practices.

Equity, Expectancy, and Commitment

A comprehensive approach to commitment requires combining the individual and organizational characteristics that have been identified. This can be accomplished by introducing the concepts of equity and expectancy. Not only must individuals feel their rewards are comparable with those received by others, but also these rewards must be perceived as valuable and obtainable. Consider your experiences as a student. Obviously, it is important for all students in the same class to be graded according to the same standard. This reflects an equity concern. However, whether grading rules are applied uniformly will be of little interest if the instructor fails to reward hard work. Equity loses its importance if even the best students in the class are destined to fail. Student motivation is likely to be undermined if the valued outcome of a good grade is impossible to obtain.

The same principle holds in work settings. Individuals will be motivated to remain in and contribute to organizations when rewards are felt to be equitable and when the rewards meet their expectations (Mortimer, 1974). This formulation, of course, is almost identical to that developed in our discussion of motivation.

Several independent research projects support the points made here. For example, among managers, the greater the rewards received by individuals, the greater their commitment to the organization (Grusky, 1966). Organizational rewards are obviously linked to positions in the managerial hierarchy. Commitment also appears to be increased by having overcome obstacles on the way to obtaining organizational rewards and by the reference groups that people use in evaluating their success.

When the focus shifts to very different forms of work, the same patterns hold—although the routes to involvement and commitment are quite different for different work settings. For instance, an analysis of the Roman Catholic priesthood in the United States found that commitment results from a desirable net balance of rewards over costs that is realized by one who participates in the role of priest role rather than in a feasible alternative role such as marriage (Schoenherr & Greeley, 1974). As British actors move toward the apex of the acting hierarchy, more positive sources of commitment become available to them, such as receiving critical acclaim, being sought after for choice parts, and receiving a steady income from acting (Layder, 1984).

Among miners, who have a very dirty and dangerous occupation, an "occupational subculture of danger" generates commitment (Fitzpatrick, 1980; Vaught & Smith, 1980). The miners develop a complex of beliefs, patterns of behavior, norms, and values that serve to provide a sense of security for the workers. They also have elaborate games and dramatic performances, including an "initiation ceremony" in which workers' genitals are greased, as obstacles to be overcome on the way to commitment. The initiation ceremony is also a form of side bet; once a person has passed through the ceremony, he has paid the price and thus would want to continue receiving the rewards that mining had to offer. To leave mining would result in paying the price but not receiving the benefit.

No matter how it is achieved, work commitment, like job satisfaction, is a positive reaction to work. However, not every reaction is sweetness and light. We now turn to that other side of things.

Alienation

> I stand in one spot, about two- or three-feet area, all night. The only time a person stops is when the line stops. We do about thirty-two jobs per car, per unit. Forty-eight units an hour, eight hours a day. Thirty-two times forty-eight times eight. Figure it out. That's how many times I push that button. . . .
>
> It don't stop. It just goes and goes and goes. I bet there's men who have lived and died out there, never seen the end of that line. And they never will—because it's endless. It's like a serpent. It's just all body, no tail. It can do things to you. (Terkel, 1974, pp. 221-222)

These are the words of an assembly-line spotwelder as reported by Studs Terkel in his well-known book *Working*. This worker's description of his job illustrates that working can have its negative aspects.

The 1970s witnessed the publication of several similar books such as Stanley Aronowitz's *False Promises: The Shaping of American Working Class Consciousness* and Barbara Garson's *All the Livelong Day: The Meaning and Demeaning of Routine Work*. These were widely read and discussed in the media. The U.S. government even sponsored the publication of *Work in America* (O'Toole, 1973), which contained accounts of "blue-collar blues," "white-collar woes," and "managerial discontent." The titles reveal the major themes of these works: The negative side of work is not just dissatisfaction, it is alienation.

Structural Alienation

The linkage between work and alienation has strong ties to the writing of Karl Marx. Indeed, it may become ironically true that Marx's social analyses may be more enduring than political Marxism. Marx wrote, "Work is external to the worker; it is not part of his nature; consequently he does not fulfill himself in his work, but denies himself. . . . In work [the worker] does not belong to himself but to another person" (1964, pp. 124-125). Marx was concerned with the distance between the worker and the means and ownership of the production process. This is known as *objective* or *structural alienation*.

This form of alienation is exemplified by clerical workers in the communications industry. Over the years, they have been subjected to increased managerial control. They also now have less conceptual content in their work tasks. As workers "lose control" of their work, they experience structural alienation (Vallas, 1987).

The Subjective Experience

Most contemporary research on alienation has not looked at structural alienation in the Marxian tradition, but rather has focused on subjective alienation. This research is based on how people feel about their work. There has thus been a shift in emphasis from being powerless in an objective sense to feeling powerless in a sociopsychological sense.

The prime example of dealing with alienation in social psychological terms is Blauner's now classic (1964) study of different forms of alienation found in different working conditions. He considered four forms of alienation in four industrial settings: powerlessness, meaninglessness, isolation, and self-estrangement.

Powerlessness is the first form of alienation. A powerless person is an object manipulated and controlled by other people or by some impersonal system such as technology. Powerless people react rather than act; they cannot modify the conditions of their existence. The opposite of powerlessness is freedom and control over one's own life. Blauner's research considered the extent to which people were able to move freely about in their work; their freedom to make choices, vary the pace of their work, and have control over the quantity and quality of their work; and their freedom to select their own work techniques and routine. The more freedom, the less powerlessness.

Meaninglessness was the next component of alienation Blauner considered. This is experienced when people are unable to see a connection between their own work and the completed product. As the division of labor increases and work becomes more and more subdivided, meaninglessness becomes more common. My work is meaningful when I see this writing come out in a published book. My work would be meaningless if I did all of the keyboard entering that I have done but never saw the finished product because it was simply a tiny part of a much larger whole.

The third component of alienation is *isolation* or *social alienation*. It refers to a situation in which people are unable to establish satisfactory and satisfying social relationships on the job. It can occur when the noise level is too great to permit conversation or when people are forbidden to communicate with others while working. It can also occur in situations in which one is working with a set of people who never become more than strangers.

The final component of alienation is *self-estrangement*. Here a worker is depersonalized and detached. The work has no intrinsic satisfaction. Work that is experienced as boring and monotonous would be the typical source of self-estrangement. The work is performed, but the worker is detached from the performance.

Sources of Alienation

Further insights into alienation can be found in Melvin Kohn's (1976) analysis of the sources of subjective alienation. In his analysis, Kohn first identifies two possible sources of alienation. The first is the Marxian idea of loss of control over the product of one's labor. The second source involves control over the work process itself, which Kohn believes Marx meant to include in his development of the idea of alienation.

Kohn (1976) hypothesized that aspects of the work process are more important for alienation than the actual product of one's labor:

> Work that is "external" to the worker, in which he cannot "fulfill himself," comes close to being the opposite pole of

what Schooler and I have called "self-directed" work—that is, work involving initiative, thought, and independent judgment (Kohn, 1969, pp. 139-140; Kohn & Schooler, 1973). Although many occupational conditions are either conducive to or deterrent from the exercise of occupational self-direction, we see three in particular as crucial—closeness of supervision, routinization, and substantive complexity. Insofar as workers are free of close supervision, perform a variety of tasks, and do work that is substantively complex, their work is necessarily self-directed. Insofar as workers are closely supervised, are caught up in a repetitive flow of similar tasks, and do work of little substantive complexity, their work does not permit self-direction. Believing that loss of control over the process of work is conducive to alienation, I hypothesize that being closely supervised, doing routinized work, and doing work of little substantive complexity will result in feelings of alienation. (pp. 112-113)

In discussing his findings, Kohn notes that the circumstance in which his data were collected (a 1964 national U.S. survey) was one of relative economic security. In periods of economic uncertainty, he suggests, factors such as job security might be more important than occupational self-direction. As we noted earlier, people's expectations about their work can change over time on the basis of altered life circumstances.

Kohn also concludes that neither capitalism nor bureaucracy is the primary source of alienation. When workers are not able to exercise self-direction, they will be alienated.

Environmental Determinants. Whether a worker has the freedom to exercise self-direction is generally not up to the worker. Factors in the workplace are more influential. Again, Blauner (1964) had some interesting insights. He did not simply assume that work was universally alienating. Rather, he built the idea of industrial variation into his research and identified four sources of variation.

One source was the division of labor within a particular organization. Work can be highly differentiated into small units or people can be permitted to work on a wider proportion of the production process. Another source of variation was the social organization of a particular industry. For Blauner, this involved the degree to which bureaucratic or professional standards were used in the operations of the organizations studied. Organizations vary in their emphasis on following rules and procedures. Some give workers discretion, others do not. A third source of variation was the economic structure of the industry. Blauner believed that economically marginal industries would push their workers harder and have tighter supervisory practices.

The fourth and final source of variation Blauner investigated was the technology employed. One industry he studied, printing, was then characterized by a craft technology that had been minimally affected by technological change. The next industry considered was the textile industry, which had a more advanced technology in the form of machine tending. The third industry studied was the automobile industry, which has been characterized by a more advanced production process and a more standardized product. The traditional automobile assembly line is usually thought of as the epitome of settings in which work would be alienating. The final setting was the industrial-chemical and petroleum-refining industry. Here the work is continuous-process, with highly advanced technologies. Continuous-process work involves monitoring gauges and other indicators of temperature and pressure. Workers have a great deal of discretion and the power to stop the entire process if dangerous conditions are spotted. The industries studied thus varied from craft technology, through increasing mechanization, and on to continuous-process work. This research was conducted before the widespread adoption of computers and robots.

The Role of Technology. With this background, Blauner's findings are not surprising. The printers he studied experienced little alienation on any dimension. They could set their own work pace and move about, and they had little direct supervision. The product changed constantly, and they could see the results of their work. The printers' union was a strong one, and there was social involvement. Finally, they had pride in their work and were involved in what they were doing.

Textile workers, in contrast, exhibited more alienation. These workers tended from 40 to 60 looms. Movement and the pace of work were controlled, and supervision was close, so powerlessness was experienced. There was somewhat less meaninglessness, because the finished product was seen and the workers understood their contribution to the whole. Social isolation was not experienced, because the workers studied were from the same small Southern town and knew one another. Self-estrangement was also not found, which Blauner attributes to the low educational levels of the workers studied and their minimal emphasis on self-expression.

As expected, the auto workers experienced high levels of all four forms of alienation. The assembly line moves inexorably by, with quantity, quality, and pace determined by others. The assembly line is a control mechanism, with the worker unable to choose the order or techniques by which work is done. There is also high meaninglessness, because one individual worker is a very small part of the whole. The backgrounds of the workers were very heterogeneous, with little likelihood of working with friends from outside the plant. The size of the plant made people even feel more like numbers. The monotony and lack of challenge contributed to self-estrangement. These auto workers were the classic alienated modern workers, although as Blauner notes, this sort of work is actually a small fraction of all industrial work.

When the focus shifted to the chemical operator in the continuous-process chemical refinery, the picture changed drastically. Here we are back to a situation of low alienation. Little powerlessness was experienced, because most of the work involved skilled maintenance type work and workers set their own pace and place of work. The work was largely teamwork, and the workers understood the total process and their contribution to it, so neither meaninglessness nor social isolation was experienced. There was opportunity to experiment with new jobs, and involvement with work was high.

Blauner thus found that alienation was low at both ends of the technological spectrum—in a craft industry and in a continuous-process industry. At the intermediate technological level, the highest levels of alienation were found. This has become known as the "inverted-U hypothesis." Later research tested this inverted-U hypothesis with data from 110 factories. The hypothesis received moderate support. In general, the more advanced the technology, the lower the alienation (Hull, Friedman, & Rogers, 1982).

An interesting follow-up to Blauner's work was a later analysis of the printing industry, a form of work that has undergone significant technological change as the computer has replaced traditional typesetting skills (Hull et al., 1982). The researchers studied printers at three large newspapers in New York City. These printers had been retrained to use new, automated equipment. In most ways, the retrained printers did not experience an increase in alienation. Some shifts in job attitudes were evident, but a large increase in alienation was not found.

Another replication of the Blauner work examined textile workers using 1980 data (Blauner's were from 1947). These data indicate that textile workers had experienced moderately increased alienation in the forms of powerlessness, social isolation, and self-estrangement (Leiter, 1985). The change in results is not too surprising given the many changes in the textile industry in the 33 years between the two studies. For example, ownership of textile plants has shifted from local ownership to corporate ownership. There has been an increase in the proportion of black workers. Women workers in 1980 were not as traditional in their outlooks as those in the Blauner study. Apparently, the characteristics of the Southern textile workers changed, but the industry did not; the result was greater alienation.

Can we then conclude that either structural or subjective alienation is increasing? No, we cannot. Alienation is frequently tied to deskilling, which was considered in Chapter 1. Just as deskilling of work must be demonstrated by research rather than simply asserted, so alienation must be demonstrated. It is clear from the work on deskilling that advancing technology is not causing a unidirectional movement toward lower skill requirements. It should also be clear that there is not a unidirectional movement toward alienation.

Some Additional Negative Reactions

Alienation is not the only negative reaction to work. For instance, work's effects on physical and mental health are well documented (Kahn, 1981; see also Sutton, 1984, for a review of this literature). Stress can contribute to cardiovascular and gastrointestinal problems, excessive drinking, and so on. Some work roles contain more sources of stress than others. Particular characteristics of work that contribute to stress include role conflicts, role overload, and responsibility (Katz & Kahn, 1978). Job conditions such as these interact with personality types to yield differing degrees of stress. However, both men and women report lower satisfaction and higher stress under conditions of role conflict (Coverman, 1989; Lowe & Northcott, 1988).

Low job satisfaction, another negative reaction, is significantly linked to involvement in deviant acts directed against the work organization (Clark & Hollinger, 1983; Hollinger & Clark, 1982). These acts include actual crime against an organization, such as property theft, pilferage, and embezzlement. Other forms of deviance include tardiness, sloppy or slow workmanship, and drug or alcohol use on the job.

At this point we can say that work is thus neither an entirely benign nor an entirely harmful event in the lives of workers. Even for those for whom it is not a central life interest, work produces both positive and negative reactions.

Individuals and Work: The Broader Context

Two issues have been buried in our analysis that should be made explicit. First, at the macrolevel or societal level, a satisfied and committed labor force has positive benefits for both the workers involved and society itself. Lincoln and Kalleberg's (1990) work strongly hints at the idea that Japan's advancement to prominence in the world economy has resulted in large part from its committed labor force, which is a product of national and corporate policies. Presumably, the United States could see economic and social benefits from policies that would lead to the development of work organizations that encourage satisfaction and commitment through worker autonomy. This could involve policies that would provide profit sharing and greater worker control over work and work pace.

The second issue is related but more personal. How much work satisfaction and work commitment in particular is actually good for an individual? This issue was touched on when workaholism was discussed, but the issue is broader. Many of the people talking on their cellular phones while driving their cars are simply trying to give the impression of being important and busy, but others are driven by their work. I also know people who postpone marriage or having children because of work commitments. Similarly, some people will avoid relationships entirely in the face of work commitment. Work commitment and satisfaction can thus be taken to an extreme that is harmful to individuals.

Conclusions

Why do we work? As this chapter has shown, we have many motivations for work. Some are noble, some are crass. How do we learn how to work? We learn in school, we learn on the job, and we learn in-between. The key point is that we learn constantly. Socialization is an ongoing process. We are even socialized into retirement from work.

How do we react to work? We can be satisfied with some or many aspects of our work and our work in general. We can also be committed and involved. Or we can be neither. We can go to work and have our real pleasures off the job. We can also be alienated from our work and our fellow workers.

I happen to believe that work that is fulfilling and that serves other people is extremely rewarding. I also happen to believe that I should be extrinsically and intrinsically rewarded for my work. The key point is that I react as an individual to my work.

The point of this chapter has been to trace how and why individuals and their work interact. The next chapter will examine an entirely different topic, but one that has been hinted at throughout these first three chapters: the relationships between work and social status.

■ APPLICATION

The Meaning of Work

Why do people work? Perhaps it is because they must. Precious few of us could afford to live in any kind of comfort without the income provided by paid employment. This economic function of work notwithstanding, imagine for a moment what life might be like if you did not have to go to work or school. Imagine not having to get out of bed at any particular time in the morning. How would your life change if there was no need for you to be at any particular place at any particular time? Would you continue to work or attend school? If not, what would you do with your spare time? Where would you meet new people and establish close relationships? What would you do for fun? How would you keep yourself intellectually stimulated?

Social scientists have shown considerable interest in questions such as these in their research on "the meaning of work." Generally speaking, this research focuses on questions of why people work and what people perceive to be the more valuable outcomes of their work experiences. Some researchers have taken a historical perspective, examining how work meanings have changed over time (e.g., since before the industrial revolution). Other researchers have examined work from a crosscultural perspective, arguing that the meanings people assign to their work experiences may change as they move from culture to culture.

In 1987, a team of 14 researchers known as the MOW (Meaning of Work) International Research Team published the results of a large-scale study on work. Data were collected on approximately 15,000 individuals from 8 industrialized nations around the world. All sorts of people were interviewed, ranging from the unemployed to students to professional workers. These researchers addressed a wide variety of questions in their study: How involved are people in their work? Is work a central life interest for most people? What sorts of satisfactions do people expect to get out of their work? What do people hope to accomplish in their work? Do people work for fun or for money?

Some interesting answers were revealed. Perhaps unsurprising was the finding that, for the vast majority of people, work is a highly central aspect of their lives. In fact, across all eight nations involved in the study, work was rated second only to family in terms of its importance as a life role. Work was rated as more important than community, religious, and leisure life roles (MOW International Research Team, 1987).

Perhaps this extreme centrality of work can be understood when one acknowledges the role of economic concerns. After all, economic security is probably a necessary precondition for pursuing both leisure activities and roles in the community. In fact, the MOW team discovered that economic considerations provided the primary rationale for working among respondents in their sample: "Clearly, the dominant underlying reason why people work is to secure and maintain an income to purchase needed and/or desired goods and services" (MOW International Research Team, 1987, p. 250). In the absence of such economic necessity, work might play a less central role in people's lives.

People work for more than just a paycheck, however. Consider the following finding: 86% of the respondents in the MOW sample said they would continue to work "even if they had enough money to live comfortably for the rest of their lives without working" (MOW International Research Team, 1987, p. 251).

What then are people working for? Although the answers varied widely, some general themes did emerge from the MOW study. For instance, the opportunity for self-expression appeared to be an important work outcome for a large number of MOW respondents, as did the opportunity for interpersonal contact, learning, and self-improvement.

You may be able to detect a similar pattern of meaning with respect to your work as a student. For instance, you may attend class early and study late so that you will get good grades. This is analogous to people working for the economic benefits work provides. But instead of working for an end-of-the month paycheck, the student receives an end-of-semester grade report.

Being a student obviously carries with it sources of gratification other than a grade report. Writing a term paper offers a student not only a potential route to good grades, but also an opportunity for self-expression. Coming to class raises your odds of scoring well on an exam and ensures continued contact with friends and acquaintances. Just as students assign multiple meanings to their school activities, workers appear to assign multiple meanings (economic and noneconomic) to their work activities.

It is easy to see that people attach multiple meanings to their work. What is not immediately clear is when (if ever) workers place greater emphasis on one type of meaning than on another. When do workers see their jobs primarily as a source of income and when do they see their jobs as sources of personal fulfillment and gratification? Although the results must be interpreted with caution, the MOW team's research suggests that the answer depends largely on the job's characteristics.

According to the MOW team, people who have "high quality jobs"—jobs allowing a high degree of autonomy, variety, responsibility, and the opportunity to use one's skills—tend to emphasize the importance of outcomes such as self-expression and self-improvement over economic outcomes. On the other hand, people who perform repetitive and demanding work under unsavory conditions tend to emphasize the economic meaning of work (MOW International Research Team, 1987).

Once again, a parallel can be drawn with the experiences of students. Students are unlikely to enjoy a class if the professor does nothing but read lecture notes and administer exams. Under such circumstances, students may cease to be interested by the subject matter of the class and may instead focus on what has to be done to get out of the class with a "decent" grade. On the other hand, instructors who use a variety of teaching techniques and present intellectual challenges to their students are more likely to pique student interest in the subject at hand, prompting them to interpret their classroom experience in terms of personal achievement and enlightenment.

Of course, there are alternative interpretations of the MOW team's research results. For instance, as was argued earlier in this chapter, people's work values tend to influence the type of work they choose. Their work in turn tends to reinforce these work values. Thus the fact that managers and professionals tend to place more importance on self-expression than do service and clerical workers may have as much to do with the values held by the individuals involved as with the characteristics of the jobs they hold.

However, none of this changes the fact that work is a highly central component in all of our lives, one that we could not easily do without. Working serves a variety of important functions that we could not easily perform if unemployed. Although "it is true that nobody prevents the unemployed from creating their own time structure and social contacts, from sharing goals and purposes with others or from exercising their skills as best they can, . . . [t]he psychological input required to do so on a regular basis under one's own steam entirely is colossal" (Jahoda, in Sayers, 1988, p. 731).

■■■ SUGGESTED READINGS

A complete bibliographical entry for each work cited here can be found in the reference section at the back of this book.

Blauner, *Alienation and Freedom* (1964), is a sociological classic that shows how alienation varies across industries and organizations.

Lincoln and Kalleberg, *Culture, Control, and Commitment* (1990), is destined to become a classic in my opinion. It is not mindless praise of the Japanese approach to work, but a careful examination of how people become committed to their work and the consequences of such commitment for workers, their employers, and the larger society.

Mortimer and Simmons, "Adult Socialization" (1978), is a major summary of the research on socialization for work. The emphasis is that socialization for work continues throughout life.

O'Toole (Ed.), *Work in America* (1973), is somewhat dated but still presents a useful series of findings about how people react to their work and some suggestions for improvement.

4 Status and Occupation: The Vertical Dimension

Which would you rather be—a golf pro or a caddie? a lawyer or a paralegal? an engineer or a technician? Most people would choose the more prestigious occupation of each pair. Why do we tend to rate one as better than the other? And who decided that one is more prestigious than the other? I will try to answer these and other questions in this chapter. I will also deal with the topics of social class, status, power, income, and privilege. These are elements of what I like to call the *vertical dimension* of work.

What is the "vertical dimension"? Recall the distinctions made in Chapter 2 among blue-collar, white-collar, managerial, and professional jobs? These types of jobs are obviously different in the type of work performed and skills required. But the terms have implications that reach far beyond the nature of the work performed. They also tell us something about the income, status, and social class of the people who hold them.

The point is that people focus on work as a central defining characteristic with which to describe themselves and others. For the overwhelming majority of us, work defines our placement on the vertical dimension. The exceptions to this generalization are part of a cruel irony. Only the very wealthy and the very poor do not work, thus their place on the vertical dimension is not determined by their work.

In the following pages, I will sharpen the definition of the vertical dimension, but it should be clear that social class, status, income, and so on are extremely important components of the social order. A note: Most of the research that forms the basis for this chapter has been conducted with white males. Where appropriate, I will bring in issues of gender, race, religion, and ethnicity into the discussion here, although Chapters 6 and 8 will focus directly on these topics.

The Basic Relationship: Work and Social Status

The relationship between the kind of work people do (or their occupations) and their social status (or placement on the vertical dimension) is extremely strong. Blau and Duncan (1967), in one of the most influential books on this topic, note that in "the absence of hereditary castes or feudal estates, class differences come to rest primarily on occupational positions and the economic advantages and powers associated with them" (p. vii). In most modern societies, the status we are born with will not necessarily be our status forever. Rather, our position on the vertical dimension is a function of our individual vocational and economic achievement.

Some easy examples illustrate the importance of work for social status. Members of wealthy families such as the Rockefellers and Kennedys are known for their work, primarily as politicians, and their status is given to them for their work. In popular television shows, Bill Cosby's "Dr. Huxtable" has high status because he is a physician, not because he is an African-American; and "Murphy Brown" has her status determined by her work as a television news anchor, not because of her gender.

Measures of Occupational Status and Prestige

Extensive efforts have been made to calibrate or measure this strong relationship between occupations and social status. Sociologists would like to develop measures or scales that could be used over time and across generations. It would also be convenient if we could have measures that could be used in different countries so that we could make international comparisons (Haller & Bills, 1979). As might be expected, there is not yet agreement on the "one best way" to measure the status of various occupations, even though there have been a lot of good tries.

One major emphasis has been in measuring occupational prestige. *Prestige* is something accorded to an occupation. No person or occupation "has" prestige, it is only something given by other people. We constantly receive reminders from other people about our own place in the status hierarchy, and we have our own subjective views of our own and others' status (Faunce, 1989). Prestige scales have been developed to formalize these subjective measures of status. These formal efforts to measure occupational prestige date back at least to the 1920s (Haller & Bills, 1979).

The most influential attempt to measure occupational prestige was published in 1947 and is known as the North-Hatt or NORC (for National Opinion Research Center) scale (see Reiss, 1961, for a comprehensive review of the scale's development). This study was designed to determine the standards of judgment people use in evaluating occupational status. It also was concerned with the standards used to determine the relative desirability of various occupations. And, most important, the study was designed to determine the way in which a national sample would rate the relative prestige of a wide range of occupations.

The prestige ratings for some 90 occupations were obtained in this study. It is interesting that the reasons respondents gave for ranking an occupation highly contained the same mix of intrinsic and extrinsic factors that were discussed in Chapter 3 with regard to job satisfaction, including pay, security, service to humanity, and ability to use intelligence. People's opinions about the prestige of occupations is apparently based on the same "bundle" of factors they use to evaluate their own work.

Since the publication of the North-Hatt study and scales, there have been several other major attempts at developing occupational prestige scales that include a wider range of occupations than was contained in the original study (Hodge, Siegel, & Rossi, 1964; Hodge, Treiman, & Rossi, 1966; Siegel, 1971). The NORC scale is presented in Figure 4.1. It contains prestige scores for 90 occupations. The scores were obtained by having survey participants rank the standing of occupations on a scale of 1 to 9. These scores were then converted into the NORC metric of 0 (low) to 100 (high).

A separate prestige scale for women—the *Bose Index*—has also been developed; it includes prestige scores for housewives (Bose, 1973; Bose & Rossi, 1983). This research found slightly different prestige scores if the incumbent in an occupation was designated as a woman or a man. The basic scores were minimally affected. The Bose Index is presented in Figure 4.2.

Attempts have been made to develop prestige scales that are universally applicable to any society. Researchers have found that even though nonsocialist industrial nations and urban sectors of nonindustrial nations in Europe shared common hierarchies, formerly socialist industrialized nations in Europe and rural nonindustrial nations had different hierarchies (Haller & Bills, 1979; Penn, 1975; Treiman, 1977). Now that the socialist-nonsocialist distinction has essentially disappeared, it remains to be seen whether the prestige hierarchies in the formerly socialist nations of Eastern Europe will begin to resemble those in the West. In general, all of these studies have shown a great deal of similarity in the prestige hierarchies of most industrialized nations. The vertical dimension of work is thus quite stable over space.

There is indirect evidence that such stability also exists over time. A study found very slow change in the occupational hierarchy in Philadelphia from 1789 to 1969 (Tyree & Smith, 1978). Bankers and bakers had not changed location on the vertical dimension in both periods. This study could not use prestige scores, of course, because these scales were not available for the earlier period, but the researchers did have evidence about wealth.

Alternative Measures of Occupational Status

The prestige scales that have been developed to measure the vertical dimension of work have not satisfied all analysts because they are indirect and based on people's opinions. One simpler alternative is the use of U.S. census categories. These are very close to the various forms of work, discussed in Chapter 2: professionals; proprietors, managers, and officials; clerks and kindred workers; and so on. These categories form unique groupings, with different political, economic, and social points of view (Edwards,

FIGURE 4.1 NORC Scale of Occupational Prestige, 1947*

Occupation	Score
U.S. supreme court justice	96
Physician	93
State governor	93
Cabinet member in the federal government	92
Diplomat in the U.S. Foreign Service	92
Mayor of a large city	90
College professor	89
Scientist	89
U.S. representative in Congress	89
Banker	88
Government scientist	88
County judge	87
Head of a department in a state government	87
Minister	87
Architect	86
Chemist	86
Dentist	86
Lawyer	86
Member of board of directors of large corporation	86
Nuclear physicist	86
Priest	86
Psychologist	85
Civil engineer	84
Airline pilot	83
Artist who paints pictures that are exhibited in galleries	83
Owner of factory that employs about 100 people	82
Sociologist	82
Accountant for large business	81
Biologist	81
Musician in a symphony orchestra	81
Author of novels	80
Captain in the regular army	80
Building contractor	79
Economist	79
Instructor in public schools	79

FIGURE 4.1 Continued

Occupation	Score
Public-school teacher	78
County agricultural agent	77
Railroad engineer	77
Farm owner and operator	76
Official of an international labor union	75
Radio announcer	75
Newspaper columnist	74
Owner-operator of a printing shop	74
Electrician	73
Trained machinist	73
Welfare worker for a city government	73
Undertaker	72
Reporter on daily newspaper	71
Manager of small store in a city	69
Bookkeeper	68
Insurance agent	68
Tenant farmer — one who owns livestock and machinery and manages the farm	68
Traveling salesman for a wholesale concern	68
Playground director	67
Policeman	67
Railroad conductor	67
Mail carrier	66
Carpenter	65
Automobile repairman	63
Plumber	63
Garage mechanic	62
Local official of labor union	62
Owner-operator of lunch stand	62
Corporal in the regular army	60
Machine operator in factory	60
Barber	59
Clerk in a store	58
Fisherman who owns a boat	58
Streetcar motorman	58
Milk-route man	54

FIGURE 4.1 Continued

Occupation	Score
Restaurant cook	54
Truck driver	54
Lumberjack	53
Filling station attendant	52
Singer in a night club	52
Farm hand	50
Coal miner	49
Taxi driver	49
Railroad section hand	48
Restaurant	48
Dockworker	47
Night watchman	47
Clothes-presser in a laundry	46
Soda-fountain clerk	45
Bartender	44
Janitor	44
Share-cropper — one who owns no livestock or equipment and does not manage farm	40
Garbage collector	35
Street-sweeper	34
Shoe-shiner	33

Source: Adapted with the permission of The Free Press, a Division of Macmillan, Inc. from *Occupations and Social Status* by Albert J. Reiss, Jr. with Otis Dudley Duncan, Paul K. Hatt, and Cecil C. North. Copyright © 1961 by the The Free Press.

1943). They also have economically distinct standards of living, with quite different intellectual and social standards of life. However, these census distinctions offer too many possibilities for inaccuracies and misleading placements. For example, U.S. census categories would place a corporate chief executive lower on the vertical dimension than a nurse.

A more rigorous measure than census categories that does not rely on subjective judgments as do the prestige scales is the *socioeconomic index* (SEI), which was developed by Duncan in 1961 (in Reiss, 1961), using 1950 census information about the education and income of people in various occupations. The SEI is an "objective" indicator of status in that it links education and income into a single status measure for each occupation. SEI sores were developed by calculating the proportion of people in a particular occupation who had more than a high school diploma and who earned more than $3,500 (a considerable amount in 1950) (see Duncan, in Reiss, 1961, pp. 120-124, for details).

The SEI was originally developed as an extension of the NORC work. The SEI is highly correlated with both the original NORC prestige scale and the more recent one developed by Siegel (1971) (see also Duncan, Featherman, & Duncan, 1972). The major differences are that some occupations, such as clergy or professors, score lower on the SEI than on the prestige scales, while others, such as business occupations, score higher on the SEI than on the prestige scales. In general, however, the scales are essentially interchangeable (for a recent debate on this subject, see Grusky & Van Rompaey, 1992; Hauser & Logan, 1992; Rytina, 1992a, 1992b).

Having described all of these measures of occupational status, I must confess that, for our purposes, it does not matter which of these highly sophisticated analyses we consult. All show the same thing: Different occupations have clearly different placements on the vertical dimension, regardless of the measure used. The real question is, Why do they have different placements?

The Role of Education

Education is clearly a crucial factor in determining a person's placement on the vertical dimension. Few of us would dispute the strong relationships among education, occupation, and earnings. But the relationship between education and work is more complicated than simply the number of years of schooling yielding particular forms of work or a particular occupation. *Certification*, rather than number of years of schooling, is the key variable here. A person might have some college, but without the certification of

FIGURE 4.2 The Bose Index

Occupation	Incumbent	
	Females	Males
1. Box packer	16.6	16.0
2. Fruit harvester, working for own family	25.0	28.8
3. Assembly line supervisor in a manufacturing plant	57.5	51.6
4. Fireman in a boiler room	32.2	37.8
5. Landscape gardener	34.5	39.4
6. Beautician	47.4	44.2
7. Delivery truck driver	31.6	31.7
8. Salad maker in a hotel	19.9	20.1
9. Electrical engineer	78.8	79.8
10. Florist	50.0	46.5
11. Stenographer	56.3	56.4
12. Practical nurse	58.4	61.5
13. Garbage collector	15.9	20.5
14. Circulation director of a newspaper	60.9	56.6
15. Metal container maker	32.2	32.4
16. Locomotive engineer	54.7	59.6
17. Vegetable grader	16.1	25.6
18. Flour miller	23.3	27.9
19. Electric wire winder	34.9	37.8
20. Short order cook	17.7	26.0
21. Stock broker	80.9	80.8
22. Post office clerk	42.8	48.1
23. Carpenter	47.2	53.2
24. Wholesale salesperson	42.9	42.0
25. Tool machinist	44.1	52.6
26. Key punch operator	45.1	52.3
27. Shirt maker in a manufacturing plant	25.9	34.0
28. Bookkeeper	53.4	55.1
29. Hotel chamber maid (F)/Hotel bedmaker (M)	13.8	12.5
30. Chiropractor	76.6	76.6
31. High school teacher	64.4	71.5
32. Yarn washer	14.7	13.5
33. Social worker	56.6	60.6

FIGURE 4.2 Continued

Occupation	Incumbent	
	Females	Males
34. File clerk	42.5	39.7
35. Warehouse clerk	28.7	31.7
36. Dental assistant	60.3	57.7
37. Administrative assistant	67.0	67.9
38. Hotel manager	69.1	68.9
39. Office secretary	62.2	57.4
40. Janitor	10.0	15.1
41. Building construction contractor	79.4	77.3
42. City superintendent of schools	85.0	82.4
43. Owner of a factory employing 2,000 people	82.5	86.9
44. Blacksmith	26.6	30.3
45. Warehouse supervisor	48.4	55.6
46. Coal miner	26.6	26.6
47. Floor finisher	30.8	38.5
48. Cotton farmer	30.1	29.7
49. Butcher in a shop	30.4	44.7
50. Babysitter	18.3	17.8
51. Assembly-line worker	26.6	36.9
52. Laundry worker	17.6	15.9
53. Police officer	52.9	55.0
54. Welder	42.9	49.1
55. Advertising executive	80.4	75.6
56. Sociologist	71.2	72.7
57. Private secretary	66.0	69.1
58. Feed grinder	20.4	17.3
59. Housewife/househusband		
wife	43.6	—
husband	—	23.8
60. Waitress/Waiter	24.4	27.2
61. Housekeeper	29.5	23.1
62. Car dealer	53.8	57.5
63. Mayor	92.1	90.3
64. Boardinghouse keeper	28.2	26.9
65. Rag picker	5.8	5.9
66. Cashier	42.3	43.3

FIGURE 4.2 Continued

Occupation	Incumbent	
	Females	Males
67. Book binder	32.4	33.8
68. Stock clerk	32.7	28.1
69. Lawyer	91.7	90.6
70. Pastry chef in a restaurant	36.9	28.1
71. Electrician	64.7	57.2
72. Supervisor of telephone operators	61.9	61.3
73. Manager of supermarket	61.5	55.9
74. Office manager	70.8	66.3
75. Typist	48.7	46.6
76. Someone who sells shoes in a store	33.0	31.3
77. Insurance agent	60.6	62.2
78. Power house engineer	66.1	63.5
79. College professor	87.5	87.5
80. Piano tuner	43.9	31.3
81. Truck driver	38.5	37.2
82. Parking lot attendant	13.8	10.9
83. Washing machine repairman	41.7	30.3
84. Automobile refinisher	38.8	27.5
85. Physician	90.1	95.9
86. Maid (F)/Household day worker (M)	16.6	15.9
87. Floor supervisor in a hospital	64.5	54.1
88. Bell hop	17.3	9.4
89. Textile machine operator	31.7	31.6

a college degree, the status outcome would be the same as if there were no college experience (Faia, 1981).

Any analysis of the relationship between education and the vertical dimension must recognize the multifaceted nature of education (Kerkhoff, Campbell, & Trott, 1982). A school may be public or private, Ivy League or non-Ivy League. The type of degree one earns and the number of years of schooling may also vary. These variations lead to variations in occupational earnings, authority, and control. A person with an MBA degree from an Ivy

FIGURE 4.2 Continued

Occupation	Incumbent	
	Females	Males
90. Architect	82.7	88.1
91. Hospital lab technician	63.8	66.7
92. Dress cutter	34.0	31.9
93. Telephone operator	48.1	49.1
94. Hospital aide	33.3	30.0
95. Accountant	69.9	74.4
96. Rubber mixer	22.4	28.8
97. Registered nurse	71.2	72.8
98. Plumber	56.4	52.5
99. Manager of a factory employing 2,000 people	71.9	72.8
100. Typesetter	47.2	46.5
101. House painter	44.7	29.8
102. Person living on welfare	5.3	1.9
103. Person who repairs shoes	30.9	26.3
104. Car hop	15.2	9.9
105. Artist	62.8	58.6
106. Grade school teacher	68.4	64.5
107. Auto mechanic	49.4	45.2
108. Hairdresser	44.4	38.8
109. Inspector in a manufacturing plant	51.3	47.8
110. Cattledriver working for own family	32.5	35.9

Source: "Prestige Standings of Occupations as Affected by Gender," by C. Bose and P. Rossi, 1983, *American Sociological Review*, 48, pp. 327-328. Copyright © 1983 American Sociological Association. Reprinted with permission.

League school thus has greatly different earnings potential than a bachelor's in English from a small state college. Community college entrants suffer an occupational penalty when compared with four-year college entrants, even when controlling for the number of years of schooling eventually completed (Monk-Turner, 1983).

Not only are there between-school differences in regard to the outcomes for work, but also there are important differences within schools (Griffin & Alexander, 1978). These within-school differences are known as *tracks*. Tracking begins before high school, but becomes most visible in the high-school years. Some schools have official labels for tracks, such as *gifted, vocational,* and *academic.* Others do not have official labels for tracks, but they exist even in the absence of labels.

The importance of high-school tracks is vividly seen in an analysis of a high school in the Northeast (Rosenbaum, 1975). The social-class composition of this school was quite homogeneous because children of affluent parents attended a nearby private school and children of the least affluent dropped out of school, leaving the high school largely white and working-class. There were five distinct tracks in this school. Students in the upper tracks generally experienced increases between the 8th and 10th grades in their IQ test scores, while students in the lower tracks tended to have their IQ scores reduced.

Proponents of tracking suggest that by grouping students on the basis of their perceived abilities, more able students will benefit from the more advanced materials to which they are exposed, the faster pace with which they can move because they are not held back by the less gifted, and the support provided by peers, counselors, and teachers. Less able students are purported to benefit from having materials presented that will be relevant to their futures, from not having to suffer in competition with the more able, and from having materials presented at a pace they can handle.

Critics note that tracking provides more resources for exactly the students who need them least. The critics also note that tracking leads to a high-school status system in which those in the lower track are looked down on as being somewhat stupid. In addition, those in the lower tracks are denied access to teachers and curricula that would allow them to compete with the more privileged members of their cohort (Alexander, Cook, & McDill, 1978; Bowles & Gintis, 1976; Persell, 1977; Rosenbaum, 1976). All of this is bad enough, but it seems that tracking also contributes to and perpetuates social inequality. Higher-status students have been shown to be "streamed disproportionately" into college-preparatory curricula (Alexander et al., 1978, p. 65).

Tracking does not end with high school. Students in lower tracks, if they pursue additional education at all, are much more likely to matriculate to a community college. Even at a university with an open-admissions policy, a form of tracking persists. The City University of New York (CUNY) experimented with an open-admissions policy, which was successful in bringing large numbers of minority students to the university's campuses. At the same time, minority-group members were much more likely to be enrolled in the two-year schools and much less likely to be enrolled at the more elite senior campuses (Lavin, Alba, & Silberstein, 1981). Minority students at the two-year schools were also more likely than whites to be enrolled in vocational curricula, which reduces their chances of eventually entering four-year schools. Paradoxically, the advantages of open admissions did reach the targeted groups—minority students. At the same time, white students actually benefited more from the open-admissions policies as more whites entered the system at all levels.

The relationships between education and occupational status are thus very complex; the analysis here only touches the surface. The nature of the education that people receive has a clear effect on their placement on the vertical dimension. It is not the only determinant, however. For children of elite families who possess a high level of resources, college education has little effect on their occupational attainment (Tinto, 1984). But for nonelite families, the type of college education their children receive may play an important role in subsequent occupational attainment. Education is thus not the sole determinant of placement on the vertical dimension. The question remains, however: What does determine occupational status?

Why Do Occupations Vary on the Vertical Dimension?

One of the most enduring and most debated questions in sociology is, How does one explain stratification in society? The basic debate is among the proponents of three models: the functional model, the conflict model, and the structural model. Each has a different view of status and a different explanation for why some occupations have more prestige and income than others.

The Functional Model

The roots of the functional model in American sociology can be traced back more than 50 years (Parsons, 1940), with its clearest articulation in the work of Davis and Moore (1945). The basic argument is that for society to exist, it needs to have a variety of tasks performed. Individuals must be motivated to fill the positions (occupations) that perform these tasks. Motivation to fill the tasks must be based on the differential rewards—whether in terms of enjoyment, accomplishment, or compensation—that are linked to the various positions. Differential rewards would be unnecessary if all tasks were equally important, equally pleasant to perform, and equal in their requirements of ability and talent. Such is not the case, however.

Differential Rewards. Because there is a "differential scarcity of personnel"—that is, more people interested in some jobs than others—differential rewards are necessary. After all, we want to make sure that the essential, functionally important positions attract enough people to do the job. The more difficult and important the position and the scarcer the personnel, the higher the rewards must be. For instance, the position of CEO carries with it more functional importance than the position of executive secretary. The firm might be able to struggle along without the services of an executive secretary until another could be hired. But the survival of the business might be threatened by the absence of the individual CEO, whose vision guides all of the organization's activities. Hence the higher pay for CEOs. Or consider "high steel" workers, who walk girders far above the ground. They receive premium pay for their willingness to perform this difficult and hazardous, yet essential, task.

The differential rewards lead to a stratified society, with different statuses ascribed to members of the population. However, the basic functionalist argument is that such stratification is unavoidable. The status of occupations is affected by the differential importance of occupations to society, variations in the requirements of the occupations, and differences in the kinds of abilities necessary to fill the positions. Positions must be differentially rewarded to ensure their occupancy by competent personnel.

Functionalists all agree with this basic argument, but they disagree on such issues as how the importance of various positions is determined, whether existing social-class distinctions prevent talent from being developed, and whether people who undergo extensive training for difficult positions need greater rewards (Davis, 1953; Moore, 1963a, 1963b; Tumin, 1953, 1963).

The last point—whether people who undergo extensive training deserve greater rewards—is a good example of the weaknesses of the functional theory. It suggests that high reward levels are necessary to induce people to undergo difficult and extensive training periods, as in colleges and universities and professional schools. But "what tends to be completely overlooked, in addition, are the psychic and spiritual rewards that are available to the elite trainees by comparison with their age peers in the labor force" (Tumin, 1953, p. 390). "Trainees" often enjoy privileges that are beyond the reach of their cohorts in the working world. For example, exchange programs often provide college students with the opportunity to study abroad while pursuing their education. Many people would consider such an opportunity more than sufficient inducement to undergo training. Other rewards are greater income over a lifetime of work, higher prestige, greater opportunity for self-development, the opportunity to delay adult responsibilities while one completes the training, and access to leisure and freedom. Still, despite these rewards, not everyone is willing or able to undergo the difficulties of studying for access to these highly rewarded positions (Davis, 1953, p. 396).

There are other weaknesses in the functional theory that even the most casual of observers would note. The extremely high salaries of sports or rock music stars are frequently cited as a clear contradiction of the notion that people are rewarded in proportion to their contribution to society. However, these highly visible roles have notoriety, but not eminence (Hope, 1982). Also, if one were to take the average salaries of, say, all basketball players in colleges and professional basketball leagues or all rock musicians, then the salary figures would be much lower. At the same time, the functional theory has a hard time explaining why some college football coaches are paid more than the presidents of the colleges for which they coach. Similarly, the exorbitantly high salaries of some corporate executives seems to fall outside of the explanatory power of the functional approach.

Supporting Evidence. The functional theory will not be proven or disproven with words, however. Verification through empirical research is needed. Unfortunately, such empirical testing has been quite rare because of the difficulties involved in developing the necessary controls to permit adequate testing. For instance, to truly isolate the relationship between rewards and functional importance, we would have to identify jobs that differed in functional importance but were identical in all other respects. In addition, the functionalist view of society is a dynamic one, because the stratification system is constantly emerging (Borgatta, 1960). It would be necessary to anticipate the future to determine what the differentiated rewards of today should be, and no one has yet been able to do that. Given these limitations, most attempts to test the functional approach have used historical data.

For example, one study examined patterns of military pay during periods of war and peace. If the functional theory is correct, military pay should rise during times of war, because the military are more important at those times. The data essentially confirmed this hypothesis (Abrahamson, 1971).

Another study examined executive compensation in large U.S. business firms as indicated by their place in a *Forbes* magazine directory (Broom & Cushing, 1977). It found a limited relationship between the magnitude of executive responsibility (an indicator of functional importance) and executive compensation. Also, executives of large corporations were paid more than executives of small corporations. These findings tend to support the contentions of functional theory. However, the same study found no relationship between company performance and executive compensation. Even more puzzling are the findings that executives in "essential" industries such as pharmaceuticals, food, steel, and textiles were paid less than executives in less essential industries such as beer, cosmetics, soft drinks, and tobacco. Here again we see the elusiveness of the concept of functional importance.

Functional importance often depends on the relationships between individual role performance and the success of the employing organization (Jacobs, 1981). There are three possible relation-ships. In the first, the performance of some employees greatly helps the total performance of the organization. For example, sales personnel are crucial for most automobile dealerships. How-ever, auto dealerships typically hire many sales personnel, reward them moderately, and retain few over time. In the second relation-ship, good individual performance makes very little difference for the organization, but poor performance can have serious adverse consequences, as in the case of airline pilots and their airlines. Pilots are highly rewarded, although their performance is closely monitored. The final relationship is one in which individual per-formance has little or no effect on the organization, as in many factory jobs. As you might expect, these jobs are not well compen-sated. This research thus yields mixed support for the functional-ist position that essential employees are rewarded handsomely and have more control over their work.

Some limited support for functional theory can be found in the work of Cullen and Novick (1979), who examined prestige and income (as rewards) and other characteristics of some 267 occu-pations using U.S. census data. They found that prestige and income were greater for occupations that require talent and train-ing and have greater perceived importance. Physically demanding work was low in prestige but tended to be associated with greater income. Outdoors, or "outside" work, was also associated with greater income. Cullen and Novick speculated that fewer people can fill jobs that require talent and training, and fewer want to fill physically demanding jobs, so employers offer higher rewards to attract workers. However, the prestige of physically demanding work remains low.

A follow-up study found that task complexity and required education were significant predictors of occupational earnings, as functional theory would predict (Cullen, 1985). Some occupational groups earned more because they were able to control educational requirements. It is the professional occupations that are most able to influence legislation that requires certain levels of education. The professions can thus control at least one aspect of their reward system. This line of reasoning shades directly into the conflict model, as we will see shortly.

The problem with all of these studies is that they have neither proven nor disproven the functional approach. We have seen limited support for some propositions derived from the approach, but we have also seen large flaws and inconsistencies. Function alone does not explain why some occupations have more status than others. Other forces must be at work.

The Conflict Model

The conflict approach to explaining social stratification has historical roots even deeper than those of the functional model. In fact, the conflict model can be traced back to the writings of Karl Marx (1967) and his emphasis on the ownership of capital and the control of economic conditions. Conflict theorists have updated Marx by arguing that control of power in the workplace, rather than ownership, determines class position (Dahrendorf, 1959).

Class Distribution of Power and Wealth. The key to the conflict approach is the idea of class. Dynamic social forces, such as political and ideological movements, determine the distribution of power and wealth between classes. Furthermore, there is a tendency for the relative class positions of individuals and families to be maintained over time.

According to the conflict model, people in positions of control or ownership within the workplace use their power to maintain their privileged class positions. In contrast, the functional model holds that status varies with the functional importance of a job or the availability of people to fill it.

Exploitation is a central element in conflict analysis. Those who profit from the production process (that is, owners and top executives) do so by appropriating more income than their actual contributions to the production process warrant. In other words, somewhat less than the full value of what is produced is returned to workers in the form of a wage. In addition, the dominant class has social and political power stemming from its control over surpluses. With political power and control over resources, the dominant class can also shape the development of society and of culture. This is called the *conflict approach* because of the inherent conflict between those who exploit and those who are exploited. It is important to realize that the conflict approach does not consider the motivations or reactions of the people involved in the process.

The most recent comprehensive theoretical statement of the conflict perspective is found in the work of Wright (1979; see also Wright, 1978; Wright & Perrone, 1977), who formulates three basic class "locations": the *bourgeoisie* (property owners), the *petty bourgeoisie* (farmers and tradespeople), and the *proletariat* (wage earners). Three contradictory class locations are in opposition: *managers, small employers*, and *semiautonomous employees* (self-employed craft workers). As Figure 4.3 shows, the contradictory class locations rank between the two extremes of the basic class locations and are essentially what are often called *middle-class positions*. The percentages given in Figure 4.3 are Wright's estimates of the percentages of the population in each class location.

Classical Marxian formulations predicted that the basic bourgeoisie-proletariat distinction would become more pronounced, but actually the so-called petty bourgeoisie sector has grown in our society (Steinmetz & Wright, 1989).

Wright defined the classes on the basis of (a) economic ownership or control over investments and the accumulation process, (b) control over the physical means of production, and (c) control over the labor power of others (Wright, 1979, p. 27). An extension of Wright's approach adds "control over human capital" as a new dimension (Schervish & Herman, 1986). The point here is that employers can control the training and experience of their employees. This approach also suggests that control in real life varies from full control, through partial and then minimal control, and finally to no control whatsoever. Wright talks about a simple presence or absence of control.

Even though many predictions from the Marxist perspective did not work out, it would be a mistake to dismiss the conflict approach altogether. Control of ownership, means of production, labor power, and human capital give some occupations a tremendous social advantage. There is considerable prestige associated with "owning your own business," even if that business is just a small shop. Even in the absence of ownership, a manager's ability to control the flow of resources and rewards gives him or her

FIGURE 4.3 The Relationship of Contradictory Class Locations to Basic Classes in Capitalist Society

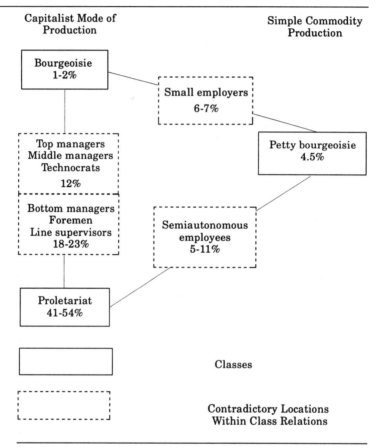

Source: Erik Olin Wright, 1978, *Class, Crisis and the State.* London, England: Verso Editions/NLB—Figure 2-1, p. 63.

considerable power. If we look back at the discussion of the professions in Chapter 2, we can see exactly how this set of occupations fights to maintain its control and thus status.

Supporting Evidence. From the conflict perspective it is easy to see why the dominant classes would want to see work deskilled and broken into simpler tasks. Deskilling would increase control by dominant classes by reducing the amount of control exercised by workers. As was noted in Chapter 1, evidence in regard to deskilling is not conclusive. But that is only one element of the conflict perspective.

A more important aspect of the conflict approach is a social psychological issue: *class consciousness*. Marx predicted that the working class would become more aware than the owners of the differences in their power and control in society. However, the research on this issue has done little to clarify the relationship between class and class consciousness (Giddens, 1973).

One study looked at how individuals defined their own class placements. Basically, those in positions of authority placed themselves in the middle class, while those without such authority placed themselves in the working class (McNamee & Vanneman, 1983). Another found that self-employed manual workers such as construction workers, painters, and truck drivers did not identify with the working class and were more politically conservative. They also earn demonstrably more than their organizationally employed counterparts (Form, 1982).

An interesting twist to class consciousness can be found in an analysis of taxi drivers in Boston. Among those who lease their cabs, there was a tendency toward "bourgeoisification." The lessees were no longer employees and did not regard themselves as such. Consciousness was thus affected by this form of linkage to ownership. Leasing also provided advantages for the cab fleet owners, because they could avoid worker's compensation, unemployment insurance, and social security costs. The drivers had the advantage of not having to report all of their fares (Russell, 1983).

Two additional aspects of class consciousness should be noted. First, in a major study of affluent industrial workers in Great Britain, Goldthorpe and associates (Goldthorpe, Lockwood, Bechhofer, & Platt, 1969) found minimal evidence of class consciousness but ample evidence of "commodity consciousness." The workers and their families were avid consumers and paid little attention to the class issue. But when times turn bad, the class consciousness issue might become more important, especially when the workers are no longer able to buy commodities. None of these studies, therefore, has provided strong support for Marx's notion that workers would become resentful toward those who control their labor.

However, one study of class consciousness does affirm the conflict approach. There is compelling evidence of strong class consciousness among business elites in the United States and Great Britain (Clawson & Neustadtl, 1989; Domhoff, 1967, 1971; Mills, 1957; Useem, 1982, 1984). This upper-class consciousness contributes to collective political and economic activity in an ironic, upside-down twist of traditional Marxian notions of class consciousness. Marxists predicted that the strongest class consciousness would develop among the working classes; instead, it has developed at the upper-class level through people's memberships in country clubs, service on common boards of directors, and frequent interactions with one another. It would appear, then, that the conflict model explains reality no better than the functional model.

The Structural Approach

Both the functional and the conflict approaches have explanatory power, but neither has received full empirical support. Some theorists have therefore tried to develop a model with more power to describe the variations among occupations on the vertical dimension. An approach that combines elements of both functional and conflict theory, known as the *structural approach*, has been developing rapidly over recent years.

Merging the Functional and Conflict Approaches. The functional approach would say that the determinant of occupational status is the difficulty and importance of the work, both within the organization and in society as a whole. The conflict approach would say that occupational status is determined by the ongoing struggle among social classes for power and resources. Thus the rewards associated with occupation can at least partially be understood in terms of a functionalist perspective, with those that are more complex and require more skills receiving more rewards. The effects of class, the key variable in the conflict perspective, come in terms of hierarchical positions in organizations.

The strength of the structural approach lies in its capacity to use ideas from both the conflict and functional perspectives. From

the conflict perspective it borrows the explanation for the maintenance of huge gaps between the tops and bottoms of large organizations. The functional perspective contributes an explanation for
the highly elaborate pay scales that some organizations develop.
These represent attempts to develop rational schemes for appropriately rewarding highly differentiated work.

The basic argument of the structural approach is a simple one:
Positions within work organizations are structured in a hierarchical way. Individuals have some mobility and move in and out of
those positions. Just think of military organizations. There are
ranks of officers and enlisted personnel that are present before
and after particular individuals are in those ranks. In most
business firms there are set numbers of positions at particular
levels, with usually a single presidency, a set number of vice-
presidencies, and so on. When a person resigns, retires, or dies, a
vacancy is created that presents a mobility or promotion opportunity for another person. This creates what is known as a *vacancy
chain* (White, 1971). Someone must then be promoted into the
vacant position, and his or her position then becomes open and
available. Hypothetically openings would occur all the way down
to the bottom of the organization.

The issue is not really so simple, of course. Hierarchies in
different organizations and in different industries vary widely in
form and scope. There are more job titles in organizations that are
large and bureaucratic, leading to more gradations in status
(Baron & Bielby, 1986). A professionalized labor force and organi-
zation-specific skill gradations also create more job titles. For
example, one organization might have the job grades of Mechanic
I, Mechanic II, and Mechanic III, while another organization
might only have one job level for mechanics. We cannot understand variations in occupational status unless we account for
differences in organizational hierarchies.

Patterns of Inequality. Different organizations have different
hierarchies, but they all place some employees above others. To
structuralists, the interesting question has been, What patterns
do organizations develop to stratify employees? In other words,
what are the patterns of inequality? Patterns of inequality seem

to vary, depending on the organization's industry, job ladders, ports of entry, and policies.

Industries, as well as organizations, are a source of inequality patterns, according to structuralists (Baron, Davis-Blake, & Bielby, 1986; Pfeffer & Langton, 1988). For example, one study found differences between service industries and manufacturing industries in terms of the manner in which inequality is structured (Nelson & Lorence, 1988).

Other theorists use the idea of "job ladders" (very similar to vacancy chains) to describe the inequality structures. In the federal government, for example, there can be several clerical ladders, several administrative ladders, and multiple professional ladders (DiPrete, 1987a, 1988). Promotions take place within ladders. For example, clerical workers can be on a word-processing ladder or a data-analysis ladder. For the most part, promotions would take place within specific ladders. For a long time there was no movement between ladders or between tiers of ladders: For example, clerical workers did not move onto the administrative ladder. Recently, however, people have begun to move between tiers. Upper-level clerical workers have been able to move into entry-level administrative positions. As organizations expand or contract, new and extended ladders or vacancy chains may become available (Stewman, 1986).

Organizations typically also have several "ports of entry" (Grandjean, 1981). A person's port of entry into an organization usually determines what job ladders or vacancy chains are available. People are hired into administrative units that may well be their home for the duration of their careers. My port of entry was as a new faculty member at the rank of instructor at Indiana University. One of my best friends entered the University at Albany in the admissions office. He has remained on this ladder, rising to the position of assoicate director of admissions.

The port of entry can actually exist beyond the doors of the organization. In Japan, some employers have semiformal agreements with high schools to hire students on graduation. Competition is not within the organization, but within and between schools (Rosenbaum & Kariya, 1989).

After a person has passed through a port of entry, several types of mobility are possible. In *contest mobility*, a pattern roughly representative of the U.S. educational system, all participants are completely free to move up. In contrast, in *sponsored mobility*, those people who are to move up are selected and sponsored from the outset, as in the educational system in Great Britain (Turner, 1960). Another type is *tournament mobility* (Rosenbaum, 1979b), which is analogous to a basketball tournament: If you win in the first round, you are eligible for the second round; if you win there, you are eligible for the third round, and so on. If you do not win, then you are no longer eligible to move ahead. For almost all forms of work, educational status determines the particular tournament in which an individual will compete. After beginning the competition, the person involved will compete for an upward move. If he or she loses, then that particular vacancy is gone, probably forever.

The important point about patterns of mobility is that the status system in organizations is structured in advance. The number of positions and their relative status are fixed at a point in time. The reasons for the fixedness lie in attempts both to maintain and gain power (the conflict model) and to be rational (the functional model). Over time, the arrangement of positions will be altered as power is exerted, politics are played, and the market operates, although the alterations will be slow and slight. Technological change also plays an important role here. There is a growing belief that many middle-management positions will be eliminated because of the advent of information-handling computers. This would shorten the job ladders.

For another example of the interaction of functional, conflict, and structural perspectives, consider the salaries of National Basketball Association players (Wallace, 1988). Three classes of factors determine salaries: (a) human-capital (conflict) factors, which include draft position, placement on the all-rookie team, and years of experience; (b) performance (functional) factors, which involve player performance or merit and include points scored, rebounds, and shots blocked; and (c) structural factors, which include player positions (center, point guard, etc.), team played for, and race. The structural factors are the most important in salary determination, but the key point here is that the explanation of salary differences depends on all three types of factors in combination. Rather than looking for a single explanation, we will draw on the functional, conflict, and structural perspectives as we look at individuals and the vertical dimension.

How Are People Placed on the Vertical Dimension?

How do people get placed on the vertical dimension? This is one of the most fundamental questions about society. After all, we want to know whether our hard work will get us ahead. We want to know if there is hope for promotion. As a parent, I had to decide whether it was worth saving so my children could go to college. The basic question then becomes, Is our status almost fixed at birth or are there opportunities for everyone?

The question has intrigued scholars throughout recorded history. It currently receives major attention from sociologists, economists, philosophers, theologians, and even biologists. Within sociology it has been the dominant issue for more than 20 years, spurred largely by Blau and Duncan's (1967) landmark study of occupational mobility. The study of various forms and meanings of mobility literally took off in response to that research.

Continuities and Comparisons

By and large, there have not been important shifts in mobility patterns in the United States, specifically in the ability to increase one's status. However, consistent and minimally changing patterns have been found, starting with a study of white men in Indianapolis in 1910 and 1940 (Rogoff, 1953) and continuing with studies undertaken into the 1990s:

> In this century, there has been essentially no trend in the
> relative mobility chances of American men whose fathers held
> differing occupations. To put the matter crudely, but correctly,
> there has been no change in the odds that a man of low-status

> origin will achieve high rather than low occupational
> standing relative to the odds that a man of high-status origin
> will achieve high rather than low occupational standing.
> (Hauser & Featherman, 1977, p. 169)

However, although the patterns of relationships between the occupations of a father and his son have remained unchanged, upward mobility appears to have increased and downward mobility decreased, at least until the mid-1970s (Featherman & Hauser, 1978; Hauser & Featherman, 1977).

Upward mobility has increased because the occupational structure has changed. There are fewer low-status positions (such as unskilled work) and more high-status positions (such as professional work) (Pampel, Land, & Felson, 1977). There have also been industrial shifts, such as the decline in agriculture and the increase in services. These shifts have contributed to the increase in managerial and professional jobs. Of interest, too, is that some of the shifts have had counteracting effects. For instance, in agriculture there now are fewer owners but more professional and clerical workers because of the growth of agribusinesses (Singelman & Browning, 1980). This phenomenon can be explained by the structural approach.

As the demand side of the labor market has changed in terms of the kinds of work available, so too has the supply of workers in terms of their credentials, and this has had an interesting outcome in terms of mobility. Because there are increasingly more college graduates in the labor force, there is a weaker relationship now between fathers' and sons' occupation than in the past. College graduation tends to cancel out the effects of origin or a father's status (Hout, 1988).

Some interesting patterns in regard to mobility emerge when national comparisons are made. For example, there are strong similarities between Australia and the United States (Hauser & Featherman, 1977). An analysis of Canada and the United States found no difference in trends in mobility in either country and no difference in the overall mobility patterns (McRoberts & Selbee, 1981). A comparison between Great Britain and the United States revealed that the British stratification system is somewhat more closed, with less intergenerational mobility (Treiman & Terrell, 1975a); this study also found that, despite large differences in the educational systems, the role of educational attainment in occupational mobility is very similar in the two countries.

The pattern is quite different when a comparison is made between the United States and Poland. Meyer, Tuma, and Zagorskin (1979) found that father-to-son occupational mobility was considerably less in Poland than in the United States. This is mainly attributable to the large traditional agricultural sector in Poland; when farmers' sons were excluded from the analysis, patterns similar to those in the United States were found. Polish educational attainment had a much larger effect on occupational attainment than education in the United States. In Poland, the educational system has stronger allocative powers, is more highly selective, and is more differentiated in terms of both type of school and clear distinctions being made between levels of school. The Polish school system thus has tracks that have much stronger effects than those in the United States.

Comparisons between Japan and the United States have revealed that Japanese mobility is based on age and seniority (Kalleberg & Lincoln, 1988), whereas that in the United States is linked to job characteristics, including the promotional policies of employing organizations.

Status differentiation, then, is present in all societies, although its openness or rigidity varies over time and space. Apparently, some consistency is found in the way people are placed on the vertical dimension. The question remains: How do they achieve a particular status?

Factors in Status Attainment

As it turns out, the status-attainment process is quite complex. Many social, individual, and environmental factors are involved in the process of choosing and preparing for an occupation. In turn, that occupation is a major determinant of a person's status.

Social and Individual Factors

Research on status attainment got its major impetus from Blau and Duncan's (1967) study. They used the SEI, which was described earlier, as their measure of occupational status. Their basic findings are presented in Figure 4.4. This diagram indicates that a man's occupational status in 1962 (at the right of the diagram) was determined by his father's occupation (bottom left) and its contribution to the son's education and first job, together with the contribution of the father's education to the son's education, which then also has a direct link to the son's first job and 1962 occupational status.

This basic model has seen spin-offs in several directions. For example, when grandfathers are added to the model, a son-father-grandfather congruence in occupational status has been found, particularly when farmers are excluded from the analysis (Goyder & Curtis, 1975). This is difficult to do, of course, given the agricultural basis of the society two generations ago, but occupational status inheritance is nonetheless very high. In a similar vein, both the paternal grandfather and the mother's occupation are significantly associated with the son's occupation. However, the association with the father's occupation remains the strongest (Beck, 1983).

The critical role of education in the status-attainment model has served as the basis for another major research tradition in its own right: the *Wisconsin model*, which takes its name from the University of Wisconsin, where most of the research was undertaken. This model is presented schematically in Figures 4.5 and 4.6. This approach adds social psychological factors, such as the encouragement of teachers and parents, the plans of friends, and individuals' aspiration levels (see Alexander, Ekland, & Griffin, 1975; Alwin, 1974; Haller, Otto, Meier, & Ohlendorf, 1974; Porter, 1974; Sewell & Hauser, 1975; Sewell, Hauser, & Featherman, 1976; Yuchtman & Samuel, 1975).

The Wisconsin model also adds mental ability and intelligence, which is mediated by significant others in shaping both school performance and educational and occupational aspirations. The Wisconsin model does *not* question the basic link between parents' occupational level and sons' educational and occupational attainments, but it does seek to refine the explanation of the relationship and improve the explanation's predictive power.

Another important research tradition has emphasized the importance of family advantages for status attainment (Jencks et al.,

FIGURE 4.4 Blau and Duncan's Model of the Stratification Process

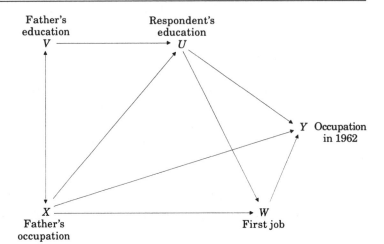

Source: Adapted with the permission of The Free Press, a Division of Macmillan, Inc. from *The American Occupational Structure* by Peter M. Blau and Otis Dudley Duncan. Copyright © 1967 by Peter M. Blau and Otis Dudley Duncan.

1972, 1979, 1988). One primary mechanism by which this is accomplished is schooling, with the children of the affluent staying in school longer.

This research reaches the vital conclusion that it is schooling level that makes a difference. Completing college is much more critical than simply attending college. Again, the idea of the importance of the credential is evident here, because a person who lacks only one credit for graduation is no better off than a person who drops out of college during the first year. The message here should be quite clear for all college students.

Research on status attainment has revealed several other important patterns. The most important are those involving gender, race, and ethnicity; these will be addressed in Chapters 6 and 8.

There is an additional component of the status-attainment process that throws some interesting light on the ways in which individuals move through the system. There is systematic evidence that social ties—who you know—do play an important role in a person's status attainment (Granovetter, 1973; Lin, Vaughn, & Ensel, 1981; Lin, Ensel, & Vaughn, 1981). The important social

FIGURE 4.5 A Social Psychological Model of Post-High School Achievement

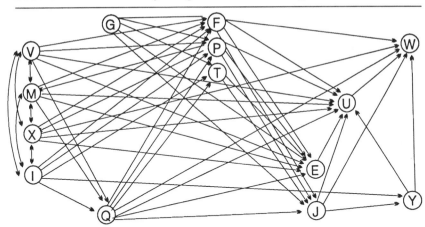

Source: From *Education, Occupation, and Earning: Achievement in the Early Career* (p. 92) by W. H. Sewell and R. M. Hauser, 1975, New York: Academic Press. Copyright © 1975 by Academic Press. Reprinted with permission.

FIGURE 4.6 The Influence of Socioeconomic Background on Earnings

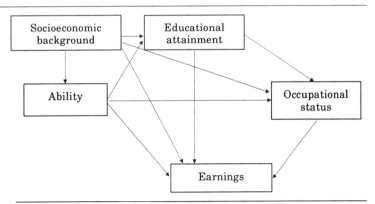

Source: From *Education, Occupation, and Earning: Achievement in the Early Career* (p. 49) by W. H. Sewell and R. M. Hauser, 1975, New York: Academic Press. Copyright © 1975 by Academic Press. Reprinted with permission.

ties are "weak ties" or linkages that are not part of an individual's immediate social circle. Apparently, people hear about jobs through casual acquaintances rather than from close family or friends.

Although all of these other factors relating to family and individual characteristics are powerful and cannot be ignored, luck is also an important ingredient in status attainment (Jencks et al., 1972, 1979, 1988). People with identical backgrounds can end up with quite different status in the labor market. This makes sense, of course, because the whole status-attainment process takes place in situations in which people cannot control their entire destinies. Being in the right place at the right time certainly cannot be overlooked.

Environmental Factors

Time is also a factor in a larger sense. At a given time in a given society, depending on the level of socioeconomic development, the relative influence of social origins and education on occupation and status may be different. In the stage of early industrialization, for example, there may not be enough jobs that require high levels of education, so the effects of educational attainment would be reduced (Lin & Yauger, 1975).

One other important environmental factor to be noted here is that there are regional differences in the status-attainment process. The idea was expressed in such past lore as "Go West, young man, go West." That was where the opportunities were perceived to be. Studies in the Unites States (Lane, 1968; Logan, 1976, 1978; Mueller, 1974) Israel (Semyonov, 1981), and Japan, (Grusky, 1983) have revealed that "opportunity structures" vary by region of the country. Regional variations reflect the tendencies of industries to cluster in different locations. Pennsylvania is famous for its steel industry, West Virginia for its coal mines, and Texas for its oil fields. As Logan (1978) points out, "The fortunes of almost everyone in Detroit depend upon the fortunes of the automobile industry" (p. 409). More recently, job opportunities in high-tech industries have presented themselves in areas such as "Silicon Valley" in central California.

The status-attainment process just outlined is largely an individualistic, human-capital approach. Here *human capital* refers to the skills, credentials, experience, and other characteristics that individuals accumulate over time and which improve their attractiveness as potential employees. Individuals acquire human capital through their family, education (both formal and informal, such as on-the-job training), social ties, and environmental circumstances as they move into the work marketplace (Coleman, 1988; Wholey, 1990).

This heavy reliance on the human-capital approach has been criticized as being too individualistic (Kerkhoff, 1976). This criticism can be muted if we reconsider the structural approach.

The Structural Approach and the Placement of Individuals

Industries

At the broadest level, the structural approach considers differences between industries. For instance, there are more opportunities for advancement in expanding than in contracting industries. Obviously, the link between status attainment and individual worker characteristics is much weaker in some industrial sectors than in others. In fact, studies have revealed differences in status attainment among industrial sectors that cannot be explained by examining the characteristics of the individuals employed in those sectors.

For instance, Beck, Horan, and Tolbert (1978) distinguished between a *core* industrial sector that is dominated by large oligopolistic corporations and a *periphery* industrial sector that is made up of smaller firms operating in a more competitive environment. These investigators found differences in employee earnings between the core and the periphery that could not be accounted for by the characteristics of the individuals in those sectors. More specifically, Beck et al. (1978) found that people earn more in the core sector than in the periphery, regardless of their human capital, gender, race, or ethnicity. In addition, the link between individual worker characteristics and earnings was much stronger within the core sector than within the periphery.

The significance of this study is its demonstration that status attainment cannot be accurately predicted solely from knowledge of workers' individual characteristics. Rather, one must also account for broad structural factors. For example, the individual's education and choice of industry can be equally important. The value of the structural approach for explaining status attainment is that it takes all such factors into account. There are important differences in status-attainment patterns in different industries.

Organizations

Why does the status-attainment process differ by industry? One reason is that career paths are shaped by organizational structures. If the typical organization in an industry has many divisions and many levels of hierarchy within each division, then the chances that an employee will rise rapidly through the hierarchy are rather low. The movement will be from a position at one level to one at the next highest level. Opportunities for promotion are also affected by the way top positions in the industry are filled, whether from outside or from within an organization. Opportunities for attaining a higher occupational status are higher in industries where most of the top-level positions are filled from the internal labor market.

Individual human capital factors, such as education and family background, have variable effects in internal labor markets (Spilerman, 1977). The human-capital factors have a strong effect in some careers but only weak effects in others. The returns to individuals from their human-capital investments depend on whether the "port of entry" was a core or peripheral industry and what kinds of opportunities are linked to that port of entry. The person with a college degree enters the organization at a different entry port than the person with a high-school degree, and the opportunities that follow from the entry are also different.

There are interesting twists and turns in regard to internal labor markets. One study found that laboratory workers had internal labor markets in chemical and oil firms but not in hospitals. In the latter setting, domination by physicians blocked mobility by actually eliminating internal labor markets for the lab workers (Schroeder & Finlay, 1986).

In a *New York Times* article, Kilborn (1990) reports that some large U.S. corporations are openly reducing the number of layers in their hierarchies and socializing their workers to expect to reach career plateaus rather than seek continued advancement. The explanation here is partially demographic: There are large numbers of so-called baby boomers in the system. The answer is also based on the current trend in many organizations to thin their management ranks. As we have noted, technological innovations, such as increased computer usage, apparently will reduce the number of managerial levels. In any event, internal labor markets will remain neither constant in form nor consistent in all situations.

For many people, promotions are an important part of their journey through internal labor markets. Promotions are used by organizations as a form of efficiency, because organizations need to recruit for higher levels (Rosenbaum, 1979b). The premise here is that organizations will promote those who perform well. Although the promotion rate declines with age—the older a person, the less likely a promotion—education increases the rate of promotion and extends the age at which promotional opportunities are available. Noncollege graduates may be moved up in their youth to positions of responsibility and then have little promotional chance later. College graduates face more of a linear decline of opportunities over time. Even in periods of economic decline, college graduates in the 30-to-34 age group are minimally affected. For both college and noncollege graduates, an early promotion is required to receive further promotions, which is consistent with the idea of tournament mobility introduced earlier.

Although individuals' career prospects generally decline as they move up in an organization, there are exceptions (Stewman & Konda, 1983). Four *microstructures* can affect career prospects. The first is the grade ratio within the organization—that is, the number or percentage of people at each grade. In organizations that have many people or a large percentage of the work force at high grade levels (as is the case in many professionalized organizations), the opportunity structure is greater than in a more "bottom-heavy" organization. The second microstructure is the nature of the vacancy chains used by an organization (see Stewman, 1975). The third microstructure is the managerial-selection processes used, with insiders versus outsiders being critical here. Fourth and finally, cohort size—the number of people at a stage who are eligible for promotion—is important. If cohort size is small, then promotional opportunities are greater. Extrapolating from this, promotional opportunities will be less for people of the baby-boom generation than for the surrounding generations. Similarly, individuals in occupations that are in short supply will have strong promotional opportunities, as was the case with people with computer skills in the initial phase of computerization.

Two *triggering mechanisms* also affect the promotional-opportunity structure (Stewman & Konda, 1983): (a) the growth rate of the organization or industry and (b) the exit rates of the personnel involved. If the industry is growing or there are many exits, then promotional opportunities increase. On the other hand, if the industry is not growing or everyone stays in the organization, then promotional opportunities are limited.

One final factor should be noted: whether an individual has been identified as a "star" early in his or her career. Such identification enhances promotional opportunities for an extended period of time. Even in the case of such identity, of course, the basic structure of careers is one of declining opportunity with age.

To summarize, organizations impinge on career outcomes in two ways. First, the division of labor among jobs (internal labor market) and among organizations generates a distribution of opportunities and rewards that often has nothing to do with the incumbents. Second, organizational procedures for matching workers to jobs affect the distribution of rewards and opportunities within and across firms, influencing the likelihood of career success. Organizations can thus be viewed as independent contributors to career patterns and social mobility (Baron, 1984).

Conclusions

This chapter had several purposes. The first was to establish the strong linkage between work and social status. Included in this relationship are strong interrelationships between education, earnings or income, and social status. We next sought to explain these relationships by examining the functional, conflict, and structural approaches, finding insights from each, but with the structural approach emerging as the most powerful explanation. The chapter then turned to a consideration of the ways in which people are placed on the vertical dimension through their work. Here it was noted that the processes and outcomes are quite consistent over time and space. We next examined the factors involved in status attainment as it has been analyzed in recent years. Finally, we considered the structural approach to the placement of individuals, with its emphasis on the importance of organizational and industrial factors.

Almost all of the studies cited in this chapter were based on data from white males. In chapter 6, the major focus will be on women and the vertical dimension, thus providing continuity with the present chapter. Chapter 8 will deal with race, religion, and ethnicity. Both chapters also will deal with nonvertical aspects. But before dealing with those issues, we must understand the horizontal dimension of work, which has to do with job content and labor markets.

■■■■ APPLICATION

Downward Mobility

David Patterson was a practical man. All his life—from his youth in a rundown working-class district of Philadelphia to his adulthood in the affluent suburbs of New York—he had made rational decisions about the future. David had a talent for music, but he studied business. He had a flair for advertising, but he pursued a job in the computer industry. He wore his rationality proudly. Having steered clear of personal indulgence, he had a lot to show for his efforts: a beautiful home, two luxury cars, a country club membership, a rewarding executive job, and a comfortable, stable family. The Philadelphia slums seemed a million miles away and a million years ago.

When David's boss left frantic messages with the secretary, asking him to stay late one Friday afternoon, his stomach began to flutter. Only the previous week David had pored over the company's financial statement. Things weren't looking too good, but it never occurred to him that the crisis would reach his level. He was, after all, the director of an entire division, a position he had been promoted to only two years before. But when David saw the pained look on the boss's face, he knew his head had found its way to the chopping block. (Newman, 1988, pp. 1-2)

This is only the first chapter in David Patterson's story of downward mobility. Unable to find a job that offered similar pay and prestige, David and his family soon joined the millions of Americans who, over the past 10 to 15 years, have been forced to descend the vertical dimension. No longer able to afford the niceties to which they have become accustomed, the downwardly mobile must be content to take their place among the less financially fortunate. With the loss of a privileged position comes a loss of power and status. For the downwardly mobile, the connection between work and status is all too clear.

As mentioned in this chapter, economic expansion during the middle part of this century resulted in an overall trend toward upward mobility in this country at least until the mid-1970s. However, more recent trends have been in the direction of economic decline, especially in some industries. For instance, the insurance industry entered a phase of radical retrenchment during the mid-1980s, triggering a wave of mergers and layoffs (Newman, 1988). This wave left some employees clambering to keep their places in the occupational hierarchy. Thus downward mobility may be in part a function of broad structural factors, such as poor economic health in a particular industry or industrial sector.

However, downward mobility probably cannot be attributed entirely to the state of the economy. Another contributing factor is the sheer number of people competing for jobs of high occupational status. Consider the plight of the baby-boom generation. Baby boomers represent a demographic anomaly—a huge mass of Americans born between 1946 and 1964, most of whom are highly educated and ambitious. It was not long ago that these individuals were labeled "yuppies" to signify their upwardly mobile status. However, as more and more of them entered the labor market, something had to give. There simply was not enough money or high-status jobs to fulfill the aspirations of their generation.

As a result of these dynamics, many older baby boomers are being forced to descend the ladder of success, and younger professionals are finding fewer opportunities for occupational advancement. As one might expect, these barriers to advancement have caused considerable frustration. According to trend-analysis specialist Arnold Brown (in Pollan & Levine, 1992):

> [Baby boomers] were raised to believe that if they did what they were supposed to they would be rewarded. When they got good grades, their allowance was increased. They continued to apply this lesson throughout life. But now they're doing what they're supposed to but no longer getting rewarded. . . . They're working hard but not being promoted. This has led to a great deal of anger. (p. 31)

Obviously, many aspiring individuals are not getting what they expected in terms of occupational status. Baby boomers have invested heavily in their human capital, only to reap a disappointing return on their investment.

You might ask yourself, "Doesn't this conflict with the notion that occupational status and compensation are related to the human capital possessed by employees?" Perhaps, but occupational status depends on more than just the characteristics of individual workers. For baby boomers, the plenitude of workers has offset any potential gains in occupational status to be realized from their investment in education. The very presence of so many people in the job market has driven down wages for occupations that, although functionally important, can easily be filled. In this case, the functional model of occupational status proves very useful for explaining downward mobility.

The phenomenon of downward mobility is hardly restricted to upper-middle-class workers such as David Patterson. Between 1981 and 1986, nearly 2 million blue-collar and white-collar workers experienced permanent job displacement (job loss because of a plant closing or elimination from an organization's hierarchy) (Newman, 1988). Many of these displaced workers will be unable to find equally good work, if they stay in the labor force at all. By comparison, roughly 780,000 managerial and professional employees suffered displacement during the same period. Thus, although managerial and professional employees are not immune to downward mobility, far more working-class people are affected.

In the presence of so much downward mobility, conditions are ripe for conflict between groups whose members have no desire to fall from their positions on the vertical dimension. If the conflict model of occupational attainment has any validity, the future occupational status of different classes will be determined at least partly by the outcomes of power struggles among these groups. To the extent that economic hardship dictates additional pruning of the organizational hierarchy, patterns of downward mobility may come to reflect the interests of those who own and control the means of production.

■■■ SUGGESTED READINGS

A complete bibliographical entry for each work cited here can be found in the reference section at the back of this book.

Blau and Duncan, *The American Occupational Structure* (1967), was the major turning point in the analysis of the vertical dimension. It opened the doors for status-attainment modeling and set the stage for the development of the structural explanations stressed in this chapter.

The Wisconsin model with its emphasis on the influence of multiple factors for placement on the vertical dimension is clearly specified in Hauser and Featherman, *The Process of Stratification* (1977).

Two major studies have been conducted by Christopher Jencks and his associates: Jencks, Smith, Acland, Bane, Cohen, Gintis, Heyns, and Michelson, *Inequality: A Reassessment of the Effect of Family and Schooling in America* (1972); and Jencks, Bartlett, Corcoran, Crouse, Eaglesfield, Jackson, McClelland, Mueser, Olneck, Schwartz, Ward, and Williams, *Who Gets Ahead?* (1979). Both works document the factors associated with placement on the vertical dimension, including family, education, and luck.

Mills, *The Power Elite* (1957), is a sociological classic that documents how people can keep their wealth and power through their connections with one another.

Mills' arguments are updated in Useem, *The Inner Circle* (1984).

5 Labor-Market Sectors: The Horizontal Dimension

In the last chapter we saw how work and status are related—in other words, we investigated the *vertical dimension* of work. In this chapter we turn work "on its side" to deal with issues of how to differentiate among groups of people on the basis of what they do in different occupations. I call this the *horizontal dimension*.

Probably the easiest way to understand the nature of the horizontal dimension is to begin with some examples. Among my friends, one is a lawyer, another is a banker, another sells heavy machinery, yet another is a physician, and I am a professor. We are all roughly equivalent in terms of our status, or our positions on the vertical dimension. Our income is about the same, and we live in the same neighborhood. At the same time, the nature of the work we do is very different.

I have another close friend who is an elementary-school music teacher. We both teach, so our work—or our *placements* on the horizontal dimension—is essentially the same. However, our *positions* on the vertical dimension are quite different.

Thus our topic is differentiation. We will look at ways proposed to understand the differentiations among forms of work. In Chapter 2, we identified varieties of work in a rather descriptive manner. Our purpose here is to be more analytical.

The Nature of the Horizontal Dimension

The subject matter of this chapter has been a central focus of such classical writers as Emile Durkheim (1933) and Adam Smith (1937), who referred to it as the *division of labor* and used it as the cornerstone of their analyses. In fact, they saw the division of labor as the key to the whole social order. More recently, Peter Blau (1977) developed a theory of the social structure that considers the division of labor and the distribution of power as the two most important forms of social differentiation in society.

These formative theorists' emphasis on the importance of the division of labor might lead us to believe that the horizontal dimension would be a dominant issue in research on work. This has not been the case, however, because sociologists have had a near fixation on the vertical dimension. Furthermore, those who have tried to differentiate among jobs in terms of what people do have not yet come up with an approach on which they can agree.

The sociologists who have focused on the horizontal dimension at least agree that it is the complement to the vertical dimension of work. The vertical dimension is concerned with hierarchy and differential status; the horizontal dimension is concerned with the nonstatus aspects of work such as its degree of complexity or the extent to which work involves dealing with people, data, or objects. It is also possible to compare different forms of work in terms of how much physical dexterity is required or how much mental activity is used (Parcel & Benefo, 1987). It is hypothetically possible to compare different forms of work on almost any criterion, and that has been part of the problem.

To simplify matters, however, we will concentrate here on distinctions that appear to bear particularly useful fruit for the understanding of work. We will thus consider only three ways of analyzing the horizontal dimension: the situs approach, the job-content approach, and the labor-market-sector approach.

The Situs Approach

One group of sociologists has approached the question of how to classify jobs on the horizontal dimension by drawing a distinction between situs and stratum (Benoit-Smullyan, 1944). A *stratum* is a category of individuals or positions placed above or below other categories on the vertical dimension. A *situs* does not have this hierarchical ranking; instead, it is a category of individuals or positions placed on the same level with other categories, without the evaluation of rank.

An early attempt to develop the situs idea tried to develop a set of occupational categories in the form of "parallel status ladders" (Hatt, 1950). This effort did not really work out, because the investigator was unable to come up with truly equivalent status ladders for all forms of work.

In their analysis of the situs approach, Morris and Murphy (1959) defined situses in terms of 10 distinct societal functions. For instance, all jobs related to manufacturing were grouped within one situs, and all jobs related to aesthetics and entertainment were considered to belong to another situs. The 10 situses they identified are listed across the top in Figure 5.1.

Morris and Murphy also attempted to show how the various jobs within situses compare with one another in terms of status or occupational prestige. For example, as Figure 5.1 illustrates, the owner of a large factory would enjoy considerably higher status than a machinist, even though both jobs fall within the manufacturing situs. Morris and Murphy were able to identify jobs belonging to different situses that nevertheless share roughly equivalent levels of prestige. Returning to Figure 5.1, we find that the factory owner and the orchestra conductor are both depicted as enjoying high levels of occupational prestige, even though the two occupations belong to different situses.

Morris and Murphy found some support for these notions when they asked a sample of undergraduate students to place a set of occupations into situs versus status categories as shown in Figure 5.1. To a considerable degree, the students' perceptions of where these occupations should fall corresponded with Morris and Murphy's theoretical predictions.

This situs idea has had limited usage among sociologists. One study found that situs is a good predictor of people's work values (Mortimer & Lorence, 1981; Samuel & Levin-Epstein, 1979). For instance, in terms of the values of *collectivism* versus *individualism*, those employed in the aesthetics and entertainment

FIGURE 5.1 Theoretical Situs Locations of Selected Occupations Determined by Sample of Student Raters

					SITUSES					
Prestige Rank Quartiles (Student Ratings)	1 Legal Authority	2 Finance & Records	3 Manufacturing	4 Transportation	5 Extraction	6 Building & Maintenance	7 Commerce	8 Aesthetics & Entertainment	9 Education & Research	10 Health & Welfare
1	Supreme Court Justice Lawyer	City Manager	Owner of a large factory	President of a railroad		Architect		Conductor of a symphony orchestra	College President	Physician Minister
2		Banker	Biologist for a pharmaceutical company	Airline Pilot	Geologist in an oil company	Building Contractor	Advertising Executive Commercial Artist		Philosopher County Agricultural Agent	Welfare Worker
3	Policeman	Book-keeper	Machinist		Farmer Forest Ranger		Manager of a hardware store	Radio Announcer Singer in a night club	Music Teacher	Fireman
4	Prison Guard	Cashier in a Restaurant	Restaurant Cook	Mail Carrier Truck Driver	Coal Miner	Waiter in a resturant Garbage Collector	Milk Route Man	Barber		

STRATA

Source: From "The Situs Dimension in Occupational Structure," by R. T. Morris and R. J. Murphy, 1959, *American Sociological Review,* xxiv, 2.

situs were found to be more individualistic and those in the health and welfare situs more collectivist. Keep in mind the relationship between work and values, which was discussed in Chapter 3: Work values are reinforced by the type of work one does.

In my opinion, the lack of sociological interest in the situs concept is a mistake. Some of its ideas complement ideas derived from other approaches to the horizontal dimension, such as the job-content approach.

The Job-Content Approach

One way to look at the horizontal dimension is in terms of the extent to which the content of work deals with data, people, or things. The job-content approach is based on the growing utility and visibility of the *Dictionary of Occupational Titles* (DOT), which is published by the U.S. Department of Labor (1939, 1949, 1965, 1977, and 1991).

The DOT was developed as a reference manual to be used in local offices of the U.S. Employment Service. Since 1939, it has been used in career counseling and vocational education.

The data in the DOT are based on extensive on-site observations and are available on computer tape for the research community. Thus, the DOT has provided researchers an easily accessible and rich source of information with which to work. This source has stimulated considerable research on job content over the past decade. However, because social scientists cannot easily dictate the type of data provided by the DOT, researchers are limited to working with the information it currently provides. That fact has shaped job-content research.

The *Dictionary of Occupational Titles*

The 1977 version of the DOT was a real breakthrough because it was much more useful for research. It contained descriptions of some 12,099 *occupations*, which are considered to be aggregations of jobs. (Recall from Chapter 1 that jobs represent the type of activity that people perform when they are employed; occupations represent the positions filled.) Several million specific jobs are held by members of the U.S. labor force. The U.S. census groups all of these jobs into 441 broad occupational categories that contain the DOT's 12,099 occupations.

Each of the 12,099 occupations is represented by a nine-digit code in the DOT, such as 781 684 030. Our interest is the middle three digits: These are the measures of work complexity. They indicate how concerned each occupation is with data, people, and things. Relatively simple tasks are given high numbers, and more complex tasks are given lower numbers. Figure 5.2 is the section of the DOT that explains the contents of the data, people, and things categories.

In the example just given, the middle three digits are 6, 8, and 4. This particular occupation is shoemaking. The worker must compare data ("6") in the form of size of pieces of leather, take instructions from supervisors ("8"), and manipulate the shoe materials ("4").

FIGURE **5.2** Definitions of Data, People, and Things Codes

DATA (4th digit)	PEOPLE (5th digit)	THINGS (6th digit)
0 Synthesizing	0 Mentoring	0 Setting-Up
1 Coordinating	1 Negotiating	1 Precision Working
2 Analyzing	2 Instructing	2 Operating-Controlling
3 Compiling	3 Supervising	3 Driving-Operating
4 Computing	4 Diverting	4 Manipulating
5 Copying	5 Persuading	5 Tending
6 Comparing	6 Speaking-Signaling	6 Feeding-Offbearing
	7 Serving	7 Handling
	8 Taking Instructions-Helping	

Definitions of Worker Functions

DATA: Information, knowledge, and conceptions, related to data, people, or things, obtained by observation, investigation, interpretation, visualization, and mental creation. Data are intangible and include numbers, words, symbols, ideas, concepts, and oral verbalization.

0 Synthesizing: Integrating analyses of data to discover facts and/or develop knowledge concepts or interpretations.

1 Coordinating: Determining time, place, and sequence of operations or action to be taken on the basis of analysis of data; executing determination and/or reporting on events.

2 Analyzing: Examining and evaluating data. Presenting alternative actions in relation to the evaluation is frequently involved.

3 Compiling: Gathering, collating, or classifying information about data, people, or things. Reporting and/or carrying out a prescribed action in relation to the information is frequently involved.

4 Computing: Performing arithmetic operations and reporting on and/or carrying out a prescribed action in relation to them. Does not include counting.

5 Copying: Transcribing, entering, or posting data.

6 Comparing: Judging the readily observable functional, structural, or compositional characteristics (whether similar to or divergent from obvious standards) of data, people, or things.

FIGURE 5.2 Continued

PEOPLE: Human beings; also animals dealt with on an individual basis as if they were human.

0 Mentoring: Dealing with individuals in terms of their total personality in order to advise, counsel, and/or guide them with regard to problems that may be resolved by legal, scientific, clinical, spiritual, and/or other professional principles.

1 Negotiating: Exchanging ideas, information, and opinions with others to formulate policies and programs and/or arrive jointly at decisions, conclusions, or solutions.

2 Instructing: Teaching subject matter to others, or training others (including animals) through explanation, demonstration, and supervised practice; or making recommendations on the basis of technical disciplines.

3 Supervising: Determining or interpreting work procedures for a group of workers, assigning specific duties to them, maintaining harmonious relations among them, and promoting efficiency. A variety of responsibilities is involved in this function.

4 Diverting: Amusing others. (Usually accomplished through the medium of stage, screen, television, or radio.)

5 Persuading: Influencing others in favor of product, service, or point of view.

6 Speaking-Signaling: Talking with and/or signaling people to convey or exchange information. Includes giving assignments and/or directions to helpers or assistants.

7 Serving: Attending to the needs or requests of people or animals or the expressed or implicit wishes of people. Immediate response is involved.

8 Taking Instructions-Helping: Helping applies to "non-learning" helpers. No variety of responsibility is involved in this function.

THINGS: Inanimate objects as distinguished from human beings, substances or materials; machines, tools, equipment and products. A thing is tangible and has shape, form, and other physical characteristics.

0 Setting-Up: Adjusting machines or equipment by replacing or altering tools, jigs, fixtures, and attachments to prepare them to perform their functions, change their performance, or restore their proper functioning if they break down.

FIGURE 5.2 Continued

Workers who set up one or a number of machines for other workers or who set up and personally operate a variety of machines are included here.

1 Precision Working: Using body members and/or tools or work aids to work, move, guide, or place objects or materials in situations where ultimate responsibility for the attainment of standards occurs and selection of appropriate tools, objects, or materials, and the adjustment of the tool to the task require exercise of considerable judgement.

2 Operating-Controlling: Starting, stopping, controlling, and adjusting the progress of machines or equipment. Operating machines involves setting up and adjusting the machine or material(s) as the work progresses. Controlling involves observing gauges, dials, etc., and turning valves and other devices to regulate factors such as temperature, pressure, flow of liquids, speed of pumps, and reactions of materials.

3 Driving-Operating: Starting, stopping, and controlling the actions of machines or equipment for which a course must be steered, or which must be guided, in order to fabricate, process, and/or move things or people. Involves such activities as observing gauges and dials; estimating distances and determining speed and direction of other objects; turning cranks and wheels; pushing or pulling gear lifts or levers. Includes such machines as cranes, conveyor systems, tractors, furnace charging machines, paving machines and hoisting machines. Excludes manually powered machines, such as handtrucks and dollies, and power assisted machines, such as electric wheelbarrows and handtrucks.

There are wide variations in the extent to which these job-content categories are present in the labor force. Figures 5.3, 5.4, and 5.5 show how the jobs people have rate on each level of the scales for data, people, and things.

The DOT also includes information on:

- the training time required for the job (both general education and specific vocational preparation);
- 11 aptitudes, such as motor coordination or finger dexterity;

FIGURE 5.2 Continued

4 Manipulating: Using body members, tools, or special devices to work, move, guide, or place objects or materials. Involves some latitude for judgment with regard to precision attained and selecting appropriate tool, object, or material, although this is readily manifest.

5 Tending: Starting, stopping, and observing the functioning of machines and equipment. Involves adjusting materials or controls of the machine, such as changing guides, adjusting timers and temperature gauges, turning valves to allow flow of materials, and flipping switches in response to lights. Little judgment is involved in making these adjustments.

6 Feeding-Offbearing: Inserting, throwing, dumping, or placing materials in or removing them from machines or equipment which are automatic or tended or operated by other workers.

7 Handling: Using body members, handtools, and/or special devices to work, move, or carry objects or materials. Involves little or no latitude for judgment with regard to attainment of standards or in selecting appropriate tool, object, or material.

Note: As each of the relationships to people represents a wide range of complexity, resulting in considerable overlap among occupations, their arrangement is somewhat arbitrary and can be considered a hierarchy only in the most general sense.

Only those relationships that are occupationally significant in terms of the requirements of the job are reflected in the code numbers. The incidental relationships that every worker has to data, people, and things, but that do not seriously affect successful performance of the essential duties of the job, are not reflected.

Source: U.S. Department of Labor (1977).

- 10 temperaments or personal traits, such as the ability to deal with people or to perform under stress;
- 5 interest factors, such as preference for concrete versus abstract work;
- 6 physical demands from the job, such as strength or ability to see things; and
- 7 working conditions, such as presence of noise or extreme heat.

FIGURE 5.3 Distribution of U.S. Jobs Within Data Levels

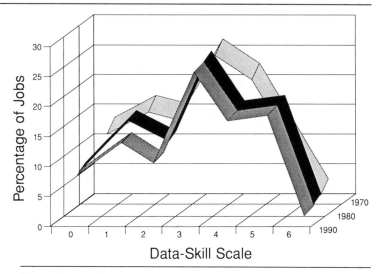

Source: From "Occupational Transformation in United States Economy, 1970-1990: Is There any Middle-Range Jobs Reduction?" by Mahmoud Kashefi. Reprinted with permission of author.

FIGURE 5.4 Distribution of U.S. Jobs Within People Scale

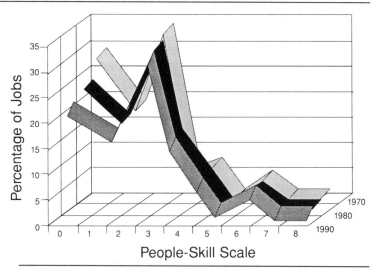

Source: From "Occupational Transformation in United States Economy, 1970-1990: Is There any Middle-Range Jobs Reduction?" by Mahmoud Kashefi. Reprinted with permission of author.

FIGURE 5.5 Distribution of U.S. Jobs Within Things Levels

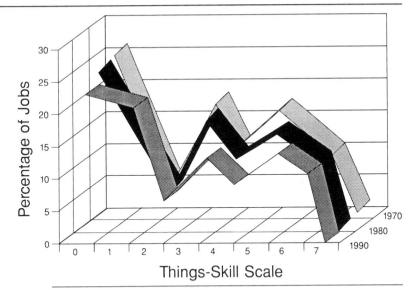

Source: From "Occupational Transformation in United States Economy, 1970-1990: Is There any Middle-Range Jobs Reduction?" by Mahmoud Kashefi. Reprinted with permission of author.

All in all, 44 such measures (see Figure 5.6) have proved a great resource for researchers.

Underlying Dimensions of the DOT

One of the more interesting uses of the DOT has been Cain and Treiman's (1981) examination of the interrelationships among the 44 measures listed in Figure 5.6. Using a subsample of 10% of all DOT occupations, Cain and Treiman did a statistical analysis to determine which of the 44 variables were related to one another. In doing so, the researchers were trying to determine if the different jobs in the DOT could be distinguished on the basis of a relatively small number of dimensions or factors. The results, presented in Figure 5.7, indicate that the 44 variables can be combined to form 6 factors, each representing an underlying dimension by which DOT occupations can be differentiated.

By a wide margin, substantive complexity of the job emerged as the strongest factor. Thus when attempting to differentiate

FIGURE 5.6 Information in the DOT

Variable Label	Description
Worker functions	
DATA	complexity of function in relation to data
PEOPLE	complexity of function in relation to people
THINGS	complexity of function in relation to things
Training times	
GED	general educational development
SVP	specific vocational preparation
Aptitudes	
INTELL	intelligence
VERBAL	verbal aptitude
NUMER	numerical aptitude
SPATIAL	spatial perception
FORM	form perception
CLERICAL	clerical perception
MOTOR	motor coordination
FINGDEX	finger dexterity
MANDEX	manual dexterity
EYEHAND	eye-hand-foot coordination
COLORDIS	color discrimination
Temperaments	
DCP	direction, control, and planning
FIF	feelings, ideas, or facts
INFLU	influencing people
SJC	sensory or judgmental criteria
MVC	measurable or verifiable criteria
DEPL	dealing with people
REPCON	repetitive or continuous processes
PUS	performing under stress
STS	set limits, tolerances, or standards
VARCH	variety and change

FIGURE 5.6 Continued

Variable Label	Description
Interests	
DATACOM	communication of data vs. activities with things
SCIENCE	scientific and technical activities vs. business contact
ABSTRACT	abstract and creative vs. routine, concrete activities
MACHINE	activities involving processes, machines, or techniques vs. social welfare
TANGIBLE	activities resulting in tangible, productive satisfaction vs. prestige, esteem
Physical demands	
STRENGTH	lifting, carrying, pulling, pushing
CLIMB	climbing, balancing
STOOP	stooping, kneeling, crouching, crawling
REACH	reaching, handling, fingering, feeling
TALK	talking, hearing
SEE	seeing
Working conditions	
LOCATION	outside working conditions
COLD	extreme cold
HEAT	extreme heat
WET	wet, humid
NOISE	noise, vibration
HAZARDS	hazardous conditions
ATMOSPHR	fumes, odors, dust, gases, poor ventilation

Source: From "The Dictionary of Occupational Titles as a Source of Occupational Data," by P. Cain and D. Tremain, 1981, *American Sociological Review,* 46, Table 1, p. 258. Copyright © 1981 by the American Sociological Association. Reprinted with permission.

among jobs in terms of their content, we must obviously consider substantive complexity. (Recall also from Chapter 4 that job complexity is a factor in determining a job's status.) The second factor,

FIGURE 5.7 DOT Occupational Factors

Factor 1: SUBSTANTIVE COMPLEXITY

GED	general educational development
SVP	specific vocational preparation
ISTELL	intelligence
DATA	complexity of functioning with data
REPCON	repetitive or continuous processes
NUMER	numerical aptitude
VERBAL	verbal aptitude
ABSTRACT	abstract and creative vs. routine, concrete activities
MVC	measurable or verifiable criteria
CLERICAL	clerical perception
SPATIAL	spatial perception
PEOPLE	complexity of functioning with people
FORM	form perception
TALK	talking
DCP	direction, control, and planning
VARCH	variety and change
DATACOM	communication of data vs. activities with things

Factor 2: MOTOR SKILLS

FINGDEX	finger dexterity
MOTOR	motor coordination
MANDEX	manual dexterity
THINGS	complexity of functioning with things
FORM	form perception
SPATIAL	spatial perception
SEE	seeing
REACH	reaching
STS	set limits, tolerances, or standards
MACHINE	activities involving processes, machines vs. social welfare

FIGURE 5.7 Continued

Factor 3: PHYSICAL DEMANDS

LOCATION	outside working conditions
STOOP	stooping, kneeling, crouching, crawling
EYEHAND	eye-hand-foot coordination
CLIMB	climbing, balancing
STRENGTH	lifting, carrying, pulling, pushing

Factor 4: MANAGEMENT

DEPL	dealing with people
DCP	direction, control, planning
PEOPLE	complexity of functioning with people
TALK	talking
TANGIBLE	activities resulting in tangible satisfaction vs. prestige
SCIENCE	scientific, technical activities vs. business contact
DATACOM	communication of data vs. activities with things
DATA	complexity of functioning with data

Factor 5: INTERPERSONAL SKILLS

SJC	sensory or judgmental criteria
FIF	feelings, ideas, facts
INFLU	influencing people
MACHINE	activities involving processes, machines vs. social welfare

Factor 6: UNDESIRABLE WORKING CONDITIONS

HAZARDS	hazardous conditions
ATMOSPHR	fumes, odors, dust, poor ventilation
HEAT	extreme heat

Source: From "The Dictionary of Occupational Titles as a Source of Occupational Data," by P. Cain and D. Tremain, 1981, *American Sociological Review,* 46, Table 8, p. 267. Copyright © 1981 by the American Sociological Association. Reprinted with permission.

which was found to be only half as strong a basis for classifying jobs as the first, reflects the motor or sensory skills required. The third factor is based on strength and brawn, rather than motor skills. The fourth factor involves organizational or administrative skills. The fifth factor contains items related to working with feelings and ideas and influencing people. The sixth and final factor distinguishes occupations with undesirable working conditions.

Cain and Treiman correctly caution that these results are dependent on the occupations included in the DOT and the statistical technique they used. Nonetheless, the results reveal a relatively small number of important factors we can use to distinguish among job types.

Shortcomings of the DOT

The DOT as a source of information about the content of work is not without its problems. First, the data do not contain information on matters such as career ladders or transfer routes within the occupations. Second, the DOT overemphasizes production process occupations, because of the prevalence of clerical, sales, and service occupations (Miller, Treiman, Cain, & Roos, 1980, pp. 191-193). For example, some 70 kinds of "sewing machine operators, garment" were analyzed, but only 6 kinds of secretaries were analyzed (Cain & Treiman, 1981, p. 260). Third, some occupations were analyzed many times, while others were not analyzed at all. Fortunately, the fourth and fifth DOT editions do not undervalue occupations mainly held by women, as did the third edition.

Fourth, the DOT underdetails professional and managerial occupations (Spenner, 1990). This shortcoming may partly reflect the difficulties involved with specifying the content of certain forms of professional and managerial work. It is not easy to generalize about what managers and professionals do. Regardless, the lack of detail obstructs attempts to understand and describe these types of jobs, which are quite important in our present economy.

A major problem with using the DOT as a basis for developing the horizontal dimension is that job content is not and cannot be completely independent of the vertical dimension. For example, the amount of training required is considered in the DOT. But training is also a component of a job's *status*. As much as social scientists would like to do so, there is no way to develop a completely "pure" horizontal dimension.

Power is another important component of both status and work content, but it is not even captured in the DOT derivations. Quite obviously, power is closely associated with the vertical dimension, but it also can be distinct from it. Some 30 years ago, David Mechanic (1962) provided an insightful analysis of the power held by people in relatively low-status positions. At that time, university departmental secretaries could control the flow of paper and thus, literally, the fate of junior faculty members. That situation has changed to some extent with the advent of personal computers, but the power of department secretaries remains high because of their centrality in university organizations.

In a related vein, a study of architectural firms found that staff architects who have specialized and esoteric expertise have power above and beyond their status in the official hierarchy (Blau, 1979). Apparently, in work settings in which the power distribution is not absolutely fixed, and this would be in the vast majority of organizations, some people have power above and beyond that conferred by the formal position. This would particularly be the case in professional work, where an individual's power and influence are often more closely related to standing in the profession than to position within the organization.

Job complexity is another component of both the horizontal and vertical dimensions. Although complexity is obviously a major component of job status (see Chapter 4), there can be more or less complexity in particular work settings without differences in status.

Spenner (1983) thought of both complexity and power in a manner that is highly relevant for the horizontal dimension. His focus was on skill levels of jobs. He notes that there are two components that should be conceptualized and measured. The first is *substantive complexity*, which is based on the level, scope, and integration of mental, interpersonal, and manipulative tasks in a job. The second is labeled *autonomy-control*; it is analogous to power and is based on the idea that a worker has more or less room in which to initiate and conclude action and to control the content, manner, and speed with which a task is done.

This nice combination of complexity and autonomy-control appears to be at the heart of the horizontal dimension. And despite the fact that the DOT does not directly measure either factor, it has allowed sociologists to take a major step in the development of the horizontal dimension.

The Labor-Market-Sector Approach

The job-content approach to the horizontal dimension is explicitly concerned with the horizontal dimension of work. The labor-market-sector approach is fundamentally concerned with the vertical dimension of work, because it has emerged out of the literature on status and income attainment. However, the approach does provide a means to join the situs and job-content approaches. Furthermore, it is a potentially definitive approach to horizontal differentiation.

Dual Labor Markets

A key concept in the labor-market-sector approach is the *dual economy*, which was introduced in Chapter 1. The *core economy* consists of highly productive and highly profitable oligopolistic industries. The *peripheral economy* consists of highly competitive industries composed of small companies that realize low profits and low productivity. Related to the dual economy is the *dual labor market*. The primary labor market has high wage jobs, good working conditions, and internal labor markets; the secondary labor market has low-wage jobs, poor working conditions, and an absence of internal labor markets (Zucker & Rosenstein, 1981, p. 870).

Figure 5.8 shows how four major studies categorized industries in the dual economy. These findings indicate a great deal of agreement for most industries but sharp differences for others. Quite obviously, each study proceeded from different assumptions. Although no overall single classification of industries is available, the classifications in Figure 5.8 demonstrate that huge differences exist between at least some labor markets (Hage, 1989).

Unfortunately, the core-periphery distinction is too simplistic for use in differentiating among jobs on the horizontal dimension. We therefore need a different perspective on labor-market sectors.

Industrial Sectors

Kaufman, Hodson, and Fligstein (1981) tackled the difficult problem of determining how many different industrial sectors exist. They took into account 10 variables that might be used to describe industrial sectors or to distinguish industrial sectors from one another. For instance, they considered the size of the industry, the industry's concentration (i.e., how many firms were competing in the industry), the industry's labor intensity (e.g., the proportion of operating expenses that go to pay labor costs), and several other variables. The result was 12 distinguishable industrial sectors:

1. oligopoly (organizations with high values on all variables, such as IBM and General Motors),
2. core (manufacturing),
3. wholesale,
4. periphery (services, some manufacturing),
5. small shop (retailing, physicians and dentists),
6. core utilities and finance,
7. peripheral utilities and finance,
8. core transport,
9. peripheral transport,
10. local monopoly (health services and construction),
11. education and nonprofit, and
12. agricultural.

Subsequent analyses have identified additional sectors. For example, there are core and peripheral sectors in sports and entertainment; consider the difference between professional and high-school football coaches (Smith, 1983). There also appear to be core

FIGURE 5.8 Placement of Industries in the Dual Economy

Industry Group	Beck, Horan, and Tolbert (1978)	Bibb-Form (1977)	Hodson (1977)	Tolbert, Horan, and Beck (1980)
Agriculture, forestry, and fisheries	periphery	excluded	periphery	periphery
Mining				
metal mining	core	core	core	core
coal mining	core	core	core	core
crude petroleum and natural gas	core	core	core	core
nonmetallic mining and quarrying	core	core	periphery	core
Construction	core	core	core	core
Durable manufacturing				
lumber and wood products	periphery	core	periphery	periphery
furniture and fixtures	periphery	core	periphery	periphery
stone, clay, and glass products	core	core	core	core
metal industries	core	core	core	core
machinery, except electrical	core	core	core	core
electrical machinery, equipment, supplies	core	core	core	core
transportation equipment	core	core	core	core
professional and photographic equipment	core	core	core	core
ordnance	core	core	core	core
miscellaneous durable manufacturing	periphery	core	core	periphery
Nondurable manufacturing				
food and kindred products	periphery	periphery	core	core
tobacco manufacturers	periphery	periphery	core	core
textile mill products	periphery	periphery	periphery	
knitting				periphery
dyeing and finishing				core
textile and floor coverings				periphery
yarn, thread, and fabric mills				core
miscellaneous textile mills				periphery
apparel and other fabricated textiles	periphery	periphery	periphery	periphery
paper and allied products	core	periphery	core	core
printing, publishing, and allied industries	core	periphery	periphery	core
chemicals and allied products	core	core	core	core
petroleum and coal products	core	core	core	core
rubber and miscellaneous plastic products	core	core	core	
rubber products				core
miscellaneous plastic products				periphery
leather and leather products	periphery	periphery	periphery	
tanned, finished				periphery

FIGURE 5.8 Continued

Industry Group	Beck, Horan, and Tolbert (1978)	Bibb-Form (1977)	Hodson (1977)	Tolbert, Horan, and Beck (1980)
footwear	core			
leather products, except footwear			periphery	
not specified nondurable manufacturing	periphery	periphery	periphery	periphery
Transportation				
railroads and railway express service	core	core	core	core
street railways and bus lines	core	core	periphery	periphery
taxicab service	core	core	periphery	periphery
trucking service	core	core	periphery	core
warehousing and storage	core	core	periphery	core
water transportation	core	core	periphery	core
air transportation	core	core	core	core
petroleum and gasoline pipelines	core	core	periphery	core
services incidental to transportation	core	core	periphery	periphery
Communication				
radio broadcasting and television	core	core	periphery	core
telephone (wire and radio)	core	core	core	core
telegraph (wire and radio)	core	core	core	core
Utilities and sanitary services				
electric light and power	core	core	state	core
gas, steam, and supply systems	core	core	state	core
electric-gas utilities	core	core	state	core
water supply	core	core	periphery	periphery
sanitation services	core	core	periphery	periphery
other not specified utilities	core	core	periphery	periphery
Wholesale trade	core	periphery	periphery	
motor vehicles and equipment				periphery
drugs, chemicals				core
dry goods and apparel				periphery
food and related products				core
farm products				periphery
electrical goods				core
hardware, etc.				periphery
machinery and equipment				core
metals and minerals				core
petroleum products				periphery
scraps and waste materials				periphery
alcoholic beverages				core

FIGURE 5.8 Continued

Industry Group	Beck, Horan, and Tolbert (1978)	Bibb-Form (1977)	Hodson (1977)	Tolbert, Horan, and Beck (1980)
paper and its products				periphery
lumber and construction				periphery
wholesalers, n.c.c.				periphery
not specified				periphery
Retail trade	periphery	periphery	periphery	periphery
Finance and insurance	core	periphery	periphery	core
real estate	core	periphery	periphery	periphery
Business and repair services	periphery	periphery	periphery	periphery
Personal services	periphery	periphery	periphery	periphery
Entertainment and recreation services	periphery	periphery	periphery	periphery
Professional and related services	core	periphery	periphery	
offices of physicians/dentists				core
hospitals/convalescent institutions				periphery
legal services				core
educational services				periphery
museums, etc.				periphery
religious organizations				periphery
welfare services				periphery
nonprofit organizations				periphery
engineering and architectural				core
accounting, auditing, bookkeeping				core
miscellaneous professional				core
Public administration	core	core	state	core

Source: From "Taxonomies of Institutional Structure: Dual Economy Reconsidered," by L. Zucker and C. Rosenstein, 1981, *American Sociological Review*, pp. 800-882. Copyright © 1981 by the American Sociological Association. Reprinted with permission.

and peripheral sectors in government; some employees of local government, such as sheriff's deputies or town assessors, seem to be at the periphery given their low wages, poor working conditions, and limited opportunities for advancement. With the addition of a peripheral sector that contains hustling and illegal work, we would have the model of the horizontal dimension depicted in Figure 5.9.

FIGURE 5.9 Labor-Market Sectors

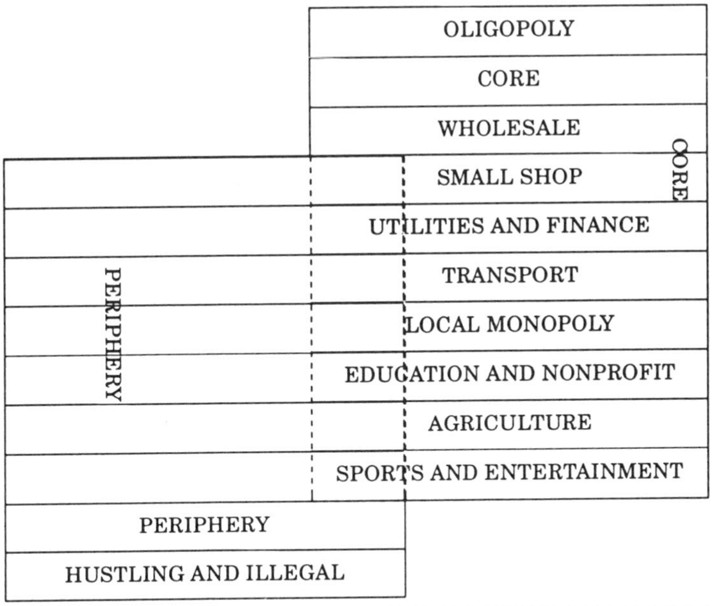

Note that this new model incorporates elements of both the labor-market-sector and situs approaches. The distinction between core and periphery allows us to accommodate previous research on labor-market sectors, which was summarized in Figure 5.6. Also, the industrial sectors included in the new scheme strongly resemble the situses theorized by Morris and Murphy (1959), which were diagramed in Figure 5.1. The combination of these two approaches allows us to make much finer distinctions among jobs than would be possible using either approach alone.

The model in Figure 5.9 shows that most of the jobs within certain industries (e.g., oligopolies such as auto manufacturing) exhibit core labor-market characteristics (e.g., high wages, good working conditions, and opportunities for advancement). The jobs in other industries (e.g., illegal industries such as prostitution) are clearly on the periphery. Still other industries offer employment in both core and periphery labor markets. For example, within the transportation industry, a job with Amtrak might very well exhibit core characteristics, while a job with the local taxicab service would probably be relatively low-paying, insecure, and dead-end.

Notice that knowledge of both the labor-market sector and the situs contribute to our understanding of different types of jobs. Jobs in the transportation industry differ predictably from jobs in other industrial sectors. However, not all jobs within the transportation sector are the same. Distinguishing between core and peripheral markets in the transportation industry gives us some understanding of wages, working conditions, and advancement opportunities.

A Final Consideration

Combining elements of the dual labor-market idea with elements of the industrial sector approach goes a long way to describing the horizontal dimension, but the picture is not complete. We still need to add some elements of the job-content approach, particularly the dimensions dealing with substantive complexity and autonomy-control. Complexity in terms of data, people, and things could be added as well. Thus within each sector, work would also vary in terms of job content, as depicted in Figure 5.10. It would then be possible to place any form of work or any occupation at the appropriate point on the horizontal dimension.

A model such as this reveals much more about the nature of work than simply knowing an occupational title. For example, the practice of law takes place in a wide variety of settings. The solo practicing lawyer who relies on finding accident victims (the "ambulance chaser") in order to develop suits for damages would be in the small shop periphery sector, with moderate to low substantive complexity and autonomy and control. The partner in a Wall Street law firm would be in the small shop core sector, with much higher complexity and autonomy-control ratings. The lawyer who is employed by General Motors would be placed in the oligopoly sector.

Before concluding our analysis of the horizontal dimension, note that horizontal (and vertical) aspects of work are not fixed for all time. Just as industries or firms can shift from core to

FIGURE 5.10 Within-Sector Differentiation

		high	low
		Substantive Complexity	
OLIGOLOPOLY		**Autonomy Control**	

		high	low
		Substantive Complexity	
HUSTLING ILLEGAL		**Autonomy Control**	

S E C T O R S   to

periphery and vice versa, particular jobs can shift within a sector. For example, declining profits in the printing industry contributed to changing technology, with computerization, more routinized tasks, and a decline in the work's skill requirements. Printers' jobs might have shifted from the core to the periphery if the union representing the printers had not been able to secure guarantees for its members. They then welcomed the technological change for the sake of efficiency (Wallace & Kalleberg, 1982). However, if they had not accepted the changes and as a result the industry's profits were to decline too far, then the industry itself would shift to the periphery.

Longshoremen offer another example of a shift in skill requirements in a single sector (Finlay, 1983). Their work was affected greatly by the development of containerized cargos and cargo ships. The result was the development of two labor markets. Crane operators for containerized cargo ships remained at the core, but the labor market for other longshoremen moved to the periphery.

The horizontal dimension itself is vital and dynamic. A study of job content in Canada, for example, found that for both men and women there were more entry-level jobs in 1980 that required the ability to deal with high cognitive complexity and verbal activity than in 1930 (Hunter, 1988). Jobs that required gross motor activity (sheer physical strength) had declined. In its shifting nature, the horizontal dimension is like the vertical dimension.

Conclusions

In this chapter we have considered how work varies along the horizontal dimension. A reasonable question to ask at this point might be "So what?" What have we gained from our discussion of "situses," "labor-market sectors," and "job content"?

One thing we have gained is an understanding of why people of generally equal status can have widely different points of view about personal, political, economic, and social issues. The friends that I mentioned at the beginning of this chapter are all at the same status level, but some are Republicans and some are Democrats. The point is that our work shapes our attitudes and beliefs through our interactions with co-workers. Additional important aspects of the horizontal dimension will be seen as we progress through the remaining chapters.

I have intentionally not dealt with one major aspect of the horizontal dimension (and the vertical, as well): placement by ascription. Hidden in the analyses presented here is the sad fact that discrimination and prejudice still survive on the basis of age, race, ethnicity, and gender. These issues will be addressed directly in upcoming chapters. An understanding of how work varies on the horizontal dimension (as well as how this variation relates to the vertical dimension of work) is crucial to an understanding of these issues.

In this chapter, I have attempted to develop an approach to the horizontal dimension of work that is consistent with current theoretical and empirical developments in the field. I have also attempted to develop an approach that will yield insights into the ways in which work and workers are distributed across the horizontal dimension. Work that is substantively complex in the educational sector is different than that which is substantively complex in the manufacturing sector. It is not certain that the sectors that have been identified are those that would ultimately serve as the best bases for understanding horizontal differentiation, but they offer a promising start in that direction.

A major advantage of the approach suggested here is that it can be linked directly to the vertical dimension. Aspects from the job-content approach—substantive complexity and autonomy-control—have been shown to be closely related in many instances to the vertical dimension. The development of the labor-market-sector approach arose from attempts to understand status and income-attainment processes along the vertical dimension. Despite these relationships, the horizontal dimension remains an important dimension of work.

■■■ APPLICATION

"Pulsating Organizations"

As mentioned toward the close of this chapter, the horizontal dimension is a dynamic one. The content of work is periodically altered as new technologies emerge. The availability of jobs in certain industrial sectors fluctuates with the economic fortunes of the firms involved. Any number of things can happen to change the landscape on the horizontal dimension. Some of these changes are temporary, and some them are quite permanent.

One of the more striking recent developments with regard to the horizontal dimension has been an apparent shift away from core labor-market jobs and toward jobs on the periphery. This is to say that, of the jobs available today, a greater proportion are located on the periphery than was the case only a few years ago. This shift has resulted in part from increases in the numbers of service-sector jobs, many of which are located on the periphery. However, part of the shift from core to periphery must be attributed to the emergence of so-called pulsating organizations.

What are "pulsating organizations"? Faced with mounting economic pressures, many organizations have adopted novel labor-utilization strategies in recent years. One such strategy has been to shed a large proportion of the organization's permanent labor force, replacing these workers with part-time employees who are called in only when needed (Sorge & Streeck, 1988). Thus the organization takes on employees during periods of peak activity and quickly cuts back on the number of workers employed when consumer demand wanes or when a production cycle ends. Toffler (1990) calls such firms "pulsating organizations."

In a 1978 corporate survey, 94% of the polled firms (including those in the construction, manufacturing, transportation, trade, finance, and service sectors), "employed flexible [i.e., temporary] workers and had a work force differentiated between core and buffer employees" (Pfeffer & Baron, 1988, p. 264). Such corporations keep excess labor costs to a minimum through a variety of means, including the use of short-term contracts, subcontractors, and hire-and-fire policies (Hyman, 1988). Also, the employment of part-time workers can be in the economic interests of labor-intensive firms because many part-timers are not protected by national job legislation. Their employers are exempted from paying various taxes or contributing to benefits plans on their behalf.

One result of the emergence of these pulsating organizations has been an increase in the incidence of *contingent employment* (Block, 1990). Those who experience contingent employment have been displaced from their permanent jobs and so must seek temporary or part-time employment. In many cases these employees have been effectively shifted from the core sector of the labor market to the periphery.

One way to illustrate the increasing prevalence of contingent employment is to consider the recent growth in the number and size of firms competing in the temporary help services (THS) industry. Providing much of the labor power needed by pulsating organizations, the industry almost doubled in size during the 1982 to 1985 period in terms of payroll size and number of employees. The growth of the THS industry even outstripped that of the burgeoning computer-equipment industry by 21% from 1970 to 1984 (Pfeffer & Baron, 1988). Other findings complement these data, showing an expansion in the incidence of employment in the periphery in the United States over the last several years (Block, 1990; Harvey, 1990).

But is contingent employment a good or a bad thing? How you answer this question depends on your perspective. For instance, it is quite plausible that the increasing prevalence of temporary and part-time positions is making it easier for working women to coordinate their working and nonworking lives. Single mothers who cannot afford child care may benefit from the flexibility offered by temporary and part-time employment. In fact, such positions may represent the only available alternative to welfare or unemployment for some single mothers. Also, a position in the temporary labor force may prove particularly suitable for anyone who desires freedom of movement into and out of the labor force. Finally, some people may be attracted to contingent employment because of the variety it provides in terms of work settings, work content, and interpersonal contacts.

On the other hand, contingent employment does have its down side, especially when compared to core labor-market jobs. Although temporary or contingent employees may be paid a competitive wage, the lack of job security associated with contingent employment often threatens financial security. Also, many temporary and part-time employees have no opportunity for advancement within the organizations for which they work. Finally, contingent employees are less likely than permanent employees to enjoy benefits such as retirement and employer-sponsored health care. These arrangements are "a source of insecurity and adversity for those outside the core labor force" (Hyman, 1988, p. 50). Regardless of your particular perspective, however, the emergence of pulsating organizations and contingent employment has clearly changed the landscape of the horizontal dimension.

■■■■ SUGGESTED READINGS

The *Dictionary of Occupational Titles* (DOT) is a basic tool for analyzing the horizontal dimension. It is given a complete, if rather technical, assessment in Miller, Treiman, Cain, and Roos (Eds.), *Work, Jobs, and Occupations* (1980).

A simplified account of work in the marginal sector is found in Hodson and Sullivan, *The Social Organization of Work* (1990).

6   Gender and Work

My values tell me that we should not have to think or write about gender and work, but my observations tell me that sexual harassment and discrimination based on gender do exist. It does not take a sociologist to scent something unusual about the fact that we have had no women U.S. presidents. As my friend and colleague Chris Bose has noted, gender is a pervasive "organizing principle in the world of employment" (Bose, Feldberg, & Sokoloff, 1987, p. 2). Gender *does* make a huge difference in the world of work.

This chapter focuses on women. The analysis of women in the labor force is complex and complicated. The enormous political and philosophical battle over the Equal Rights Amendment in the United States in the 1970s and 1980s is indicative of the emotions felt by people of many persuasions about women in the labor force. The role of women in the military remains a heated issue. Another, but not unrelated complication, springs from the linkage between women, the family, and childbearing and child rearing. Even the issue of abortion is part of the complicated scenario, because some women have chosen abortion for the sake of their careers. Men do not have to make such a choice. It is also difficult to disentangle differentiation by age, race, and ethnicity, because work is different for young black women than for middle-aged white women. Yet another complexity and complication is that of sexuality, because sexual attraction does occur at work.

My hope is that this chapter will recognize the complexities and complications, as well as the subtleties, that are implicit in the topic. At the same time, I will attempt to keep the presentation as simple as possible. The first topic is the rate of women's participation in the labor force. We then turn to a consideration of the factors affecting that participation and then to a consideration of the social and psychological aspects of this participation. The chapter will then turn to an analysis of women and the vertical dimension, because Chapter 4 dealt with data from men only. The next topic will necessarily be segregation and discrimination as these phenomena apply to women and work. The final topic will be women in nontraditional work.

Women in the Labor Force

Women have always worked, whether on rural farms or in urban boardinghouses (Bose, 1984). However, their work often has not been counted because it has not been paid employment. The focus here is on paid work, or *women's labor-force participation* (WLFP).

WLFP data are most instructive (see Figure 6.1). Both World War I and World War II were periods of increased WLFP. During World War I, the numerical increase in the number of women workers was slight, but women shifted from domestic work to work in offices and factories as industries became mechanized and routinized. After that war, conditions returned to "normal" until World War II, when WLFP increased dramatically (Greenwald, 1980).

The World War II period of the early 1940s was one of profound changes for women and work. The large influx of women into the labor force resulted from increased wartime-production needs and the absence of men. There were high wages and lots of job opportunities for women during this period (Anderson, 1981). A key factor during this war was that older married women were the most employed. Before World War II, those women who were in the labor force were predominantly young and single.

After World War II, there was tremendous pressure on these working wives to return to their homes and resume their "proper" roles as housewives (Fox & Hesse-Biber, 1984). There was, in fact, a slight decline in WLFP, but it began to increase again, a pattern that continues. Currently, 57.5% of women are in the paid labor force (U.S. Department of Labor, 1991). The major contribution to the increase has been married women (Fox & Hesse-Biber, 1984).

FIGURE 6.1 Percentage of Women in the Paid Labor Force, 1890-1980

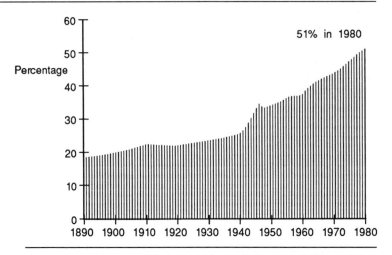

Source: From *Women at Work* (p. 14) by M. F. Fox and S. Heese-Biber, 1984, Albany, NY: Mayfield Publishing Company. Copyright © 1984 by Mayfield Publishing Company. Reprinted with permission.

Through 1960, the increase was from older married women returning to the labor force or entering it for the first time. More recent increases have come from the entry of women of all ages into the labor force.

The distribution of women in the labor force is uneven. One fourth of all working women are found in only five occupations: secretary, bookkeeper, elementary-school teacher, waitress, and retail sales clerk (Spitze, 1988a). Spitze also notes that half of all employed women are in just 17 occupations. Even when women are in predominantly male occupations, they are usually concentrated in the lowest-paying subspecialties (Jolly, Grimm, & Wozniak, 1990; Reskin & Roos, 1990). Later we will further examine the distribution of women in various kinds of work.

Within the United States, there is little difference between cities in their occupational distribution by gender (Stolzenberg & D'Amico, 1977). But internationally, the level of economic development is related to WLFP. In Israel, which has a well developed economy, patterns of WLFP are very similar to those in the United States (Izraeli, 1979). A study of 162 countries found that higher levels of economic development were related to greater integration of women into the labor force, at least in certain sectors such as clerical, transportation, and communications (Nuss & Majka, 1983). However, an analysis of eight West African towns revealed that there was considerable variation in WLFP based on both local values and the opportunity structure (Peil, 1979). Married women were less likely to work.

There is an additional aspect of the international situation that is relevant for WLFP. In fully industrialized countries, some industries have turned to export processing or "runaway shops" (Safa, 1981) in order to find and use cheap labor. There are several consequences of this for WLFP. Where the cheap labor is found, there will be an increase in WLFP, because it is frequently women who will take jobs with low wages. This creates an industrialized underclass in these locations. At the same time, this pattern could affect WLFP in industrialized nations such as the United States because American women have found the peripheral sector of the economy to be a source of many jobs (Snyder, Hayward, & Hudis, 1978). The full impact of this trend has not yet been felt.

Factors Affecting Women's Labor Force Participation

We have already encountered a couple of political and economic reasons for women to participate in the labor force: the scarcity of male workers during war and some industries' need for low-paid labor. Many other factors affect WLFP. In Chapter 3 we considered the issues of socialization and motivation for work. These processes are the same for women and men. There are important differences, however, in the content of the socialization process. There are also important differences in the adult experiences of women, particularly in terms of events surrounding marriage, family, and fertility. Finally, the demand for labor in various industries affects WLFP.

Socialization. Gender differences in socialization begin early in life. There are sharp differences in "boys' work" and "girls' work" in both family chores and paid employment for people from 2 to 17 years old (White & Brinkerhoff, 1981). Family structure and background made little difference in the assignment of things such as basic family chores, with the gender division of labor occurring at a very early age. These differences continue through schooling with clear distinctions found in terms of basic vocational counseling, training, and apprentice programs (Roby, 1981).

After an extensive review of the research on the subject of socialization, Fox and Hesse-Biber (1984) conclude:

> Of all the groups that socialize the sexes for different roles, two of the most important institutions are the family and the school. Almost immediately after birth, parents sex-type their children and respond differently to boys and girls. They regard daughters as softer, quieter, and more delicate, and sons as stronger, bolder, and more active.
>
> Although parents and others clearly characterize girls and boys in different ways, it is more difficult to determine the actual behavioral differences between male and female children, because differences can be specific to certain age periods and subject to the social context in which they occur. Researchers agree on only two items about early sex differences: girls are more verbal, and boys are more aggressive. Some persons would take this a step further and argue that these differences indicate early female inclinations toward people-oriented occupations and male inclinations toward more task-oriented occupations.
>
> This brings us then to the long-debated argument over whether the origin of sex differences is a function of *nature* (or biology) or *nurture* (or experience). From our examination of these major perspectives, we conclude that biological differences between the sexes are just a starting point in the development of sex-role differences and their occupational consequences. Biology may influence certain tendencies, but these differences are strengthened by the child's social environment. In addition, the "cognitive perspective" on development stresses that the children themselves play an active part in their development by selecting, organizing, and acting on the messages they receive about sex-appropriate and sex-inappropriate behavior and occupational roles.

The family is the earliest socializing experience. But schools soon join in and intensify the process of socializing males and females and influencing their occupational outcomes. School influence on the destinies of females comes through a variety of social arrangements and processes, including the following:

1. Boys and girls are segregated, tracked, and funneled into different groups, activities, classes, and courses.
2. The imagery in books, texts, and readers depicts boys and men as the doers, goers, and makers of ideas, places, and things; girls and women are spiritless observers.
3. The schools structure power and authority so that children see males in superordinate and females in subordinate positions.
4. Teachers prefer male students despite girls' good behavior, and teachers more actively interact with boys, not just in reprimands, but also in instruction, careful listening, and opportunities for response.
5. Guidance staffs covertly and overtly reinforce traditional cultural definitions of masculinity and femininity.

Each of these educational processes and arrangements operates toward the following final outcomes.

1. They lower girls' esteem and depress their confidence so that as they progress through school, they become less confident about their accomplishments and the adequacy of their entire gender group.
2. They form self-defeating attributions of success and failure.
3. They inhibit the development of growth and potential so that between adolescence and adulthood, when male IQ's are still rising, women are making few gains.
4. They restrict development, particularly of the mathematical, technical, and scientific skills that are required of 75% of the majors in higher education and 75% of all well-paying jobs. (pp. 67-68)

Socialization involves more than the institutions of the family and school. There is also strong peer pressure to behave in what the times consider traditional sex-role fashion. Any parent knows that attempting to urge a child to move in directions contrary to peer pressures is essentially a losing battle. These socialization patterns then interact with the opportunity structure to yield traditional "feminine-type" jobs with low pay and little opportunity for advancement. Both the family and the school will probably continue to operate in these ways, because both institutions are highly resistant to change. Even a reduction in the sex-typing in textbooks and readers would take a generation to have any impact.

Marriage and Family

Socialization is only part of the picture. Most women and men marry. Being married used to reduce the likelihood of WLFP, but this pattern has declined (Eriksen & Klein, 1981). Married women now are nearly as likely to work as unmarried women. The one exception is when the husband's income is very high. In that case, the wife is less likely to work (Spitze & Spaeth, 1979).

Family Finances

A 1980 Roper Organization survey (Fox & Hesse-Biber, 1984) asked the following question: Are you working primarily to support yourself, to support your family, to bring in extra money, or for something interesting to do? The results from the answers to this question are shown in Figure 6.2. Economic factors reign supreme, with 46% reporting that they work to support themselves or their family; 43% worked to bring in extra money. Only 14% replied that they were working because they wanted something interesting to do (not a bad motivation in its own right).

Working wives' economic contribution to the family is significant. Among wives who work full-time, year-round, their contribution to the family income approaches 40% of total family income (Fox & Hesse-Biber, 1984, p. 31). Of course, for single, divorced,

FIGURE 6.2 Women's Reasons for Working

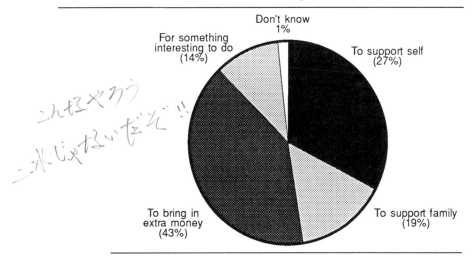

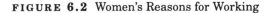

Source: From *Women at Work* (p. 30) by M. F. Fox and S. Heese-Biber, 1984, Albany, NY: Mayfield Publishing Company. Copyright © 1984 by Mayfield Publishing Company. Reprinted with permission.

or separated women, work is often their sole means of support. Changed marital laws and divorce provisions have drastically reduced the likelihood that alimony and child-support payments will constitute total support. And because the divorce rate continues to climb, especially among young women, the economic motivation for working will continue to increase.

Geographic Mobility

Geographical mobility is a rather complicated issue. The higher the husband's occupational prestige, the greater the demands to migrate because of better employment opportunities elsewhere in the country (Duncan & Perrucci, 1976). The probability of the whole family moving is thus greater when the husband has high occupational prestige. Wives' work typically has much less effect on family migration. Obviously, wives' continued employment is hampered by family migration. However, some wives who had been unemployed find that migration puts them into the work force, perhaps because old ties are broken and new opportunities appear attractive.

Women who see themselves as the primary providers for themselves or their families are as willing as men to migrate (Markham, Macken, Bonjean, & Corder, 1983; Markham & Pleck, 1986). However, if they did not see themselves as the primary provider, then they were less likely than men to be willing to move. The presence of a husband thus has a strong effect on WLFP. Needless to say, dual-career families face severe problems when both spouses' jobs require geographical mobility.

Family Roles

Despite the importance of a wife's work to family finances, the husband's work often takes priority when conflicts arise. Factors such as his career pattern, the amount and type of time demanded of the husband (shift work or overtime work), and geographical mobility requirements could all affect a wife's decision to take or refuse a job (Mortimer, Hall, & Hill, 1978). Certain types of husbands' jobs simply make it more difficult for wives to work.

The husband may not be available for household work if he works constantly changing shifts or moonlights with two or more jobs, and so the wife by default must take responsibility for running the home. Similarly, a husband's job that requires absence from home for long periods of time, such as long-distance truck driving or traveling sales, makes it difficult for wives to work, especially if there are children but no child-care arrangements.

Interactions in the family setting also appear to affect WLFP. Husbands' attitudes towards their wives' working may be more important than the wives' own attitudes in determining whether wives work (Chenoweth & Maret, 1980). For example, wives' employment, their attachment to their work, and their earnings have an effect on husbands' perceptions of the decision-making process in the family. Husbands whose wives go to work tend to believe that their wives' decision-making power has increased (Huber & Spitze, 1981, 1983). Wives' previous earnings experience and the number of children are also important determinants of their husbands' attitudes.

Fertility

One key factor associated with WLFP has been the presence of small children, which is closely, but not perfectly, related to the marriage issue. The presence of small children was a major inhibitor of WLFP, but this pattern is changing. There was a decline in the importance of the presence of children under 6 years of age for the 1940-1960 period, which was before the real surge in WLFP (Waite, 1976).

More than likely, fertility will continue to decline, because of the costs of childbearing and the costs of staying home (Huber & Spitze, 1983). In addition, the rising divorce rate, the decreased economic rewards from having children, and the reduced psychological benefits (because children often move away at adulthood) will also contribute to a decline in fertility.

Career plans and plans to have children are developed together (Waite & Stolzenberg, 1976). The point here is that for married couples the idea of career and family plans cannot be assumed to be simply a matter of rational calculation. The matter is neither rational nor simple. On the one hand, unwanted pregnancies do occur. If a woman gets pregnant and she loves her career, what is she to do? The options all have high costs. I have friends who have opted for abortion in these situations. I have had other friends decide to have their babies, with either the husbands or the wives leaving their career paths. Sometimes, plans to have children just do not work out. In still other cases, the "biological clock" runs out. There are many other possible permutations here, of course, like having twins or triplets, rather than just one baby to care for, or rationally planning to have two children and then having one or both die. For single women, of course, parenthood creates a huge dilemma in regard to work, TV character Murphy Brown aside.

Through all of this, the fact remains that the presence of small children reduces WLFP (Smith-Lovin & Tickameyer, 1978), even though the effect now is not as large as it was. Fertility does strongly affect wives' employment in the short run (Cramer, 1980). As their youngest children near school age, however, many women return to work. If women are having fewer children, then the impact of fertility on employment will continue to decrease, because less time will be spent out of the labor force.

Demand for Labor

Our focus so far has primarily been on factors that affect the supply of women in the labor market. We know less about the demand for such participation, aside from the demand for inexpensive labor in the peripheral labor market.

An exception is a small body of research on the way that an organization's previous experience with female employees affects its recruitment and selection of additional female employees. For example, an analysis of data from 24 large U.S. banks found that those with a history of employing women in management positions were most likely to have above-average WLFP (Szafran, 1984). Once an employing organization has moved beyond the employment of only a few token women (Kanter, 1977a), they will probably continue to hire women at all levels.

The labor markets within which organizations operate also will affect their WLFP demand. If the labor market contains increasing numbers of highly qualified women, then their demand for such women will increase. For example, there has been an almost startling increase in the percentage of women lawyers in Wall Street law firms (Epstein, 1980, 1981a). These firms were male bastions of the first order only a short time ago. Although the women in these law firms still face problems ranging from advancement to love relationships, their numbers and percentages have increased dramatically. This increase at least partly results from the labor markets in which the law firms operate. Many of the top law-school graduates are now women.

This same pattern would appear to be evident in other forms of professional and managerial work, although strongly entrenched patterns of discrimination and segregation remain. However, given the distribution of grades and leadership positions in college classes (a fair portion of which go to women), it seems impractical for a business firm to refuse to hire women for managerial positions.

As a sidelight, it is interesting to note the impact that WLFP has on men in the workplace. A study of federal workers found that as the proportion of women in work groups increased, the social solidarity among male workers decreased. Male workers also received greater social support from female workers (South, Bonjean, Markham, & Corder, 1983). The somewhat surprising finding apparently resulted from more frequent interaction between men and women.

Women's Experience of Work

Up to this point our focus has been largely on structural factors and their effects on WLFP. Another major consideration is how women generally think about work and how they react to the work they do.

Orientations and Attitudes Toward Labor Force Participation

Women's and men's orientations toward WLFP cover the whole spectrum, from "A woman's place is in the home," through "Equal pay for equal work," to "All power to all women." Staid economists write of women's "taste for housework" (Cain, 1966) or "taste for market work" (Sandell, 1977). As you can see, opinions widely vary. However, sociologists seem to agree that orientations toward WLFP are a consequence of early socialization, ongoing experiences, and perceived future prospects.

Like most orientations, those toward WLFP begin in the home. Traditional sex-role socialization contributes to the lower value that girls place on work and to their more traditional occupational orientations (Rosen & Aneshensel, 1978). However, girls ranging from kindergarten age to college age whose mothers are employed have less-traditional views of marital and sex roles (Fox & Hesse-Biber,

1984, p. 50). These daughters also see women as more competent than do daughters of nonemployed mothers, and they view women's accomplishments more positively. Women with employed mothers are more likely to plan to work themselves, particularly if their mothers have enjoyed their work.

Whether women or men have mothers who are in the labor force will soon become a moot point. Most mothers and fathers will be working, and thus most children will grow up to be men and women who accept WLFP.

The development of orientations toward WLFP does not stop with childhood, of course (Ferree, 1980; Mason, Czajka, & Arber, 1976). Orientations toward WLFP are shaped continually as people move through their careers. The interaction between orientation and experience is complex. Spitze and Waite (1980) argue that sex-role attitudes respond to, rather than affect, early work experiences. However, they also suggest that women with a strong taste for paid employment may behave early in their career in such a way as to maximize the benefits of long-term employment. For instance, a young career woman may aim for a job in a core industry or hold out for a management-trainee position instead of accepting a clerical job.

For married women, family roles are also important. A strong orientation toward family can weaken involvement with work (Statham, Vaughn, & Houseknecht, 1987). However, many women value and seek a balance between work and family.

Perceptions about the future availability of job opportunities affect women's aspirations and their willingness to invest in higher education (Ferber & McMahan, 1979; Fox & Faver, 1981). Ferber and McMahan believe that women's high expectation levels, high investments in education (especially in formerly male-dominated fields), increasing labor-force participation, and decreased fertility will reinforce one another and contribute to a reduction of the male-female earnings gap. This, of course, remains to be seen.

Reactions to Work

How people feel about their work depends on the work itself, the rewards it brings, and their orientation. The two main areas in

which researchers have investigated women's reactions to work
have been job satisfaction and mental health.

Job Satisfaction

There have been several studies directly concerned with comparisons of female and male job satisfaction. The findings here are
mixed. Current research has found that men and women are
apparently equal in job satisfaction and commitment to working
(Lorence, 1987c; Shaw, 1985).

How people (both men and women) feel about their work
depends on the work itself and the rewards it brings, plus their
points of reference. A variety of factors have been linked to women's
job satisfaction. For instance, women with more education and with
an urban background were found to be more likely to be dissatisfied
than men with comparable backgrounds, probably as a consequence of not having their skills and training fully used (Miller,
Labovitz, & Fry, 1975). The job satisfaction of blue-collar women
was most affected by intrinsic and financial rewards from their
jobs (Loscocco, 1990a). For female clerical workers, perceived
opportunities for training and the full use of one's skills were
strongly associated with job satisfaction (Grandjean & Taylor,
1980). Autonomy appears to be a factor as well (Lorence, 1987b).
It must be realized, however, that women are often segregated
into occupations that minimize the likelihood of exercising autonomy and supervisory authority (Jaffee, 1989).

Perhaps one of the most important factors in job satisfaction is
day-to-day work conditions (Miller, 1980). That factor is directly
linked to satisfaction for both men and women, although there are
slight differences in the conditions that were important for men and
women. Men are more affected by closeness of supervision, organizational structure, their position, and job protection, while women
are more affected by the substantive complexity of their work, the
dirtiness of the work, the number of hours worked, and their income.

Another important variable in the job-satisfaction equation is
the comparison or reference group people use. Hodson (1989) found
that women reported higher satisfaction than men, despite objectively poorer jobs. The use of different comparison groups, plus the
fact that men have been socialized to be more willing to vocalize their

dissatisfaction, leads to this gender difference. This type of idea is supported by Loscocco and Spitze's (1991) research in which women reported lower satisfaction as they began to compare their work and its rewards with those received by men.

Mental Health

Another individual WLFP outcome is mental health. Work setting and job conditions have a significant effect on women's reactions to their work. For instance, female medical students were found to be more dominant, independent, and active than women educated in other fields (Mandelbaum, 1978). The women medical students also exhibited different personality traits than male medical students. For example, the women scored higher than the men on measures of self-confidence, autonomy, and aggression, while scoring lower on deference and need for affiliation.

Another study of women found that job conditions that encourage self-direction are related to effective intellectual functioning, openness, and flexibility. In this case, however, the pattern is basically the same as that found for men (Miller, Schooler, Kohn, & Miller, 1979).

Work is not always good for women's mental health. Competing demands at work, as well as the absence of demand and challenge, lead to stress at work—slightly more for women than for men (Lowe & Northcott, 1988). But the demands of home and family are a much bigger source of stress for women. A major study found that married women tend to be in poorer mental health than married men (Gove & Geerken, 1977). Employed men and employed women without children experience essentially equal numbers of demands; married employed women, however, have more demands on them than do married men.

Of particular interest is that this research found that nonemployed wives have even more demands on them. While it would seem that married employed women have more demands on them than married unemployed women, Gove and Geerken (1977) suggest that it is the *kinds* of demands experienced that makes the difference. Apparently the demands of children and housework can adversely affect mental health. This research also found that employed men expressed the lowest levels of loneliness and desire to be left alone. Married employed women expressed higher levels of these feelings, and married unemployed women expressed the highest levels.

Women's Labor Force Participation and the Vertical Dimension

If we think back to Chapter 4, we can remember the rather straightforward link between work and social status. The chapter outlined the extensive and rather conclusive research in regard to the linkages among prestige, status, education, and income. However, most of the research was carried out by and dealt with white males. Unfortunately, the results cannot simply be applied to women.

The complicating factor is that gender interacts with occupation in the prestige and status ratings of occupations. A very simple example of this can be found in research carried out with a sample of college students (Powell & Jacobs, 1984a, 1984b). The students were asked to indicate the prestige ratings for both male and female nurses, architects, construction workers, and so on. Men in traditionally "male" occupations received higher prestige scores than did their female counterparts. At the same time, women in traditionally "female" jobs received higher scores than did men in the same jobs. When the students were asked to rank women in male-dominated occupations or men in female-dominated occupations, occupation proved to be more important than gender in determining prestige. The income and educational requirements of the occupation were still the most significant determinants of the prestige given to the incumbents. Therefore, the basic relationships explored in Chapter 4 operate for both men and women. However, because of the lower prestige generally accorded "female" occupations, the gender factor basically harms women and benefits men (Bose & Rossi, 1983; Tyree & Hicks, 1988).

There seems to be ample evidence that occupations that have predominantly women incumbents receive lower prestige scores than do male occupations and that the income differentials are even sharper. At the same time, most prestige studies have included only highly stereotypical female occupations, such as nurse or secretary (Bose & Rossi, 1983). Until we achieve a situation of gender neutrality, the extent to which an occupation is perceived to be male or female will continue to make a difference in its prestige and income. Research clearly indicates, however, that occupation is ultimately the strongest predictor of prestige and income.

Women Versus Men

There are both similarities and differences in the placement of men and women on the vertical dimension. One area in which similarities have been found is in the socioeconomic-achievement process. Research that used the basic Wisconsin model (described in Chapter 4) found the same patterns of socioeconomic achievement for both women and men, although education was more central and social origins less important for women (Featherman & Hauser, 1976a). For both men and women, there were improvements in socioeconomic status between 1962 and 1973, although female earnings dropped slightly during that period.

Another finding of similarity between women and men is that women and men generally attain the same mean level of occupational status. The pace and scope of achievement are different, however. Men have more upward mobility, and their status levels increase over their work lives, with most of the increases in the early years of their careers. But men achieve their highest status more slowly than do women, because they have more steps along the way (Marini, 1980; Rosenfeld, 1979, 1980). On the other hand, the clerical and semiprofessional occupations so often filled by women have higher status than do many traditionally male blue-collar occupations. But women in these occupations tend to stay at the same level throughout their careers. Job shifts by women from one of these female occupations to another do not raise their status, but job shifts to other occupations have the potential to do so.

These findings of similarities between women and men in terms of socioeconomic achievement have been criticized. The findings of similarity may be affected by an overrepresentation of successful women in the samples of employed women. Women who can afford not to be in the labor force will stay out of it unless they can find a job commensurate with their education. If these women entered the labor force, they would not achieve occupational statuses in keeping with their education and thus the similarity in pattern would not be found (Fligstein & Wolf, 1978).

Even at the same prestige level, there are task differences that vary by sex identification, according to McLaughlin (1978). These task differences on the horizontal dimension are such that "male" job tasks have greater earnings potential. If, for example, aggressiveness is highly rewarded and males are more aggressive, then their rewards will be higher. At the same time, it must be recognized that characteristics that are valued and rewarded can shift over time. If, as many observers are suggesting, we are moving toward a more androgynous society, it may well be that the affiliative skills of women will prove to be an alternative route to achievement (Kaufman & Richardson, 1982).

Differences between men and women at the same basic prestige level have been examined in several studies of college and university faculty members and administrators. It has been repeatedly found that women are more likely to be found in lower tenure-track ranks or in nontenured positions and also receive lower salary levels (Fox, 1981, 1985; Pfeffer & Davis-Blake, 1987; Pfeffer & Ross, 1990; Rosenfeld, 1981). There are many reasons for these differences, including less incidence of continued employment primarily because of pregnancy, greater unwillingness to make geographical moves, sex segregation by discipline, and intrauniversity differences in salary and other reward structures. In addition, males receive greater returns on their human-capital attainments, such as obtaining advanced degrees such as the doctorate (Fox, 1985). Some of these patterns do appear to be changing as a consequence of affirmative action and attitudinal changes on the part of both men and women (Ferber, Loeb, & Lowry, 1978; Rosenfeld, 1981), but colleges and universities remain places where discrimination and segregation persist.

As the studies of universities and colleges attest, there are important female-male earnings differences, even when the actual work is very similar, based on DOT measures. At the same time, there are some hints that the differences may be decreasing as a result of affirmative-action policies and changing patterns of WLFP itself (Kemp & Beck, 1986).

Male-female pay differentials are not limited to the United States. There are substantial differences in earnings between men and women in all industrialized nations (Roos, 1983; Treiman & Roos, 1983). There are some interesting international twists and turns. For example, the dual labor-market system in the United States is associated with a large gender gap in income; in contrast, countries such as Norway and Sweden have less labor-market segmentation and a smaller income gap (Rosenfeld & Kalleberg, 1990).

Factors Associated With Working Women's Status

In this section we will examine the factors that have been studied in regard to the location of women on the vertical dimension. Among the factors to be considered are the occupation of women's mothers, education, labor-force experience, and the industrial sectors and organizations in which women are employed. The conclusion that we will come to is that both individual (human-capital) explanations (such as mothers' roles, education, and experience) and structural explanations (such as industrial sector) are required for a complete understanding of vertical dimension placement (Rosenfeld, 1979).

Mothers' Occupation

The first factor to be considered is the role of mothers. Most early analyses of women's intergenerational mobility compared daughters' occupations with those of their fathers. These were similar to analyses of males' intergenerational mobility. No surprise, then, that research in this tradition found stronger relationships for father-son mobility than for father-daughter mobility.

Rachel Rosenfeld's (1978a) research included mothers' occupations in her analysis of daughters' occupational outcomes. She argued that there were three reasons for doing so. First, if the mother worked, this had an effect on the family's socioeconomic status. Second, mothers are important role models for daughters.

There is extensive evidence that when the mother has been employed, the daughter will be more likely to be employed and to be employed in less typically female occupations. Third, because women are concentrated in relatively few occupations, adding the mothers' occupation into the analysis will improve the prediction of where daughters will be located in the occupational system. Rosenfeld's (1978a) research findings support these arguments. She concludes:

> Mother's occupation is a significant dimension of women's intergenerational occupational mobility. Whether or not the mother worked outside the home and what occupation she held, given that she was employed, affect daughter's location. When only those cases are considered in which the mother had been employed at the time the daughter was 15, the effect of mother's occupation is relatively more important than that of the father in predicting daughter's occupational destination. In other words, mother's work matters for daughter's occupational location. The same conclusion has been reached with respect to girls' and young women's occupational aspirations and with respect to the occupational attainment of certain selected subgroups (primarily college graduates). The findings here allow generalization to the occupational mobility process for adult women. (p. 45)

Rosenfeld further notes that as increasing numbers of women work outside the home, the importance of the mother's occupation may well increase and may be important in terms of understanding a son's occupational locations.

Education

The role of education in women's location on the vertical dimension is complex. Education pays off for both men and women—in fact, it is the most critical factor for both, although men get more return on their investment in education than do women. Furthermore, single women receive a higher return on education than do married women (Treiman & Terrell, 1975a).

As far as the effects of parental background are concerned, mothers' education and occupation had a stronger effect for women than did the fathers' education and occupation for men (McClendon, 1976; Treiman & Terrell, 1975a).

Further insights into the complex role of education are provided by an analysis of the effects of post-high school education (Sewell, Hauser, & Wolf, 1980). The initial finding confirmed the notion that post-high school education has a greater effect among men than among women. The researchers also found that the first job has a greater effect on the current job than does education. Subsequent analyses revealed that the status of women's first jobs was higher than men's. When this first-job status was controlled, the continuing influence of schooling on subsequent status attainment was higher among women than among men. In other words, for men, post-high school education is an important determinant of their first job, which in turn is an important determinant of their current job. For women, post-high school education is a weaker determinant of first-job placement, but the effects of this education will continue to be exerted on eventual occupational location. For example, a woman with a college degree might obtain a job as a secretary as her first job but then be able to move into a managerial position over time. A man with similar credentials would move into the managerial level at the outset.

An interesting twist to the role of education is provided by an analysis of job shifts. When men shift from one job to another, they are changing full-time jobs. Women's job shifts frequently (more than 25%) involve shifts in or out of part-time employment (Felmlee, 1982). Education is an important factor for women in obtaining full-time employment after part-time work, but education does not play a significant role in women's shifts from full-time job to full-time job. The reason is apparently an absence of career and promotion opportunities for many women, whose jobs are essentially dead-end.

Labor Force Experience

The labor force experience of women has also been shown to be related to their location on the vertical dimension. Women with less-extensive and less-continuous employment experience have fewer opportunities to move to higher positions and have less gains in occupational rewards over their work lives (Rosenfeld, 1978b). Work experience is an investment in human capital. Women who have invested in a career and developed seniority and job-specific skills are more likely to be promoted than women who have not, even though they tend to realize relatively few additional benefits from the promotion (Felmlee, 1982).

There is an odd twist to the work-experience factor. Particular forms of work experience can actually have negative consequences for women. A big part of the earnings gap between men and women is based on women's concentration in low-paying, heavily female jobs in which there is less ability to exercise authority and control the means of production (Roos, 1981). Apparently, work experience outside of heavily female jobs has positive effects on achievement and status, but experience in typically female jobs has the opposite effect.

Industrial Sector and Organizational Practice

The industrial sector in which women are employed is also thought to be important in the location of women on the vertical dimension. Most research has found women concentrated in economically weak sectors (e.g., Bibb & Form, 1977). A more detailed analysis of industrial sectors found women to be underrepresented in some core industries, such as wholesale trade, transportation, communication, and utilities, where males have high earnings (Bridges, 1980).

There is some evidence from a major core sector—state and federal government work—that provides interesting insights into gender and the vertical dimension. Women employed by government have benefited from policies that have permitted them to move from one job ladder to another (DiPrete, 1987b; DiPrete & Soule, 1986, 1988). This most commonly occurs as women move from the top of the clerical ladder onto the bottom of the administrative ladder. The administrative ladder opens up a whole new set of opportunities. However, not all clerical work puts a woman in a position to become eligible for the civil-service exams that enable the move to a new ladder (Steinberg, Haignere, &

Chertos, 1990). Of course, in the public-employment sector, as in all other organizations, there are wide variations in practices in different agencies (Baron & Newman, 1990).

Organizational practices can keep women from achieving greater occupational status with little regard to efficiency or rationality (Bielby & Baron, 1983). For example, restaurants tend to employ either waitresses or waiters, with little or no regard for waiting skills. Similarly, when an organization has men and women in the same occupation, they are frequently given different titles. Factories employ female assemblers and male operatives to do the same work.

Summarizing

As you can see, there is no single determinant of women's location on the vertical dimension. It would appear that having mothers who have worked contributes to women working in nontraditionally female occupations. In most cases, educational requirements for such positions will be rather high. Education thus has a continuing and strong influence on occupational status, because it offers some prospect of upward mobility. Higher education is also related to more intensive and continual experience in the labor force. However, the tendency for women to be employed more often in peripheral industrial sectors will probably continue.

Additional factors operate against women in their efforts to attain higher-status jobs. For example, women tend to know fewer persons in networks who can assist them in finding new and better jobs (Campbell, 1988), they receive less encouragement for advancement (South et al., 1987), and they receive less on-the-job training (Wholey, 1990). The process of placement on the vertical dimension thus continues to contain many areas of inequity and inequality.

Discrimination and Segregation

My daughter recently graduated from college. The keynote speaker at the commencement ceremony was a graduate of the college who has had a smashingly successful career in film and the arts—a wonderful role model for the women and men who graduated that day. Unfortunately, she is not the typical woman worker.

The work and life of the more typical woman worker is well captured by Fox and Hesse-Biber (1984):

> The ordinary working woman is typically a working mother in her thirties; she attended and probably graduated from high school. She has little or no college experience, and therefore does not work in those higher-paying professional, technical, or managerial occupations that require college degrees and specialized training. She works, for example, in the typing pool of a large corporation, on the assembly line of a manufacturing firm, or she is a file clerk in an insurance company. She is the woman who waits on you when you shop for clothing—or she is the woman who stitched the clothing. She is also the woman who serves you at your favorite restaurant, cashes your check at the bank, answers your telephone call for information, or washes and cuts your hair at the beauty parlor.
>
> Most likely, however, she holds a white-collar job (42% of employed women are in white-collar occupations), and most likely the job is clerical. The majority of women are typists, secretaries, bookkeepers, and clerks (the "pink-collar" occupations—white-collar occupations held predominantly by women). Thirty-five percent of employed women hold clerical positions, and women account for more than three-fourths of all clerical workers. The other major white-collar occupation for women is sales. Most women in sales work are in the retail trades, where they hold the lower-paying positions; for example, as clerks and department-store saleswomen.
>
> The next largest occupational category for women is the services field (20 percent of employed women in 1979), where, again, women outnumber men. Within the services occupations, women work mostly in the food-services field as waitresses or in the health- and personal-services field as nurses' aides, orderlies, attendants, hairdressers, and cosmetologists. Cleaning and private-household work is also common.

Blue-collar occupations, where male workers predominate, account for only about 15 percent of employed women. Most blue-collar women workers hold the lower-paying operative jobs; they are the assemblers, inspectors, wrappers and packers, or operators of machinery (such as sewing machines). Few women are employed in the more lucrative blue-collar craft jobs.

Although the occupations of "ordinary" women workers are quite diversified, they share some important characteristics. They are highly segregated by sex—most women are employed in occupations that are dominated by women. Furthermore, the skills or attributes required by their work are usually considered "female traits," and such beliefs guide the hiring practices of employers. For example, women in blue-collar occupations are hired as operatives because women are believed to have greater manual dexterity than men. Women are sewers and stitchers because they are believed to be better suited to do "fine detail" work. Similarly, most typists are women because it is said that their "superior" manual dexterity allows them to type faster than any man. (The belief that women have greater manual dexterity than men is supported by some research. However, manual dexterity is certainly as important for surgery, for example, as for sewing or typing, but we hear little argument that surgery is therefore "women's work.")

Another characteristic shared by these diverse occupations is that they tend to be dead-end positions that are unstable and among the lowest paid. Within white-collar, blue-collar, and service categories women earn about three-fifths the wages paid to men in the same occupational groups . . . and women's unemployment rates are higher. Women's jobs also provide little opportunity for advancement in the organizational hierarchy. And it is rare that a woman's job requires that she supervise male workers. (pp. 97-99)

The patterns that Fox and Hesse-Biber so well describe result partly from discrimination and segregation. Although sex-role socialization (discussed earlier in this chapter) undoubtedly contributes to women's disadvantaged position on the vertical dimension, the evidence that we will examine makes it very clear that discrimination and segregation are also powerful explanations.

There is a delicate issue here. In a series of analyses of entrants to medical school (medicine is an elite occupation for both women and men), it was argued that the fact that a lower proportion of women premedical students actually enter medical schools than men premedical students is based on socialization and the availability of attractive alternatives to medicine (Cole, 1986; Fiorentine, 1987). An alternative argument is that these differences in medical-school enrollment are a consequence of lingering discrimination and segregation (Gross, 1989). Who is right? They both are. The explanations must be used in combination.

Discrimination and segregation frequently tend to be lumped together, even though they have distinct meanings. *Discrimination* refers to "institutional arrangements whereby certain categories of people are either excluded from or disadvantaged in the distribution of power, property, or satisfaction" (Alvarez, Lutterman, & Associates, 1979, p. x). *Segregation* involves disparities in the allocation of jobs and promotional opportunities (Halaby, 1979b). Discrimination involves unequal pay or other rewards for equal work. Discrimination is the broader concept, because discriminatory hiring practices lead to segregation on the job.

Socialization for Work

Patterns of job discrimination and segregation begin early. A study of the first jobs of 10th and 11th graders found significant segregation by gender. There are boys' jobs and girls' jobs. Girls worked fewer hours and typically earned lower wages. This "harbinger of things to come" meant that job types dominated by girls received less pay (Greenberger & Steinberg, 1983).

As noted earlier in this chapter, discrimination and segregation have been part and parcel of the school system, with boys and girls treated differently. There appear to be some changes taking place in these patterns, but the force of tradition here is difficult to overcome. These patterns persist into professional schools. In a nationwide study of medical schools, Bourne and Wikler (1978) found little overt "actionable" discrimination, but a "discriminatory environment" that existed on the basis of understandings of commitment and success that were based on male sex-role stereotypes and family roles. This contributed to channeling into particular specializations within medicine. A study of law schools found that when women were a small minority ("tokens"), there were performance pressures, social isolation, and role entrapment. This pattern was modified in situations in which women made up a higher proportion of the student body (Spangler, Gordon, & Pipkin, 1978).

Employment Practices

Once people complete their education and move into the labor force on a full-time basis, whatever patterns of discrimination and segregation that are present in the hiring organization and in the labor market in general come into operation. The long-term trends in occupational segregation were quite constant until the 1970s, when a decline in segregation began that has continued to the present (Jacobs, 1989). The Civil Rights Act of 1964 and subsequent legal decisions have had a truly dramatic effect in this area (Christensen, 1988).

The focus of legislation and court action has been *affirmative action*, which requires organizations to take steps to provide women (and other disadvantaged groups) with equal employment opportunity. Some people have the mistaken idea that affirmative action gives women advantages over men, even if the women are less qualified. That is not the case. Affirmative action opens up women's opportunities for jobs only if the women have the proper credentials.

The real test now for discrimination is in terms of promotion and advancement in positions for which this is possible; this is known as the "glass ceiling" problem. For managerial personnel and professionals, the 1990s will be the time of testing, because the large number of women recruited into entry-level managerial and professional positions will be ready for promotion, partnerships, tenure, and the like. Competent women should be promoted just as quickly and as frequently as competent men.

The key factor in women's lack of opportunity is access to power, and evidence shows that women have not had that access (Kanter, 1977a, 1977b, 1977c, 1979; Wolf & Fligstein, 1979a,

1979b). They will not have it, either, as long as they remain a small proportion in particular occupational settings.

As a disadvantaged group in the labor market, women tend to have jobs with less variety, diversity, independence, and control than do men (Baron & Bielby, 1982). Contrary to popular impressions, proportionately more women than men operate machines in their work (Form & McMillen, 1983). These are simple hand-tools or machines that perform repetitive tasks and restrict mobility. Women are thus exposed to machines that have potentially alienating effects because of their lack of control over the machines. Women are also more likely to suffer from the negative effects of technological change. Despite these differences, men and women have similar attitudes toward technology, technological change, and job satisfaction (Form & McMillen, 1983). Both women and men like their machines.

Pay Differentials

There is widespread agreement (and widespread dismay) that women are paid less than men (see Coverman, 1988; Stevenson, 1988; Treiman & Hartman, 1981). Despite the economic necessity that often drives them to work, women are still paid approximately only 60% of what men are paid for the same work.

Clearly, pay differentials are not based on choices made by women. Women simply do not choose lower-paying work for the sake of convenience, and they do not choose work on the basis of ease in entering and leaving a job. Economic theories based on differential productivity of men and women have also been found wanting (Brown, Moon, & Zoloth, 1980; England, 1982, 1984; Ragan & Smith, 1981). Economic theories of choice, turnover, and productivity simply do not explain pay differentials. This is not to say that economic factors are unimportant, only that explanations based on classical assumptions of economics are way off the mark.

A study of a large business firm found that pay practices are such that women receive unequal pay for equal work and employment practices result in gender segregation on jobs and promotion opportunities (Halaby, 1979b). In this study, the actual employment practices were more important than the pay practices in producing inequities, but both were operative. Note that these outcomes are the result of decisions made in organizations that are mostly run by men.

There is growing agreement that the disparities are indeed based on the fact that women are concentrated in (segregated into) jobs that are heavily female (England, 1982, 1984; England & McLaughlin, 1979; Halaby, 1979b; Roos; 1981). Even in a situation in which wage discrimination has been virtually eliminated by law (such is the case in Australia), occupational segregation, coupled with discontinuous career patterns and part-time work, continues to depress the earnings of women (Jones, 1983).

There are important differences among organizations and labor-market sectors in terms of the extent of discrimination and segregation practiced. Although segregation has declined more rapidly in the public than the private sector (Wharton, 1989), an analysis of the pay system for workers in Washington state found that the pay in predominantly male jobs was higher than in predominantly female jobs (Bridges & Nelson, 1989). Public employment thus does not eliminate pay differentials.

The matter is even more complex than this, however. It has been found that when the nature of the tasks performed (measured by the DOT) was held constant, women still received less pay (England & McLaughlin, 1979). This type of finding has led to the development of a drive for comparable worth. As Steinberg (1984) notes:

> Equal pay for work of equal value, more commonly known as comparable worth, represents the newest development in the evolution of policy to achieve labor market equality for women. It concerns whether work done primarily by women is systematically undervalued because it has been and continues to be done primarily by women. The consequence of systematic undervaluation is that the wages paid to women and men engaged in women's work are artificially depressed relative to what the wages would be if the jobs were being performed on the free market by white men. (p. 15)

Determining comparable worth is a formidable task: A huge number of factors must be considered. With the continual refinement of instruments such as the DOT, the task will become easier.

The opposition to comparable worth will remain strong, however, because of economic, political, and social reasons. These same reasons would seem to explain the existing patterns of discrimination and segregation.

Reasons for Discrimination and Segregation

There are abundant explanations for discrimination and segregation. These range from Marxian analyses of women as part of the oppressed and exploited class controlled by capitalists and by men (Quick, 1977; Sokoloff, 1980) to blaming the victim by arguing that women bring discrimination and segregation on themselves by discontinuous work and high turnover rates. As in the case of most such arguments, the best explanations appear to be more in the middle (Coverman, 1988).

Attempts to "blame" capitalism for discrimination and segregation have been met with increasing opposition based on empirical research. U.S. industries that use "massed labor" do not exhibit more segregation (Bridges, 1982). Furthermore, a study of the former Yugoslavia found more gender segregation in that socialist system than was present in the United States (Putnam, 1990).

Nor do women seem a likely source of the employment and pay practices that put them at a disadvantage. Some critics have claimed that women gravitate toward easy or flexible work, or that typically considered "women's work." On the contrary, the work that women do requires a great deal of energy. In fact, employed women expend more energy than do their male counterparts (Bielby & Bielby, 1988). Also, women in predominantly female jobs report that their jobs are neither flexible nor easy to mesh with family responsibilities (Glass, 1990).

We are thus left with inconclusive explanations for segregation and discrimination. Certainly patriarchy and capitalism play roles. So does tradition. Also to be considered is the political arena surrounding the passage and interpretation of laws. Clearly, various federal and state legislative acts and regulations have reduced discrimination and segregation. We also know that women are more likely to win sex-discrimination cases if they involve collective cases or class actions (Burstein, 1989). Currently, women win more than half of all sex-discrimination cases. Nevertheless, discrimination and segregation remain areas of legal battle.

Comparable worth also remains a battleground. Whether comparable-worth advocates will be able to convince legislators and others to enact legal means that enforce comparable-worth requirements is not yet known. To do so threatens the interest of those who favor the present arrangements; employers, men, and women can be found on both sides of this particular issue. It remains an area of continuous change.

Nontraditional Work

More and more women are entering and staying in occupations that were traditionally male, such as surgeon and road construction worker. These are jobs that have been dominated by men in the past and therefore carry with them a masculine stereotype. At the same time, men are entering and staying in occupations that were traditionally female, such as elementary-school teacher and receptionist (Williams, 1989). In this final section, we will consider why men and women choose nontraditional work, how careers advance within such work, and which particular problems are faced by people in such work.

Orientations

As noted earlier in this chapter, the likelihood of women's participation in the labor force is influenced by the working experience of their mothers. The exposure to alternatives to traditional work appears to be another key factor in developing a taste for such work. For example, when there is a lot of experience with typically male tasks, such as working with cars, women are more likely to have traditionally male factory jobs (Padavic, 1991). Experience, then, is one element in choosing nontraditional work.

Higher levels of education, together with recent employment experience, are also associated with less-traditional outlooks toward work (Mason et al., 1976). The matter is not simply educational level, however. It has been found that men in traditionally female curricula and women in traditionally male curricula in college were more like their sex peers than their curricular mates in terms of their work values. Men remained more concerned with extrinsic values and women more with intrinsic values (Lyson, 1984). A related study found that people's gender was more salient in occupations dominated by the opposite gender and that occupational competencies were more salient in same-gender occupations (Macke, 1981). Both these findings can be interpreted in terms of the number or proportion of men and women in nontraditional work. For example, when there are relatively few women in traditionally male occupations or curricula, gender will be more important and more noticed.

Time on the job appears to be another important consideration. A study of women in nontraditional skilled and semiskilled work found that during their first year of work on these jobs, the women were concerned with the challenge of surviving and succeeding. New skills had to be learned, self-confidence had to be developed, and the women had to get along with frequently troublesome male co-workers. For the women who remained in the work for a second year, the areas of concern changed to the more traditional concerns of skilled and semiskilled workers—the nature of the work, working conditions, and relationships with management (McIlwee, 1982).

Quite similar findings are reported in another study of men and women in nontraditional work (Schreiber, 1979). This work is interesting because it documents the orientations of both men and women in such work, as well as dealing with the women and men who were in traditional occupations in the first place. Both women and men in work traditionally associated with their own gender were concerned about the arrival and behavior of newcomers of the opposite gender. Both women and men were concerned about matters such as their own and the newcomers' appearance, their language (could they swear?) and other aspects of interpersonal interaction.

Sexuality does become an issue in situations of nontraditional work. The military is but one organization that, until quite recently, has cited problems of sexual attraction as a reason for excluding women from crucial roles. In the military's case, sexual attraction between men and women in combat has been neither proved nor disproved as a critical problem.

Careers

The career prospects of people in nontraditional work are affected by the numbers of people involved and the strength of the female and male traditions involved. An analysis of a military-service academy found that women have been accommodated but not assimilated. The opportunity structure and the power system were strongly characterized by the prevalence of a male value system that limits women's military roles (DeFleur, 1985). In a different male venue—truck driving—Lembright and Reimer (1982) found that male sponsorship from a husband or boyfriend reduced problems of low pay and harassment for women truckers. In both situations, the force of tradition was a strong influence.

Research on women lawyers reveals a very different pattern. Epstein (1980, 1981a) found truly dramatic changes in the numbers and proportions of lawyers in government work and in major Wall Street law firms. These law firms are among the most prestigious and powerful in the United States. Epstein attributes these changes to the Civil Rights Act of 1964, lawsuits, the actions of law-school personnel in the recruitment process, and changing attitudes toward women's competence and equality. The result is the presence of women in specialties formerly reserved for men such as litigation and corporate work. At the same time, the women lawyers still faced problems of access to some specialties, some resistance from clients, and concerns about promotion to partnership (similar findings have been reported for England; see Podmore & Spencer, 1982). They also experienced serious problems with their personal lives, particularly in terms of marriage and children, with a sizable number making the painful choice to forgo one or both sets of interpersonal relationships.

This same problem with marriage and interpersonal relationships is also noted in studies of women in business management (Brown, 1979). Large business firms employ larger numbers of women, but the chances for rising to top management may be greater in small firms. The possibility of women's movement into top-management positions is influenced by the attitudes and actions of the people (men) with whom they work. Many male executives do not perceive women as "ready" for the managerial climb (Kaufman & Fetters, 1983). At the same time, the climb requires that a woman be superwoman if she wants to fulfill other roles in life (Ferree, 1987).

One major source of segregation noted earlier is the lack of access by women to positions of power and authority. Even when such access is gained, career problems continue to plague them. Women in nontraditional positions of authority over men and women evoke different reactions on the part of subordinates than do men in equivalent positions (Mayer, 1979). Authority positions can also involve clear breaks with traditional family and sex roles that can be resisted by both women and men. A study of male and female supervisors in a federal bureaucracy initially found that female subordinates of female supervisors reported less job satisfaction, lower group morale, and a higher perception of the supervisors' behavior as controlling and particularistic than subordinates reported for male supervisors. Closer examination of the data revealed that when the actual power of the supervisors was controlled, the differences between male and female supervisors was significantly reduced. When men and women supervisors had equivalent status in the organization, similar voice in decision making, and equal amounts of autonomy, there was little difference in subordinates' perceptions (South et al., 1982). As more women enter supervisory positions, the perceived differences between women and men will probably be reduced.

Problems in Nontraditional Work

People in nontraditional work face several problems. When their numbers are small there is likely to be social isolation and even ostracism. Career advancement may be hindered or blocked. For women, work-time demands may be so great that marriage and child care suffer. Their performance may have to be well above average in all spheres of life just to be perceived as adequate. These same problems are faced by people who are in a weakened minority position because of age, race, or ethnicity.

On the gender dimension, there is the unique problem of sexual harassment. *Sexual harassment* means taking advantage of another person. It has nothing to do with mutual sexual attraction. Although there are instances of female versus male, male versus male, and female versus female harassment, the dominant problem is men harassing women. Such harassment can take the form of (a) expecting or demanding sexual favors in exchange for a promotion, a course grade, making a sale, or retaining a job or (b) continued unwanted sexual advances, such as being felt, pinched, or otherwise made to feel like a sex object.

The key to harassment is power, which explains a good part of the motivation for harassment. Women with the least power are the most likely to be overtly harassed (Gruber & Bjorn, 1982). Harassment is found throughout the occupational hierarchy, but it tends to take more subtle forms at higher levels. As would be expected, women who have been harassed are less satisfied with their work in general (O'Farrell & Harlan, 1982). As would also be expected, there are clear differences between women and men in how they define harassment (Konrad & Gutek, 1986).

At some time, perhaps, the topic of this section on nontraditional work will seem quaint. Currently, however, we are left with the situation in which one is startled by the voice of a woman airline pilot or perhaps worried by the presence of a male elementary-school teacher.

Conclusions

This chapter has examined women and work. (We did not touch on unemployment and underemployment, which may well have more serious implications for women than for men.) Although there have been massive changes in recent years, many aspects of women and work would appear unchanged and perhaps unchangeable. Childhood socialization will probably continue to treat boys and girls differently. Women will retain childbearing responsibilities, even though there may be alternatives available for child care. Entrenched attitudes will take at least a generation to be changed in any significant manner. Men in powerful positions will use that power to attempt to maintain their positions.

Despite these inertial tendencies, major changes suggest that others will follow. We can expect continued movement to reduce sex-role stereotyping and training in educational institutions. We can also expect continued movement toward more equitable hiring, promotion, and pay practices. We also can probably expect to see employment practices develop that will facilitate the merging of work and family obligations. The gender dimension is thus the scene of change, as is the age dimension to which we next turn.

■■■ APPLICATION

Unintended Affirmative Action Consequences

The concept of affirmative action was born in the late 1960s in response to perceptions of ongoing inequality in employment practices. Several years after the passage of the 1964 Civil Rights Act, two presidential executive orders were issued with the intent of ensuring compliance with the act, which explicitly prohibits discrimination in employment on the basis of gender, race, color, religion, or national origin. In some cases, these executive orders also provided for the implementation of corrective measures in situations showing evidence of past discrimination in employment and employment practices. The idea was to encourage a proactive approach to correcting historic discriminatory patterns and to move actively in the direction of equality in employment practices. Although these executive orders originally applied only to agencies and contractors of the federal government, many private corporations have since adopted such affirmative-action policies.

There is little question that the architects of the affirmative action concept had the best interests of women and minorities in mind when these executive orders were passed. Indeed, affirmative-action plans probably have been useful tools for attracting qualified female and minority applicants to jobs for which they have not traditionally applied, resulting in the hiring of these individuals into jobs typically dominated by white males. By this criterion, affirmative action might very well be judged a reasonable success. However, recent research suggests that affirmative action can have unintended negative consequences that were not initially predicted by those who formulated the affirmative action idea.

To understand the potential negative consequences, consider the situation that female job applicants face under affirmative action. Imagine, for example, that you are a candidate for the job of marketing director in a large retail organization. You are competing with several others for the job, all of whom have qualifications similar to yours. The only difference between you and your competitors is that you are the only woman applying for the job. Now imagine that you have been offered the job, not solely on your job qualifications, but on the basis of your qualifications *and* your gender.

How would this make you feel? Would it bother you to find out that your gender had something to do with your preferability as a potential hire, or would you view this fact as irrelevant? Would you think of yourself as the best candidate for the job, or would you be forced to question your own credentials? Finally, how do you think the gender issue would affect the way other employees viewed your presence in the organization?

Recent research suggests that preferential selection on the basis of gender can have marked effects on women's attitudes and behaviors. For instance, Heilman, Simon, and Repper (1987) found that females selected as task leaders on the basis of their gender suffered negative self-evaluations compared to females hired on the basis of merit. "When selected on the basis of sex, women devalued their leadership performance, took less credit for successful outcomes, and reported less interest in persisting as leader; they also characterized themselves as more deficient in general leadership skills" (Heilman et al., 1987, p. 62).

A similar conclusion was reached in a study conducted by Heilman, Lucas, and Kaplow (1990). These researchers found that, among people who question their ability to perform a job effectively, knowledge that they were preferentially selected on the basis of their gender negatively influences their perceptions of their task performance and their willingness to persist at the task. This relationship was found to hold for both men and women. Particularly striking was the finding that women are more likely than men to question their abilities in the first place. The women in the Heilman et al. (1990) study assumed they lacked competence in the absence of information to the contrary.

The findings from these studies strongly suggest that affirmative-action plans can produce inadvertently negative effects on worker's self-perceptions. However, preferential-hiring processes also can influence workers' perceptions of a variety of aspects of their work organizations. For instance, Chacko (1982) discovered that "women who perceived that they were selected [for managerial jobs] because of their sex had less organizational commitment, less satisfaction with their work, with supervision, and with their co-workers . . . than women who felt sex was not an important factor in their selection" (p. 199).

Finally, the effects of preferential hiring do not stop with the individual being hired. Affirmative-action policies can potentially affect the way new hires are viewed by others both within and outside the workplace. Jacobson and Koch (1977) report that women appointed to leadership roles on the basis of their performance are evaluated more favorably than are women appointed on the basis of their sex. These women also receive more credit for group success and are less likely to be blamed for group failure.

Another particularly striking finding is that women in the labor force are less likely to become attracted to occupations if there is the perception that the women already employed in those occupations were selected on the basis of their gender rather than on the basis of their competencies (Heilman & Herlihy, 1984). Apparently women become disinterested in occupations when they suspect they will not be evaluated on the basis of their merit. This has drastic implications for affirmative action given its goal of attracting greater numbers of women and minorities into occupations traditionally dominated by men.

The point of this presentation is not to suggest that affirmative action is bad. However, these findings do suggest that how a corporation conducts an affirmative-action program is just as important as having the program in the first place. As was stated earlier in this chapter, affirmative action is not intended to provide women with advantages over men, regardless of qualifications. It is intended to attract highly qualified female and minority applicants to the job market. The research reported here suggests that applicant qualifications should be emphasized and characteristics that are irrelevant to performance (such as gender and race) should be deemphasized when hiring decisions are described. This should reduce the likelihood that applicants or others in an organization will perceive hiring decisions as strictly gender-based. Attention to such issues may be necessary to ensure that affirmative action accomplishes what it is intended to accomplish without harming those it is intended to benefit.

■■■ SUGGESTED READINGS

Women have always worked, even if they were not counted as part of the official labor force. This is amply documented in Bose, Feldberg, and Sokoloff with the Women and Work Research Group, *Hidden Aspects of Women's Work* (1987).

The most balanced and complete overview of women and work is found in Fox and Hesse-Biber, *Women at Work* (1984).

The relationships between being married, having children, and being in the work force is carefully analyzed in Huber and Spitze, *Sex Stratification* (1983).

Kanter, *Men and Women of the Corporation* (1977a), has become a classic in its own time. The concepts of tokenism and empowerment are developed here.

7 Work Throughout the Life Course

I recently visited with two rather elderly uncles. Both are retired, and both have health problems. One uncle has a lucrative retirement package from his former employer and a wide circle of cronies from his former job. The other uncle lost his retirement benefits because his former employer went bankrupt. All of his former friends were transferred out of the area shortly before the bankruptcy. These uncles can be contrasted with Matilda White Riley, an octogenarian sociologist who is still employed and writing and researching. How have these three people come to such different places at the end of their work lives? That question addresses the main issue of this chapter.

Along the way, we also will consider other phases of the typical work life. I think of my young friend Ian, who helps me with some yard work: He soon will be old enough to mow the lawn with my riding mower. Another young friend, Jane, "pet sits" for us when we are out of town. They are learning about work as they are growing up. They attend the same school. Both get good grades and already are "tracked" as "gifted" students. All of these experiences will be relevant for their future work.

Many of the people I know who are working in mainstream situations also think about their age and their careers. My son is an army officer who has very clear ideas about the age at which he should reach higher ranks. I have a close friend in her mid-50s who is earning her doctorate. She worries about being able to get an academic job because of her age.

Although these examples are not necessarily representative of the total population, they do serve as a starting point for examining the factor of age as it intersects with the other aspects of work we have been considering. In addition, age itself makes unique contributions to the understanding of work.

Age and the Individual at Work

Throughout the book, we have occasionally examined individual responses to various aspects of work. We begin here by examining the ways in which age interacts with an individual's commitment or involvement with work.

Job involvement is volatile in the initial stages of the work career but increases as workers grow older. In other words, a young person usually has a lot of interests that compete with his or her commitment to the job or the employer. As a result, he or she may sometimes seem gung ho about the job and eager to do anything—and sometimes seem to prefer doing almost anything but working. Perhaps this on-and-off commitment results from the fact that entry-level jobs generally do not allow much autonomy or encourage creativity, perhaps because young people do not always see the link between commitment to the job and career advancement.

By the middle stage of their careers, however, people begin to see very clearly that job involvement affects later career achievement. Generally, if a person is highly involved—spending time with co-workers, taking work home, volunteering for extra assignments—and there are indeed opportunities, then the person's career is enhanced (Lorence, 1987; Lorence & Mortimer, 1985). Still, the key to involvement is the person's position in the social structure. People in higher-status jobs, where the opportunities for achievement are greater, tend to become more involved and committed.

Like their younger counterparts, older workers' involvement with their work tends to remain high or even increase if opportunities are present. However, older men and women in the United States generally have been found to be more committed to their work than their younger counterparts (Loscocco & Kalleberg, 1988), especially when internal labor markets are present (Loscocco, 1990b). But if a career is perceived to be at a dead end, involvement will decline.

Another aspect of the individual, subjective response to work is *work satisfaction*. There is a positive correlation between age and work satisfaction: Worker satisfaction increases with age. This relationship is mediated by work rewards, meaning that those who expect rewards and receive them feel satisfied. Of course, older, more experienced workers generally have higher reward levels available to them in the form of pay and job security. And frequently more intrinsic rewards are available, such as the opportunity to do work that the person considers meaningful (Mottaz, 1987a).

The bottom line is that the way people respond to their work is affected by both age and opportunities.

Perspectives on Age and Work

In previous chapters, we encountered differing sociological viewpoints. For instance, Chapter 5 presented the situs, job-content, and labor-market-sector approaches to analyzing and understanding horizontal differentiation among jobs. Similar distinctions can be made in the ways sociologists view the role that age plays in people's work experiences. My colleague Russ Ward (1984) has identified several perspectives on aging. The two most useful here deal with age stratification and life course.

Age Stratification

The age stratification approach focuses on the way in which age is a dominant criterion by which people are placed in the social structure (Riley, 1971; Riley, Johnson, & Foner, 1972). Consider the professional athlete. Athletes are viewed as being "over the hill" at very clearly defined ages. One sport, professional golf for men, overtly recognizes age stratification with its Senior PGA Tour. Age stratification is also used to classify people in terms of their eligibility to participate, as in age limitations for Little League baseball. It can also be seen in terms of age qualifications for political office. Mandatory retirement practices constitute another form of age stratification.

A major work-related issue that can be discussed in terms of age stratification is *age discrimination*. Discrimination occurs when age, rather than other qualifications, is used as the major criterion for hiring, promoting, or dismissing workers. I recently had a conversation with a business executive who was just older than 50. He was the head of one international division of a major office-equipment company. This particular company had just adopted a policy of not promoting managers who were not in their 40s to the top level of corporate management, thus precluding this executive's further advancement. In this case the policy was informal, because a formal, published policy of that sort would probably be illegal.

Age stratification is related to the horizontal dimension. Often certain types of work are disproportionately populated by people of a certain age group. For instance, sports and rock music are the venue of the young for the most part; judges tend to be older. It is also a fact that both younger and older workers are more likely be found in peripheral sectors—the smaller companies, the less desirable industries, the realm of self-employment. The core sectors are disproportionately populated by middle-aged adults. Chapter 8 has more on this subject.

Life Course

The other major perspective is that of the *life course* (Elder, 1981; Hareven, 1978). Biological, psychological, and social aspects of life are recognized as changing with time. In addition, work itself is a dominant event in the life course (Ward, 1984, p. 133). We tend to recognize prework experience as one major stage of life, the working years as another stage, and retirement as another.

The life-course approach also can include various phases or stages in work histories. For the sake of simplicity, the rest of the chapter will take this life-course perspective and deal with young workers, adult workers, and older workers.

Young Workers

As was noted in Chapter 1, in the United States the labor force is defined as including only people 16 years and older. This age limit is arbitrary and thus often distorts our understanding of who does and does not work. Actually, more youths are in school until 18 than are in the labor force (Ginzberg, 1981). However, the U.S. National Commission on Employment and Unemployment Statistics decided in 1979 that there were enough young people over 16 in the labor force that this was the age at which their experience should be monitored.

It is evident that a lot of work is performed by young people who are not yet part of the official labor force. Many youths less than 16 have part-time jobs while in school and full-time jobs in summers (Ginzberg, 1981). Household chores, baby-sitting, lawn mowing, paper routes, and farm work are widespread work activities performed by many youths. Some become involved in elite athletic competition. At the other end of the spectrum are those who engage in various forms of hustling work, including drugs, prostitution, and thievery of various sorts. None of these forms of work is counted in official counts or measures of the labor force.

When does a person stop being a young worker? For the purposes of labor-market analyses, young workers are defined as "young people between the ages of 16 and 24, but with special focus on those between 16 and 19 years of age" (Ginzberg, 1981, p. 13).

Workforce Participation

The dominant characteristic of young workers is their high rate of unemployment. Table 7.1 indicates the high unemployment rates of young workers in the labor force in April 1984 and February 1991. The table reveals strikingly higher levels of unemployment for the youngest segment of the labor force, as well as striking white-black differentials. (The table also reveals some decrease in black unemployment at all levels between 1984 and 1991.) The reasons for these patterns are well known—low educational levels, low skill levels, and, by definition, low experience levels. With age, as human capital is acquired—in the form of education, skill, and experience—the unemployment rate goes down.

TABLE 7.1   Unemployment Rates by Age and Race, 1984 and 1991

| | Unemployed in Each Category (%) | |
	1984	1991
White Men, All Ages	6.7	6.9
16 to 19	16.4	18.4
20 to 24	10.5	11.3
White Women, All Ages	6.3	5.5
16 to 19	15.4	16.4
20 to 24	8.7	6.9
Black Men, All Ages	17.7	13.4
16 to 19	41.4	37.6
20 to 24	29.5	23.3
Black Women, All Ages	15.0	11.1
16 to 19	44.6	34.5
20 to 24	26.9	18.6

Source: U.S. Department of Labor. (1984, May). *Employment and Earnings, 31,* 15-16 (Table A-4), and (1991, February) *38,* pp. 13-14 (Table A-4).

Young people really tend to be segregated into certain types of jobs. Much of the work of the young is in marginal positions in peripheral sectors. Adolescents can be found working mostly in food services (such as fast-food outlets), retail sales and cashier work, clerical positions, manual labor, semiskilled and skilled labor, and cleaning. These jobs vary widely in opportunities for initiative, autonomy, and interaction with other people. The developmental significance of such work thus varies, although none of these jobs provides many opportunities for learning (Greenberger, Steinberg, & Ruggiero, 1982).

All adolescents tend to be disadvantaged in the labor market, but some are more so than others. As noted in the previous chapter, there are clear differences between the jobs held by male and female 10th and 11th graders (Greenberger & Steinberg, 1983). Girls usually work fewer hours and at lower wages than boys. Furthermore, a study of minority females in a central city found that they tended to receive only the minimum wage. There is a triple disadvantage here in terms of being female, having minority status, and coming from a poor background (Farkas, Barton, & Kushner, 1988). There is actually a quadruple disadvantage, because being young is also a major disadvantage—at least in terms of work.

One area that would be interesting to explore would be the impact of after-school work on subsequent careers. Some people think that such work interferes with schoolwork, or that the money earned is used for cars, car expenses, or drugs. Other people see after-school work as a form of contribution to good work habits and responsibility. This is an area in which research is needed.

Transition to Adult Work

The transition from young worker to adult worker takes place when people leave school and attempt to enter the full-time labor force. Because some people enter the civilian labor force directly out of high school while others delay their entrance until after college or graduate and professional school, this transition can quite obviously occur at widely varying times. In addition, some people do not enter the labor force directly after they finish school. Some delay entering the labor force by traveling. Young people from Australia and New Zealand, for example, regularly "trek" around the world before settling to work back home. Others do not enter the labor force because they cannot find work. Still others are at home with small children.

Another factor here can be service in the military. When the draft was used to fill the ranks, military service competed with employment for young workers' time. Today military service is an intentional form of work. When young workers leave the military, as when they finish their schooling, they may not be absorbed immediately into the labor force (Mare, Winship, & Kubitschek, 1984). The transition is neither automatic nor necessarily smooth.

How does the transition to adult work take place? The following three patterns in the transition to adult work have been identified.

1. *Straight pattern*. Those who make the transition with little or no difficulty have qualifications that employers seek and also have family support to draw on.

2. *Interrupted pattern*. Those who are unable or unwilling to move directly from school to work have not acquired the necessary credentials, because they are undergoing emotional turmoil or are confused about their aims and goals. They need time to sort out their feelings, conflicts, and goals.

3. *Disturbed pattern*. Those who are poorly prepared, alienated, or of minority status, or those who have police records are not acceptable to most employers and so find getting and holding a job unrewarding and frustrating. As an alternative, this group often drifts into illicit activities (Ginzberg, 1981, p. 72).

The phase of transition from youth to adulthood is one of the major turning points in the life of the individual. It typically contains several important life events: the end of schooling, first real job, and marriage. Several writers (Elder, 1974, 1978; Neugarten, Moore, & Lowe, 1965) have noted "normal" or "appropriate" times when these events take place. There is also a "normal" ordering of such events, with schooling to be completed before marriage.

For white males with the same level of schooling, nonnormative ordering (such as early or late marriage or marriage before the completion of schooling) is associated with lower earnings at later career stages (Hogan, 1980). Unfortunately, as increasing numbers of men extend their education and attend college, graduate, and professional schools, there will be increasing instances of nonnormative ordering, because pressure to marry also increases with age. Those who marry before completing school, at whatever level, earn less over their lifetime than those who complete a degree first.

The importance of an orderly transition is also applicable to women. In our society, most adult women work at some time in their lives, but the life event of having children is still very important. The timing of childbearing is thus a problem. Having children at a young age is detrimental to the transition to adult work both because it is viewed as nonnormative and because of the absence of child-care facilities. Having children later is more "normal," but it interrupts career progress.

So far, we have considered the human-capital side of the transition phase: the accumulation of knowledge and experience. Thus an important element is missing from these conclusions: the labor market, or the number and distribution of jobs for the cohort of individuals going into the labor force. If there are no jobs, the process may be disturbed and disorderly. The transition to adult work thus depends on a mix of human-capital and labor-market factors.

Adult Workers

The transition to adult work does not mean that age becomes meaningless. On the contrary, adult workers are differentially located in the labor force by age, and hiring and promotion decisions also seem to be affected by the age of adult workers. In addition, age has somewhat different implications for women than for men.

Distribution in the Labor Force

A study by Kaufman and Spilerman (1982) gives us a more precise idea of the types of work adults are likely to have at different phases of adulthood. These researchers were intrigued by the idea that some jobs are more easily performed by younger workers. Other jobs require long training and thus would be staffed by older workers. Kaufman and Spilerman (1982, p. 833) identified the following five types of occupational-age distributions:

1. Occupations that are heavily represented by younger adult workers include entry-level positions and jobs that are related to new technologies.

2. Occupations in which middle-aged workers are concentrated include the senior positions in job sequences (supervisors, foremen, and managers).

3. Occupations with high concentrations of adult workers are primarily those that allow workers

flexibility in setting their rates of work and in scheduling their hours. Contracting—that is, shrinking—types of occupations also fall into this category.

4. Occupations with uniform age distributions or relatively equal numbers of people in different age groups, such as the professions and craft occupations, usually have longer tenure, often spanning most of an individual's working life.

5. Occupations that have U-shaped age distributions—that is, they are densely populated by both younger and older people but have few middle-aged workers—have jobs that are less desirable and which offer poor advancement.

Kaufman and Spilerman (1982) present data for males older than 17; the data were collected in the 1970 U.S. census and by and large confirm the patterns just described.

Occupations in which younger adult workers are overrepresented include a cluster that involves heavy physical labor, such as electrical line workers, stock handlers, and warehouse persons. Another cluster comprises entry-level occupations that could lead to advancement, such as assemblers, bank tellers, and drafters. Police officers also were found in the younger set of occupations. Computer repair persons and programmers tend to be younger, demonstrating the effects of working with new technology.

Middle-aged occupations were dominated by occupations with supervisory and middle-level tasks—school administrators, sales managers, vocational counselors. These occupations are reached by promotion, with entry credential and retirement requirements. Airline pilots were also a middle-aged occupational group, because long training is required and health and retirement policies restrict the number of older workers.

Occupations with concentrations of older workers included those involving self-employment, such as barbers, tailors, and taxi drivers. Occupations that permit flexible time schedules are also in this category, such as real estate salespeople, cleaners, and guards and watchmen. Railroad and apparel workers are also found in this category, because these industries have suffered declining employment, and seniority rules protect the older workers.

The uniform, or flat, age distributions were found among craft occupations, such as carpenters, electricians, and typesetters. The "free" professions, such as dentists, doctors, and lawyers, also had flat age distributions, with some slight overrepresentation of older workers because of the physical ease of the work and the ability to be self-employed. Younger workers were somewhat underrepresented because of the training requirements.

The U-shaped distribution was found in such occupations as food-service workers, elevator operators, gardeners, and counter clerks. Pay in these occupations is low, and there are really no promotional prospects. Thus they tend to be filled mostly by those with reduced prospects elsewhere: the youngest and oldest workers.

Age and Unemployment. Although it would appear from the preceding list that there are occupational advantages to being middle-aged, it is unfortunately true that adults who become unemployed face more difficulty than other groups of workers in finding subsequent work (Osterman, 1988). The fact of being laid off is a shock in and of itself; the inability to find new work compounds the problem. Such layoffs are now rather commonplace among middle-level and even higher-level managers as organizations "downsize," or become smaller. Even supposedly secure public-sector, civil-service jobs are affected these days by layoffs and staff reductions.

This matter of downsizing and layoffs demonstrates that there are important industry effects in the age distribution for occupations (Kaufman & Spilerman, 1982). Industries that are contracting in size typically reduce their personnel through layoffs in reverse order of seniority—that is, last hired, first fired. Those who remain tend to be older and thus skew the age distribution. Those who leave voluntarily also tend to be younger workers, who have more appeal in the external job market and thus an easier time finding a better job. In contrast, expanding industries hire young workers. If the expanding industry is heavily dependent on new technology, then new hires are even more likely to be young and recently trained (see also Simpson, Simpson, Evers, & Poss, 1982).

Policy Implications. In the 1980s, many industries contracted in an attempt to cope with reduced profits or to become more competitive in the international marketplace. Large numbers of middle-level (usually middle-aged) workers were laid off. Many had a hard time finding work equivalent to their former jobs, because in a time of high unemployment they had trouble competing with the younger, more recently trained workers. The economic recession of the early 1990s exacerbated the problem. The scope and prevalence of the problem is viewed by many as evidence of widespread age discrimination (Winerip, 1990).

The Age Discrimination in Employment Act, originally enacted in 1967, was amended in 1986. This legislation did not do much for displaced middle-aged workers, but it reduced or eliminated mandatory retirement, such as some organizations' rules that people automatically retire at 60 or 65. (Now university and college faculties are the only occupations in which mandatory retirement is permitted.) The result of the new rules has been an increase in the number of employed older workers and a reduction in the numbers of occupations that fall into Kaufman and Spilerman's old-age and U-shaped occupational categories.

Ironically, the ban on mandatory retirement has broadened opportunities for older workers but reduced them for the middle-aged. Aging workers at middle to upper levels in organizations now tend to stay in their jobs longer, thus expanding the number of occupations with a relatively uniform age distribution. At the same time, aging workers hold onto jobs into which middle-aged workers would normally be advancing. Thus the major effects of an altered retirement policy are felt by those in the middle-aged category.

This particular situation is just about to be critical for the baby-boom generation. In the years to come, the large size of this cohort will conflict with the occupational longevity of older workers; as a result, promotion will become increasingly unlikely for an increasing proportion of the cohort. We can also expect a larger number of middle-aged people in middle-level positions to be laid off as many organizations continue to downsize, particularly in their middle ranks.

Gender and Age. The studies we have been examining have focused on the age dimension and male workers. There is a paucity of research on female workers and the age dimension. The research that is available suggests that age may well have different effects on women's careers than on men's (Markson, 1986). One study found that women's job mobility increased with age, which is certainly not the case for men. Perhaps employers, particularly in female-dominated occupations, consider older women to be more stable employees (Felmlee, 1984).

In their childbearing years, working women may experience severe role overload. Those who stay home to care for children instead of taking a job face the problem of reentry into the labor force once they reach their late 30s and early 40s. Reentry is a problem-laden process. Their job skills may not have been used or they may have become outmoded; the women may have developed strong self-concepts as housewives and mothers and not as workers; and they may have strained relationships with husbands and children who do not support reentry into the labor force (Hood, 1983; Shaw, 1983,1985). Some women face the same types of problems because of divorce, separation, or widowhood. For working women who are not married, reentry would not be an issue, because of continual employment through their middle years.

Older Workers

The dividing line between adult workers and "older workers" is hard to distinguish. We may define those workers in their mid-60s and above as "old" (Parnes, 1981), but keep in mind that the transition to older worker does not take place overnight. As with the transition from young worker to adult worker, the transition from adult worker to older worker can take place over a rather long span of years. Otherwise, the issues that face older workers are very different from those that face younger workers. The differences are based on societal views of older people in general, corporate and governmental policies regarding mandatory retirement, and corporate and governmental policies regarding support for retired persons.

In this section we will examine older workers and consider the transition to retirement. We will not deal extensively with retired people. Technically, they are out of the labor force and thus not within the scope of this book. More practically, the amount of literature on the elderly in general is vast. We must therefore focus on how the age dimension impinges on older workers and on how work impinges on aging. By necessity, this topic is intertwined with retirement issues, as well as with death and bereavement.

Although retirement is now essentially voluntary, the average age of retirement has dropped. The expansion of public and private pension programs has increased the likelihood of early retirement for men less than 65 (DeViney & O'Rand, 1988). Until World War II, retirement occurred only if forced because of ill health or if a person had substantial private wealth (Parker, 1982, pp. 20-28). Today, those who retire not only have a better standard of living than their predecessors, but also are much healthier. There is also a noticeable trend among older people toward a more youthful outlook on life and more youthful behavior (Parker, 1982).

These positive developments are countered by a series of more negative factors. People who have youthful vitality often want to stay on the job longer, leading to pressures to raise the age of retirement or to eliminate or modify retirement policies. Economic pressures are in the reverse direction, as employers and unions seek to bring younger, lower-paid workers into the labor force (Pampel & Weiss, 1983). The results are conflicts of interest between younger and older workers. Younger workers resent having fewer promotion opportunities and paying for the older workers through increasing social security taxes. Older workers resent being relegated to nonfunctional roles or forced to make way for younger workers.

Prejudice and discrimination against older workers is a real problem. Parker (1982) notes, "What we are up against is one aspect of ageism: the systematic stereotyping of, and discrimination against, people simply because they are old, just as racism and sexism accomplish this with skin color and gender" (p. 24). Our society devalues the past, and age has low status—a situation not found, for example, in Asian societies such as China and Japan. Parker also notes that retirement has no significant social definition. Working is valued; not working is not. In addition, retirement is also viewed in terms of declining physical and mental prowess and impending death—all highly negative conditions.

Further evidence about older workers is available through the National Longitudinal Surveys (NLS), which have been examining several samples of men and women of different ages over time (Parnes, 1981). (Many of the empirical studies of women workers discussed in the last chapter were based on NLS data.) Beginning in 1966, a panel of U.S. men 45 to 59 years old were studied over a 10-year period. The results present a different picture than that drawn by Parker, primarily because most of the men in the NLS were still employed.

The most significant event that took place over the 10-year period was retirement, particularly among the oldest members of the panel of men. For those who remained in the labor force, the picture was actually quite bright. Earnings were higher in 1976 than in 1966 for both wage and salary earners. The only decline in earnings was for men who went into postretirement kinds of work. The workers remaining in the labor force also reported high levels of job satisfaction (Parnes, 1981, pp. 32-34; see also Loscocco & Kalleberg, 1988). It would seem, then, that older workers with good jobs who continue working are economically rewarded, experience feelings of success, and are quite satisfied with their work.

Older workers are little different than younger workers in these matters, with one major exception: For older workers, health is a very salient factor (Mutran & Reitzes, 1989). Continued labor-force participation is related to good health and positive work experiences. Of course, it also is related (as is the case for workers of all ages) to the availability of work.

The key issue for older workers is really retirement. There is both a "push" and a "pull" toward retirement (Hardy, 1982; Ward, 1984). The push comes from mandatory-retirement requirements and health problems, while the pull comes from pension plans that make retirement affordable and attractive. Men whose spouses are also eligible for retirement feel an additional pull. Another form of pull comes from jobs that are experienced as boring and alienating. For most people, several factors operate. If a person is becoming bored with work and a good retirement program is available, then retirement is likely.

People whose work is a central life interest have a pull against retirement. For example, female and male physicians have difficulty in planning for retirement, because they put a high value on being active and being dedicated to their profession (Quadagno, 1978). In 1990, *Science* (a publication of the American Association for the Advancement of Science) reported the case of a University of California biochemist who was fighting mandatory retirement ("News and Comment," 1990). This scientist is deeply involved with his work and wants to continue. Mandatory retirement is attractive from the university's point of view, because the costs of a new assistant professor are much less than that of a tenured professor, even if he is distinguished. For the individual involved, the issue is not cost.

A sizable minority of officially retired workers continue to work, usually on a part-time basis (Parker, 1982). Up to one third of all male retirees work, even if the work is downwardly mobile. The distribution of these older workers is much like that of younger workers, with the exception that there heavy manual labor is less likely.

Those who liked their work before retirement are those who are most likely to seek and obtain postretirement work. For example, retired executives frequently work as part-time consultants to their former employers or other companies. Other retirees write memoirs. Satisfaction with jobs entered after retirement is based on the same factors associated with satisfaction in preretirement work (Fontana & Frey, 1990).

Inasmuch as those who like their work tend to have higher-status occupations, the relationship between the vertical dimension of work and the age dimension continues past retirement. Indeed, the determinants of income after retirement were the same as those before retirement: education, occupation, and marital status (Henretta & Campbell, 1976). The nature of people's work is a dominant influence on the nature of their retirement years.

For people who do not have retirement programs, this relationship still prevails in a cruel way. People working in the peripheral sector receive low pay and poor benefits. This same inequity exists as they get old. People who were poor when they were working are

even poorer when retired. Work in peripheral sectors thus continues to have a negative effect even into old age.

Conclusions

The relationship between age and work is direct in that there are
"normal" ages at which people do and do not work. The issue
becomes more complex when we consider the consequences of the
kinds of work that young people do, the ways in which people of
different ages react to their work, the variations in the distributions of adult workers among various occupations and labor-force
sectors, and the discrimination and prejudice that may affect
workers because of their age.

There have been some obvious intersections between this chapter and earlier chapters. In Chapter 3, for example, we considered
socialization for work. Skills and values are transmitted to youths,
with the process continuing through the lifetime. In Western
societies, this activity is formalized in schooling, which is the
dominant activity of most youths. For the young, much of life is
socialization for work. There are also significant interactions
between age and the vertical and horizontal dimensions. Age and
gender also clearly interact, in the sense that the work activities
of women of childbearing age may be affected by their role. None
of the dimensions we are considering offers a single explanation
of work or of people in their work. This will continue to be the case
as we add race, religion, and ethnicity to the mix.

▬▬▬ APPLICATION

Move Over Yuppies—Here Come the Yiffies

The types of work people pursue, as well as their reactions to this
work, tend to vary with age. For example, older workers tend to
be more satisfied with their work than are younger workers; jobs

organized around new technologies tend to be populated by younger workers. And so on. However, the association between age and work does not exist in a vacuum. Some aspects of the relationship between age and work are critically dependent on a third factor: demographics. As was described in Chapter 4, workers who are members of the baby-boom generation are finding it difficult to ascend the vertical dimension, largely because of the number of people competing for jobs in their age range. The amounts and varieties of work available to those in any particular age group are likely to vary as a function of the cohort's size.

The baby-boom generation is a demographic phenomenon that has caught the attention of many social observers. Less attention has been paid to a newer demographic trend: the emergence of the "baby-bust" generation. The term *baby bust* has been applied to describe the decline in birth rates that began in the mid-1960s and lasted throughout most of the 1970s. The birth rate in the United States during the period 1972 to 1979 was 3.5 million per year, down from 4 million per year for the decade ending in 1964 (Wendling, 1988). As of 1995, most baby busters will be in or entering their 20s. Perhaps you are among their ranks.

Those who have tried to characterize baby busters have had only limited success. Some call them "yiffies" (an acronym for young, individualistic, freedom-minded, and few) (Solomon, 1992). Yiffies have been described as upbeat and as valuing a rich family and spiritual life over material rewards (Deutschman, 1992). Others report that the baby-bust generation places as much if not more emphasis on financial success as preceding generations (Wendling, 1988). All we can really say for sure is that baby busters are relatively young and that there are relatively few of them. Perhaps Solomon (1992) came closest to the mark when she concluded that, "just as the baby boomers . . . can't be categorized or managed as a homogeneous group, neither can the baby busters" (p. 59).

Baby busters do have one thing in common: They are all entering the world of work in the same demographic context. Not only will they share many of the experiences common to all young workers, but also they will have a variety of work-related experiences unique to their demographic category. For instance, they are unlikely to suffer the high levels of involuntary unemployment typical of young workers in general. Because of their relatively small numbers, a labor shortage is practically inevitable as the yiffies reach working age. This shortage will be especially acute where entry-level jobs are concerned. Wendling (1988) predicts that the number of potential new entrants into the labor force (people between the ages of 18 and 24) will be 22.7 million in 1995, a drop of 7 million from the 1980 figure of 29.7 million. Those who recruit new employees for businesses foresee a period of intense competition among firms for recruits from this shrinking pool of labor (Davids, 1988).

It may seem ludicrous to suggest low levels of unemployment given the economic conditions of the early 1990s. It is true that many industries have been in a period of retrenchment or downsizing. However, the recent recession that has spurred this retrenchment may have hidden what the *Economist* insists is a "demographic time bomb" ("Gone Fishing," 1990, p. 61). The dwindling number of labor-force entrants will almost surely mean that baby busters will be highly sought after by employers in years to come. As a result, members of the baby-bust generation can expect aggressive recruitment and retainment tactics from certain potential employers. More specifically, specialized high-technology and service industries will be in heated competition to obtain and retain young talent. Young workers with the appropriate technological training may well find themselves being wooed by many potential employers, each offering attractive incentives.

Such aggressive recruitment strategies are already being practiced in some parts of the world. For example, Japanese firms are finding it extremely difficult to find qualified young workers to fill entry-level positions. There are 2.7 white-collar job vacancies for every applicant in Japan (Guest, 1992). At one point, on-campus recruiting became so intense in Japan that universities forced businesses to refrain from recruiting students until the summer before a student's senior year. There have even been cases of "kosoku"—an unfortunate form of recruiting in which young graduates are lured to hot-springs resorts and then coerced into signing employment contracts ("Gone Fishing," 1990).

Baby busters in the United States may not experience such extreme forms of recruitment. Nevertheless, it is likely that there will be work available to the vast majority of yiffies in the coming years. Of course, the greatest demand for labor will come from particular industries and will occur at entry levels. Plenty of yuppies remain to compete among themselves for middle- and upper-level positions. Thus, although they may have little difficulty finding work, there is some question whether the baby busters will enjoy the promotional opportunities their predecessors enjoyed.

Employers may be forced to find alternatives to advancement and salary increases as means of rewarding younger workers. For example, new types of benefits such as study scholarships may be substituted for the traditional raise or promotion. To the extent that traditional promotional opportunities are blocked, work may take on a new (that is, noneconomic) meaning for the baby-bust generation.

Once again we can see how the demographic context helps to inform us about the relationship between work and age. The experiences of the baby-bust generation will be shaped not only by its age, but also by the size of both its own and the preceding age cohorts.

■■■■ SUGGESTED READINGS

A complete bibliographical entry for each work cited here can be found in the reference section at the back of this book.

Most analyses of age and work focus on older workers and retirement. A welcome exception here is Ginzberg, *The School/Work Nexus* (1981).

The most careful study of a panel of men moving through middle to older age in relation to work is Parnes (Ed.), *Work and Retirement* (1981).

Matilda White Riley is a leading student of older people. She herself is now in her 80s and is vigorously pursuing her research on a full-time basis. Her perspective on age, stratification, and work is exemplified by Riley, Johnson, and Fonner (Eds.), *Aging and Society. Volume 3: A Sociology of Age Stratification* (1972).

Ward, *The Aging Experience* (1984), gives a balanced perspective on the aging process and contains a good bibliography.

8   Race, Religion, and Ethnicity

Race, religion, and ethnicity are touchy subjects. However you deal with them, you are bound to step on someone's feelings and beliefs. If you avoid the ugly labels and stark realities, then the discussion is bland and hollow. If you attach racial, religious, or ethnic adjectives to particular forms of work—"black athlete," "Jewish lawyer," "Mexican migrant worker"—you can sound like and actually be a bigot. At the same time, it is foolish to ignore the fact that members of various racial, religious, and ethnic groups are over- and underrepresented across the spectrum of work.

We are dealing here with a topic of intense feeling. The Los Angeles riots of 1992 were about more than the acquittal verdict in the first trial of white police officers accused of beating black motorist Rodney King. Rather, the riots reflected a deep and abiding sense of injustice and oppression that stemmed from perceived discrimination. That discrimination extends into the work world.

We are also dealing with an issue whose face changes rapidly and has been changing, I hope, for the better. In 1992, at my university, the University at Albany (New York), graduation ceremonies included a series of academic and leadership honors, fully half of which went to African-American and Latino students. The very next week I returned to my alma mater, Denison University (Granville, Ohio), for a class reunion—my first after 36 years. My classmates were uniformly white, Anglo-Saxon, and Protestant (the proverbial WASPs) and went into work that was much the same, such as banking. Thankfully for Denison, and probably for banking, times have changed. Managerial and professional work is no longer a WASP male bastion.

Change has also taken place in the names used to designate various minority groups. Today, *African-American* is preferred by many over the noun and adjectival use of "black," and *Latino* is preferred by some to "Hispanic." At the same time, we have echoes of the past in the names of such esteemed organizations as the United Negro College Fund and the National Association for the Advancement of Colored People and university departments such as those of Chicano Studies. In honor of the fact that research in this area has been done in different eras, I will use the terms used when the research was done as we examine the interstices between work and race, religion, and ethnicity.

Race, religion, and ethnicity intersect with the aspects of work that we have already considered. For example, in terms of individual reactions to work, it has been found that blacks experience lower levels of workplace satisfaction than whites (Tuch & Martin, 1991); the basis for this difference is in the objective job rewards received. In the last chapter, Table 7.1 showed the ways in which age and race interacted in terms of unemployment rates. We learned in Chapter 5 that the peripheral sectors of the horizontal dimension are where many immigrants are employed. Race can have an even stronger influence on work than the vertical dimension, which Chapter 4 showed to be critically important. For example, the unemployment experience of whites and nonwhites is quite similar among people with low tenure in their work; but when cutbacks reach those who have more seniority, nonwhites are more likely to be laid off than whites (DiPrete, 1981). This difference may result from the concentration of nonwhite workers in industries that are particularly sensitive to economic downturns. Whatever the mechanism, consideration of race is significant to our understanding of the sociology of work.

It is easier to see that race, religion, and ethnicity affect people's work experience than to define what each term is by itself. Ethnicity can involve religious affiliation as well as national origins. Race can be used in broad categories (e.g., white versus nonwhite) as well as in more rigorous categories. In a similar manner, religion can be used broadly (e.g., Judeo-Christian versus Islamic) or more narrowly (e.g., Protestant versus Catholic).

So how do we define race, religion, and ethnicity? They will be treated here in terms of their social definitions. By this I mean that if a people is defined by others, by itself, or both in terms of its race, religion, or ethnic origin, then it constitutes an identified minority group.

Horizontal Dimension

As noted earlier, change is a key factor in any discussion of how work is linked to race, religion, and ethnicity. The same is true of the horizontal dimension, which pinpoints the labor-market segments in which people work. For example, in the American South, a huge majority of blacks once performed agricultural work, both as slaves and as emancipated people. There has since been a dramatic shift away from agricultural work, however (Coleman & Hall, 1979; Wadley & Lee, 1974). It is partially linked to black migration to the North, but it is more strongly linked to changing employment patterns in the South itself. There has been a much wider distribution of blacks in all sectors of the labor force in the South (Tsonc, 1974), so much so that some observers began to view the South as the place of greatest opportunity for blacks (Rhee, 1974). In part, the shift resulted from new forms of industry moving to the South. For example, the extension of the tourist industry to Hilton Head Island, South Carolina, altered the work of the Gullah blacks who inhabited the island and who had led independent, agriculturally based lives. As the resort industry grew, increasing numbers of native blacks took low-skill jobs (chambermaids and caddies) at the resort. Despite the low wages, resort work is seen as a positive alternative to work in the fields (Thomas, 1980).

Agricultural work remains important, especially for new immigrants. Jamaican migrant farm workers, for example, perceive their work as a possible source of upward mobility for themselves and their children (Foner & Napolic, 1978); American-born black migrant farm workers have no such perception. An analysis of undocumented Mexican workers in South Texas found that the typical migrant first works on a farm or ranch and then moves into an urban area (Jones, 1984).

Agricultural work has been the point of entry for many immigrants throughout U.S. history. Indeed, it is how Northern and Western European immigrants who came to the United States in the early 1800s made a living. For example, Scandinavian and German immigrants moved to settle the rich farmlands of the Midwest.

A major change took place after 1880. The later migrants from Southern, Central, and Eastern Europe more typically moved to the cities, where industrial jobs were located. In a major study of these later immigrants and of black migrants to urban areas, Stanley Lieberson (1980) found that neither group had especially desirable jobs. But the European immigrants tended to have jobs in the manufacturing sector, while blacks were concentrated in service jobs.

Research dealing with race, religion, and ethnicity and the horizontal dimension in the late 20th century has been concentrated in the areas of dual labor markets and labor-market sectors. The dual-labor-market perspective has yielded the somewhat surprising finding that there are not large differences in racial representation in the core and peripheral markets (Beck, Horan, & Tolbert, 1978, 1980; Tolbert, Horan, & Beck, 1980; Zucker & Rosenstein, 1981). In other words, the ratios of blacks and whites employed in the two markets are very similar.

At the same time, individuals' positions in these dual labor markets can vary with race. Disadvantaged groups are disadvantaged in both core and peripheral sectors. An analysis of black industrial workers revealed that they were hurt disproportionately when manufacturing operations were moved overseas (to so-called runaway shops), were relocated in the United States, or were automated (Bonacich, 1976). However, black men are more disadvantaged in terms of pay in the peripheral sector than they are in the core sector (Daymont, 1980). For example, the pay differential between white and black taxi drivers is greater than the pay differential between white and black schoolteachers.

A clearer picture of horizontal differentiation emerges when we consider labor-market sectors. For example, government employment offers greater opportunities for black workers than the transportation industry does (Kaufman & Daymont, 1981). More black lawyers are found in public-sector employment than in the private sector (Cappell, 1990). It also appears (although I can cite no research to back up my statement) that the entertainment industry offers relatively favorable opportunities for blacks.

Other ethnic, religious, and racial groups also experience inter-sector occupational differences. Lieberson (1980, p. 2) notes that every president of the United States thus far has been of old (Northern and Western) European origins. John Kennedy, a Roman Catholic, faced extreme pressure when he ran for president in 1960. Lieberson also found that Poles and Italians are dramatically underrepresented as board members or officers in large corporations in the Chicago area in comparison with their proportion in that metropolitan area's population. He notes that Roman Catholics and Jews (even more so than Roman Catholics) are seldom found as senior officers in banking.

Labor-market sectors thus are differentiated in terms of their racial, religious, and ethnic composition. It is also critical to note that the distribution of people within sectors is uneven, with minority groups subject to discrimination and segregation and thus differential placement on the vertical dimension (Kaufman, 1983).

Vertical Dimension

The intersection between the vertical dimension and race, religion, and ethnicity is evident to the most casual observer. Membership in a minority group is often clearly associated with differences in social status, privilege, and opportunity.

Perhaps because the problem is so visible, the bulk of the research on race, religion, and ethnicity has dealt with the vertical dimension. Furthermore, the bulk of the literature in the last three decades deals with blacks, with lesser attention paid to other racial and ethnic groups. Earlier, because of Nazism, the focus was on Jewish people and work. These and other groups, despite their differences, are alike in the fact that they have experienced discrimination in the work setting.

Discrimination

Any consideration of the intersection between racial, religious, and ethnic factors and the vertical dimension must begin with the issue of discrimination. *Discrimination* may be defined as long-lasting inequality in well-being among individuals based on their "color, gender, or ethnic ties. . . . It can also be defined as differences in pay or wage rates for equally productive groups" (Cain, 1984, p. 2). We are concerned with more than economic factors and thus would add differences in power and authority and other forms of work rewards such as satisfaction into the definition.

Such discrimination is systematically found in analyses of how race, religion, and ethnicity affect socioeconomic opportunity. In their major study of changes in socioeconomic opportunity between 1962 and 1972, Hauser and Featherman (1977, pp. 134-135) report that discriminatory practices remained as important barriers in that decade, even though there were slight improvements for blacks.

An examination of median earnings for year-round, full-time workers finds similar trends (Cain, 1984). The black-white earnings ratio for men has shifted from .45 in 1939 to .73 in 1982 (black men earn 73% of that earned by white men). There was a nearly identical earnings ratio for Hispanic men in 1982, the only year for which data are available. The earnings ratio for women shifted even more dramatically. In 1939 the black-white ratio for women was .38; it changed to .94 in 1982. The near parity between black and white women is offset, of course, by the fact that white women earn just 59% of what men earn. The black women's gain has only caught them up with white women. Hispanic women earn 86% of what white women earn.

Although these figures mean that equally productive men and women are discriminated against in terms of their pay (Cain, 1984), they also show that change is taking place. Aggregate occupational inequality has declined each decade from 1940 to 1980 (Fosset, Galle, & Burr, 1989). Despite the decline, of course, discrimination remains in effect.

Several factors are operative here. One study suggests that blacks are systematically excluded from higher-paying occupations; this, of course, lowers their average earnings (Snyder &

Hudis, 1976). Some theorists have argued that the earnings gap can be explained in terms of differences in human capital, such as number of years of schooling or years of experience; or in geographical location, such as South versus non-South. However, these explanations are inadequate. In fact, it appears that blacks receive fewer rewards for their educational attainments than do whites (Hanushek, 1982). If these analyses are correct, then access to both occupations and earnings within occupations are subject to discrimination.

Sources and Causes of Discrimination. Any explanation of racial, religious, and ethnic discrimination must explore *organizational* or *institutional discrimination.* Alvarez (1979) defines it as

> a set of social processes through which organizational decision making, either implicitly or explicitly, results in a clearly identifiable population receiving fewer psychic, social, or material rewards per quantitative and/or qualitative unit of performance than a clearly identifiable comparison population within the same organizational constraints. (p. 2)

Much institutional discrimination can be attributed to employers seeking lower costs. Some analysts argue that the problem is unique to capitalists seeking cheap labor both domestically and overseas (Bonacich, 1972, 1976). I would counter that this sort of exploitation occurs in noncapitalist systems as well, because any organization would seek cheap labor, regardless of its race or ethnicity or its domestic or overseas location. Racial, religious, and ethnic minorities that have few alternatives will work for lower wages (Marks, 1981; Wright & Perrone, 1977). This pattern is found today in the case of Palestinians in Israel and Vietnamese in the United States.

While the practices of organizational owners and managers have contributed to discrimination, so too have the activities of unions. European immigrants at the turn of the 20th century had a difficult time gaining access to the craft unions (Lieberson, 1980). For blacks the situation was even worse. Exclusion from craft unions meant exclusion from craft jobs. Even today, craft unions (plumbers, electricians, and so on) appear to discriminate against black workers who seek entry into the union (Leigh, 1978). However, industrial unions (auto workers, truck drivers, and so on) appear not to so discriminate and do not exclude a disproportionate number of black men from union coverage. Once they get into a union, minority members do not experience as much discrimination as their nonunion counterparts, because unions tend to have agreements with employers about wages, seniority, and working conditions. It should be noted that employment in the public sector typically involves union membership, which may be one reason that its employees more accurately reflect the racial and ethnic makeup of the local community.

Some research has found that geographical location is also important in regard to discrimination. For example, organizations that rely on local community residents as their customers, such as banks, will be more responsive to local community characteristics than organizations that do not serve the local area (Szafran, 1984). They hire more minority workers.

Discrimination is not purely institutional. Workers in general seek to maximize their own positions and use discrimination as a means to keep their incomes and benefits higher than those of the groups against which they discriminate. Exactly who gains from discriminatory practices is the subject of a lively and as yet inconclusive debate (see Beck, 1980, for a review of this literature). The radical interpretation is that racism is supported by capitalists who stand to gain by fractionalizing the working class, pitting one group against another, and that both whites and blacks suffer economically because of racism (Reich, 1971; Szymanski, 1976). Other data suggest that white workers actually do gain by having blacks at the economic periphery (Beck, 1980). What is lost in some of this debate is that blacks systematically lose, whether or not white workers gain.

In addition to purely economic factors there are also cultural or value explanations that must be considered. Beliefs about the inferiority or superiority of particular racial, religious, and ethnic groups contribute to discriminatory practices (Christiansen, 1979). Although it is difficult to disentangle the economic factors from the noneconomic, it would appear that economic factors are at the root of discrimination.

Shifting Patterns of Discrimination. Not so long ago, minority-group status was found to be negatively related to promotion in the military. Blacks consistently faced longer times for rank promotions even when such objective criteria as civilian education, scores on the Armed Forces Qualifications Test (AFQT), and occupational type were controlled (Butler, 1976; Nordlie, 1979). The U.S. Army revised its affirmative-action plan, partially on the basis of findings such as these. Today the military is far less blatant in its discriminatory practices.

Discrimination is also in flux in other areas of society. Wilson (1978) has argued, and Hout (1984) has demonstrated, that race is becoming less significant than class factors in the employment patterns of blacks. Prior to the 1960s, a preponderance of blacks were in lower social classes. Today, however, blacks have reached the middle class and in some cases the upper class. Apparently, gains in black employment and status have created more class differences among this group than existed before the 1960s (Hout, 1984; Wilson, 1978). To a large extent, black gains can be attributed to the growth of public-sector employment. As discriminatory practices have abated, there have been significant black gains.

While race may be declining in importance, the pattern is unclear in regard to ethnicity. Some theorists argue that in recent years we have become less likely to identify whites by their ethnic background; others are not so sure (Alba, 1990; Hirschman, 1991). However, even within the public sector, there is evidence that full equality has not been achieved. Significant differences still exist in occupational level and pay between Mexican-Americans and Anglos (Taylor & Shields, 1984).

Migration and Immigration

Today, sizable numbers of professionals, technicians, and craftspeople are entering the United States from nations such as India, South Korea, Taiwan, and the Philippines; this has been described as a Third World "brain drain." Many of these workers enter the primary labor market (Portes & Manning, 1985). Such has not always been the case, however. Immigrants—especially from minority groups—

have typically entered the labor force at the bottom of the occupational ladder.

As Lieberson (1980) points out, new immigrants tend to find occupational niches:

> As for special niches, it is clear that most racial and ethnic groups tend to develop concentrations in certain jobs [that] either reflect some distinctive cultural characteristics, special skills initially held by some members, or the opportunity structure at the time of their arrival. In 1950 among the foreign-born men of different origins there were many such examples: 3.9 percent of Italians in the civilian labor force were barbers, eight times the level for all white men; 2.5 percent of the Irish were policemen or firemen, three times the rate for all white men; more than 2 percent of Scottish immigrants were accountants, about two and one-half times the level for whites; 9.4 percent of Swedish immigrants were carpenters, nearly four times the national level; 14.8 percent of Greek immigrant men ran eating and drinking establishments, 29 times the national level; and 3.3 percent of Russian immigrant men were tailors or furriers, 17 times the rate for all white men. These concentrations are partially based on networks of ethnic contacts and experiences that in turn direct other compatriots in these directions. (p. 379)

This pattern is continuing with the arrival of Latin American and Southeast Asian immigrants, many of whom are finding niches in food-service and assembly work.

For American-born blacks migrating from the South to the North and West, the pattern has been quite different. True, the jobs they found were, like immigrants' jobs, at the bottom of the ladder—in sanitation, maintenance, personal services, and other service positions. But, according to Lieberson (1980), from the very outset of black migration to the North, blacks were excluded from work in the core sector, while European immigrants were able to gain access to manufacturing jobs in the core. The movement of sizable numbers of blacks to the North actually reduced the negative disposition that other whites had toward new European groups. The employment patterns were exacerbated by labor unions that feared economic competition and by residential segregation with its attendant differentiation in schooling. It would also appear that black migrants to the North were hampered by the poorer schooling they received in the South before migrating (Hogan & Pazul, 1982). For all of these reasons, blacks remain lower on the vertical dimension than do immigrant groups such as the Irish, Italians, and Swedes.

Lieberson's ideas seem to make sense, but some authors have found weaknesses. Steinberg (1983) suggests that the lumping together of European immigrants is a mistake, because immigrants from rural Italy differed greatly from urban Jewish immigrants from Eastern Europe. More important, Steinberg takes Lieberson to task for ignoring the almost 90% of blacks who lived in the South in 1880 and the 77% who lived there as late as 1940. Their current situation is not explained by competition with immigrants to the northern United States, according to Steinberg.

Lieberson (1980) contrasted the situation of black migrants with that of Asian immigrants of the same era. He notes that Asians did not pose economic threats to whites, except in the West where the response to Asians was severe and violent. In addition, Asian migration was essentially stopped by immigration laws. Many Asian immigrants stayed in the West and established niches in work such as truck farming. Lieberson also suggests that attitudes toward China and Japan may have been very different from attitudes toward Africa.

In recent years, the educational attainments of both native-born and migrant Asian-Americans have equaled or exceeded those of whites. Moreover, native-born Asian-Americans have achieved parity in income with whites (Hirschman & Wong, 1981). Newly arrived Asians, however, remain far behind, perhaps because of the concentration of immigrant Chinese and Filipinos in service and retail-trade jobs.

The experiences of Cuban immigrants are also quite different. During the 1950s through the 1970s, a large proportion of Cuban immigrants settled in ethnic enclaves, most notably in Miami, Florida. There they had their own labor markets and some insulation from competition with the dominant white labor market (Wilson & Martin, 1982; Wilson & Portes, 1980).

Such enclaves have been found among other large groups of minorities; they provide a cozy harbor for fellow immigrants' enterprises and support for one another. These enclaves were found in the past among Jews in Manhattan and Japanese on the West Coast (Portes & Manning, 1985). Today there is an important Korean enclave in Los Angeles; the community was brought into the public eye during the 1992 riots. Ethnic enclaves are not limited to the United States. In Australia, for example, groups that are not fluent in English also have formed enclaves (Evans, 1989).

Enclaves do not always protect their members from discrimination. In 1980, a huge influx of Cuban refugees reached Miami. The result was that negative stereotypes of Cubans began to circulate in the community (Portes, 1984). Competitive pressures forced many new immigrant Cubans into the broader labor market, where they were identified as ethnic, and hence disadvantaged, workers. At the same time, the enclaves remained in Miami (Portes & Jensen, 1989).

Means of Improving Socioeconomic Status

As you have just seen, many minority groups have experienced improvements in their occupational and socioeconomic status. The key appears to be education, although military service may also play a role.

Blacks who get a good education tend to increase their socioeconomic status above that of their families of origin. Blacks remain disadvantaged, however, because they cannot convert their schooling into higher-status occupations as readily as whites (Featherman & Hauser, 1976b, 1978; Stolzenberg, 1975). However, at the higher end of the vertical dimension, blacks are making gains. The higher the level of certification, the greater the returns on education. There is evidence to suggest that blacks who are intelligent and creative are "sponsored" within the educational system by both teachers and peers (Porter, 1974; Portes & Wilson, 1976).

For Hispanics, schooling and fluency in English are both part of their human capital. When Hispanic men speak English "very well" and have completed at least 12 years of school, their occupational achievement is close to that of white non-Hispanic men in the same geographical area (Stolzenberg, 1990).

The other way for racial and ethnic minorities to improve their socioeconomic status is service in the military. There minority group members can learn skills and behaviors that can be transferred to the civilian labor force. The evidence on this route is mixed, however. One study reports that among one set of Mexican-Americans and blacks studied, veterans generally had higher incomes than nonveterans by occupational category (Browning, Lopreato, & Polson, 1973). In contrast, another study found that the 1964 civilian earnings of former draftees were equal to or lower than those of nonveterans, that military service does not facilitate postservice economic achievement, and that the job training received in the military is not relevant to civilian jobs (Cutright, 1974). The discrepancies may result from the comparison of different groups. Draftees, of course, would be different from volunteers. Furthermore, both of these studies are based on rather dated samples of military personnel.

A more recent study found that volunteer military service was linked to positive financial gains for black and Hispanic personnel, particularly during their time in the service (Phillips, Andrisani, Daymont, & Gilroy, 1992). The gains diminished somewhat once the people retired from the service.

Structural Factors

Research on the vertical dimension and race, religion, and ethnicity increasingly reveals the importance of the structural aspect. In other words, the organizational context is a key factor in determining economic outcomes for nonwhites (Baron & Newman, 1990).

In general, the public sector has been found to have the most open and equal opportunity structure (DiPrete, 1987b; DiPrete & Soule, 1986). To be promoted in the public sector, however, it is vital to be in positions that are eligible to take examinations for advancement (Steinberg, Haignere, & Chertos, 1990). Minority workers face the risk of being caught in an affirmative-action labor market, which would render them unable to move into other positions in the larger organization (Durr, 1993). In this situation, a person might be able to move from the position of Affirmative Action Officer 1 to Affirmative Action Officer 2 but not be able to get out of the affirmative-action "loop."

Other structural factors relate to local economies. For example, minority opportunities are greatest in local economies that are growing rapidly and have a high percentage of union jobs (Stearns & Coleman, 1990). A study of 1,200 U.S. cities found that the level of Hispanic political representation and the size of the local public-sector employment system were also related to minority job success (Mladenka, 1989). These findings provide some cause for optimism, but it is still the case that ethnicity and race play roles in the distribution of jobs on the vertical dimension.

Interaction of Gender With Race, Religion, and Ethnicity

Race, religion, and ethnicity interact with gender with some strange twists and turns. For example, on average, black women earn less than white women or black or white men (Fox & Hesse-Biber, 1984). At the same time, among professional and technical workers and managers, black women have had somewhat higher levels of earnings than white women. This anomaly is explained in part by the prevalence of so many black women in nonelite positions where there are large earnings differentials between black and white women. There is also some evidence that black women professionals stay in the labor force more consistently than white women and over longer periods of time, which would give them more seniority and more opportunities for promotion (Wallace, 1980, p. 61).

In the professions and semiprofessions, black women are concentrated in teaching, social work, and nursing, just as with white women. At the same time, while approximately 40% of all professionals are women, black women have constituted more than half of all black professionals since 1940 (Fox & Hesse-Biber, 1984). Some authors have suggested that "loopholes" in racial discrimination have permitted black women to take advantage of educational opportunities and that black families may have encouraged their daughters, rather than their sons, to continue with their education.

There is also a rather interesting argument that black professional women enjoy a positive effect from the "double negative" of being both black and women (Epstein, 1973). The argument is that the two negatives cancel each other out: Being black negates the deficiencies attributed to white women professionals, such as seeking husbands in the professions or being more likely than men to leave the labor force. In addition, the black professional woman, being rather unique, may have a better bargaining position with organizations that want to appear open-minded (she fills the categories of both black and woman) and may have stronger motivations to succeed, given the reduced likelihood that her spouse will achieve high socioeconomic status. The idea that black women benefit from double negatives has been attacked in several studies. According to Fox and Hesse-Biber (1984), there are more obstacles than advantages in the educational system for black women; the concentration of black women in teaching, social work, and nursing hardly increases their bargaining power for more rewarding or better-paying work; and black women tend to have lower aspirations for professional work than do black men. Nonetheless, the anomalous pay differential between white and black women in the professions remains. The strongest explanation appears to be that black women's work histories are less interrupted than white women's. If black women are married to black men, their husbands are likely to be paid less than white men, and thus the continuous income is needed.

Black women have a long history of labor-force participation. In times of slavery, they were very much a part of the labor market. After slavery ended, black women continued to participate in the labor force because of economic pressures. As already mentioned, black women who are married to black men tend to need additional income because their husbands are likely to have low incomes. For black women who are not married or whose husbands are absent, work is necessary for self-maintenance and the care of children. The proportion of black families maintained by women is much higher (40.5%) than is the case for white families (11.6%) (U.S. Department of Labor, 1980).

Black women and female workers from other racial and ethnic groups tend to be concentrated in the same kinds of work as women in general, except that minority-group members tend to be on the lower end of the scale. The processes by which minority women attain positions and their related social and economic status are largely the same as for other groups in the labor force, with a couple of exceptions: Black women get more return for their education than black men (Treiman & Terrell, 1975b), and English language skills turn out to be more important than educational level for Hispanic women (as for Hispanic men), which is the key to mobility for other groups (Cooney & Ortiz, 1983).

Conclusions

This chapter is the last on the patterns of occupational distribution and the last of three dealing with matters that seem to determine occupational discrimination: gender; age; and race, religion, and ethnicity. We have not dealt with all types of workers who are subject to discrimination and prejudice. For example, we have not considered those who have physical or mental handicaps or those who have same-sex preferences. Hate and fear continue to face all groups that are identified as different.

Change was stressed in this chapter, as well as in Chapters 6 and 7, because the issues have been changing—albeit very slowly. The changes have largely resulted from governmental action, which in turn reflects public opinion and social movements. Government actions can be sweeping and horrifying, such as those in Germany that produced the Holocaust, but they also can be subtle and muted, like those enforcing affirmative-action regulations. Changes also occur as members of racial and ethnic groups move into areas of the vertical and horizontal dimensions that were formerly closed or seldom entered.

It is perhaps a dream that race, religion, and ethnicity, along with gender and age, will in the future make no difference in regard to work. There does seem to be movement toward that dream, but the movement is glacial, and it meets strong resistance. Much of the resistance comes from organizations—the subject of the next chapter—which are by nature highly resistant to change.

■■■ APPLICATION

When the Trouble Is in the "System"

Practically everyone has encountered discrimination in their lives. Perhaps it was something as simple as being excluded from a neighborhood club because you were "the new kid on the block." Perhaps it was something more serious, such as being turned down for a job because you did not "fit the applicant profile." Even if you cannot recall having been personally discriminated against, you are almost certain to have witnessed discriminatory behavior on the part of another. It is an unfortunate truism that overt discrimination is far from rare in our society. All of us can recognize such discrimination, even those of us who have not experienced it personally.

There exists another, often more subtle form of discrimination with which people are sometimes unfamiliar. Here I refer to the type of discrimination that is a built-in part of "the system," a form of discrimination that results from adherence to established policies and procedures that work to the disadvantage of one group relative to another. The "system" may be small (for example, a local public school) or large (for example, a national government). The discrimination may be intentional or unintentional. In any case, such "institutional discrimination" can be an insidious source of occupational disparities among people of different races, ethnicities, or religious affiliations.

Piven and Cloward (1989) offer a striking illustration of institutional discrimination in their analysis of Americans' voting patterns. These authors make a persuasive argument that the right to vote has been systematically obstructed for certain groups in the United States by voting requirements. For instance, at earlier stages in our history, poll taxes and literacy tests effectively prevented the poor and uneducated (that is, black) citizenry from casting ballots in important elections.

Piven and Cloward (1989) also argue that the logistics of voter registration currently make it difficult for the underprivileged to participate in the electoral process. For instance, many sites for voter registration have limited weekday hours. Piven and Cloward (1989) argue that these limitations make voter registration difficult for many working-class people who do not have the discretion to leave their hourly wage jobs, even for the time required to register to vote. Piven and Cloward note with irony that

> in the United States, the formal right [to vote] is virtually universal, a condition much celebrated in the political culture. . . . At the same time, the ability of large numbers of people to act on the right to the franchise is impeded by a series of procedural obstructions embedded in the voter registration process. Those obstructions are selective in that they are more likely to interfere with voting by the poor and unlettered than by the better off and educated. (Piven & Cloward, 1989, p. xxiv)

What forms does institutional discrimination take in the workplace? Consider the following scenario: An employer who is interested in providing her employees with a strong incentive for good performance decides to institute a strict policy of promotion from within. She will fill all future high-level vacancies in the organization by promoting current employees to higher levels. New employees will be hired to fill entry-level positions only. This policy, she presumes, will motivate lower-level employees to maintain high levels of performance so that they will be viewed favorably when promotion opportunities arise.

Such a system seems readily justifiable. Indeed, employees who perceive opportunities for advancement may be more motivated than employees who suspect they might be passed over for a promotion. After all, what is the point of working hard in your job when the boss goes outside the firm to fill higher-level positions?

But the wisdom and fairness of promoting from within becomes questionable when we consider an additional factor: Because of past discriminatory hiring practices, nonwhites are vastly underrepresented in the organization. Now consider the effects of the internal-promotion policy. Because new hires are restricted to entry-level positions only, highly qualified whites—and nonwhites— are ineligible for hire into attractive, high-level positions within the organization. A system that was designed for a seemingly legitimate purpose has effectively perpetuated unequal opportunities between whites and nonwhites.

Systems that promote intergroup disparities are bound to stir some debate. However, it is important to be aware of the potential for institutional discrimination because it is sometimes implicit and often unnoticed. Failure to recognize the dynamics of institutional discrimination can result in blindness to existing ethnocentrism. It can also result in biased perceptions of others and false conclusions about the causes of their behavior.

For example, consider the findings (presented earlier in this chapter) that blacks, generally speaking, achieve lower levels of occupational status than whites. This finding probably reflects the operation of many factors, including institutional discrimination. Blacks' lower levels of occupational status may reflect restricted access to higher education, which in turn may reflect deficiencies in the primary and secondary school systems in primarily black-populated inner cities, which in turn may reflect the decay of inner-city economic infrastructures resulting from "white flight" to the suburbs, which in turn may result from high crime levels brought on by rampant poverty, and so on, and so on, and so on. We can refer to such complex chains of obstruction as *vicious cycles* (Jhabvala, 1977).

The point is that, although overt discrimination may be playing a role here, there are also other interrelated characteristics of the system that very likely influence the occupational attainments of minorities. A failure to recognize such institutional factors might lead one to erroneously conclude that minorities attain lower occupational status because they are somehow inherently less able than other groups. As Kanter (1979) argues, "Sometimes institutional [racism and sexism] impacts on people's opportunity in a way that makes them appear to deserve their lack of mobility, but this is instead a function of limited situations" (p. 55).

■■ **SUGGESTED READINGS**

Alba, *Ethnic Identity* (1990), argues that ethnicity and, to some degree, religion are declining in their importance as a basis of differentiation in the United States. Other theorists disagree, but it is an interesting argument.

Discrimination by race, religion, or ethnicity has been pervasive for a long time. A careful analysis of this phenomenon can be found in Alvarez, Lutterman, and Associates, *Discrimination in Organizations* (1979).

Lieberson, *A Piece of the Pie* (1980), presents a thoughtful and provocative analysis of the experiences of black and white immigrants to urban areas and their work there.

In what has become the most influential book on the subject, *The Declining Significance of Race* (1978), William J. Wilson argues that issues surrounding social class and the vertical dimension, rather than race, have had the most serious and negative effects on African-Americans.

9 The Organizational Context

Organizations are the context in which work takes place. This point has been made repeatedly, but what does it mean? Let us begin with a very simple example—a fast-food restaurant such as McDonald's or Burger King. Workers all wear the same uniforms. Very few employees would argue about that. The restaurant also always charges the same price for its food. There is no haggling, bargaining, or bartering with customers: The price is set by the company. In other words, employees' on-the-job overt behavior is set by the company. But more subtle things also go on here. There are company rules that govern who becomes crew chief. There are also company rules regarding who gets hired in the first place.

You might say, Well, that is a trivial example. What about real jobs in the real world of work after college?

Sorry, but things are not that much different. Suppose you go to work for a bank. The first thing you will notice is that darn uniform. In a bank it is a dark suit for a man and a suit or "proper" dress for a woman. Banks also have clear rules that govern the approval of loans. Banks also have policies for the processes of hiring new workers and promoting them once hired.

If we move from these simple observational kinds of examples into research-based studies, we find that the same points are made. For example, Fine (1990) found that workers' time is structured in all restaurants. Both internal and external pressures make certain periods of the day very hectic, while other periods are quiet. Restaurant workers must adjust and negotiate their free time within organizational constraints. The free time they find to have a cup of coffee or to smoke is not selected on their terms, but on the restaurant's.

Another study dealt with the ways in which people behave outside of work. Christenson, Hougland, Ilvento, and Shepard (1988) examined the ways in which middle managers in corporations participate in community affairs. They may join the Rotary Club or Kiwanis, be on the board of the local symphony, or otherwise become active in local events. The determining factor in participation is company norms. Companies vary in the degree to which they expect (demand) that their managers be active in local affairs and in the degree to which they pay for such social activities as joining a country club. One interesting fact is that people who have become involved in the community are less likely to transfer to another community, even when the move means a promotion. Local involvement could thus mean a loss of promotion potential. Apparently, these company norms are strong ones.

The point is that organizations affect people's behavior both on and off the job. This chapter will investigate how organizations do so and how some are changing the way they relate to their employees.

Employment in Organizations

Organizations provide the contemporary work setting for both the employed and self-employed. The vast majority of workers are employees, although 7.5% of the labor force is self-employed in nonagricultural pursuits and 84% of agricultural workers are self-employed (U.S. Department of Labor, 1992). These figures have changed little during the 20th century. Nonagricultural self-employment involves work such as restaurant ownership, household maintenance, skilled trades such as painting or electrical work, automobile or appliance repair work, and other small-business ownership.

Self-employment does not mean an escape from the organizational context. One's customers and suppliers are most likely to be organizations rather than individuals. And one must always deal with government agencies. Consider an average restaurant.

Health and sanitation requirements are enforced by a government organization. So too are regulations regarding employees and their pay and taxation. On the private side, there are creditors such as banks. There are also credit-card companies such as Visa and American Express. Even for the self-employed, then, the organizational context is pervasive.

For the balance of the nonagricultural labor force, organizational employment dominates. The data on such employment are revealing in several ways. First, only one tenth of 1% of all organizations have more than 1,000 employees, but those few employ more than 14% of the labor force. Thus large organizations are a dominant component of contemporary work (Tausky, 1984, p. 61). Approximately 75% of all organizations have fewer than 10 employees, but these smaller organizations employ slightly more than 15% of the labor force. Did you notice that both large and small organizations have close to the same proportion of all employees?

Another important point concerns small organizations. Many are new and suffer from the liabilities of newness and smallness (Carroll & Delacroix, 1982; Stinchcome, 1965). Thus they have a hard time surviving; there is a high "death rate" (see Whetten, 1980) among small and new organizations. As a result, work in such organizations may be precarious. As will be seen later in this chapter, the size of the organization is also important in other ways.

Although small organizations are important, most work is carried out in larger organizations. These tend to grow larger over time for a variety of reasons (Hall, 1991). The primary focus of this chapter will be on work in relatively large-scale, complex organizations. There will be two major thrusts in the analysis. The first will consider the role that organizations play in the distribution of people on the vertical dimension, with issues of gender, age, race, religion, and ethnicity being considered where appropriate. The second thrust will consider organizations as the immediate setting of work. In Chapter 3 we saw how people respond to their work. Here we will take this issue further and consider how work has been and might be changed to enhance its quality for the people involved.

Organizations and the Vertical Dimension

Organizations are not only the contemporary work setting, but also agents of stratification in contemporary society. Organizations distribute people into positions. The positions have differential rewards attached to them. These facts may seem obvious, but only relatively recently, as the structural approach has developed, has the organization itself been considered an element of the vertical dimension.

This section borrows heavily from James Baron and colleagues' extensive research on the interaction between organizations and the vertical dimension (see Baron, 1984; Baron & Bielby, 1986; Baron, Davis-Blake, & Bielby, 1986; Baron, Dobbin, & Jennings, 1986; Baron, Jennings, & Dobbin, 1988; Baron & Newman, 1990). Baron's analyses are based on data about the *promotion paths* in 100 California firms. Promotion paths are the same as career ladders and vacancy chains, which were discussed in Chapter 4. Baron begins his analysis with the observation that the division of labor among jobs and organizations leads to a distribution of opportunities and rewards that is independent of any particular employee. Some organizations pay more than others and have higher promotion rates; others pay less and have fewer promotion opportunities. The organization, not the worker, is the determinant.

Internal Labor Markets

Baron's primary focus is internal labor markets and the factors that affect career outcomes within organizations. Previous discussions of internal labor markets have stressed that the concept includes promotions, transfers, and demotions within an organization (Stewman, 1986). The idea of job ladders, whereby employees can proceed from entry-level to higher-status jobs, is also very prominent (Baron & Bielby, 1986; Baron, Davis-Blake, & Bielby, 1986).

Before we proceed with an analysis of internal labor markets, note that the basic decision to hire or not hire in the first place has important ramifications. Organizations may have discriminatory hiring procedures. On the other hand, hiring procedures that may seem to discriminate can be rational. Few business firms would hire women to serve as sales representatives in Saudi Arabia, for example. To reduce the incidence of discriminatory practices, many enlightened organizations have established formal hiring standards. Formal hiring standards tend to be established in organizations that (a) have a strong need to train workers, (b) are in industries that are characterized by rapid technological change, and (c) have internal labor markets (Cohen & Pfeffer, 1986).

We can now return to a consideration of what happens once a person is employed by an organization. What are the factors that determine how easily and how frequently employees are promoted? Baron's analyses reveal several organizational characteristics that affect internal labor markets. Perhaps it is no coincidence that the factors he focuses on are also those that have been integral to organizational theory: size, growth, demography, technology, and environment.

Size. The relationships between size and the vertical dimension exist but are ambiguous (Hall, 1991). On the one hand, researchers such as Hodson (1984) conclude that "[a]t the company level, organizational size appears to be the most significant determinant of earnings" (p. 345). The bigger the organization, the higher earnings tend to be. Hodson further notes that at the industry or sector level, the extent to which capital investment is required is the most important determinant; in this case, the greater the capital investment, the higher earnings tend to be.

Hodson's research demonstrates that organizational size and industrial sector interact in interesting ways in regard to gender. Large organizations tend to be more bureaucratic and thus have procedures that grant employment and promotion based on performance, which benefits women. At the same time, capital-intensive industries, such as investment banking, are largely staffed by men, which gives men in general a huge advantage in regard to wages.

Other researchers discount the importance of organizational size. Granovetter (1984), for example, agrees that large organizations have more hierarchical levels and more openings in the internal labor market, but that the large number of small organizations should really be the focus of research. Granovetter reports that while the proportion of the labor force employed in small establishments or organizations has declined in this century, more than 25% of the labor force is employed in establishments of fewer than 100 workers and that 72.5% of the labor force is employed in organizations of fewer than 1,000. He reasons that smaller organizations will not have highly developed internal labor markets.

Granovetter also found a somewhat different reality in smaller establishments that are part of larger firms. Middle- or upper-level managers in these smaller establishments would have access to internal labor markets within the larger firm, so they could possibly move from one small establishment to another. For blue-collar production workers and most white-collar workers in the smaller establishments, however, the kinds of internal labor markets assumed to be present in large organizations simply do not exist.

Baron's (1984) research revealed that large organizations in prosperous industries have greater numbers of hierarchical levels and hence greater promotional opportunities, particularly (again) for managerial and professional personnel. These organizations will also have higher pay scales at all hierarchical levels, because most will be unionized. In addition, executives and professionals ensure that they are paid well themselves, and their pay levels will generally pull up other wages in the organization.

In industries that are characterized by small establishments, such as retailing and restaurants, there is less prosperity in general and so pay and promotional opportunities will be less. The same conclusion would appear to hold for employment in the public and not-for-profit sectors. However, museums with wealthy patrons and school districts in wealthy suburbs do present greater opportunities for their employees than do their less-affluent counterparts.

The lesson for employees and prospective employees is that large and prosperous organizations pay more and have more opportunities for promotion.

Growth. Organizational size is essentially a static variable. Closely related to size, however, is the more dynamic factor of *changes* in organizational size. Most of the emphasis has been on organizational growth, although some attention has been paid to shrinking size.

Changing organizational size is closely linked to the industry or sector in which an organization is located. It is quite well established that profitability is strongly related to the growth of industries (Lieberson & O'Connor, 1972). Thus it is not too surprising that there are increased internal promotional opportunities in growing organizations (Bielby & Baron, 1983; Rosenbaum, 1979a).

Baron (1984) notes that there have been few studies of the consequences of organizational shrinkage. Nevertheless, some research suggests that seniority policies disproportionately harm minorities and women, who tend to be among the last hired and thus the first fired when an organization downsizes (Schervish, 1983b). Common sense also suggests that contraction would limit chances for mobility in almost all situations.

Demography. Although clearly not an organizational variable, demographic factors outside of organizations and the demographic profile of their own employees affect movement and attainment on the vertical dimension (Baron, 1984). Chances for mobility are greater for members of small birth cohorts, such as children of the Great Depression. At the same time, the baby-boom generation has found chances for mobility to be severely limited in the absence of strong economic growth.

Within an organization, the age structure has been shown to be important. When organizations are staffed at the top by relatively young workers, as is the case in the semiconductor industry, other young workers, seeing little or no chance for advancement, will leave and join startup firms (Brittain & Freeman, 1980). Organizations that have extensive numbers of older workers exhibit much greater opportunities for mobility as the older workers retire.

Gender distributions are also important. When such a distribution in an organization is highly skewed in favor of males, the women who are present are treated as tokens and are in a collectively powerless position. Token individuals are very visible, and their actions are more easily observed than are those of the dominant group's members (Kanter, 1977a; Spangler, Gordon, & Pipkin, 1978). When a woman does advance rapidly in a highly gender-skewed organization, others tend to be skeptical about her capabilities: Was the advancement because the organization wanted to exhibit its token woman or was it possibly because she slept with her male boss? These kinds of questions are not asked about men in the "fast track." When the gender distribution is more even, such questions are less frequently raised. This same basic point, minus the issue of sexual activity, would hold for minority-group members and their demographic distribution.

The demographic factor contains one additional point of interest. Organizations that have many women or minority-group members tend to be poor and to pay employees poorly (Baron & Newman, 1990).

Technology. Technology, or the way organizations do things (not just machinery), is an important variable in the vertical dimension (Baron, 1984). The technology variable is a complicated one, because most organizations use several or many technologies. The technology used to handle administrative matters is different from those used to handle production and marketing.

Organizational operations that use routine technologies, as is the case in much production and administrative work, offer little in the way of promotion opportunities, because the work can be easily routinized and thus filled by almost anyone. But organizations that include bureaucratic or professional specializations have longer chains of opportunity and hence offer more chances for promotion (Baron, Davis-Blake, & Bielby, 1986; Kelley, 1990).

Environment. The major focus of organizational research and theory in recent years has been organizations' environments. In this context, an environment includes the social, political, and economic factors that are outside of and which affect an organization. Three theoretical models—population-ecology, resource-dependence, and institutional—give us insight into how organizational environments affect the vertical dimension.

The first of these approaches is the population-ecology model (Hannan & Freeman, 1990), which tries to look at *populations* of organizations—that is, all organizations of a similar type in a similar industry. For example, personal-computer manufacturers would be one population of organizations. College-textbook companies would be another. These populations of organizations either survive in their environments (are adaptive) or are doomed to extinction by going out of business.

Adaptive organizational forms, such as the fast-food restaurant franchise organization, are successful because they have been able to adjust to changes in the larger environment. Fast-food franchises have succeeded in part because they have coped with the high cost of labor by developing jobs that are less than full-time. These jobs do not carry pensions and other fringe benefits, as full-time jobs in restaurants might.

The population-ecology model has been criticized because (a) it downplays the importance of choices made within the organization; (b) it removes issues of power, conflict, disruption, and social class from organizational analyses; and (c) it ignores what organizations do in and to their environments (Hall, 1991; Perrow, 1979; Van de Ven, 1979). Nonetheless, the model does sensitize us to the ultimate test of organizational effectiveness—survival—and to the role of environmental factors in organizations' development and survival.

As an alternative to the extreme environmental determinism of the population-ecology model, other organizational theorists have proposed the resource-dependence model (Pfeffer & Salancik, 1978; see also Hall, 1991). The name of the model—resource-dependence—emphasizes the high degree to which organizations are dependent on their environments for basic resources of financial support, customers, suppliers, and personnel.

This approach views the organization as an active participant in the organization-environment relationship. Organizational leaders make strategic choices about how to deal with the environment from among a set of alternatives. These choices may include whether to enter or remain in a particular environmental niche (Chandler, 1962; Child, 1972) or how actively an organization will try to manipulate its environment. The obvious example here is when U.S. companies try to have government tariffs or other blocks placed on foreign competition. This happens both ways, of course. The resource-dependence model does not imply that an organization's choices are necessarily rational or moral—just that an organization does react to and act on environmental pressures.

Baron (1984) has noted several insights provided by this approach. First, environmental dependence leads to internal changes. For example, organizations that are dependent on government contracts or are subjected to intensive regulatory pressures have shown substantial improvements in job opportunities for disadvantaged workers. Another insight is that individuals and organizational subunits that deal (successfully) with key aspects of environmental uncertainty will be rewarded more highly. It is no accident that lawyers who have been promoted out of the legal departments of large corporations are now the CEOs of those corporations. Legal issues have been critical, and legal departments and their lawyers have reaped the rewards when they have been successful. Baron also suggests that when organizations are interdependent, shared practices will develop, including ways of managing human resources.

The third theoretical model is useful at this point. The institutional model stresses that the proliferation of personnel-management associations, human-resource consulting firms, government agencies, unions, and business schools has diffused personnel practices across organizations, industries, and locales (DiMaggio & Powell, 1983; Zucker, 1988). In addition, organizations mimic one another when they have no other clear signals about how to operate. This results in *isomorphism* or homogenization within similar organizations.

Implications for Human-Resource Policy

The many insights generated by the three models of organizational environments lead to the conclusion that *monocausal arguments* are inadequate for explaining organizational personnel policies (Baron, Jennings, & Dobbin, 1988, p. 509). These personnel or human-resource policies are crucial, because they are the determinants of what happens to people in organizations.

Baron and his colleagues describe several patterns for human-resource policy that exist within particular industries or fields of organizations. First, banking, insurance, and trade firms have both centralized personnel functions and formal policies about jobs, salaries, and promotions; these functions and policies lead to long-term employment and extensive internal labor markets. Second, mass-production industries use centralized personnel functions, job analyses, and employment record keeping as adjuncts to scientific management, tying employees to the mass-production process and reducing internal labor markets; this pattern also is related to high turnover. Industries that use advanced technologies (such as petroleum or utilities) develop personnel practices that reduce turnover and stress long-term employment.

Baron, Dobbin, and Jennings (1986) come to the conclusion that organizations take different sizes and shapes and that those sizes and shapes affect opportunities for advancement. They consider it simplistic to give capitalists, managers, or workers the entire credit for shaping organizational behavior. The beauty of this conclusion is that it does not deny the relevance of economic, psychological, management, or sociological explanations of why and how the vertical dimension varies from organization to organization. Rather, it accepts multiple explanations of this complex phenomenon.

Organizations and the Individual

Now that we have a better idea of the organizational factors that structure opportunities for advancement, we can examine the ways in which organizations affect individuals. Three of the most important are (a) individual mobility within the organization, (b) the individual's day-to-day experience of work, and (c) job complexity and individual satisfaction.

Individual Mobility

How do organizations sort out the individuals to be promoted? One approach to understanding individual mobility in organizations is an economic approach. Just as the price of a particular commodity can be thought to reflect its value among consumers, the wages, salaries, and promotions offered to a particular employee can be thought to reflect that employee's value to the organization. Higher quality products can command higher prices than products of lower quality. Employees with better training and higher qualifications can command higher wages and greater upward mobility than employees with less human-capital value.

Just as commodity prices vary as a function of fluctuations in supply and demand, so too can an individual's job opportunities and wage levels vary as a function of the supply and demand for workers with similar credentials and qualifications. The world's finest snowmobile might not sell at any price to residents of the Arizona desert. Even a highly trained physician might have trouble finding a job in a city that is experiencing a glut of doctors.

These concepts are of considerable value for understanding mobility in organizations. According to conventional economic theory, workers are sorted out along the vertical dimension on the basis of their worth to the organization (their human capital) and on the basis of existing supply and demand. However, many additional factors influence worker mobility. Unfortunately, economic theorists have failed to consider many of these factors. As Baron (1984) states, "The question of which workers are matched to which jobs does not appear problematic to neoclassical micro-theorists." The problem is that the question of how workers are matched with jobs is indeed problematic. The sorting of people within organizations raises serious questions about the utility of economists' supply-and-demand approach. Organizations do not and perhaps cannot act in economically rational terms in their selection and evaluation processes. Other factors affect an individual's progress in an organization, and they vary with the stage of employment.

The first stage, of course, is the selection of workers. Employers often use a "credentialist" system in which the possession of a particular credential, such as a B.A., M.B.A., or Ph.D. is taken as the sole indication of a person's capabilities (Berg, 1971; Collins, 1979; Meyer, 1977). The prestige of the college or university that is granting degrees has also been shown to affect the level at which people enter their employing organizations (Rosenbaum, 1981). The credential (not years of schooling) and its source serve as a signal to the employer and to fellow workers about what a person probably is like.

Once a person is in an organization, the situation continues to be one in which the predictions of neoclassical economists would not be confirmed, because promotions and advancement are hardly based on completely rational grounds. For example, in the large industrial firm she studied, Kanter (1977b) found a process of *homosocial reproduction,* or the use of gender, race, social background, and family status to determine who will advance in the organization. Only those who are similar to the decision makers in these characteristics—those with homosocial characteristics—stand much chance of promotion. As you might expect, white, college-educated, Northern European males have the best chances.

Another complication for neoclassical economists is that the evaluation of performance once a person is in the organization is itself ambiguous and vague. The higher the worker is in the hierarchy, the greater the ambiguity and vagueness of evaluation standards (Dornbusch & Scott, 1975). The job description of a company president is typically much less specific than that of a clerk in an office. At the other end of the spectrum, it is difficult for organizations to assess how well new employees are performing in relation to the job requirements (March & March, 1978). Evaluations of performance take place only periodically.

On the basis of performance evaluations, some people advance and others do not. A key factor here appears to be early career stardom (Kanter, 1977b; Rosenbaum, 1979a). People who are identified as stars early in their careers are put on fast tracks in their organizations. The designation as stars is likely to remain with the individuals unless they conspicuously make repeated blunders. Role expectations and self-fulfilling prophecies operate here; in other words, those who are watching and evaluating employee performance often see what they expect to see. They will tend to see stars' performance through rose-colored glasses. Also, organizations may escalate their commitment to earlier decisions so that they do not look foolish (Baron, 1984).

Whether or not personnel decisions are rational does not matter if the people involved believe in the system. If such rationality is a myth, then it is one that is largely accepted by those who participate in and contribute to it. At the same time, although behavior in organizations is not totally random, mobility is subject to a series of factors beyond individual or organizational control (March & March, 1977). For the organization, the lack of rationality might not make much of a difference. If the initial selection criteria, with their focus on academic credentials, bring bright and trainable people into the organization, the issue of who is or is not mobile is irrelevant. For the individuals involved, of course, it matters a lot.

Experience of Work

It has been well documented that the organizational context is a
critical component in individuals' placement on the vertical dimension. The organizational context also has an indisputable
effect on individuals' experiences of work through the immediate
work arrangements they face each day. As Chapter 3 concluded,
organizational work is less alienating and more satisfying than
common stereotypes would suggest.

There are important differences, however, in individuals' organizational work experiences, and these are related to the individuals'
relationships to their organizations. In a summary of their almost
20-year research program on job conditions and personality, Kohn
and Schooler (1982) concluded that

> [p]osition in the organizational structure has a widespread
> impact on other conditions of work. Ownership results in
> doing substantively more complex work, at higher levels of
> income, but with a greater risk of losing one's job or business.
> Bureaucratic firms and organizations provide substantively
> more complex work, more extensive job protections, higher
> income, physically lighter work, and fewer hours of work.
> Higher position in the supervisory hierarchy results in
> substantively more complex, less routine, less closely
> supervised, and physically lighter work; higher levels of pay;
> and more hours of work per week. In short, the three facets of
> position in the organizational structure have similar effects
> on substantive complexity and job income, but decidedly
> different effects on the number of hours worked and on job
> protections and job risks, with ownership maximizing risk
> and bureaucratization maximizing job protections.

For our purposes here, two of the factors listed by Kohn and
Schooler—position in the hierarchy and degree of bureaucratization—are important. The issue of ownership, while interesting, is
less relevant because it is an unlikely work condition for most people.

The important point, then, is that people who work in well-
developed bureaucracies and who are higher on the job ladder
tend to have more complex jobs and higher incomes. Those who
prefer to lessen their personal accountability and have secure

employment should therefore find a mid- to low-level job in a highly bureaucratic organization. Such a job, unfortunately, is not likely to have much status or to pay very well.

One additional example of how the organizational context affects the individual's work experience is of particular interest to me. It seems that there are "departmental effects" on faculty research, the infamous "publish or perish" measure of productivity. Faculty members in departments that are improving have increased rates of publication. Faculty in downwardly mobile departments have decreased productivity (Allison & Long, 1990). The same may be true for other types of workers: A demoralizing environment seems likely to depress any worker's productivity.

Job Complexity

Chapter 3 pointed out that workers tend to be more satisfied when their jobs are complex and involving. Job complexity has a strong positive relationship with such personality factors as self-confidence, flexibility, and self-direction, meaning that job complexity reinforces these personality characteristics. On the other hand, job complexity and the amount of distress experienced on the job have a negative relationship, so that those who have complex jobs tend to be more satisfied. Those are the relationships between job complexity and the individual. What we are concerned about here is how job complexity, organizational structure, and the individual interact.

Apparently, it is exactly those people who have the potential to experience mobility in the organizational setting who have the kinds of work that offer the substantive complexity that is so important for mental well-being. To be precise, people in managerial and professional occupations are the ones who most often have jobs that are complex, challenging, and interesting—and therefore satisfying. For other organizational workers, the job is typically less complex, more routine, more boring, and less satisfying. Because dissatisfied workers are unproductive and more prone to leave, organizations have been trying to find ways of altering work conditions to make them more satisfying, particularly for people at lower hierarchical levels.

Organizations and Change

Advocates of organizational change come from different camps. Some see organizational change from a political perspective and wish to see more power in workers' hands and less in capitalists'. Others take a more humanistic stance toward work and see organizational change as a way to improve the lives of the individuals involved.

The sources of change are both internal and external. External sources of change include labor unions, government actions (for private organizations), and social-movement groups (McKelvey, 1982). The civil rights legislation of the 1960s is probably the classic case here, because the gender, racial, religious, and ethnic compositions of organizations became and still are becoming altered by this externally induced change. The major force for change these days is management, which sees organizational change as a way to increase productivity and hence profitability or efficiency. Currently, the changes most often sought are in job redesign, worker participation, and the adoption of the "Japanese" approach.

Job Redesign

Whether change is pursued from a humanistic or capitalistic motive, the impetus typically comes from the top of the organization. Job redesign, which reorganizes jobs to make them more complex and satisfying, is clearly a form of organizational change arranged by management, although workers also must be involved in its implementation.

According to Tausky and Parke (1976, p. 532), jobs can be redesigned by one of three ways:

1. *Job rotation*, or the movement by a worker from one workstation to another, either every few hours or day to day; the tasks remain designed as they were, but the worker shifts among a limited set of tasks.

2. *Job enlargement*, in which the tasks stay as they were, but a limited set are grouped together into a job, thus providing the worker more variety at a

workstation; this sort of variety is sometimes referred to as *horizontal loading.*

3. *Job enrichment,* or *vertical loading,* which combines variety with complexity and discretion.

As we noted, *variety* has to do with the number of operations to be performed; *complexity* involves the sequence, timing, and coordination of the variety; and *discretion* incorporates the decisions required to deal with complexity.

Vertical loading of a task, however, requires a bit more flesh than the bare bones we noted; in a fundamental sense it resembles the vertical integration of a firm. A series of operations that come before and after a single task are grouped together so that the overall task has a discernible unity. For example, instead of simply feeding a machine, the worker with an enriched job would set up and feed the machine, then inspect the output, accept, reject, or repair the output, and, if necessary, adjust or even perhaps repair the machine. Thus, variety, complexity, and discretion are joined in the design of an enriched job.

Of the three forms of job redesign, job enrichment is obviously the most far-reaching form and has received the most attention. Enrichment efforts are frequently carried out in conjunction with other forms of organizational change, including various worker-participation schemes and attempts to develop work-group solidarity. Enrichment programs are also carried out in a context of the workers' own expectations and experiences, the wider organizational setting, the presence or absence of unions, and an environmental context that includes economic and political considerations. It is these contextual factors that impinge on enrichment programs and make an assessment of their results very difficult.

The evidence that is available in regard to enrichment programs is mixed. Numerous case studies report successful implementation of enrichment programs (for extensive references to these studies, see Nystrom, 1981; Tausky & Parke, 1976). At the same time, other research has reported mixed results or outright failure. Part of the problem is that job redesigns cannot be isolated from their milieu, because other organizational variables often change at the same time (Nystrom, 1981). These other variables include the redesign of work groups, wage incentives, training, altered physical facilities, and the establishment of new information systems.

A great deal of attention has been focused on the Saab and Volvo automobile-assembly programs in Sweden. Both auto makers have experimented with their production processes, abandoning the traditional assembly line and installing "a new production system involving assembly by parallel groups, employees having control over pace, products moving to component materials, and employee groups moving along with their product, all tied to a common transportation system" (Nystrom, 1981, p. 278). While the workers are generally satisfied, production costs are higher. Other aspects of the Swedish experience also should be noted. The group assembly section of the Saab assembly plant has attracted workers who were already highly motivated. In sections of the plant that still used traditional assembly methods, the staffing is heavily dominated by young women who had emigrated from Finland. Note here how the gender and ethnic factors find their way back into our analysis. The Finnish women get the least desirable and lowest-paying work. Nystrom concludes that, despite the publicity that these enrichment efforts have received, it is premature to judge success or failure.

The importance of workers' expectations in redesign efforts can be seen in several studies that Nystrom reviewed. Particularly interesting are two cases in which redesign efforts apparently contributed to less satisfaction with the work being performed. This outcome was attributed to the fact that expectations about the new work arrangements were raised before the new work designs were implemented and that the new work arrangements did not fulfill the raised expectations.

Worker characteristics have another important relationship with work-redesign programs. Nystrom suggests that in some instances it is high-performing workers who volunteer for job-enrichment experiments. There is also evidence that when workers are given the power to select their own co-workers, they are highly selective and so the work group is not wholly representative.

In general, labor union leaders and regular members tend to rank job redesign lower in their priorities than the more traditional concerns of earnings and job security (Nystrom, 1981).

Indeed, if job-redesign efforts lead to increased productivity, labor union members believe that they should receive the rewards, not the owners or management.

Enrichment programs almost always involve feedback to workers on their performance. Thus these programs make workers more accountable for the quantity and quality of their work (Tausky & Parke, 1976). Accountability in turn may contribute to increased productivity. Indeed, one study found that productivity sharply rises with an increase in individual accountability and declines as accountability declines (Tausky & Chelte, 1983). Such accountability may not be the only factor important in redesign efforts or in productivity overall, but it certainly appears to be critical.

Not all work can be redesigned to make it more satisfying and less alienating. The organization has to have the financial resources to permit redesign. New equipment and new physical arrangements are typically required. If the organization is in a marginal industry, it is less likely to have the financial resources available for such redesign efforts, and the poorest jobs are likely to be found in just those organizational settings. Only rather affluent organizations can really attempt redesign. The workers involved also must be interested in having their work made more complex. This is not always so. Careful thought also has to be given to how any gains from redesigned work are to be distributed. Job redesign is clearly not the answer to all workplace problems.

Worker Participation

Job redesign affects the manner in which labor is divided in the making of products or the delivery of services. It is a slight alteration of the horizontal dimension within organizations. Worker participation, on the other hand, can be a dramatic, even radical, departure from traditional hierarchical forms.

Worker participation can range from benign systems of consulting with workers, through the participation of workers in management decisions, to worker ownership. Varying degrees of worker participation are closely intertwined with the power arrangements in organizations and thus could be considered in the next chapter. I will deal with worker participation here, because it is frequently linked to job redesign efforts. Participation schemes obviously take place in organizational settings.

The link between worker participation and job-redesign programs is rather common in the United States. For example, the experience of a General Foods dog-food plant in Topeka, Kansas, has served as a model for altering organizational arrangements (Walton, 1980). This particular program received national television and newspaper coverage. Walton (1978) describes the operation:

> Three rotating shifts were used to operate the plant [24] hours a day, [5] days a week. On each shift, one self-managing team was responsible for the "process" segment of production and another for the "packaging" segment. The teams numbered from [7 to 14] operators, large enough to embrace a set of interrelated tasks and small enough to permit face-to-face meetings for making decisions and for coordination. Activities usually performed by separate units—maintenance, quality control, custodianship, industrial engineering, and personnel—were built into the responsibilities for each team. For example, team members screened job applicants for replacements on their own team. (pp. 219-220)

The transfer to the work group of personnel screening and other decision making is typical of a limited form of worker participation linked to job redesign. The continued success of any worker-participation program depends on management's continued backing. In the case of the dog-food plant, this backing eroded over time. In the end, there was little actual shift in power from management to the workers. What was shifted was only what management wanted shifted.

At the opposite extreme is employee ownership, which is described by Woodworth (1981):

> The mechanisms by which employees come to obtain ownership of a business are at least fivefold: (1) Crises—a plant closing due to bankruptcy or relocation; (2) Company Benefits—part of a corporate rewards program intended to interest and satisfy employees; (3) Gifts—an offering of the stock of one's company to the employees usually by a retiring

entrepreneur or an ideologist benefactor; (4) Takeovers—the seizing of control by workers who demand a voice and a piece of the business; (5) New Collectives—the spontaneous creation of a new enterprise by individuals who share democratic values in consensus decision making and communal property. (pp. 195-196)

Two points about employee ownership must be noted before we continue. First, employee ownership is impossible for governmental organizations, although a high level of worker participation is possible. Second, takeovers, while conceptually possible, are possible in fact only when state laws and regulations have an orientation toward private property that is very different from those in capitalistic systems.

Employee ownership with extremely high levels of worker participation is more common in other economic systems. The former Yugoslavia, for instance, had its era of worker control of the workplace (see Obradovic, 1972; Rus, 1972; Tannenbaum, Kavcic, Rosner, Vianello, & Wieser, 1974). The workers elected councils that in turn elected management. Referenda were held to decide major organizational issues. Power in the organizations rose from the bottom, rather than working from the top down. This approach was very successful for more than 30 years, but the tragic regional and ethnic strife in what was Yugoslavia have apparently destroyed the system.

Another example of intense worker participation is found in the Israeli kibbutz system (see Tannenbaum et al., 1974, for a complete description), which uses intentional work-role rotation, including rotation into managerial positions. A major difference between the kibbutz system and the employee-ownership system of the former Yugoslavia is that the kibbutz is not the major vehicle for Israel's economic activity (Warner, 1981).

Additional approaches to worker participation are various schemes linked to the idea of "industrial democracy" or worker-participation social movements. Most such activity has occurred in Europe (see Thorsrud, Sorensen, & Gustavsen, 1976). Industrial democracy and worker participation take many forms, ranging from increased worker participation at the sociotechnical level through worker or union representation on boards of management or boards of directors. Such schemes have been implemented in both state-owned and privately held organizations.

There is a strong relationship between social and economic conditions and the extent to which worker participation and representation is supported by both workers and management. In general, levels of worker participation and representation increase in periods of economic growth and stable social conditions, while they decrease in more difficult times (Brannen, 1983).

Most observers note clear differences between Europe and the United States in terms of the magnitude and forms of worker participation. In many European countries, at least an operational level of agreement exists among government leaders, labor spokespersons, and social scientists in regard to the value of restructuring work-role relationships (Miles, 1981). There it takes the form of greater worker participation in work-related decisions and worker representation on corporate boards. Such is not the pattern in the United States, where the issues of pay and employment security are more central to workers and unions. It would appear that programs designed to increase worker participation in the United States will be supported only when management sees a clear link with increased productivity and labor sees no threat to job security or pay.

Such major changes are unlikely because of power and money. Worker participation requires an investment in training and the willingness of management to give up some of its prerogatives (Russell, 1988; Tausky & Chelte, 1988). From a union perspective, worker participation reduces worker solidarity, threatens grievance procedures in unionized situations, and suppresses unions in nonunion situations (Fantasia, Clawson, & Graham, 1988). As a result, both workers and management in the United States have opposed worker-participation programs.

The Japanese Approach

In recent years there has been a great deal of interest in borrowing Japanese managerial systems. The reasons are simple: Japanese firms have been very successful in world markets, and Japanese workers have been shown to be highly productive.

In his review of the Japanese experience, Tausky (1984) notes that Japanese education stresses discipline and that Japanese culture emphasizes collective, rather than individual, ends. The context is thus clearly different from that in the United States, which makes a difference in the importability of this Japanese product. Still, there are many U.S. efforts to import certain practices common to the Japanese approach.

Consistent with the larger culture, the Japanese approach has a strong collective orientation. Employees hired in a given year are promoted as a group, rather than divided, with some individuals on the fast track. Employers are paternalistic, offering housing programs, family allowances, day care and medical facilities, and group travel arrangements. After a probationary period, workers receive permanent employment. Wages are relatively low but are supplemented with a bonus system that is linked to a firm's profitability for the preceding time period (Lincoln & Kalleberg, 1985; Lincoln, Kalleberg, Hanada, & McBride, 1990).

Permanent employment and bonuses based on group performance create a strong bond between employees and employers. It is in the employees' interests to produce work that is high in quality and quantity, because the company's success contributes to both individual and collective benefits. The relationships between employers and employees are nonadversarial.

Note that the Japanese approach is not universal in Japan. Most women are excluded from such work. The country also has peripheral industries in which work is not secure and paternalism is not present.

An interesting fact, too, is that this Japanese approach is not really new to the United States. The Lincoln Electric has had a pay system linked to productivity for 50 years (Fein, 1976). The Lincoln system is tied to collective accomplishment. The company's workers perform fast and hard, and they receive very high bonuses each year. Much more of the company's profits go to management and workers than to stockholders.

Although Lincoln has been visited by many other managers over the years, there has been little emulation, perhaps because the system is seen as too "radical" (Fein, 1976, p. 513). At the same time, Ouchi (1981) has found examples of successful implementation of

Japanese-type programs in companies such as IBM and Hewlett-Packard.

What all of these programs share is a clear redefinition of the role of individuals. When individual accomplishment is stressed, there is little likelihood of successful implementation of such approaches. The most likely prospects for successful implementation in the United States would appear to be high-technology organizations, which are very labor-intensive and require highly collaborative work. Also note that these systems are nearly impossible in nonprofit work situations, unless there were wholesale restructuring in the ways in which government agencies, public universities, hospitals, museums, and the like are funded and evaluated.

One other technique that has been borrowed from Japan is the quality control (QC) circle. In QC circles, work groups meet with supervisors to discuss production and quality problems and propose solutions. The proposed solutions are subject to management approval. The QC-circle approach has gained rapid acceptance in many U.S. organizations, but Tausky (1984) sees little likelihood that it will have a lasting effect because of the continuing adversarial relationship between employers and employees. Tausky concludes:

> The programs we have reviewed have promise, but fall short of coming to grips with the underlying dilemma of adversarial relationships. Until that problem is resolved, no scheme is likely to extend its effects beyond rather restrained improvements. Adversarial relationships are not handily detectable in strike statistics; their results are usually more subtle because they inhibit concern with higher productivity and better quality. There is, it seems to me, no mystery about the personnel policies that are sufficiently potent to stimulate substantial gains in cooperation. With the twin policies of secure jobs and profit sharing, the perception of a shared fate emerges. Without such a perception, adversarial relationships will most likely persist. (1984, p. 147)

I concur, with the caveat that something comparable to profit sharing must be developed for work in the public sector. The American emphasis on individuality may impede efforts to improve the quality of work life. But developing a sense of shared futures and rewards could dramatically change U.S. workers' relationship with employing organizations.

Conclusions

This chapter began with the observation that contemporary work is organizational work, and it ended with the note that organizational change could dramatically affect individuals' experience of work. In between we saw the power of organizations in their role as the arbiters of attainment on the vertical dimension. We also saw that organizations are clearly affected by their own environments. The final consideration was various approaches to changing the organizational dimension that have appeared in the literature and in practice.

The forms of organizational change analyzed at the end of the chapter generate from both inside and outside organizations. Organizational management is the dominant internal source of change as it seeks to raise productivity and minimize costs—regardless of whether an organization is public or private. External sources of change include labor unions, government actions (for private organizations), and social-movement groups.

Regardless of the source of change, organizations are highly resistant to it. By their very nature, organizations are designed to be stable. It is thus unrealistic to expect rapid or deep changes in the organizational dimension of work. Most forms of change that we have been considering are essentially tinkering, and this is likely to be the pattern of the future. Larger-scale changes would appear to dependent on shifts in power within both organizations and the wider society. The next chapter further considers the role of power.

■■■ **APPLICATION**

Organizational Culture

While attending an academic conference recently, I happened to bump into a former colleague of mine. We stopped to chat for a moment, and during our conversation she informed me that she had just changed jobs, moving from a prestigious university in the Northeast to a school of somewhat less distinction in the South. It seemed unlikely to me, given her stature in the academy, that she had been asked to leave her former job. Out of curiosity, I asked her why she had chosen to give up her high-status post for a position in a less-prominent institution. After struggling momentarily to find the right words, my former colleague responded, "Well, I just didn't like the 'feel' of the place. I was there for seven years and I never really felt at ease. There was just something negative about the environment. The people, the policies; almost everything about the place seemed hostile or unfriendly. I much prefer the school where I'm working now."

Most of us can probably relate to the experiences of my former colleague. It is not uncommon for people to describe organizations using terms such as "friendly," "aggressive," "trusting," "cooperative," and "competitive." Perhaps you have attended schools where you sensed a great deal of competition among students and faculty. On the other hand, perhaps norms of trust and cooperation have been more common in your experience. In any case, it is not unusual for such characteristics to be attributed to organizations.

How can an entity such as a university be perceived as hostile? After all, hostility is an attribute of human beings. To speak of an organization in this way implies that the organization has the status of a living human organism. Obviously, it is not. However, many organizational researchers have argued that, although they may not be hostile or friendly per se, organizations can possess distinctive cultures (see, for example, Ouchi & Wilkins, 1985; Schein, 1985; Schneider, 1987). Such cultures are part of the organizational dimension. They influence and are influenced by the people residing in the organization.

The term *organizational culture* is used quite a bit, but, unfortunately, researchers have not used this term consistently and have not defined the concept clearly. However, it is generally

accepted that the term refers to the norms for appropriate be
ior that pervade an organization. It also refers to the va
espoused and adhered to by a majority of the organization's members. According to researchers of organizational culture, these norms
and values are transmitted to all organization members, sometimes
in the form of specific policies and procedures, and sometimes in
the form of "war stories" or "corporate myths" that are passed from
person to person by word of mouth.

Although there is some debate over how *culture* should be
defined, there is little debate, at least among laypersons, that
organizations possess distinctive cultures. Sometimes these cultures are reflected in depictions of organizations in the popular press
and advertising media. For instance, 3M Corporation stresses the
importance of innovation in its corporate culture.

In their bestselling book *In Search of Excellence*, Peters and
Waterman (1982) describe the cultures of many successful U.S.
companies. They describe Digital Equipment Company as having
a "fetish for reliability" and report that McDonald's places tremendous emphasis on virtues of "Q.S.C. & V." (quality, service, clean-
liness, and value). To take an example from this chapter, consider
the topic of worker participation in organizations. An organization
in which workers participate in the making of decisions might be
described as having a participatory culture. Such an organization
may be populated with individuals who value the opportunity to
contribute to the decision-making process. Norms may develop
that motivate employees to behave in ways that facilitate participation. In fact, explicit rules may exist that require employees to
fulfill their participatory role, such as rules requiring attendance
at important work-group meetings.

Where do organizations' distinctive cultures come from? Perhaps they come from the surrounding environment. For instance,
the strong collectivist orientation observed in some Japanese
firms might be described as an aspect of organizational culture.
This culture is distinguishable from the individualist culture that
is more typical of U.S. companies. Although organizational cultures
need not necessarily reflect the cultures of the societies in which they

are embedded, it appears that this is one aspect of culture that firms have adopted from their surrounding environments.

Another possible source of organizational culture may be the values professed by the organization's founder (see, for example, Schein, 1985). Promotional messages for the Dean Witter investment firm imply that the individualized treatment received by the firm's clients reflects a philosophy first espoused by the company's founder.

Other aspects of organizational culture may reflect accumulated values, beliefs, and norms espoused by individual organizational members. According to this view, an organization's culture is a reflection of those values, beliefs, and norms that are commonly held by a large number of organizational inhabitants.

When it comes to understanding people's work behaviors and experiences, is culture really as important as factors such as organizational size, opportunities for advancement, or job design? Many culture researchers would argue that culture is at least as important as these other factors. In fact, some might argue that culture is the most important organizational characteristic to consider when seeking an understanding of organizational life. Such arguments are based on the assumption that the particular norms and values that make up an organization's culture shape the organization's structure and operations rather than the other way around.

Such an assumption is reflected in work by Schneider (1987), who suggests that organizations attract and select individuals whose attributes (value systems and beliefs) are compatible with those shared by existing organizational members. Schneider also predicts that individuals who do not fit the organization's culture will tend to leave. This process of "attraction, selection, and attrition" yields organizations that are populated by particular kinds of persons who value particular kinds of goals and who prefer particular means for achieving those goals. Thus, according to Schneider, organizational inhabitants do not merely react passively to the organizational context. Rather, "the behaviors of people in pursuit of organizational goals determine the processes and structures that evolve in organizations" (Schneider, 1987, p.

443). As Schneider states so simply, not only does the place make the people, but also "the people make the place."

■■■ **SUGGESTED READINGS**

A complete bibliographical entry for each work cited here can be found in the reference section at the back of this book.

Kanter, *Men and Women of the Corporation* (1977), already was mentioned in the chapter on gender. It is equally useful here, because it provides a rich description of life in a large corporation.

Organizations influence us in many ways. Hochschild, *The Managed Heart* (1983), describes how an airline attempts and sometimes succeeds in influencing even the emotions of its flight attendants.

Another rich description, this time about morality and organizational decision making, can be found in Jackall, *Moral Mazes* (1988).

The first three books mentioned here have all been based on research in the private sector. A glimpse of work in the public sector can be found in Lipsky, *Street Level Bureaucracy* (1982). Lipsky shows how workers develop their own sets of norms and values that allow them to cope with their organizations and clients.

Another look at work in the public sector is provided by Miller, *Enforcing the Work Ethic* (1991). Miller's research focuses on the meanings that develop in interactions on the job.

10   Power and Control in the Workplace

Power is an ever present fact of work life. When I am playing dean and the president's office calls, I jump. I frankly do not jump as high when I am playing professor and a colleague calls.

Every chapter in this book, in one way or another, has been concerned with power and control. The issue of deskilling, discussed in the first chapter, concerns employers' attempts to maintain power over workers by reducing the scope of their jobs. Chapter 2 revealed that managers and executives occupy positions of power and that professionals exercise power in relationships with clients and with others in related occupations. Most white-collar and blue-collar work is characterized by the relative absence of power. Chapter 3 discussed autonomy, which essentially concerns the power that individuals have to control their own work.

The vertical dimension (Chapter 4) can be viewed exclusively from a power perspective, although I believe that this is too narrow an interpretation of status. On the horizontal dimension (Chapter 5), autonomy is one of the defining characteristics for different types of jobs, and core or monopoly sectors have power over peripheral or competitive sectors. The influence of gender, age, race, and ethnicity (Chapters 6 through 8) can also be viewed from a power perspective. Feminist scholars, for example, consistently view male-female economic and status differentials from the perspective of male efforts to maintain dominance. Almost all analyses of sexual harassment start with an assumption of a power differential between the harasser and the harassed.

302

Most recently (Chapter 9), we saw that efforts to restructure the organization to increase worker participation and satisfaction involve shifts in power arrangements. As you can see, power and control are dominant components of all aspects of work.

If we have already covered power issues in every chapter, why have I provided a separate chapter on the subject? There are several reasons. First, there are some loose ends from the discussion of the organizational context that should be brought together into a coherent conclusion. Second, there is an additional approach to power distributions in organizations—*empowerment*—that is separate from the issue of worker participation. Third, so far we have only obliquely considered labor unions and their efforts to alter power arrangements, and we need to bring them fully into the analysis. Finally, the influence of the broader political system has not yet been analyzed.

Power Defined

The simplest and most widely used definition of *power* is this: "A has power over B to the extent that he can get B to do something that B would not otherwise do" (Dahl, 1957, pp. 202-203). (For additional considerations of the power concept, particularly in the organizational context, see Bacharach & Lawler, 1980; Bierstedt, 1950; Blau, 1964; Dornbusch & Scott, 1976; Emerson, 1962; Etzioni, 1961; Hall, 1991; Kaplan, 1964; Pfeffer, 1981; Weber, 1947). Note that this definition specifies two roles: a power holder (A) and a power recipient (B).

This simple definition can be modified easily for our purposes. For instance, "Men have power over women to the extent that men . . ." or "Organizations have power over their workers to the extent that organizations. . . ." It is possible to consider social classes, industrial sectors, gender groupings, or any social unit within this basic definition of power. Power can also operate at the individual, interpersonal level in work settings, as when Jill (a sales representative) convinces Joan (also a sales rep) that Joan should dress more stylishly for both female and male clients.

One other point needs to be made: Power is sometimes exercised without the intention of the power holder. It is possible for the power recipient to perceive that some power holder—an organization, a superior, a member of the opposite sex—is attempting to wield power when that is actually not the intention. However, if the power recipient perceives an action as an exercise of power and behaves accordingly, then power has been exercised, regardless of the power holder's intentions. If your boss's passing comment about what a mess your office is induces you to stay late to clean up, then A (your boss) has definitely gotten B (you) to do something that B (you) would not otherwise do. If you overhear your boss comment to one of his friends that the office is getting too messy and you stay late to clean it up, then A has definitely gotten B to do something that B would otherwise not have done, even though the boss did not have the intention to have you (specifically) clean up the mess. Most of the time, of course, the power holder does intend to exercise power.

Power Versus Participation

The basic power issue in organizations is that employers and workers have conflicting goals and values (Hill, 1981). Employers want workers to produce goods and services efficiently so those goods and services can be sold profitably. Workers want to earn as much as they can with minimum discomfort and inconvenience. Both parties have some power over the other to achieve their goals, which they try to exercise in the workplace. For instance, workers can get an employer to improve working conditions through a union or through a worker-oriented human-resources department. The employer can get workers to speed up production by threatening doom or by rhapsodizing about the organization's position in the industry.

As has been intimated throughout this book, power and control over workers' activities tend to be concentrated in the hands of management. To the extent that workers gain control over their activities—that is, achieve some measure of autonomy—they bring the power arrangements closer to balance. The previous chapter noted that worker-participation schemes are now being adopted at many companies; those programs essentially transfer some decision-making power from managers to workers. Conceptually, we can set management power and control against worker participation and autonomy. In reality, of course, the relationship is seldom so clear-cut.

If participation decreases managerial power, why would managers ever want to institute worker-participation programs? Aside from humanitarian ideals, the reasons often include the idea that allowing workers to have more control increases their commitment and thus their efficiency—and company profits. From the workers' point of view, participation programs would seem completely desirable, because they increase worker autonomy and control. You might be surprised to learn that some workers do not want the opportunity to participate more in the workplace. We will get to that point in a bit.

First we need to review some of the factors that other chapters have indicated increase worker autonomy, involvement, and participation: age, experience, training, professional status, and organizational structure. Another important factor is workers' orientations or attitudes toward work in general (Brannen, 1983), which develop out of individual background, social conditions, and the immediate work situation. This factor is what will help us solve the riddle of why some workers do not value participation. As noted in the last chapter, workers' involvement and participation are also related to the wider political and economic context. When the economy is humming along and profits are flowing, everyone tends to be happier about the work experience. But when times are tough and organizations are either cutting costs or working in overdrive to stay competitive, the power issue becomes more salient.

Needless to say, managers' orientations toward worker participation also have bearing on power issues within organizations. Brannen (1983) studied the orientation of managers toward worker participation during the 1970s, which was an era like this one in which there was an interest in increasing citizen participation and power. Brannen's study was conducted largely in Europe, where there is generally more worker participation than in the United

States. Brannen noted some common orientations toward participation among managers:

> Most managers expressed interest in the idea of
> participation. Few managers defined participation in terms of
> sharing the decision-making process with the workforce. For
> most managers across industry and across managerial
> occupations participation was about communication and
> consultation, a means of involving the workforce and
> increasing their commitment in order to increase efficiency.
> (Brannen, 1983, p. 95)

For most managers, then, worker participation was considered a means to the same end as always: more efficient production to achieve greater profits. All in all, Brannen (1983) concludes, "Participation is considered by management only when there are threats to managerial authority, and paradoxically in order to maintain it" (p. 96).

Brannen noted that there are variations in managerial orientations. Managers with a leftist political orientation were more in favor of worker participation than those of opposing political views. Managers in areas such as personnel or industrial relations were more disposed toward worker participation than line managers were. Senior managers, interestingly enough, were less threatened by the idea of worker participation than their more junior colleagues. There was also some variation by economic sector, with the industrial sector more favorable toward worker participation than the service sector and the public sector more positive than the private sector.

Another part of Brannen's (1983) study was an analysis of worker orientations toward participation. First he admits to having studied mostly workers in the core labor market. In the peripheral labor market, workers are less likely to have the "organization, knowledge and understanding" that are essential to a feeling of participation. Then Brannen (1983) makes an important observation:

> However, even in the primary segments with strong potential
> and at a time of high public interest, the data indicate that
> [while] there was a general demand for greater participation,

> there was also a general acceptance of the existing authority
> structure of the enterprise. Despite some signs of a cultural
> change, with a heightening of expectations, particularly
> [among] younger workers, the data appear to suggest that
> most workers are uninterested in participating in their work
> organizations other than in relatively limited ways at the
> socio-technical level. Their values represent no basic
> challenge to managerial authority. (p. 80)

If Brannen's conclusions are sound, it would seem that many workers are not particularly interested in achieving greater participation in decision making. They are perfectly content to let the managers make the decisions that affect their work lives. Brannen's view is thus that worker-participation schemes like those discussed in Chapter 9 have little likelihood of altering the basic power arrangements in organizations.

This conclusion is reinforced by two other bits of evidence. One study examined orientations toward worker participation in Sweden, a country with a strong tradition of participation (Albrecht, 1981). It found that while interest in and demands for worker participation were high, they were countered by broad trends toward the concentration of power in the hands of managers. Thus the expression of interest in participation may have arisen from workers' sense that they were losing power.

Another study analyzed levels of participation in labor-management committees designed to increase worker participation (Leitko, Greil, & Peterson, 1985). The workers who were members of such committees actually participated in decision making very little. Apparently, the workers' own orientations and those of the managers on the committees were to blame. Both workers and managers had been socialized to expect workers' nonparticipation.

Are you getting the impression that worker-participation programs have little effect on the power arrangements within organizations? You may be right. Managers understandably have very little interest in losing power, and workers as a whole appear to be unwilling and unable to assume power through participation in decision making. Some analysts even suggest that worker participation weakens the power of workers by reducing their inclinations to unionize and wield power as an organized group

(Fantasia, Clawson, & Graham, 1988). Power arrangements are affected by more than worker-participation schemes, however, and the next sections discuss other ways of increasing workers' power in organizations.

Empowerment

The idea of empowerment is closely tied to the work of Kanter (1977b), who largely focused on women in big organizations. The basic idea behind empowerment is "to alter the distribution of power in work settings so that those who have been powerless in the past are given more opportunities to control their destinies" (Miller, 1981, pp. 247-248). Empowerment has obvious ramifications for those disadvantaged because of their age, gender, race, or ethnicity, as well as for the professional-client relationship (Miller, 1981).

According to Kanter (1977a), empowerment must begin with a realization of the nature of power in the organizational work setting. She notes:

> Power has both a job-related and a social component. It is associated with the exercise of discretion, the chance to demonstrate out-of-the-ordinary capacities in the job, handling uncertainties rather than routine events; with access to visibility; and with the relevance of the job to current organizational problems. As is well known, organizations also have an informal power structure coexisting alongside of the formal delegation of authority, which is influenced by formal arrangements but may or may not correspond to official hierarchical distinctions. Thus, power is also accumulated through alliances with sponsors, successful peers, and up-and-coming subordinates. To empower those women and others who currently operate at a disadvantage requires attention to both sides of power. (pp. 275-276)

Kanter (1977a) further makes specific suggestions for implementing empowerment. To deal with the formal, job-related side, she recommends flattening the hierarchy. For example, an organization with 10 levels of management between the president and the frontline employee might cut back to 5 levels. Kanter also suggests spreading the discretion to make important decisions more evenly throughout organization (a process called *decentralizing*). She believes that these changes would benefit both subordinates and superiors. Subordinates would participate in more decisions, while superiors would be freed from watchdog-type supervision and could engage in more planning. Also, work groups would gain more autonomy. Thus both superiors and subordinates would be empowered.

The informal side of power arrangements is often a more difficult problem, because it involves individuals' attitudes. To create the atmosphere for empowerment, Kanter suggests opening up the channels of communication so that everyone, not just a select few organizational members, have more access. Also, Kanter suggests spreading knowledge of how the organization functions as an overall system. Both techniques would permit access to information previously controlled by those "on the inside."

As a way of empowering those in the later stages of their career, Kanter suggests a sponsorship program. Senior employees would groom and train younger employees. These senior employees could then be rewarded for the number of younger individuals they successfully sponsor, with the result that both are empowered. Kanter also advocates increasing the numbers of minorities and women in organizations (to prevent tokenism) and enhancing opportunities through job redesign.

The implementation of these sorts of programs would lead to more effective organizations, according to Kanter. Of course, empowerment movements always face resistance, because giving some people more power is usually perceived as taking it from others. Nonetheless, Kanter believes that the costs of leaving some workers relatively powerless are too high for both disadvantaged workers and the organizations that employ them.

Evidence in support of Kanter's approach is found in a study of male and female supervisors in a large federal bureaucracy (South, Bonjean, Markham, & Corder, 1982). The researchers note that the stereotype of female supervisors is a negative one, with such frequent descriptions as "mean," "bossy," "domineering," "capricious," and "excessively bureaucratic." They found that female subordinates generally rated their female supervisors as more particularistic and controlling than their male supervisors. The more interesting finding, however, was that female supervisors got better ratings when they had actual power. In that circumstance, female subordinates placed a higher value on membership in their own work group and felt greater job satisfaction; their perceptions of supervisor favoritism and close supervision decreased.

Unfortunately, according to South et al. (1982), the negative side of these findings is what normally influences the workplace:

> Ironically, however, a major obstacle to the admission of women to positions of authority may well be managers' application of the "mean and bossy" stereotype, not only to powerless female supervisors, but also to all female supervisors. This stereotype may thus take on the status of a self-fulfilling prophecy: If executives think that female supervisors are rigid and authoritative, play favorites, and foster low group morale and job dissatisfaction among their employees, they are more likely to assign female supervisors to low-status, unimportant, and powerless positions in the organization. And, as we have seen, powerlessness, among both male and female supervisors, breeds these very traits. (p. 252)

Changing such deep-seated stereotypes is difficult. However, it appears that more women and minorities are likely to be empowered in the future, if only on the basis of sheer numbers. Affirmative-action hiring has led to increasing numbers of women and minorities entering the labor force in positions with the potential for advancement to supervisory and managerial levels. As these individuals move through their organizational systems, some empowerment will be inevitable.

Empowerment changes the power arrangements within organizations, as do worker-participation strategies. But they are both the result of pressures within organizations. Altered power arrangements can also occur as a result of pressures from outside organizations. One of those sources of pressure is labor unions, to which we now turn.

Labor Unions

Labor unions are a relatively recent phenomenon in the United States. It was not until the New Deal era of the 1930s that the Norris-LaGuardia Act (1932) and Wagner Act (1935) granted unions protection and recognition. Legislation in later decades (Taft-Hartley, 1947, and Landrum-Griffin, 1959) prohibited certain union activities, but the basic government protection and recognition remained.

Despite the official tolerance of unions, a clear minority of workers are union members. Less than 16 percent of the nonagricultural labor force is represented by organized labor (U.S. Department of Labor, 1993). The percentage of this labor force that is represented by unions has shown a steady decline since its 1945 high of 36 percent (Tausky, 1984).

The distribution of union power within the United States also is uneven. Some 20 states have so-called right-to-work laws that ensure workers may be hired whether or not they are union members. These states are primarily in the South and Southwest (Tausky, 1984). This is at least a partial explanation for the wholesale movement of some Northern and Eastern industries to the Sunbelt. The relative weakness of unions there is based on a combination of management practices, worker characteristics, and characteristics of both unions and the industries in these areas (Simpson, 1981).

Some researchers believe that Sunbelt workers and communities are becoming more enthusiastic about unions. However, their zeal is tempered by the constant threat that companies might transfer manufacturing operations overseas, where labor costs less. It appears that the general climate in the South will remain antiunion (Robinson & McIlwee, 1989).

Worker Attitudes Toward Unions

In the United States, people join and participate in unions for a variety of reasons. The basic, and obvious, reason for favorable attitudes toward unions is dissatisfaction with the workplace (Getman, Goldberg, & Herman, 1976; Kochan, 1979). The most critical factors, especially for blue-collar workers, involve economic issues, such as wages, job security, and fringe benefits (Farber & Saks, 1980; Kochan, 1979; Schriesheim, 1981). Other factors include the gap between workers' desire to participate in decision making and their actual ability to do so (Brett, 1980) and levels of commitment to the organization (Alutto & Belasco, 1974). The exact reasons why a particular set of employees would want to unionize vary with the particular work situation and social setting. For example, in a business firm with a strong program of employee stock ownership, the more stock an employee owns, the less interested he or she is in union membership (Rosenstein & French, 1985). A study of working-class consciousness in Spain during the Franco regime found that recent rural migrants to cities were less resentful of the managerial class than were more affluent workers, who tended to be more militant. Apparently, the affluent workers had a clearer sense that they had little opportunity for further advancement in that system (Logan, 1981). Sometimes union actions in response to arbitrary firings or poor wages become more extreme than the workers originally intended, perhaps because they become more militant and develop greater class consciousness as the actions proceed (Fantasia, 1988). There is thus not just one factor that determines attitudes and actions in regard to unionization, but rather a combination of factors unique to particular work situations.

Collective Bargaining

The basic tool of unions is *collective bargaining*, in which worker representatives make labor agreements with employers. This technique, which was developed by blue-collar unions, "is now so well known and effective that other occupations are adopting it: clerical workers in large firms, government workers at all skill levels, and various levels of professional workers such as nurses, teachers, and airline pilots" (Form & Huber, 1976, p. 772).

Collective bargaining assumes an adversarial relationship between labor and management. Each side attempts to gain as much as possible, while giving up as little as possible. For labor, the gains come in the form of economic benefits, employment security, extra holidays and vacations, and greater control of the work process. For management, gains come in the form of keeping labor costs down and retaining control of the work process.

Oddly, U.S. unions have had little interest in the power issues of job content and design. In fact, some theorists suggest that worker-participation schemes, management-employee councils, and other power-sharing techniques are actually welcomed and encouraged by management as a means of weakening unions (Brody, 1980). These gestures lessen worker dissatisfaction and alienation and thus their motivation to form a union.

The "ultimate" weapon in collective bargaining is the strike by labor (union members refusing to work) or the lockout by management (managers refusing to let them work). Strikes are now infrequent: typically less than one tenth of 1% of the total working time per year (U.S. Department of Labor, 1993). Labor unions have been far more militant in the past.

Collective bargaining in general and decisions to strike in particular do not take place in a vacuum. The social and economic contexts of a particular collective-bargaining situation are critical. Strikes can be viewed as rational when there is low unemployment, regardless of the attitudes of employers or the extent to which the government is favorable to unions. Conversely, it would not be rational to strike when unemployment is high (Smith, 1979). Plant size, degree of industry unionization, and union size also affect the length, extent, and frequency of strikes. For example, in heavily unionized industries, strikes were broader (involving more workers), shorter, and more frequent than they were in less unionized industries (Britt & Galle, 1974). The context in which collective bargaining is carried out thus has important consequences for the outcome.

In the past decade or so, the social and economic context has been rather unfavorable for unions. Many unionized industries in the United States, such as the automotive and steel industries, have been facing intense foreign competition. In fact, unions have made wage and other concessions to employers in order to maintain the job security of union members. Were the situation to turn around, unions would obviously demand these concessions and more back from employers.

The key question here is, Does collective bargaining actually alter power arrangements? As Tausky (1984) asks,

> Does unionism pay? Generally, yes. What is harder to answer is how much it benefits union members. Since an answer to "how much" depends on comparison between union and nonunion wages (and benefits), we should notice that union wages also affect nonunion employers. They too may follow along, at least roughly, in order to avoid unions. But it does appear that among employees doing approximately similar work, over the past [20] years there has been a 5 to 20% wage advantage in the private sector for union versus nonunion pay, with the low side of this estimated advantage for unionized federal workers and state and local public employees. (p. 129)

Other analysts are less sanguine about collective bargaining's benefits to union members. For one thing, it is hard to separate the effects of collective bargaining on wages from the effects of more general economic upturns and downturns and the effects of changes in a particular industrial sector (Form & Huber, 1976). It also seems that the victories of unionized workers have a positive effect on nonunionized plants but a negative effect on the nonunionized workers in plants that are not fully unionized (Leicht, 1989a). These workers may not receive pay increases and other benefits. Collective bargaining has also had mixed results for women and minorities. Industrial unions have narrowed black-white income differentials (Baron, 1984). Craft unions, on the other hand, have systematically excluded minority workers. For women, the picture is different. Both teaching and nursing are highly unionized (as are some lower-status jobs in services), and collective bargaining has increased the power of these semiprofessions. Of course, women who have heavy household responsibilities have trouble finding time to participate in union activities (Cornfield, Filho, & Chun, 1990). As is the case for men, it is nonunion jobs that provide the potential for the greatest returns and prestige for women.

According to Form and Huber (1976), the real impact of unions has been in the area of working conditions:

> Unions reduce conflict at the local level, solve grievances on the plant floor, decrease the arbitrary authority of foremen, demand consultation on changes in wage rates, and secure adherence to seniority rules. In short, unions have forged a common law for everyday problems at the plant level and have institutionalized conflict in economic bargaining. Unions everywhere have stimulated governments to assume some of the burdens resulting from economic instability, such as unemployment insurance, old age benefits, medical insurance, and price stabilization. (p. 776)

In short, collective bargaining has made the relationship between managers and workers less volatile, made working conditions more tolerable in many small ways, and even shown government policy makers what workers value.

The answer, then, to our basic question is, yes, unions have contributed to alterations of power arrangements in work. Workers' economic gains have been slight; labor's share of the total economic pie appears to have changed little over time (Form & Huber, 1976, p. 775). But in terms of control over working conditions, unions have had an important influence.

Unions and the Larger Society

We have seen that unions and government have had a mutual effect in the United States. Government has the power to legitimize or tolerate union activity. Unions can pressure government to provide economic security for all workers. But Tausky (1984) warns that we cannot take unions and collective bargaining for granted:

> For the largest share of the world's workers these activities are still either not permitted or stunted. Outside North America and Western Europe, collective bargaining is found in comparatively few nations. In the rest, unions are either absent altogether—as in China, Indochina, and the major OPEC countries—or so tightly controlled by the government that the unions resemble an arm of the state—as in Russia, Cuba, Eastern Europe, and most of South America.

> The reasons for suppressing or controlling unions involve
> power and economics. Autonomous unions represent a
> challenge to the concentration of power in a government's
> hands, as the suppression of Polish unions [by Poland's
> communist government in the early 1980s] unmistakably
> illustrates.
>
> In addition to the power issue, but tied to it, is the
> economic dimension. The amounts of money invested in
> different sectors of an economy are directly determined by
> government if the economy is not open to organized demands
> for wage hikes and consumption goods. Organized pressure
> for such gains can be avoided if unions are prohibited or
> tightly regulated. Clearly, we should not expect a reversal of
> current policies toward unions in nations with a history of
> centralized power. (p. 118)

A crucial point is somewhat buried in the above quotation. Without governmental recognition of unions, there is little likelihood that power arrangements will be altered on a large scale, even in the face of massive worker protests. At the same time, unions have the potential for exercising a great deal of power. In communist Poland, for example, the government made a strong but ultimately unsuccessful effort to crush the union-based Solidarity movement.

Ironically, where unions are officially recognized, as in the United States, they have not wielded nearly as much power in the wider political context. England at least has its Labour party. In the United States, however, such direct linkages are absent. At one time, there was a close linkage between organized labor and the Democratic party, but this linkage has been weakened in recent years. Currently, unions have little broad political power. Perhaps U.S. labor unions are relatively uninvolved in politics because of our egalitarian ideals. The United States has always been characterized by low levels of class consciousness, and U.S. trade unions have always been relatively apolitical (Brody, 1980).

The future of U.S. unions appears rather bleak. Workers who have the least desirable jobs are the most likely to organize (Pfeffer & Davis-Blake, 1990). However, employers who have felt threatened by incipient unionization have simply closed the affected plant or office and transferred the work to another, nonunion location (Cornfield, 1986, 1987, 1989; Leicht, 1989b; Perrucci, Perrucci, Targ, & Targ, 1988). Even the rumor of such closings weakens the potential for unionization. Employers who can afford to do so try to provide enough benefits to keep unions out of the picture (Cornfield, 1986). Technological change is also operating against unions, particularly in manufacturing, which is the sector in which unions have traditionally had their greatest strength. Unless offices turn into factory-like operations, it appears that union membership will continue to decline.

Political Context of Work

The discussion of labor unions mentioned their relationship with government. That is just one of the ways that political structures interact with work. For example, Chapter 2 explained how an occupation's professional status arises from licensure and certification by the state, which controls the numbers of practitioners of that profession and thereby maintains the profession's power. Aspiring professions attempt to gain recognition from the state, while established professions in the same field fight to keep them out. Ebbs and flows of power among lawyers, accountants, and bankers in the area of financial management and among physicians, nurses, and physicians' assistants in the area of health care are based on events in the political arena. It is no accident that the headquarters of most major professional associations in the United States are in Washington, D.C., or that state associations have their headquarters in state capitals.

Two other aspects of the political environment affect many workers. Both were mentioned in the discussion of unions. Labor legislation is a governmental response; class conflict is a societal response.

Labor Legislation

Laws have encouraged and discouraged various forms of work activities in countries around the world (Stern & Whyte, 1981).

For example, legislation in Sweden and Norway paved the way for reforms of the work environments in those countries (Deutsch, 1981).

In the United States, laws and regulations have had major impacts on gender, age, racial, religious, and ethnic discrimination in the workplace, although many inequities remain. For example, the number of women in coaching and administrative positions in college athletics has increased as a result of Title IX and Equal Employment Opportunity (EEO) regulations. An unintended consequence, however, may be a sex-segregated structure in athletics, with women coaching women's teams and men coaching men's teams (Abbott & Smith, 1984). The "big-ticket" items in college athletics remain football and men's basketball, so that a power differential will undoubtedly continue. In addition, the role of athletic director remains a largely male position.

Another important focus of legislation has been workers' wages and hours. Economic crises, such as depressions and recessions, have typically been followed by greater protections and extensions of wage and hour coverage to more workers (Steinberg, 1982).

Earlier, we noted that unions' greatest impact may have been in their lobbying for unemployment insurance and other measures that provide workers with basic economic security. Unionization has also affected minimum-wage legislation. States with high levels of unionization are more likely to have progressive minimum-wage laws (Steinberg, 1982). The adversarial relationship between unions and employers is also a manifestation of class conflict, which is another way of understanding work.

Class Conflict

The class-conflict approach sees workers as pitted against owners and managers. In other chapters we have considered the class-conflict approach and found it less than useful as the basis for understanding the nature of work or as the dominant source of change in work. In Chapter 1, for example, we considered the issue of deskilling. Class conflict theorists hold that owners and managers systematically seek to deskill work to increase their measure of control over workers. Empirical evidence does not offer strong support for that position. In Chapter 2 we considered the extent to which the executive elite could be considered a class that acts in its own behalf. The evidence here appears to be stronger. Nevertheless, this elite is unable to impose its will completely, which suggests some additional weakness in the class-conflict approach.

The class-conflict approach has also been applied to the political context of work. One basic issue is whether class consciousness serves as the basis for attempts at worker control on the part of owners and managers. The evidence indicates that this is only a partial answer for the forms of contemporary work.

A second basic issue is whether class consciousness is at the core of movements designed to alter social relations at the workplace, such as those to change laws regarding wages and hours or to eliminate gender discrimination. After an extensive review of labor movements and social movements, Landsberger (1976) concludes that class consciousness is not the core phenomenon: "A class-conscious working-class movement with revolutionary potential, of the kind envisaged in the early part of this century, is over and done with: atrophied by success in economically developed societies; subject to repression by governments of all political colors in the developing nations" (p. 870).

Although class consciousness is not now a force in the West, it certainly has strong potential in areas such as South Africa and other settings where oppression of entire classes of people still occurs.

If class-conscious social movements do not play the crucial role in the political arena surrounding work, what does? The answer appears to lie in a point that has been made repeatedly in this book: Work is carried out in organizations. Organizations have a powerful role in every society, but they are even more powerful in a country like the United States. As I have written elsewhere (Hall, 1991):

> [T]he modern organization is a legal entity, just like the individual person. Legality is granted by the state, itself a legal creation. While the individual is given a set of rights and responsibilities by the state, rights and responsibilities are extended to organizations. These rights, coupled with size, give organizations an enormous amount of power within the state. The state or government is more comfortable

dealing with other organizations than with individual
persons, and thus tends to provide more preferential
treatment to organizations in areas as diverse as taxation or
rights to privacy. (pp. 15-16)

The political arena surrounding work is composed of organizational actors: corporations, the government, labor unions, professional associations, and social-reform organizations on both the
political right and left. Powerful organizations, not social classes,
are thus the key political actors in this country.

Conclusions

Power has been a consistent theme throughout this book, because
power is part of work itself. In this chapter I have attempted to
complete the analysis of the relationship between work and power.
My view is that power arrangements in organizations are subject
to change. Altering the balance of power at work is difficult, given
the organizational setting in which work is carried out, but the
labor movement, attempts at empowerment, and programs of
work reform have all altered existing patterns. Having said this,
I would also note that widespread, revolutionary changes in power
arrangements are extremely unlikely simply because owners and
managers have more power than workers. The sheer possession
of power tends to lead to its perpetuation.

Our focus so far has been work itself. In the next chapter, the
focus will shift. We will consider how work affects family life and
individual health.

■■■ APPLICATION

Symbols and Sources of Power

Where does power reside on your university campus? Perhaps you
should consider the lay of the land. Jeffrey Pfeffer did just that in
his 1981 book, *Power in Organizations*. In examining a partial

map of the hillside campus at the University of California at Berkeley, Pfeffer noted that the more powerful academic departments (in this case, physical science departments) were located higher up on the hillside than less powerful departments (e.g., forestry, education, and public health). Does Pfeffer's discovery apply to your school? Do some departments enjoy prime locations while others are tucked away where nobody ever sees them? Which are housed in the newest or best maintained buildings? Which (if any) are housed in neglected and drafty structures that have not seen a coat of paint in 15 years? Are these differences symbolic of differences in departmental power?

Symbols of power are not restricted to university departments. Important-sounding titles, convenient reserved parking spaces, executive washrooms, company cars, and large offices appointed with leather sofas and plush carpeting are just a few of the easily recognizable symbols of individual power in organizations. If you know what the symbols are, you may be able to identify powerful organizational actors with little or no prior knowledge of the organization's structure. Often the power holder parks just outside the front door and rides the elevator to his or her office on the top floor.

Symbols are more than just indicators of power, however. They may also play an important role in the exercise of power. Consider for a moment Dahl's (1957) definition of power, which was presented earlier in this chapter: "A has power over B to the extent that he can get B to do something that B would not otherwise do" (pp. 202-203). This definition makes clear the role of persuasion (if not coercion) in the exercise of power. When used assiduously, symbols can provide the power holder with a valuable tool for persuading others and for justifying the use of power in the first place.

One of the most important symbols used by power holders is political language. Power holders sometimes use political language to justify their actions and to obfuscate any conflict of interest that may exist between the power holder and those who are subject to that power. For example, how would you react if, as you arrived at work one morning, your boss took you aside and explained that from that point forward you would be doing the work of three people, with no increase in pay? You might be tempted to go looking for another job. But what if instead your boss explained that your job was being "enlarged" so that you would enjoy "more variety and a greater sense of responsibility"? Suddenly the new arrangement has a different ring to it.

The point here is not to suggest that power holders are inherently malevolent or deceitful. Also, it is unlikely that many attempts at job redesign are initiated with absolutely no concern for the interests of workers. However, this example does serve to illustrate the importance of language as a tool for highlighting points where interests converge and smoothing over points of conflicting interests. Thus political language is a crucial means of persuasion by which the powerful may gain acceptance for their decisions.

Aside from language, other symbols or symbolic activities are associated with the effective use of power. Pfeffer identifies ceremonies as serving important symbolic functions for power holders. Consider the ceremonies that surround the selection of a new president or supreme court justice. The pomp and circumstance (and sometimes intense scrutiny) that are associated with such selection processes serve in part to legitimate the successor's power in the eyes of others. Sometimes these ceremonies are little more than token rituals. In other cases they involve a careful assessment of the potential successor's character and qualifications. In either case, the existence of a formal induction procedure is symbolic of the power inherent in the position.

Of course, symbols do not a power holder make. We can all probably think of examples of powerless puppet leaders surrounded by the symbolic trappings of power but possessing little in the way of genuine influence. The British royal family, for instance, although clearly in possession of some clout, wields far less power than might be inferred from observations of the regal symbols that surround it. Power is not necessarily inherent in one's position.

What, then, are some of the sources of substantive power in organizations? Some of these were described earlier in this chapter. For example, the possession of specialized knowledge or skill is associated with power in organizations. If you are the only one who really understands the computer network where you work, you are clearly in a position of power. You might be able to use your "irreplaceability" as a source of leverage for convincing others (including management) to act on your behalf. In this case, as the saying goes, "Knowledge is power."

The preceding example is really a special case of a more general rule. Generally speaking, the more dependent others are on you, the more power you hold (Pfeffer, 1981). Such dependence is typically created when people are in possession of something that others need or value, such as specialized knowledge or some other resource (perhaps money or materials). In either case, the level of power enjoyed will vary as a function of the scarcity of the resource. When what you have is quite rare, your power is augmented. When what you possess is commonly available, you will enjoy little leverage.

Finally, power can derive from one's position in the organization's communication network. This includes formal as well as informal channels of communication (Kanter, 1977a). Belonging to the same exclusive social club as the company president may give you access to power not enjoyed by other members of the organization. The ability to communicate informally with a top organizational official may prove just as valuable from a power standpoint as the ability to communicate via "proper channels." In fact, informal communication may be more efficient and effective than formal communication, especially if the organization is highly bureaucratized. In that case, informal power structures complicate the formal hierarchy.

■■■ SUGGESTED READINGS

A complete bibliographical entry for each work cited here can be found in the reference section at the back of this book.

Worker militancy has not ended. Fantasia, *Cultures of Solidarity* (1988), offers ample proof of the development and outcomes of militancy.

Unions face severe threats from the closing of plants and offices. The far-reaching impact of plant closings can be vividly seen in Perrucci, Perrucci, Targ, and Targ, *Plant Closings* (1988).

Tausky, *Work and Society* (1984), provides a solid overview of the contemporary role of unions.

11 The Dynamics of Work, Family, and Health

Some years ago I had the pleasure of living in Burlington, Vermont—a lovely city in a lovely part of the world. Just outside of Burlington was a large plant and office facility of IBM, and so I naturally became acquainted with several IBM employees. One day, one of these friends asked me, "What does 'IBM' stand for?" I replied, "International Business Machines, of course." The friend then said, "No, you're wrong. It means 'I've Been Moved.'"

He was referring, of course, to the IBM policy of that time of moving its managerial and professional personnel around the country and the world. IBM, along with most major corporations and the military, has personnel for whom job transfers are an expected part of work life. Even sociologists are not immune: I have made seven such long-distance moves in my career.

These moves are just one example of how work may affect family life. When people move as part of their work, their families generally move with them. This has obvious repercussions for the work of spouses, the education of children, and relationships with parents and other relatives. Despite arguments that life in the United States is becoming homogenized, there are clear differences between living in, say, upstate New York, New York City, Minnesota, and Southern California. Moving therefore requires that the whole family adjust to the subculture of the new location.

The main focus of this chapter is work-family linkages, including not only the effects of geographic mobility but also the role of children, dual-worker families, and housework. We will also consider the relationships between work, family life, and physical and mental health.

324

Work and the Family

The linkages between work and the family are complex. Part of the complexity results from changes that have taken place in family form and composition in recent years. Today we have more single-parent families and homosexual families than ever before (Schneider, 1986); even the traditional extended family, with three or more generations living together, is reemerging (Spitze, 1988b). Such variety makes the work-family relationship a complicated one to analyze. To simplify matters, the focus here will be mainly on the nuclear family: a mother, a father, and their children.

The traditional image of a family portrays the man as the only breadwinner and the woman as the housewife and mother. This is the image we tend to hold of families in our grandparents' time. However, this image is inaccurate for most families; it was not even accurate in "the good old days." An analysis of women's work in 1900 found that there was a great deal of "hidden" employment of women at that time (Bose, 1984). Unpaid farm work or work in a family-owned business was common. So, too, was taking in boarders. In any family enterprise—farm, business, or boarding-house—work and family roles are highly intertwined. Employment outside the home, in the labor force, is not a new phenomenon either, as Chapter 6 explained. It would appear that the norm is (and has been) for both husband and wife to work.

The best way to conceptualize the work-family relationship, given that both adult members of the nuclear family are likely to be in the labor force, is to consider four roles simultaneously: the female work role, the male work role, the male family role, and the female family role (Pleck, 1977). The advantage of this formulation is that it permits a simultaneous consideration of the impact of work roles on family roles and vice versa for both men and women.

Work and family roles are generally intertwined. To clarify how these roles interact, Mortimer and her associates undertook a series of studies of male college graduates in the early stages of their managerial and professional careers (Mortimer, 1980; Mortimer, Hall, & Hill, 1978; Mortimer, Lorence, & Kumka, 1986). This research involved asking a "panel" of University of Michigan graduates about their work experiences in the early years of their careers. These men were first surveyed while in college and then again 10 years later. The researchers wanted to find out how the husband's occupation relates to work-induced family strain, the wife's supportiveness of his occupational role, and his marital satisfaction.

Previous research had found that marital satisfaction generally increases with the prestige of the husband's occupation, but that this satisfaction levels off or reverses direction at the highest socioeconomic levels. Mortimer's research supported this view. The professional and managerial occupations of the men she studied have ponderous requirements for career advancement, long hours and time pressure, lots of overnight travel, and frequent geographical mobility. The men themselves tend to be deeply involved in their careers. The results for the family are often disastrous, because there is little time left for participating in family activities and sharing family responsibilities.

Before continuing, we should add two points to the conclusions reached in Mortimer's studies. First, requirements for geographical mobility are not limited to managerial and professional workers; migrant laborers, for instance, have equal if not greater mobility. By the same token, extended and unusual hours of work can be found in a host of white-collar and blue-collar jobs—the cross-country bus or truck driver or the person working two jobs come immediately to mind (Mortimer et al., 1978). Regardless of their position on the vertical or horizontal dimension of work, the vast majority of people find that involvement with work takes time away from the family.

Since the advent of women's studies and the women's movement, many researchers have focused on women's experience of the linkage between work and family life. Several have examined the forms of work that women take when they have family obligations. They have found that, in women's decisions about what types of work to pursue, they often consider factors that make it easier to fulfill both work and family obligations. The length of the journey to work and the flexibility and convenience of the work have been found to be important to women with families when such a choice is available (Eriksen, 1977; Martin & Hanson, 1985).

The flexibility and convenience of various types of work differs considerably. Professional and managerial women often allow their work to intrude on their family roles by bringing work home (the jampacked brief case) or working longer hours. The reverse is often true for working-class women: Family roles intrude on work because of inadequate child care or inflexible work schedules. Single mothers, particularly in the working class, can be overwhelmed by role overload and anxiety (Burriss, 1991).

Clearly, tradition and traditional expectations increase the burden on women. While the boss is frowning about a female worker taking time off to care for a sick child, the female worker is feeling guilty about not having enough time to make sure her child is staying healthy. It has been argued that both patriarchy and capitalism—political and economic conditions surrounding both home and workplace—explain women's difficult position (Sokoloff, 1980). The same would logically also be true for men. Whether or not we attribute the conflicts between the demands of work and family to broad capitalistic and patriarchal trends, we can clearly see that female and male work and family roles are affected by important outside forces. There are important "inside" forces as well: the children who are part of the family.

Children

As we saw in Chapter 4, in the discussion of occupational status and the vertical dimension, the family (or more accurately parents' occupations) is a critical component in children's status and income attainment. And not only do parents affect children's eventual work roles, but also even more basic is the effect of having children on parents' work roles.

Dispassionate consideration of the relationships between work and having children is difficult. Romantic imagery and religious beliefs combined with social expectations lead us to feel that somehow having children is normal. Couples who opt not to have children experience a great deal of pressure from their peers and from their parents, who may want to be grandparents. Couples who cannot have children are frequently made to feel guilty: Whose fault is it? Is it his? Is it hers? The notion that any real couple can match the "normal" couple, is, of course, highly unrealistic. The timing, number, and spacing of children depend heavily on a couple's circumstances and personal preferences. Today, fertility, or the average number of children born to each woman, has decreased because of the combined forces of industrialization, decreased infant mortality and increased levels of education, women's labor-force participation (WLFP), and divorce rates (Huber & Spitze, 1983). This change is part of the general demographic transition. Fertility and WLFP have a reciprocal relationship. In the short run, fertility has a strong impact on wives' employment, while in the long run, employment has a strong impact on fertility (Cramer, 1980). There appear to be two explanations for this relationship. The first is based on economic factors and considerations; the second is noneconomic.

Economic Factors Affecting Fertility. The economic explanation for declining fertility recognizes that people frequently delay marriage or childbearing in order to become economically established. (Keep in mind, however, that fertility is not always planned and rational, as the incidence of out-of-wedlock children attests [Spitze, 1988b].) In fact, a high rate of employment is found for young women, married or not. Women's employment rates decline with childbirth, but increase again as children age and the costs associated with raising and educating children increase (Oppenheimer, 1982).

Fertility, economic attainment, and education also have complex links. There is strong evidence that education is a major WLFP determinant: Those with the highest and lowest levels of schooling are most likely to work. In addition, both men and women tend to delay parenthood as long as they are pursuing an education. Thus the longer they pursue an education, the longer they are likely to delay parenthood. And the longer they delay parenthood, the fewer children they are likely to have.

On the other hand, early parenthood reduces educational attainment (Oppenheimer, 1982). Premarital sexual activity complicates the picture further. Women who are more sexually active before they marry and those who begin sexual activity at an early age are more likely to have children before they complete their education. Because low educational attainment is related to limited career achievement, early childbearing has been found to be negatively related to economic well-being (Hofferth & Moore,

1979; Marini, 1984). The lesson is this: Having kids at a young age lowers attainment; higher attainment lowers the number of kids a person will have.

These economic and educational factors appear to be particularly applicable to white families. Black women do not leave the labor force as often with the arrival of children, contrary to the pattern among whites (Wilkie, 1984).

The relationship between economic factors and fertility should continue to be operative in the future (Huber & Spitze, 1983). The direct costs of childbearing and the opportunity costs of staying home (such as slower career development), particularly for educated women, will continue to drive the fertility rate down. In addition, although children once had economic value as unpaid labor and as a prospective source of support when parents reached old age, the economic rewards of having children have declined.

Noneconomic Factors Affecting Fertility. The second explanation for the relationship between wives' employment and fertility is noneconomic. Many women like their work and make decisions not to have children or to limit the number that they do have so that they can continue working. One study asked young women about both their plans for labor-force participation at age 35 and the number of children they planned to bear in their lifetimes. Both married and never-married women who planned to continue working also planned to have fewer children. This relationship held regardless of husbands' income and attitudes toward wives' labor-force participation (Waite & Stolzenberg, 1976).

There is yet another factor to be considered here. There is mounting evidence that people who have children tend to be happier than those who do not (Brody, 1992). Still, some believe that the psychological costs of having children—not every child is a genius or a superb athlete—will contribute to a continuing decline in fertility (Huber & Spitze, 1983). The psychological benefits are also increasingly difficult to realize because children leave the home and community to establish their own nuclear families. My own feeling, however, is that the benefits of having children far outweigh the costs.

Dual Work Roles

Families in which both wives and husbands are in the labor force are now overwhelmingly the norm. In only 6% of American families is the husband a full-time participant in the labor force and the wife a full-time homemaker in the home (Fox & Hesse-Biber, 1984).

Whether a wife works often depends on the economic contribution she can make to her family by working. In lower-income and lower-status families, wives' contributions are a substantial part of the family income. Wives in higher-income families are less likely to work, because it would contribute less to the total (Oppenheimer, 1982). Black women, however, are more likely to continue in the labor force as their husbands' incomes increase (Wilkie, 1984).

Dual work has the potential to disrupt family life, career decisions, and the marriage relationship. The problems are even greater when both spouses are pursuing professional or managerial careers. Let us take a look at these issues.

Impact on Family Life. Dual-worker families have great potential for role overload and role conflict. Employers demand that people be at work at particular times and in particular places. Family matters often require attention at the same particular times that a person is working but at different places. If the work role conforms to a regular 40-hour, 5-day work week, another basic issue is one of role overload, because housework tasks, family maintenance activities (shopping, child care, and affection), and other family duties all have to be crammed in at the end of the day or on weekends. If the work role requires extended or irregular hours of work or travel, the problem is worse.

The wife typically bears the brunt of these overloads and conflicts (for documentation, see Fox & Hesse-Biber, 1984; Spitze, 1988b). This is because traditional role expectations, which are held by both husbands and wives in many instances, dictate that wives take charge of child care, cooking, cleaning, and the like. These traditional role expectations come about for a variety of reasons. Women and men are still socialized into such expectations, and married people's own parents have expectations about how their children should act. Other social institutions also reinforce traditional expectations. When a child is sick, for example, schools overwhelmingly call the mother before calling the father, and it is the mother who is expected to stay home with a sick child.

Because of these role expectations, married women in the labor force tend to give precedence to the family. Married men are more able to keep their work and family roles separate without trading off one against the other (Bielby & Bielby, 1989). This is not necessarily a negative for all women, however, because many women value a balance between work and family and make clear and conscious trade-offs (Statham, Vaughan, & Houseknecht, 1987).

Overloads and strains are particularly acute in three areas (Fox & Hesse-Biber, 1984, pp. 181-187). First are housekeeping standards, which involve the quality of cooking, decorating, entertaining, cleaning, and correspondence. Several options are available here. Standards can be lowered. Some activities can be eliminated, such as entertaining. Other activities can be purchased, such as cleaning and cooking, if the family is sufficiently affluent.

The second area of strain is children. But the problem with role overload in this area is more complicated than with housekeeping standards, because few parents would want to lower their child-rearing standards. Some argue that the quality of time spent with children is more important than the quantity, but if parents are not available when children need parenting or are too tired from work to have quality relationships, problems can develop. Of course, it is possible to eliminate some child-care tasks, such as driving children to various activities; going to sporting events, plays, and musical programs; or volunteering for school activities. The problem here is that if all parents eliminated these tasks, the activities themselves might suffer. Alternatively, such activities could become the domain of those parents, typically the more affluent wives, who are not in the labor force.

There is less likelihood of dual-work conflicts when young children are present, because WLFP declines (but does not necessarily stop) during such times. However, those who need or want to work often have trouble finding alternative child-care arrangements that are affordable, reliable, and convenient. Many employers have at least begun to investigate the possibility of making some sort of provisions for employees' children. My university is about to provide child-care facilities on its main campus for the first time. These will, of course, be for students, staffmembers, and faculty members. The availability of child-care facilities near the workplace increases the odds that women who have recently given birth will return to their jobs. This is a desirable outcome for organizations, because it reduces costly turnover. Organizations that set up a child-care program for employees will also probably have happier and more productive workers who are less likely to miss work (Brody, 1992). All but the most conservative are now in favor of child care at the workplace, but we still have major debates about who should pay—the parents, the employer, or the public. It is to the employers' long-run advantage to offer child care, but it is only really feasible for larger and more affluent employers.

The third area of strain in dual-work families involves the allocation of household tasks. As noted above, these tasks are allocated disproportionately to women. Even though these women may feel overburdened, most marriages are not permanent battlegrounds on the issue of who does the housework (Huber & Spitze, 1983, p. 91). People come into marriages with expectations about how household tasks should be allocated and tend to marry those who share their beliefs. If the beliefs of one spouse change, there will be negotiations to achieve a new consensus or, in some cases, a divorce.

Impact on Career Decisions. Thus far we have been considering dual-work problems and issues that occur in the family setting. If we turn the focus in the opposite direction—toward work—a different, but still perplexing set of issues can be identified. The fundamental work problem for working husbands and wives is "simply finding two jobs that will provide satisfactory employment and still allow them to live in the same area and coordinate work and nonwork schedules" (Fox & Hesse-Biber, 1984, p. 183). This fundamental problem is most acute when a couple moves to a new location or when the decision is first made to become a dual-work family. When a man and woman who are both working decide to get married and continue their work, there is little problem at first. The problems arise when one person is transferred or changes jobs (a common phenomenon), which can throw the work of the spouse into incompatibility.

When job transfers or changes do take place, there are several factors that determine the extent to which being a dual-work family affects work. One factor is the degree of occupational specialization, because more specialized work is harder to find. Another factor is the degree to which work is a central life interest; when work is not of such paramount interest, people are more willing to make compromises about the kind of work they take. A final factor is the work stages of the partners, because people at the most intense stages of their careers will have a harder time adjusting to transfers or changes on the part of their spouses.

For some professional and managerial workers, being married to a nonworking wife is a big plus. The wife is viewed as a career resource (Pfeffer & Ross, 1982). Unfortunately, if an employer expects participation by a spouse and the spouse is unavailable for such participation because of his or her own work, the employer may not be particularly understanding.

Impact on the Marriage. There is yet another area of difficulty common to dual-work families, and this is the marriage relationship itself (Fox & Hesse-Biber, 1984, pp. 186-187). The relationship can suffer if the spouses see themselves in competition for success. Some female lawyers resist even entering a relationship lest it interfere with their promising legal careers (Epstein, 1980, 1981b).

The marriage can also suffer if so much energy and emotion is put into work that little or none is left for the relationship itself. This sort of absence will not make the heart grow fonder, nor will abstinence. The result may be reduced satisfaction with the marriage (Kingston & Nock, 1987). In any circumstances, unsatisfactory marriages have the potential of breaking up, but there is some evidence that dual careers make divorce even more likely: Women who have come to dislike their husbands are more likely to consider divorce if they have the means to live independently (Huber & Spitze, 1983).

The problems that arise in a dual-worker marriage are exacerbated when one of the spouses is moonlighting with two or more jobs. One study of moonlighting during the mid-1970s found that some 21% of husbands had two jobs. Moonlighting is most common in families with young children, because of financial need. For both wives and husbands, the strain on the relationship is considerable (Dempster-McClain & Moen, 1989). Conflicting role demands lead to both marital and job dissatisfaction (Coverman, 1989).

Dual Careers. The problems affecting family roles, work roles, and relationships are intensified greatly when the dual work takes the form of dual careers (Holmstrom, 1973; Hunt & Hunt, 1977; Mortimer, 1978; Rapoport & Rapoport, 1971). These are situations in which both husbands and wives are in demanding and competitive occupations that require high levels of commitment, long hours, deep involvement, and full devotion. The stereotypical business executive, physician, lawyer, university professor, or clergy member serves as an ideal example of the forms of work that cause problems.

There is an interesting parenthetical issue here: the "two-person career" (Papanek, 1973). The two-person career is one in which there are strong expectations that a spouse be an active and integral part of a person's career. A classic example is the male Protestant minister and his wife (Taylor & Hartley, 1975). In this situation the wife is expected to share in the husband's career not only by doing things such as teaching Sunday school or leading the choir but also by dressing appropriately and acting as a "minister's wife." The two-person career can also be seen in many instances among politicians. Indeed, candidates' spouses have become integral—and sometimes controversial—components of political campaigns. Just consider the controversy that has surrounded Hillary Rodham Clinton ever since the 1992 U.S. presidential campaign. Ambassadors' wives have been shown to play a similarly visible and public role (Hochschild, 1976). Despite these examples, the two-person career is increasingly anachronistic.

The severe strains of dual-career marriages can be reduced in several ways. One spouse can become less involved in either work or family, or the spouses may take turns being intensely involved in either work or family. There can also be structural adjustments, such as flexible work schedules (flextime) or job sharing, in which the husband and wife share a single job (Fox & Hesse-Biber, 1984). Most of these approaches to reducing the strains of dual-career marriages involve diminished career involvement. Unfortunately, other people who are competitors in the same field do not diminish their involvement, which puts the less-involved person at a disadvantage.

Housework

We examined housework as a form of work in Chapter 2. Two conclusions from the analysis in that chapter are important in the present context. First, when people are married, housework is predominantly the work of women, regardless of the extent to which women participate in the labor force. Second, housework has economic value in its own right (Becker, 1981; Berk & Berk, 1983; Huber & Spitze, 1983). The point of this section is to explore how housework is affected by the dynamics of the work-family relationships that we have been describing.

All housework activities can be purchased, but only the extremely affluent or the extremely incapacitated hire someone else to take care of all their cooking, cleaning, clothing needs, building maintenance, and other housework activities. Housework tasks range from those that are done on a daily basis—cooking, doing dishes, disposing of garbage—to those that are done on an annual basis—putting up storm windows, planting flowers, and so on. These tasks require a great deal of time and effort, whether or not anyone is paid to do them.

Although both housework and "market" work are work, there are important differences. According to Schooler, Miller, Miller, and Richtand (1984), what really distinguishes housework from market work are the interpersonal and organizational contexts of housework:

> On an interpersonal level, household members are more mutually dependent for a wider range of personal needs than are fellow employees. Thus, the interpersonal relationships found in the home are generally more intense than those in the workplace. The motivation for performing the work may also be quite different in the two contexts; for example altruism may be a stronger motive in the household than in the workplace. These interpersonal factors may affect the meaning and impact of the work for the worker in the household.

At the organizational level, the family differs from usual work organizations in both its internal and external relationships. Family relationships are marked by an absence of formal definitions of supervisory roles and job responsibilities. Although societal sex-role norms obviously affect the assignment of household tasks, in most families the division of labor is not as explicit as in a paid-work setting. Furthermore, except by remote analogy, it makes no sense to specify a houseworker's hierarchical position in a formal supervisory structure or to think of the level of bureaucratization in a family. There are also fewer objective internal and external validations of work well done in the home than in the paid-work setting. Promotions, profits, or pay raises are not available as signals to the homeworker. In fact, in the home it is unclear what work must be done (e.g., is cleaning under the beds necessary?) and what standards must be met (e.g., are water-spotted glasses necessarily unacceptable?). Even obvious failure, such as the breakup of a household, is far from proof that the housework was not well done. Thus some important dimensions of paid work cannot be applied to housework. It is even difficult to fix the boundary line between housework and leisure-time activities. At what point do cooking, gardening, or furniture repair cease being household chores and become hobbies? (pp. 99-100)

Schooler, Miller, Miller, and Richtand (1984) developed an innovative research plan that permitted them to compare housework and market work. They used information from a national sample of husbands and wives in which housework was measured along the same dimensions that have been applied to market work. They compared the two types of work on such aspects as complexity, degree of routinization, the time pressure under which the work is performed, the heaviness of the physical labor involved, how dirty one gets while performing the work, and the frequency with which one is held responsible for things beyond one's control. These aspects of work have been found to be related to aspects of psychological functioning, such as effective intellectual functioning and open, flexible orientations toward other people. Note that this approach does not consider socialization activities and socioemotional support, which are a very important component of housework.

Several findings from the Schooler et al. (1984) study are of interest to us here. First, they found some differences—but more important, similarities—between the tasks that are part of housework and market work. Task complexity is related to physically heavy labor in housework but not in paid employment. Housework is more routinized than paid employment but involves more complex work with things than does paid employment. Nevertheless, Schooler et al. (1984) conclude that "if done for pay, housework would not be a particularly unusual job" (p. 121).

A major but not unexpected finding was the presence of marked gender differences in spheres of responsibility and activity. The husbands' spheres of activities concerned household repairs, while wives are responsible for and actually do a far wider array of household tasks necessary for the daily household maintenance. This pattern was found whether or not the wife worked outside the home and regardless of other important background variables such as family income, education, and number of children under age 16.

For women, the relationship between housework and psychological functioning is comparable to the relationship between paid employment and psychological functioning. In other words, more substantively complex housework (the creative, skilled tasks such as cooking and sewing) has strong relationships with flexibility in thinking and with self-directedness; heavy housework (such as scrubbing floors) reduces both flexibility in thinking and self-directedness. In addition, being held responsible for things beyond one's control was related to feelings of distress.

For men, the picture was very different. It was not the substantive complexity of work that was related to self-direction and flexibility in thinking, but the heaviness of the housework! This unexpected finding is exactly the opposite from that found in paid employment for men. Schooler et al. (1984) believe that this can be explained by the fact that doing heavy work at home may be different than that done on the job and may fulfill some aspects of the men's self-images. It is probably more fulfilling to complete painting one's house than to do similar heavy work on something that you will never see again. Another surprising finding for men was that the substantive complexity of the work they performed at home was unrelated to their psychological functioning.

Schooler et al. (1984) conclude that housework has a different meaning for women than for men because housework is an imperative for women. Men are held responsible for little housework and thus it has less meaning for them. For women, it is much more critical to their total psychological functioning.

Schooler et al.'s (1984) analysis does not give us answers to some intriguing questions. For example, is there some point at which paid employment outweighs housework as a determinant of women's psychological well-being? It would seem that the woman who is strongly involved in work and hires someone else to do the housework will have less of a personal investment in doing the housework well. In situations in which men have more household responsibilities, as a single parent or as an egalitarian spouse, does housework have greater salience for psychological functioning? Answers to questions such as these await further research.

Geographic Mobility

People and families have always moved to find food, shelter, and work. The settlement of North America by Europeans is a story of people first moving across the Atlantic Ocean and then moving across the continent in search of work. Native Americans, of course, were forced away from their traditional work as the great westward movement of Europeans occurred. People still move to find work. Part of the growth of the Sunbelt in the United States has been based on people leaving areas in the Northeast and Midwest and seeking work in the South and West.

This example might lead you to believe that geographic mobility is a pure labor market phenomenon, but it is not. There are important nonmarket redistributions of labor that involve job transfers (Sell, 1982, 1983a, 1983b). Such transfers take place at all levels of the vertical dimension but are more frequent at the higher socioeconomic levels. Those who are most likely to be transferred are higher-status men. The rate of relocation doubled from the 1960s to the 1970s and appears to be continuing unabated (Sell, 1983a).

Obviously, geographical mobility will affect the family and the work of a spouse. Some wives who were not working before the move find it easier to get a job in the new location. However, most wives who were working before the move have trouble finding a job equivalent to or better than their previous jobs. They enter new labor markets and lose their job-related social networks (Campbell, 1988; Deitch & Sanderson, 1987). These patterns are similar for married women in their 20s, 30s, and 40s. Fortunately, the effects of long-distance moves do not last beyond the first year or two (Duncan & Perrucci, 1976; Spitze, 1984).

There appears to be growing realization on the part of some employers that their demands for geographical mobility now must consider the desires and employment of spouses, but there appears to be little likelihood that job transfers will disappear. Corporate managers are developed through socialization and selection as people are placed in different locations (Sell, 1983a). The same patterns are evident in the military, higher education, and the government.

Work and Health

As we have seen, work and family life are related in complex ways. So are work, family life, and individual health. At the extremes, however, the issue is probably quite simple. People who love their work and love their families will probably enjoy good health, while those who hate their work and hate their families will not. Very few situations are that simplistic, of course, and thus the evidence in regard to work, family, and health is unclear.

One study, for example, found that married women were in poorer mental health than married men. Married employed women had more demands on them than their husbands did but fewer demands than unemployed wives (Gove & Geerken, 1977). Another study found that working married women had improved mental health because of objective changes that had occurred in their life situations—most notably, increased income. The husbands of working women, in contrast, experienced more psychological distress, because of the contradiction of traditional sex-role orientations, greater housework pressures, and greater child-care demands (Kessler & McRae, 1982).

These discrepant kinds of findings can be at least partially reconciled when a broader set of considerations is brought into the analysis. This broader consideration involves the notion of preferences for work and preferences for traditional roles. When a wife is working, but both she and her husband believe that he should be the sole breadwinner, there is a great deal of depression. Depression is least in cases in which both husband and wife work and both are responsible for the housework (Ross, Mirowsky, & Huber, 1983).

In any event, work expectations interact with family expectations and have consequences for both physical and mental health. Both work and family carry a heavy emotional content with them and each can spill over into the other sphere.

Work by itself, independent of family considerations, also has some significant effects on health. The relationships between work and health take many forms, ranging from matters of life and death to the rather mundane finding that a sense of well-being at work is related to a sense of well-being away from work (Bergermaier, Bork, & Champoux, 1984). The importance of the work-health relationship was recognized in the 1973 publication of *Work in America* (O'Toole et al., 1973; also see O'Toole, 1984). The authors noted that relationships exist between the quality of work and longevity, heart disease and other cardiovascular problems, ulcers, arthritis, and various forms of mental illness. In addition to these problems, researchers have identified linkages between work and alcohol abuse (Fennel, Rodin, & Kantor, 1981), drug abuse, and suicide.

Work in America was valuable because it helped to focus national attention on problems in the workplace. Unfortunately, it viewed most problems of work from a social psychological standpoint, with possible improvements seen as coming from improving the quality of working life and thus levels of job satisfaction. Such an approach overlooks more immediate and more radical linkages between work and health. For example, some jobs are very dangerous physically, such as coal mining (Wallace, 1987) and offshore oil-rig work (Carson, 1982).

Some sociologists see the issue of truly dangerous work from the standpoint of class conflict, with workers assuming the risks and owners reaping the benefits (Gersuny, 1981). The more physically dangerous jobs clearly involve manual work, which is usually among the lowest-paid work. There are legitimate questions in regard to who should pay how much to whom for the performance of hazardous work. Even though premium wages are paid for recognizably hazardous work, owners still make profits without themselves undergoing risks. The problem with this sort of analysis, of course, is that the same risks are present in noncapitalist systems. In every society, some workers always assume the riskier jobs, and they always tend to be lower-status workers.

Work that presents immediate physical danger is easy to identify. More difficult is the identification of health risks that do not show up immediately. For instance, what is the long-term effect of staring at a computer monitor all day? Another concern is the health risks that operate more subtly through social psychological processes. For example, considerable effort has been devoted to exploring the relationship between health and perceived role conflict, role ambiguity, and role overload (Kahn, Wolfe, Quinn, Snoek, & Rosenthal, 1964). The assumption is that the inability to fulfill work obligations because of a lack of clear understanding or because of conflicting or overwhelming demands creates stress that in turn leads to disease. However, it seems that although role conflict, ambiguity, and overload are associated with negative emotional reactions at work, links to other aspects of mental and physical health have yet to be firmly established (Jackson & Schuler, 1985).

It is also difficult to determine if certain aspects of work yield more risk than others. For example, does working long hours create a dangerous health hazard? According to a 1990 *New York Times* article:

> Among 88 million people with full-time jobs last year, nearly
> 24 percent—largely executives, professionals, self-employed
> people, journalists, bureaucrats and the secretaries and
> clerks who toil alongside them—spent 49 or more hours a

week on the job, according the Bureau of Labor Statistics. Ten years ago only 18 percent worked so much. (Cited in Kilborn, 1990)

The implication of this particular article was that long hours of work are related to physical and mental health problems. But not working is also bad for your health. People who have personal experience with unemployment are much more likely than the average citizen to fall ill or suffer an injury (Leigh, 1987). Apparently, work, too much work, and not enough work can all be hazardous to your health.

Conclusions

Work is interwoven with every facet of our lives. In this chapter I have focused on its interactions with family and health. The major conclusion is that the relationships are reciprocal. I know that my work as a college professor has affected my family. We have made cross-country moves, and we have traveled extensively. Our orientations toward work and life are different than they would have been had I become a banker in a small city in Ohio, as many of my college classmates did. Had my wife not become a teacher of cooking, which is a portable occupation, our lives would also have been different.

Some work is dangerous. Some work is dull and boring; some work makes a person feel good. Our health and mental health are affected by our life circumstances. Because our work is a dominant component of these life circumstances, our health and mental health are directly dependent on our work.

Will the patterns we have been describing and analyzing in this chapter and those that preceded it continue into the future? We will explore this issue in the final chapter. It deals with the future of work.

■■ APPLICATION

Work, Family, and the Workaholic

In this chapter we have seen how changing patterns of employment have brought with them new challenges for the integration
of work and family. Involvement with work takes time away from
family, and dual-work and dual-career families face the difficult
task of juggling many roles and responsibilities. Families respond
to these challenges in different ways. For instance, consider the
Jarrets (Rapoport & Rapoport, 1971):

> The Jarrets represent a dual-career family in which each of
> the partners has a paramount, though diverse, commitment
> to career. Family life as such has been of much less
> importance to them as a source of personal gratification. . . .
> The Jarrets differ from [other dual-career families] in their
> lack of emphasis on familism. . . . The Jarrets place relatively
> less emphasis on having a close family life and children, and
> are really only comfortable with their son now [that] he is
> older. (pp. 167-168)

Now compare the Jarrets to the Harrises:

> Participation in both family and work activities are of high
> importance to the Harrises. . . . Apart from the fact that Mrs.
> Harris's work is at a high level, the Harris family structure is
> relatively conventional. The "unconventionality" comes from
> her actual degree of career commitment. Within the family,
> however, the Harrises' expectations of their responsibilities
> and obligations—as well as their rewards and
> privileges—tend to go along conventional sex roles with only
> moderate overlap of activities. While Mr. Harris helps at
> home, he does not have unusual responsibilities there. . . .

> How do the Harrises compare with [other dual-career families] in the way they integrate their children into their work worlds? The Harrises . . . take their children to their place of work, bring home materials for them to play with, talk to them about their work, and so on. . . . While Mr. Harris does not participate very actively in the domestic sphere, it is crucial for the family that his work life is arranged so that there is a degree of flexibility [that] allows him to be available in emergencies and to be involved to some extent in the concerns of his wife. (Rapoport & Rapoport, 1971, pp. 276-277)

The Jarrets found it necessary to emphasize one life sphere, work, at the expense of the other. The Harrises, on the other hand, have been fortunate enough to have fulfilling work and family lives. This appears to result in part from the Harris's attempts to involve their children in their work lives. However, the description also suggests that the successful integration of work and family can be attributed largely to Mrs. Harris's tireless efforts.

The point of these illustrations is that work and family can be integrated in a variety of ways. Some are more successful than others. Some are more appealing than others. However, all involve a certain level of effort or sacrifice on the part of one or more family members.

The integration of work and family roles is particularly difficult under certain circumstances. For instance, family life can be severely disrupted when one or both spouses suffer from workaholism. Wayne Oates (1971) claims to have coined the term *workaholic* to describe those individuals for whom the need for work has begun to interfere with personal happiness and smooth social functioning. Since that time the term has been widely applied in the popular press to describe practically anyone who puts in a long work week. Consider the following examples offered by Allerton (1991):

> One Motorola executive begins her work day in her car by calling voice mail for her messages and phoning Europe. After 13 hours at the office, she stops only to eat dinner with her family before taking calls from Japan at home.

> An international lawyer takes advantage of his firm's 24
> hour word processing crew, sometimes going into the office at
> 10 p.m. on Saturday to fax documents, so that they'll be first
> on someone's desk Monday morning. (p. 74)

The people in these examples obviously are intensely committed to their work. So much so, at least in the case of the Motorola executive, that work seems to have taken precedence over family life.

But are these people workaholics? It depends on who you ask. Although there has been little systematic research on workaholism, several suggestions have been offered for differentiating the workaholic from the otherwise healthy hard worker. For instance, workaholics have been said to be distinguished by their distaste for leisure time (Doerfler & Kammer, 1986; Kleiner & Francis, 1987; Morris & Charney, 1983; Sheridan, 1988; Topolnicki, 1989). As Dr. Jay Rohrlich states, a "work addict" is "somebody who goes through withdrawal symptoms when he isn't working" (quoted in Sheridan, 1988, p. 31). These symptoms may include high levels of anxiety, fitful sleep, and guilt about not being in a productive mode. Often these individuals find it difficult to stop and enjoy an evening meal with their families because of the anxiety this provokes.

Workaholism can have its positive side: "The pleasures of workaholism include acclaim, passionate involvement and gratification, high income, and aesthetic pleasure in work" (Doerfler & Kammer, 1986). However, as you might suspect, workaholism can take a definite toll.

Regardless of the potential benefits associated with total dedication to one's work, there remains one striking correlate of workaholism that is almost universal: The workaholic's interpersonal relations outside of work are severely disrupted. This can put a serious strain on the workaholic's marital and family relations (Kleiner & Francis, 1987). The situation may be particularly difficult for the workaholic mother, who may be expected to fulfill traditional gender roles of homemaker and caretaker (Doerfler & Kammer, 1986). Obviously not all of these roles can be undertaken at once, especially when one is in relentless pursuit of one's work. The result is likely to be dissatisfying or conflict-filled family relations.

Several suggestions have been offered for dealing with workaholism. Workaholics who are resigned to their fate may just as well make the most of the addiction (Morris & Charney, 1983), perhaps by avoiding commitments outside of work (such as marriage) and by moving into a field of endeavor that offers high levels of gratification. Workaholics who wish to recover, on the other hand, might try some of the techniques used to wean people away from other destructive habits. Family members who wish to spend time with a workaholic should take advantage of the workaholic's tendency to schedule everything by writing themselves into the workaholic's appointment calendar (Machlowitz, 1981, cited in Kleiner & Francis, 1987). Social plans should be arranged so that they are difficult to cancel. Family vacations should be insisted upon and meticulously planned in advance (right down to a limitation on the number of business calls the workaholic can make while away).

Segmentation is another effective strategy (Kiechel, 1989). For instance, mechanistic, simple-minded rules such as "Never work at home" and "Never work past 6 p.m." can be helpful—if the workaholic abides by them strictly. Some of these strategies may make it easier for the workaholic to successfully integrate work and family, a challenge that is difficult to meet even under normal circumstances.

■■■ SUGGESTED READINGS

A complete bibliographical entry for each work cited here can be found in the reference section at the back of this book.

We sometimes forget that some work is truly dangerous. For descriptions and analyses of dangerous work, see Carson, *The Other Price of Britain's Oil* (1982), and Gersuny, *Work Hazards and Industrial Conflict* (1981).

The interplay between work and family roles and values is carefully analyzed in Huber and Spitze, *Sex Stratification* (1983).

A more radical view of the work and family relationship from a feminist perspective is provided by Sokoloff, *Between Money and Love* (1980).

12   The Futures of Work

Currently, I am on a search committee for a new athletic director for my university. We are in the process of interviewing four women and men who appear to be very well qualified for the job. One of the men we interviewed said that he did not think that college football would be around for very long, because interest in football was fading among boys as interest in soccer was growing. He could be right or wrong. If he is right, work as a football coach in college will disappear. This kind of situation makes us ask such questions as, Will there be work in the future? What kind of work will it be? Who will be working?

I do not have complete answers to these questions. If I did, I would be a millionaire and very powerful. I do think, however, that we can look at some of the issues examined in earlier chapters and begin to see what the future might hold.

What Work Is

We began our analysis of the sociology of work with a consideration of what work is and is not. Although the definitions of work, occupations, jobs, and careers that were developed have been useful, it would appear that the lines between work and nonwork are actually becoming less distinct.

For example, it is now possible to do more types of paid work at home. Technological change is the key. Given a computer and access to electronic mail, a person could enter data at home and carry out family or parent activities at the same time. I have many colleagues whose home computers are linked to their office computers, which are in turn linked to a mainframe. When I call them at home during the day, I have no idea what they are doing. They could as well be playing with the dog as analyzing data or writing journal articles.

Working at home does have potential problems. Some theorists argue that working at home brings the conflict between work and family into sharper focus; others worry that working at home will result in lower pay, especially for women. Still, the option to work at home is attractive to many people, and as the technology for doing so spreads, more people will take advantage of it.

Developments such as these will make labor-force statistics less valuable. These statistics are based on the idea that people go to work for a fixed number of hours per week. Alternative working arrangements, such as working at home, have already weakened labor-force data. So, too, do temporary workers, who are hired by companies that specialize in filling other organizations' needs for short-term help. People who are so employed may or may not show up in labor-force statistics.

Perhaps a more meaningful term than *labor force* is *work force*. This term conveys a broader picture of what work is and what it will become.

In my thinking, the whole idea of "labor" is itself dated and misleading. It conjures up too much of a factory image. It also contributes to a factory mentality in which people think that manufacturing is the only key to economic and social progress in the United States. In this I agree with John Sculley, chair and CEO of Apple Computer, who stated, "The biggest change in this decade is going to be the reorganization of work itself. In this new economy, the strategic resources are no longer just the ones that come out of the ground, like oil and wheat and coal, but they are ideas and information that come out of our mind" (Scully, 1992). Many other theorists would agree that information and knowledge are commodities of growing importance to our economy.

All too often, the term *labor* is tied to the term *industrial relations*. Cornell University, for example, has long had its distinguished School of Industrial and Labor Relations. When I taught at the University of Minnesota, I had an appointment in the Department of Industrial Relations. Despite these long and proud traditions, the idea of "industrial relations" has also become dated. Indeed, the current common term has become *human resources*. This euphemistic term comes into action as former "personnel departments" or "industrial relations departments" have become "departments of human resources." At my university, we have an Office of Human Resource Management. For some reason, this does not sit well with me.

There is another, more basic, and much more controversial issue embedded in the move away from the idea of labor force. This is the longstanding distinction between labor and management or ownership and labor. I am not suggesting that these distinctions have had no meaning and that we have resolved all the disagreements behind the violence, strikes, and work slowdowns of the past. What I am suggesting is that the older labor-management imagery has lost meaning because of the rapid and sharp increase in layoffs of management personnel, particularly middle managers, in the past decade (Capell, 1992). It would appear that the major distinction for the coming decades will be between those who have work and those who do not. There simply will not be enough work for everyone. Of course, we will continue to find income and other social-class distinctions within both categories: workers and nonworkers.

The Nature of Work

The driving force behind changes in the nature of work is technology. However, it is vital to note that technological change is not monolithic. At one extreme, some workers will be able to use technology to work independently at home or almost anywhere else. However, we will continue to have factory work that changes very little. In fact, although high-technology industries are growing very rapidly, they still account for a minority of new job openings in the United States (Etzioni & Jargowsky, 1990). It appears that a corporation such as Boeing will continue to make passenger aircraft in much the same ways as in the past. Some office work, such as data entry, will also continue to be tedious regardless of technological advances.

Although technological change is not the magic wand that will transform all work, it would be a fallacy to underestimate its role. Some forms of factory work, such as textile manufacturing, are highly amenable to computerization and robotization. In the same manner, although many professions (such as those in law, medicine, and science) require the use of considerable human judgment, more legal, medical, and scientific legwork is now being done by computer.

Technological change has always been a crucial factor in work. The development of the earliest device to till the soil was a technological change. So, too, was the development of the steam engine and the myriad other technological developments that have brought us to this point. What is different today is that we seem to be in a basic *paradigm shift*, according to noted economist Michael Porter (Scully, 1992). The old paradigm involved access to natural resources and large pools of labor. Scientific knowledge also helped through research and development programs. The new paradigm involves international competition and continual investment in research and development, training, and access to foreign markets.

This paradigm shift can be attributed to the phenomenon of space and time compression (Harvey, 1990). In a world in which communication can be global and instantaneous, the dimensions of space and time are fundamentally altered, at least where information is concerned. Transactions involving the exchange of physical objects can be accomplished only after some delay. They also may be impractical when they involve distribution over long distances. However, the emergence of high-technology data-manipulation and transmission systems has allowed for the rise of information-based industries that rely on wide-ranging and high-speed data transmission.

The compression of space and time has resulted in a dramatic growth in business-service industries such as banking, insurance, and travel (Kling & Dunlop, in press). Information has taken on the status of a commodity, allowing for the growth of businesses that deal in the exchange of information and securities—much of which is unrelated to the production of tangible goods (Harvey, 1990). These firms thrive because of technologies that allow space and time to be compressed. These same technologies have a tremendous influence on the nature and requirements of work, which increasingly requires the handling of information rather than the expenditure of physical labor.

The impact of technology is by no means limited to industries that deal in information services. New production technologies are changing the content and availability of work in firms that manufacture tangible goods. Such technologies range from computer systems that automatically control and coordinate the pace of assembly lines to computer systems that assist with the design of new products. Of course, as Carroll (1988) points out, work and workers are affected by these changes:

> Such new technologies require fewer workers but workers with higher skill and intelligence levels who can perform their jobs to some extent independently, exercising judgment and discretion, and monitoring and evaluating machine outputs. These [include] systems that enable designers to design and modify products in a fraction of the time it took formerly. Because the computer can draw the objects and present them in three dimensions on screens and can instantly show the effects of design modifications on such factors as appearance, heat resistance, air flow, and other crucial success factors, there is an enormous saving in expenditures for design and research personnel, or a given expenditure can result in a far higher payoff than formerly was the case. (p. 95)

Technological changes are highly relevant to the deskilling issue introduced in Chapter 1. Instead of a relentless grinding down of skills, we are faced instead with a situation in which greater and more skills will be needed. To be sure, repetitive tasks will not entirely disappear. Data have to be entered, and stereos have to be assembled. Robots can take over repetitive assembly work only if the assembly organization can afford to purchase them. If not, people will do the repetitive assembly work that is at the heart of the peripheral labor market. Organizations in the core will have the robots.

But what about data entry? This is a very thorny issue. Computers do an increasingly good job of data manipulation and word processing. The problem is that someone has to key in the data and the words. Technological changes have not altered this requirement. The time may come when a computer can use voice cues instead of keyed data entry, but someone will still have to read information and enter the data by voice.

There appear to be three scenarios for the future of data entry work. First, in the short term, some of it will be moved away from the core sectors in the United States. Banks and airlines already rely on data entry clerks working on distant Caribbean islands. Second, data-entry work—that done by the traditional clerical worker—would be upgraded. This has already happened at my university. In the past, typists typed the exams and papers and were tied to the typewriter for the entire workday. Now the former typists are managing accounts and budgets and doing other upgraded work. Third, data entry will take place at the point of data usage. This development is linked to the second scenario. In my university, for example, faculty members are entering their own data. No secretary will have a hand in this book. And I now prepare my own course syllabi and exams.

These three data-entry scenarios are developing simultaneously. Over the long run, data-entry clerical work will probably largely disappear. Data will be entered by people at all levels in organizations, as well as by organizations hired specifically to do so. Data-entry organizations can use temporary domestic workers or take the work overseas. These trends will eliminate clerical work as we commonly think about it. Unfortunately, they may also eliminate work opportunities for people who have lower levels of education and skills.

There are two points here that were not emphasized strongly enough in the earlier chapters.

First, education will play an ever-expanding role in work of the future—and for all forms of work. For people to keep up with technological change, education will have to be continuous. You will remember from the discussion in Chapter 2 that semiskilled and unskilled work forms are almost disappearing. This trend will continue, and increasing numbers of skills will be needed for all forms of work. These skills are acquired and honed through education and training.

Second, work will increasingly be international in scope. We have noted that a lot of work relevant to people in the United States is done overseas. I have German skis and ski bindings, Italian ski boots, and a Japanese car in my garage. As I write this, I am listening to a stereo made in China and sold through a Japanese firm. But these are trivial examples. More important are entire new markets around the world for services and goods ranging from health care and higher education to kitchen appliances and personal computers. International finance will play a crucial role in future work. International communication and travel will become more and more common and will involve a greater range of work force members. Being multilingual probably will be a major advantage for individuals.

Varieties of Work

Chapter 2 considered the various forms of work. As we look toward the future, several points stand out. First, the occupations known as professions will continue to prosper and thrive. Some individual professions, such as that of physicians, may be weakened because of developments in the overall delivery of health care, but there will be continuing and growing demands for expert knowledge. At the same time, the lines between many professions and managers or executives will blur. As we have been noting, this latter form of work is increasingly based on specialized expertise, and graduate education is now quite normal for people going into managerial work. My best guess is that we will continue to use the terms *professional*, *manager*, and *executive* much as we have in the past; however, the differences among them in training and skills used will be much less distinct. The key to all will be expert knowledge.

Many observers believe that proprietors have an important role to play in future developments. The line of reasoning is that small businesses are the crucible of new ideas for both technology and business operations. I know of no research that offers definitive proof of this argument, but there is anecdotal evidence in regard to small businesses and innovation. For instance, McDonald's started out as a single hamburger restaurant but developed into a worldwide chain that epitomizes a completely new category of restaurant. McDonald's not only has been successful but also has developed new ways to handle food preparation and customer service, methods that led the way for many others, including Arby's, KFC, and Burger King. Some of these techniques have even been applied to nonfood businesses, such as automobile oil-change operations and quick-copy shops.

The success of McDonald's points up an odd irony. If a small business is not successful, it will go out of business. If it is successful, it will grow and no longer be a small business. Or it may be purchased by or merged with another organization—also meaning that it is no longer a small business.

I have already touched on aspects of the future of clerical and industrial work. Technological change and internationalization appear to be the most important forces that will be operating.

There is a final form of work that will not be affected by all of the changes that have been described. Housework just keeps going and going and going. Love it or hate it, housework will not disappear.

The Individual Experience of Work

Chapter 3 focused on the individual and work. We examined work motivations, the ways in which work roles are learned, and the ways in which people react to their work. There are several important points that should be reiterated here. First, the idea of a hierarchy of motivations must be approached with extreme caution. It is not necessarily better to be motivated by self-actualization than by the desire for more pay. At the same time, I am not arguing that there are not value differences among motivations. Work motivated by racial, religious, or ethnic hatred is abhorrent to me. At the same time, we must realize that work carried out for "higher" motivations such as God or country also can turn ugly—as it did in Nazi Germany.

Second, individuals' motivations, learning, and reactions to work are dynamic over the life course. I am motivated by different factors now than I was 30 years ago. It would be interesting to learn the extent to which people continue to learn new work roles over the life course. I like to think that I am continually learning, but perhaps I only fall back on a repertoire of behaviors that were learned in the past. I do know that different things satisfy me now than in the past and that still other things at work are now distasteful as never before.

Third, most of us do react to work. For some people, work is their central life interest (Dubin, 1992). For others, work is simply a means to an end, something to be endured until the workday is over and dating, sporting, or other, more meaningful activities begin. Work is not a neutral event in our lives. This fact alone is ample evidence for me that improving work satisfaction is worth the effort. It does not matter if the link between work satisfaction and work productivity has not really been demonstrated, except that the evidence is pretty good that productivity leads to satisfaction, rather than the reverse. What does matter is that the activity of work should be satisfying. Employers and unions alike ought to be concerned with satisfaction in all of its ramifications.

As we look to the future, the patterns that were identified in Chapter 3 are quite certain to continue. Work that is intellectually complex, that is challenging, that provides variety, that pays well, and that provides security will continue to provide motivation and satisfaction. At the same time, there will undoubtedly be work that is boring and alienating and that pays poorly and is insecure. Although future forms of work may involve different commodities or require different types of knowledge or skill, people's attitudes toward their work are likely to be shaped by the same general factors that are important today.

How Work Is Categorized

Together, Chapters 4 and 5 presented systems for categorizing a particular occupation. The vertical dimension measures an occupation's socioeconomic status. The horizontal dimension, which is linked to the division of labor, measures an occupation's content and position in the labor market. In general, neither dimension is likely to change much in the future, although some of the specifics may shift.

Status and Occupation: The Vertical Dimension

Chapter 4 examined the linkages between work and socioeconomic status—the vertical dimension. Three points are important here. First, in my opinion, a positive morality is involved. I would rather have status linked to work than most of the alternatives. I do not think status should be linked to family, race, religion, or ethnicity. It should not be inherited.

A form of inheritance does operate in most contemporary societies. After all, the father's or mother's occupation is the first determinant of the son's or daughter's eventual status attainment. Parents' work has a lot to do with children's educational attainments and issues such as if and where children go to college, which is in turn linked to the children's status attainment. At the same time, we do not have direct and exclusive status inheritance. For most people, work is the direct source of status.

Second, status is structured in advance. Employing organizations have hierarchies, and people fill positions in these hierarchies. Let me make the point with a simple example. As I noted at the beginning of this chapter, I am on what is known in academic circles as a "search committee." This committee was formed to recruit and select a new director of athletics for my university. The current director is retiring. We are in the process of screening candidates. The top candidates are men and women who have positions as assistant or associate directors of athletics at other colleges and universities or people in the same position as directors who see a move to Albany as an advancement in their careers. The point is that the position already exists and is waiting to be filled. There are other positions around the country and world that exist and that are waiting to be filled. They can be at the entry level or the executive level. When they are filled, the incumbents' status levels are determined. Thus an individual's placement on the vertical dimension is determined to some extent by the opportunities that exist.

Third, at all levels and in all industries, employment is not permanent and secure. This point is related to the second. Obviously, organizational employment is linked to world economic, political, and social order. Words such as *layoffs, downsizing,* and *retrenchment* strike terror in employees at all levels. Banks fail, schools lay off teachers, IBM and GM downsize, and Pan American goes out of business. The workers affected go into a sort of status limbo until they find new work, at which time their status is determined by the status of their new jobs. To use the terms introduced in Chapter 4, the internal labor market, including job ladders and vacancy chains, cannot be assumed to be set and secure for all time. Even though status is attained in a structured way, the structure can change.

The future is sure to bring with it some degree of structural change. Whether this change is good or bad will depend on the perspective of those who are involved. For instance, new technologies are likely to emerge that allow semiskilled or white-collar employees to perform functions once reserved for skilled, managerial, or professional workers. Some shift in status might result. The unskilled employee might enjoy an increase in status while the status of the skilled worker erodes somewhat. Deskilling from one perspective is "upskilling" from another.

One other important point about status and the future: It appears that the linkages between educational attainment and status will become even stronger. As technological development proceeds, people who have little or no training and education will be in danger of falling to the bottom of the vertical dimension. What will not change is the strong relationship between people's work and their placement on the vertical dimension.

Job Content and Labor Markets: The Horizontal Dimension

Chapter 5 is the most abstract chapter in this book. When I teach these materials, students literally scratch their heads in puzzlement. The simple point is that very different kinds of work can yield identical placement on the vertical dimension. The horizontal dimension is a way to differentiate among those different kinds of work. To me, the horizontal dimension is more theoretically interesting than the vertical dimension, primarily because we have not been able to capture it in a conceptually clear and interesting manner. For the purposes here, perhaps it can be thought of as the distribution of work across the division of labor.

One thing that is clear is that work in different sectors leads to very different world views (Bensman & Lilienfeld, 1991). Just think of the controversy about homosexuals serving in the military. Military personnel of all ranks are nearly unanimous in their opposition. At the same time, people working in the entertainment sector have developed a very different perspective on this issue.

For the future, it appears that some aspects of job content will grow in importance, particularly substantive complexity, management skills, and interpersonal factors. Motor skills and physical demand will continue to fade as factors. As for labor-market sectors, financial and educational services will continue to grow. Agriculture and manufacturing may decline somewhat in importance, but they will not disappear.

How Workers Are Differentiated

Chapters 6, 7, and 8 dealt with patterns of differentiation. The topics are filled with emotion. People feel and act strongly about gender, age, race, and ethnicity. I have very strong feelings about each of these topics. Basically, I believe that these issues should make no difference. But they do, and to ignore the fact would mean ignoring a great deal of reality.

Gender and Work

Chapter 6 began with a consideration of the participation of women in the labor or work force. The rate of participation has increased consistently over the past several decades. It is quite conceivable that women's rate of participation will exceed that of men if they acquire the skills that organizations need in the future—such as communication and interaction skills—and if there is not enough work to go around for everyone.

Marriage continues to be an important factor in regard to women and work. Being married influences work in a number of ways, the most important of which is related to having children. Having small children reduces labor-force participation. The presence of adequate infant and child care has the potential for reducing the impact of having children, but many people believe that the children are best served by being with their mother in the early years of their lives. And because most families have more than one child, the period of being out of the labor force can either be extended or repeated, depending on the spacing of the children. Being out of the labor force does not help women's careers.

Another impact of marriage is that career decisions have to be coordinated with or are affected by the career decisions of another person. It appears that more and more people will be making such joint career decisions in the future.

Women are paid much less than men for the same work. This inequity should change as more women are promoted to top organizational and professional positions. The trend has been for the gender gap to lessen. Whether the "glass ceiling" that now keeps women in middle management will ever be completely removed is unclear at present.

Traditional lines are increasingly being broken as women take work that was formerly only the domain of men; men are also taking jobs traditionally held mostly by women. I personally doubt whether there will ever be numerical equality of men and women in all forms of work, but "women's work" that relies on good communication and interpersonal skills may become the more dominant form of employment. It will be interesting to see.

Gender differences will not go away, but they will probably decrease in importance. For some people, these changes will not be fast enough. For others, they will be too fast.

Work Throughout the Life Course

Chapter 7 examined the relationships between age and work. People can do nothing about their age, but it has some significant effects on the type of work they do. In some forms of work, such as professional athletics, age takes its toll and people have to find new forms of work. Whatever field they work in, middle-aged adults who are laid off have more trouble finding new jobs than do younger workers. Older workers are no better off in the labor market; in fact, in some organizations and some industries, there is a strong norm in favor of retirement at a certain age.

Age will become an increasingly important aspect of work. There will be many more older people in the population, because of improved health care and the aging of the huge population of baby boomers. Providing this population with adequate retirement programs and medical benefits will place major burdens on government and employers.

The aging of the baby boomers also presents other kinds of challenges to employing organizations. If there is a push toward mandatory retirement to make room for baby boomers who have skills for promotion, then retirement costs will skyrocket. But if older people are permitted to continue to work, the large number of people now moving through middle age will have to fight hard for *any* promotion. To keep workers with stagnant careers motivated, employers may have to adopt some new practices: "Baby boom-age employees will make increasing demands for the job freedom, flexibility, responsibility, and salaries associated with low- and middle-managerial [positions]—with or without the managerial titles" (Klein & Hall, 1988, p. 150).

It appears inevitable that the relationships between age and work will become more significant and controversial—socially, politically, and economically.

Race, Religion, Ethnicity, and Work

Chapter 8 examined race, religion, and ethnicity as they intersect with work. Most notably, members of minority races and ethnic groups find that certain kinds of work are harder to get than they are for mainstream workers. Historically, racial, religious, and ethnic minorities have entered the work force at the bottom. Historically, also, there have been shifts in the status of racial, religious, and ethnic groups as people have moved up the ladder.

What is the future here? Are we to take hope from the increasing numbers of people of color who go to college or from the bright minority graduates who are moving into the mainstream? Or should we despair because of resurgent religious and ethnic strife, such as that taking place in a reunited Germany and a disintegrating Yugoslavia? Even in this country, we are not immune from prejudice and discrimination—or even interracial violence, as the 1992 Los Angeles riots indicate.

Every sign of encouragement is balanced by a sign of discouragement. For example, we see huge advances by African-Americans and Hispanics in athletic performance but far less so in the management of professional sports franchises. We see the entertainment industry full of performers from all racial, religious, and ethnic backgrounds, but again we see managers from a much more limited array of backgrounds. We see outstanding performances in classrooms by Asian-Americans, but we read about quotas in college and university admissions.

Race and ethnicity will continue to influence individuals' opportunities for getting work and maintaining successful careers. The only way to change deeply entrenched patterns of discrimination is for people of goodwill to keep trying.

How Work Relates to Other Aspects of Society

Chapters 9, 10, and 11 examined the contexts in which work takes place. Another approach to the topic would be to say we are looking at the settings of work and how the settings affect the work that is done in them.

The Organizational Context

We began with work organizations themselves in Chapter 9. Employing organizations affect people on and off the job. Worker behavior on the job can be completely controlled by the employing organization, which can also shape the activities of people off the job. It is virtually impossible to escape the organizational context of work.

The key to understanding the organizational context is the idea of the internal labor market. The organization sets the rules for hiring and promotion and raises. There are also local customs in most organizations that slightly alter the official rules.

The importance of the organizational context goes deeper than promotions and raises. It also involves the way organizations view and treat their employees. Some organizations have the potential to design or redesign their work to benefit employees. However, only the prosperous ones can afford this. Organizations can also bring workers into the decision-making process, but this country's experience is that neither workers nor managers are too excited about strong worker-participation programs.

It appears that the organizational context of work is changing. For a long time, it has been better to work for a large and prosperous organization if you want promotions, raises, and job security. However, hard times have prompted many large organizations to downsize, which requires layoffs at all levels and jeopardized health and retirement benefits for many who had felt secure. "Now, the notion that a person stays with a single company for decades, remaining loyal and receiving job security and ample benefits in return, is essentially a big-company concept that may be dying" (Lohr, 1993, p. D2). Downsizing is likely to continue for a while. Thus employment in a large organization may no longer mean job security, and problems of health insurance and pensions will come to be very important public issues.

Another potential problem in the organizational context is a declining "degree of inclusion" for many employees (Rousseau, 1988). Inclusion is the link between workers and their employers. Increasingly, workers will be employed on a part-time or temporary basis. And the incidence of telecommuting or home-based employment probably will increase. These developments will weaken the temporal and physical links between workers and their employers. They may also weaken the socioemotional attachments between employees and employers.

On the other hand, certain types of workers are likely to enjoy a high degree of job security in the future. In organizations that rely heavily on automated production systems or highly technical operating systems, a small group of "core" employees is typically needed to configure and maintain these systems. Such employees, because of their high levels of expertise and firm-specific knowledge, are likely to enjoy high pay levels and steady employment (Hyman, 1988). For these fortunate individuals, the organizational context functions to ensure lucrative and stable employment.

Power and Control in the Workplace

Chapter 10 looked at attempts at altering power arrangements in the workplace, including worker-participation schemes, empowerment, and collective bargaining by labor unions. One point that was not made in that chapter is that one very important power source sits outside the employing organization—namely, governmental regulations that affect work. Occupational safety and health rules and affirmative-action hiring regulations have helped to change the behavior of employing organizations. These rules and regulations emerged out of the political process. Quite obviously, developments at the international level (such as international trade agreements) also affect our work. Local, national, and world politics will continue their influence.

One theme of recent political campaigns has been "industrial policy." This term refers to conscious and overt efforts to stimulate work. I believe that it is misguided to call this industrial policy, because "industry" (meaning the manufacturing industry) is no longer the sole or main source of employment. At the same time, it is vital to remember that all kinds of work are affected by political processes.

Dynamics of Work, Family, and Health

Chapter 11 analyzed the links between work and the family and work and health. The chapter began with a point that is obvious but seldom made: Time at work is not time with family. This is true for "intact" families (husband and wife, perhaps with children), single-parent families, and gay and lesbian families. If one or more member's work requires travel out of town or out of the country, then he, she, or they are not available for family roles. Just think how hard it must be for a single parent to travel. Also imagine how a career might suffer if a person cannot travel because of parenting obligations.

Most families have children. As noted earlier, children have a substantial effect on women's work. At the same time, working affects whether families have children. As employers begin to realize the importance of children for their workers, they will probably begin to offer more child care if and when they can afford it.

Another important linkage between work and the family is where the family lives. This is frequently decided by an employer who believes that transferring key employees around the country or world is necessary for training and experience. What employers have sometimes failed to consider is that the whole family moves: The spouse has to change jobs, and the children have to change schools. As Chapter 11 noted, dual-worker households are now and will continue to be the norm. Thus employers who frequently transfer workers may meet more and more resistance.

The final topic was work and health. Obviously, some work, such as mining, is very hazardous. It also is possible to work yourself to death. For example, Japan has seen pretty clearly documented instances of "karoshi," in which employees work so hard that they die at their desks (Watanabe, 1992). Karoshi has become a national concern in Japan.

People also can work themselves to death in the United States. Work stress contributes to cardiopulmonary and gastrointestinal problems. At the same time, not having work is also very stressful. I have a close friend who lost his banking job and did not find work for some 18 months. Needless to say, he, his wife, and his children (and his friends) all experienced great stress during that time.

Conclusions

This last example indicates the interconnectedness of all the aspects of work we have been considering. Work is a central factor in both society and individuals' lives. In our society, work is often synonymous with status and indicates something about a person's education and family background. Losing work is traumatic, because it leaves the unemployed person without a way to define his or her status. Any development in the work arena, whether or not it is as dramatic as a layoff, affects not only the worker but also his or her family. Not least of all, work-related stress affects the individual's physical and mental health. For the unemployed person, nothing is so welcome as another job that preserves or enhances status. Once reemployed, the individual once more has a well-defined place in society.

This is a good place to stop. My work here is finished and I am going skiing: Work or play?

■■■ **APPLICATION**

The Impact of Technology

At many points throughout this chapter we have referred to new technologies and how they may affect work in the future. As I frequently pointed out, the link between technology and the workplace is nothing new. For example, consider the emergence of the first assembly-line production systems. These mass-production systems were truly revolutionary in terms of their technology. They also radically altered the experiences of vast numbers of production workers. No longer were workers involved from start to finish in the complete assembly of a product. Rather, they were given one or a few isolated tasks that they were expected to repeat again and again. No longer were workers organized in tightly knit work groups. Now they were physically dispersed along an assembly line in such a way that free and frequent social interactions with co-workers were severely constrained. This historical example illustrates the dramatic impact technological developments can have on workers and the workplace.

If the impact of technology on work is nothing new, then why place particular emphasis on the subject? One reason is that recent and emerging technological innovations seem poised to change the workplace more dramatically than at any time since the Industrial Revolution. Many of these innovations have been discussed in this chapter. The introduction of personal computers and data-entry terminals has revolutionized clerical work. Systems for computer-integrated manufacturing (CIM) work in conjunction with advanced robotics to allow for unmanned assembly lines. Tools for computer-assisted design (CAD) allow technicians to do in days what once took engineers weeks or months. The effects of these innovations promise to be far-reaching and profound.

Although few observers would argue with the notion that technology is profoundly affecting workers and the workplace, little consensus can be found when describing these effects. For instance, some authors view the emergence of new technologies as a decidedly positive development. They bombard us with their glowing vision of technical wonders that are able to manipulate large amounts of information very rapidly and with little effort— to enhance control, to create insight, to search for information, and to facilitate cooperative work between people (Kling & Dunlop, in press).

On the other hand, some observers focus on the dark side of technological innovation. These authors concentrate on a darker social vision in which computerization only serves to amplify human misery: People become dependent on complex technologies that they do not understand or they are doomed to routine work, because computers have usurped the interesting intellectual tasks (Kling & Dunlop, in press).

Although both views contain a certain amount of truth, neither fully and accurately describes the effects of new technologies in the workplace. In reality, technological innovation may be positive or negative, depending on the circumstance.

Consider the purposes to which new technology may be put. A network of computers linking all the offices in an insurance firm might be installed for any of a variety of reasons. Management might be trying to increase communication and cooperation among agents. Or management might want to closely monitor (via computer logs) the activities and effectiveness of each and every insurance agent. A system dedicated to the first purpose may very well contribute to the smooth and efficient functioning of the business. A system aimed at surveillance, on the other hand, may accomplish little more than the arousal of apprehension, suspicion, and mistrust among employees.

On the negative side, there are also those who believe that computerization and automation are tools for deskilling, removing the substantive complexity from work, and leaving workers with few opportunities to use the skills they worked so hard to accumulate. In fact, quite the opposite may be the case. Consider, for example, the word-processing program I am using now. It serves my purposes adequately, allowing me to bang away at this manuscript, all the while enjoying the luxury of that forgiving backspace and delete key. It is also the exact same program and version used by the administrative assistant who does occasional clerical work for our department. Even though we both work with the same program, the administrative assistant makes much more proficient use of it than I do. I am constantly amazed at her ability to produce striking graphs, clear tables, fancy fonts, mailing labels, and so on. She can even do desktop publishing. Her level of skill far exceeds that of most if not all of the casual users in our department. Without her skills, the faculty would be unable to produce top-flight papers and documents. Thus technology is not necessarily synonymous with deskilling.

Of course, there are clear examples where technology has removed much of the human element from work. Kling and Dunlop (in press) offer the extreme example of computerized cash registers in fast-food restaurants: "[C]lerical workers input the menu items by selecting the appropriate register buttons, rather than the price of a cheeseburger or malts. This tactic enables [management] to hire clerical workers with very few math or other skills." Of course, what is deskilling to one person may be upskilling to another. Some cashiers in fast-food restaurants may feel that their jobs offer more complexity, autonomy, and responsibility than do other jobs for which they are qualified. If it were not for computerized cash registers, these employees might not have been hired in the first place.

In an attempt to distinguish modern technology's dark side from its light side, Shoshana Zuboff draws a useful distinction between technologies that "automate" and technologies that "informate" (Zuboff, 1988). Automating technologies substitute high-tech systems for human activity. With automating technologies, work that once required considerable independent judgment and skill can be performed by a machine or by a worker with minimal skill. The use of technology to automate will undoubtedly result in some deskilling and worker displacement in the years to come. Informating technologies, on the other hand, act to transform work from a physical activity into a symbolic or information-based activity. With informating technologies, work that once involved pushing, pulling, lifting, and twisting now involves monitoring visual displays, issuing electronic commands, and manipulating symbolic information rather than physical objects. The human element remains important when informating technologies are applied.

Of course, informating technologies bring with them their own problems. The skill requirements of these new technologies call for a new type of work force. Workers must engage their surroundings on an intellectual rather than a physical basis. Often the types of skills demanded by informating technologies are quite different from those possessed by the typical skilled or unskilled laborer. As Etzioni and Jargowsky (1990) note, in the absence of sufficient training it may be impossible for some workers to make the transition from the low-tech to the high-tech workplace:

> An economy that changes rapidly from basic industries to high technology . . . may be inviting a great deal of suffering. Not everyone laid off by a basic industry may be able to switch to high tech. . . . A great deal of study is needed (and is only beginning) of the social and psychic difficulties of unemployed blue-collar workers trying to switch to high tech. Those who advocate promoting high technology at the expense of basic industries must consider the possible ramifications of an ever-widening gap between the skills of the population and the jobs available, and the limits of retraining. (p. 316)

Thus it seems that even informating technologies pose a healthy challenge to the workers and workplaces of the near and distant future.

■■■■ SUGGESTED READINGS

A complete bibliographical entry for each work cited here can be found in the reference section at the back of this book.

Johnston (Ed.), *Workforce 2000* (1987), provides a set of mainly economic projections that include continued declines in the manufacturing sector and growth in the services. It also projects that higher skill levels, particularly reading skills, will be needed in the services.

Bills (Ed.), *The New Modern Times* (forthcoming), takes issue with several of the projections in *Workforce 2000*. The authors in this volume do not foresee as many changes as are projected in the earlier work.

Schor, *The Overworked American* (1992), suggests that Americans are working harder and harder with less and less in return.

References

Abbott, A. (1981). Status and status strains in the professions. *American Journal of Sociology, 86,* 819-835.

Abbott, A. (1988). *The system of professions: An essay on the division of expert labor.* Chicago: University of Chicago Press.

Abbott, A. (1989). The new occupational structure: What are the questions? *Work and Occupations, 16,* 273-291.

Abbott, A., & Smith, D. R. (1984). Governmental constraints and labor market mobility: Turnover among college athletic personnel. *Work and Occupations, 11,* 29-53.

Abrahamson, M. (1971). The functional theory of stratification: An assessment. *American Journal of Sociology, 78,* 1235-1246.

Alba, R. D. (1990). *Ethnic identity: The transformation of white America.* New Haven, CT: Yale University Press.

Albrecht, S. L. (1981). Preconditions for increased workers' influence: Factors in the Swedish case. *Sociology of Work and Occupations, 8,* 252-272.

Alexander, K. L., Cook, M., & McDill, E. (1978). Curriculum tracking and educational stratification: Some further evidence. *American Sociological Review, 43,* 47-66.

Alexander, K. L., Ekland, B. K., & Griffin, L. J. (1975). The Wisconsin model of socioeconomic achievement: A replication. *American Journal of Sociology, 81,* 324-342.

Allardt, E. (1976). Work and political behavior. In R. Dubin (Ed.), *Handbook of work, organization, and society*. Chicago: Rand McNally.

Allerton, H. (1991, January). Workaholism: Fact or fiction? *Training & Development Journal*, p. 74.

Allison, P. D., & Long, J. S. (1990). Departmental effects on scientific productivity. *American Sociological Review, 55*, 469-478.

Almquist, E. M. (1979). *Minorities, gender, and work*. Lexington, MA: D. C. Heath.

Alutto, J. A., & Belasco, J. A. (1974). Determinants of attitudinal militancy among nurses and teachers. *Industrial & Labor Relations Review, 27*, 216-227.

Alvarez, R. (1979). Preface. In R. Alvarez, K. G. Lutterman, & Associates (Eds.), *Discrimination in organizations*. San Francisco: Jossey-Bass.

Alvarez, R., Lutterman, K. G., & Associates (Eds.). (1979). *Discrimination in organizations*. San Francisco: Jossey-Bass.

Alwin, D. F. (1974). College effects on educational and occupational attainment. *American Sociological Review, 39*, 210-223.

Amante, L. (1989, October). Help wanted: Creative recruitment tactics. *Personnel*, pp. 32-36.

American Nurses' Association. (1982). *Professionalism and the empowerment of nursing*. Kansas City, MO: Author.

Anderson, K. (1981). *Wartime women: Sex roles, family relations, and the status of women during World War II*. Westport, CT: Greenwood.

Aronowitz, S. (1973). *False promises*. New York: McGraw-Hill.

Attewell, P. (1987). The deskilling controversy. *Work and Occupations, 14*, 323-346.

Attewell, P. (1990). What is skill? *Work and Occupations, 17*, 422-448.

Bacharach, S., & Aiken, M. (1979). The impact of alienation, meaninglessness, and meritocracy on supervisor and subordinate satisfaction. *Social Forces, 57*, 853-870.

Bacharach, S. B., & Lawler, E. J. (1980). *Power and politics in organizations*. San Francisco: Jossey-Bass.

Baron, J. N. (1984). Organizational perspectives on stratification. In R. Turner (Ed.), *Annual Review of Sociology*, Vol. 10. Palo Alto, CA: Annual Reviews.

Baron, J. N., & Bielby, W. T. (1982). Workers and machines: Dimensions and determinants of technical relations in the workplace. *American Sociological Review, 47*, 175-188.

Baron, J. N., & Bielby, W. T. (1984). The organization of work in a segmented economy. *American Sociological Review, 49*, 454-473.

Baron, J. N., & Bielby, W. T. (1986). The proliferation of job titles in organizations. *Administrative Science Quarterly, 31*, 561-586.

Baron, J. N., Davis-Blake, A., & Bielby, W. T. (1986). The structure of opportunity: How promotion ladders vary within and among organizations. *Administrative Science Quarterly, 31*, 248-273.

Baron, J. N., Dobbin, F. R., & Jennings, P. D. (1986). War and peace: The evolution of modern personnel administration in U.S. industry. *American Journal of Sociology, 92*, 350-383.

Baron, J. N., Jennings, P. D., & Dobbin, F. R. (1988). Mission control? The development of personnel systems in U.S. industry. *American Sociological Review, 53*, 497-514

Baron, J. N., & Newman, A. E. (1990). For what it's worth: Organizations, occupations, and the value of work done by women and nonwhites. *American Sociological Review, 55*, 155-175.

Beck, E. M. (1980). Discrimination and white economic loss: A time series examination of the radical model. *Social Forces, 59*, 148-168.

Beck, E. M., Horan, P. M., & Tolbert, C. M. II. (1978). Stratification in a dual economy: A sectoral model of earnings determination. *American Sociological Review, 43*, 704-720.

Beck, E. M., Horan, P. M., & Tolbert, C. M. II. (1980). Industrial segmentation and labor market discrimination. *Social Problems, 28*, 113-130.

Beck, S. H. (1983). The role of other family members in intergenerational occupational mobility. *Sociological Quarterly, 24*, 273-285.

Becker, G. S. (1976). *The economic approach to human behavior*. Chicago: University of Chicago Press.

Becker, G. S. (1981). *A treatise on the family*. Cambridge, MA: Harvard University Press.

Becker, H. S. (1960). Notes on the concept of commitment. *American Journal of Sociology, 66*, 32-40.

Becker, H. S. (1974). Art as collective action. *American Sociological Review, 39*, 767-776.

Becker, H. S. (1982). *Art worlds*. Berkeley: University of California Press.

Becker, H. S., Geer, B., Hughes, E. C., & Strauss, A. L. (1961). *Boys in white: Student culture in medical school*. Chicago: University of Chicago Press.

Becker, H. S., & Strauss, A. L. (1956). Careers, personality, and adult socialization. *American Journal of Sociology, 62*, 253-263.

Bell, D. (1973). *The coming of post-industrial society*. New York: Basic Books.

Benet, M. K. (1972). *The secretarial ghetto*. New York: McGraw-Hill.

Benoit-Smullyan, E. (1944). Status, status types, and status interrelations. *American Sociological Review, 9*, 151-161.

Bensman, J., & Gerver, I. (1963). Crime and punishment in the factory: The function of deviancy in maintaining the social system. *American Sociological Review, 35*, 588-598.

Bensman, J., & Lilienfeld, R. (1991). *Craft and consciousness: Occupational technique and the development of world images* (2nd ed.). Hawthorne, NY: Aldine.

Berg, I. (1971). *Education and jobs: The great training robbery*. Boston: Beacon.

Berg, I. (1979). *Industrial sociology*. Englewood Cliffs, NJ: Prentice-Hall.

Bergermaier, R., Borg, I., & Champoux, J. E. (1984). Structural relationships among facets of work, nonwork, and general well-being. *Work and Occupations, 11*, 163-182.

Berk, R., & Berk, S. F. (1979). *Labor and leisure at home*. Beverly Hills, CA: Sage.

Berk, R. A., & Berk, S. F. (1983). Supply-side sociology of the family: The challenge of the new home economics. In R. H. Turner & J. F. Short, Jr. (Eds.), *Annual review of sociology*, Vol. 9. Palo Alto, CA: Annual Reviews.

Berk, S. F., & Shih, A. (1980). Contributions to household labor: Comparing wives' and husbands' reports. In S. F. Berk (Ed.), *Women and household labor*. Beverly Hills, CA: Sage.

Berle, A. A., Jr., & Means, G. C. (1932). *The modern corporation and private property*. New York: Macmillan.

Bibb, R., & Form, W. (1977). The effects of industrial, occupational, and sex stratification on wages in blue-collar markets. *Social Forces, 55*, 974-996.

Bielby, D. D., & Bielby, W. T. (1988). She works hard for the money: Household responsibilities and work effort. *American Journal of Sociology, 93*, 1031-1059.

Bielby, W. T., & Baron, J. N. (1983). Organizations, technology, and worker attachment to the firm. In D. J. Treiman & R. V. Robinson (Eds.), *Research in social stratification and mobility*. Greenwich, CT: JAI.

Bielby, W. T., & Baron, J. N. (1986). Men and women at work: Sex segregation and statistical discrimination. *American Journal of Sociology, 91*, 759-99.

Bielby, W. T., & Bielby, D. D. (1989). Family ties: Balancing commitment to work and family in dual earner households. *American Sociological Review, 54*, 776-789.

Bierstedt, R. (1950). An analysis of social power. *American Sociological Review, 15*, 730-738.

Biggart, N. W. (1989). *Charismatic capitalism: Direct selling organizations in America*. Chicago: University of Chicago Press.

Bills, D. B. (1990). Employers' use of job history data for making hiring decisions: A fuller specification of job assignment and status attainment. *Sociological Quarterly, 31,* 23-35.

Blau, J. R. (1979). Expertise and power in professional organizations. *Sociology of Work and Occupations, 10,* 103-123.

Blau, P. M. (1964). *Exchange and power in social life.* New York: John Wiley.

Blau, P. M. (1977). *Inequality and heterogeneity: A primitive theory of social structure.* New York: Free Press.

Blau, P. M. (1980). Comments on issues raised by Messner's research. *Sociology of Work and Occupations, 7,* 425-430.

Blau, P. M., & Duncan, O. D. (1967). *The American occupational structure.* New York: John Wiley.

Blau, P. M., & Schoenherr, R. (1971). *The structure of organizations.* New York: Basic Books.

Blauner, R. (1964). *Alienation and freedom.* Chicago: University of Chicago Press.

Block, F. (1990). *Postindustrial possibilities.* Berkeley: University of California Press.

Bluestone, B., Murphy, W. M., & Stevenson, M. (1973). *Low wages and the working poor.* Ann Arbor: University of Michigan Press.

Bokemeier, J. L., & Lacy, W. B. (1987). Job values, rewards, and working conditions as factors in job satisfaction among men and women. *Sociological Quarterly, 28,* 189-204.

Bonacich, E. (1972). A theory of ethnic antagonism. *American Sociological Review, 37,* 547-559.

Bonacich, E. (1976). Advanced capitalism and black/white race relations in the United States: A split labor market interpretation. *American Sociological Review, 41,* 34-51.

Borgatta, E. F. (1960). Functionalism and sociology. *American Sociological Review, 25,* 267.

Bose, C. E. (1973). *Jobs and gender: Sex and occupational prestige.* Baltimore, MD: Johns Hopkins University Press.

Bose, C. (1979). Technology and changes in the division of labor in the American home. *Women's Studies International Quarterly, 2,* 295-304.

Bose, C. (1984). Household resources and U.S. women's work: Factors affecting gainful employment at the turn of the century. *American Sociological Review, 49,* 474-490.

Bose, C., & Bereano, P. L. (1983). Household technologies: Burden or blessing? In J. Zimmerman (Ed.), *The technological woman: Interfacing with tomorrow.* New York: Praeger.

Bose, C., Feldberg, R., & Sokoloff, N. (1987). *Hidden aspects of women's work.* New York: Praeger.

Bose, C. E., & Rossi, P. H. (1983). Gender and jobs: Prestige standing of occupations as affected by gender. *American Sociological Review, 48,* 316-330.

Boulding, E. (1980). The labor of U.S. farm women: A knowledge gap. *Sociology of Work and Occupations, 7,* 261-290.

Bourne, P., & Wikler, N. J. (1978). Commitment and the cultural mandate: Women in medicine. *Social Problems, 25,* 430-440.

Bowles, S., & Gintis, H. (1976). *Schooling in capitalist America.* New York: Basic Books.

Brannen, P. (1983). *Authority and participation in industry.* New York: St. Martin's.

Braverman, H. (1974). *Labor and monopoly capital.* New York: Monthly Review Press.

Brett, J. M. (1980). Behavioral research on unions. In B. M. Staw & L. L. Cummings (Eds.), *Research in organizational behavior,* Vol. 2. Greenwich, CT: JAI.

Bridges, W. P. (1980). Industry marginality and female employment: A new appraisal. *American Sociological Review, 45,* 58-75.

Bridges, W. P. (1982). The sexual segregation of occupations: Theories of labor stratification in industry. *American Journal of Sociology, 88,* 270-295.

Bridges, W. P., & Nelson, R. L. (1989). Markets in hierarchies: Organizational and market influences on gender inequality in a state pay system. *American Journal of Sociology, 95,* 616-658.

Britt, D. W., & Galle, O. (1974). Structural antecedents of the shape of strikes: A comparative analysis. *American Sociological Review*, *39*, 642-651.

Brittain, J. W., & Freeman, J. H. (1980). Organizational proliferation and density dependent selection. In J. R. Kimberly & R. H. Miles (Eds.), *The organizational life cycle*. San Francisco: Jossey-Bass.

Brody, D. (1980). *Workers in industrial America: Essays on the twentieth century struggle*. New York: Oxford University Press.

Brody, J. E. (1992, December 9). For the professional mother, rewards may outweigh stress. *New York Times*, p. C10.

Broom, L., & Cushing, R. G. (1977). A modest test of an immodest theory: The functional theory of stratification. *American Sociological Review*, *42*, 157-169.

Brown, L. K. (1979). Women and business management. *Signs*, *5*, 267-288.

Brown, R. S., Moon, M., & Zoloth, B. S. (1980). Incorporating occupational attainment in studies of male-female earnings differentials. *Journal of Human Resources*, *15*, 1-28.

Browning, H. L., Lopreato, S. C., & Poston, D. L., Jr. (1973). Income and veteran status: Variations among Mexican-Americans, blacks and Anglos. *American Sociological Review*, *38*, 74-85.

Burawoy, M. (1976). The functions and reproduction of migrant labor: Comparative material from South Africa and the United States. *American Journal of Sociology*, *81*, 1051-1087.

Burawoy, M. (1979). *Manufacturing consent: Changes in the labor process under monopoly capitalism*. Chicago: University of Chicago Press.

Burawoy, M. (1983). Between the labor process and the state: The changing face of factory regimes under advanced capitalism. *American Sociological Review*, *48*, 587-605.

Burnham, J. (1962). *The managerial revolution*. Bloomington: Indiana University Press.

Burrage, M. C. & Cory, D. (1981). At sixes and sevens: Occupational status in the city of London from the fourteenth to the seventeenth century. *American Sociological Review, 46,* 375-393.

Burris, V. (1983). The social and political consequences of overeducation. *American Sociological Review, 48,* 454-467.

Burriss, B. H. (1991). Employed mothers: The impact of class and marital status on the prioritizing of family and work. *Social Science Quarterly, 72,* 50-66.

Burstein, P. (1989). Attacking sex discrimination in the labor market: A study in law and politics. *Social Forces, 67,* 641-665.

Burt, R. S. (1980). Cooptive corporate action networks. *Administrative Science Quarterly, 25,* 557-582.

Butler, J. S. (1976). Inequality in the military: An examination of promotion time. *American Sociological Review, 41,* 807-818.

Cain, G. (1966). *Married women in the labor force.* Chicago: University of Chicago Press.

Cain, G. G. (1984). The economics of discrimination: Part 1. *Focus, 7,* 1-11.

Cain, P. S., & Treiman, D. (1981). The *Dictionary of Occupational Titles* as a source of occupational data. *American Sociological Review, 46,* 253-278.

Campbell, J. P., Dunnette, M. D., Lawler, E. E. III, & Weick, K. E. (1970). *Managerial behavior, performance, and effectiveness.* New York: McGraw-Hill.

Campbell, K. E. (1988). Gender differences in job related networks. *Work and Occupations, 15,* 179-200.

Capell, P. (1992). Endangered middle management. *American Demographics,* 44-47.

Caplow, T. (1954). *The sociology of work.* Minneapolis: University of Minnesota Press.

Caplow, T. (1966). Sequential steps in professionalization. In H. M. Vollmer & D. L. Mills (Eds.), *Professionalization.* Englewood Cliffs, NJ: Prentice-Hall.

Caplow, T. (1983). *Managing an organization*. New York: Holt, Rinehart & Winston.

Cappell, C. L. (1990). The status of black lawyers. *Work and Occupations, 17*, 100-121.

Carlin, J. (1962). *Lawyers on their own*. New Brunswick, NJ: Rutgers University Press.

Carlin, J. (1966). *Lawyers' ethics*. New York: Russell Sage.

Carroll, G. R., & Delacroix, J. (1982). Organizational mortality in the newspaper industries of Argentina and Ireland: An ecological approach. *Administrative Science Quarterly, 27*, 169-198.

Carroll, S. J. (1988). Managerial work in the future. In J. Hage (Ed.), *Futures of organizations* (pp. 86-108). Lexington, MA: Lexington Books.

Carr-Saunders, A. R., & Wilson, P. A. (1944). Professions. *Encyclopedia of the social sciences*, Vol. 22 (pp. 476-480). New York: Macmillan.

Carson, W. G. (1982). *The other price of Britain's oil*. New Brunswick, NJ: Rutgers University Press.

Chacko, T. I. (1982). Women and equal employment opportunity: Some unintended effects. *Journal of Applied Psychology, 67*, 119-123.

Chandler, A. D., Jr. (1962). *Strategy and structure*. Cambridge: MIT Press.

Chenoweth, L. C., & Maret, E. (1980). The career patterns of mature American women. *Sociology of Work and Occupations, 7*, 222-257.

Child, J. (1972). Organizational structure, environment, and performance: The role of strategic choice. *Sociology, 6*, 1-22.

Chinoy, E. (1955). *Automobile workers and the American dream*. New York: Doubleday.

Christensen, A. S. (1988). Sex discrimination and the law. In A. H. Stromberg & S. Harkess (Eds.), *Women working: Theories and facts in perspective* (2nd ed.). Mountain View, CA: Mayfield.

Christiansen, J. B. (1979). The split labor market theory and Filipino exclusion: 1927-1934. *Phylon Quarterly, 40*, 66-74.

Christenson, J. A., Hougland, J. G., Jr., Ilvento, T. W., & Shepard, J. M. (1988). The "organization man" and the community: The impact of organizational norms and personal values on community participation and transfer. *Social Forces, 66,* 808-826.

Clark, J. P., & Hollinger, R. (1983). *Theft by employees in work organizations: Executive summary.* Washington, DC: U.S. Department of Justice.

Clawson, D. (1980). *Bureaucracy and the labor process.* New York: Monthly Review Press.

Clawson, D., & Neustadtl, A. (1989). Interlocks, PACs and corporate conservatism. *American Journal of Sociology, 94,* 749-773.

Cohen, Y., & Pfeffer, J. (1986). Organizational hiring standards. *Administrative Science Quarterly, 31,* 1-24.

Colclough, G., & Tolbert, C. M. II. (1990). High technology, work, and inequality in Southern labor markets. *Work and Occupations, 17,* 3-29.

Cole, S. (1986). Sex discrimination and admission to medical school, 1929-1984. *American Journal of Sociology, 92,* 549-567.

Coleman, A. L., & Hall, L. D. (1979). Black farm operators and farm population, 1900-1970: Alabama and Kentucky. *Phylon Quarterly, 40,* 387-402.

Coleman, J. S. (1988). Social capital in the creation of human capital. *American Journal of Sociology, 94* (supplement), S95-S120.

Collins, R. (1979). *The credentials society.* New York: Academic Press.

Cooney, R. S., & Ortiz, V. (1983). Nativity, national origin, and hispanic female participation in the labor force. *Social Science Quarterly, 64,* 510-523.

Cornfield, D. B. (1986). Declining union membership in the post World War II era: The United Furniture Workers of America, 1939-1982. *American Journal of Sociology, 91,* 1112-1153.

Cornfield, D. B. (1987). Plant shutdowns and union decline: The United Furniture Workers of America, 1963-1981. *Work and Occupations, 14,* 434-451.

Cornfield, D. B. (1989). Union decline and the political demands of organized labor. *Work and Occupations, 16,* 292-322.

Cornfield, D. B., Filho, H. B. C., & Chun, B. J. (1990). Household, work, and labor activism: Gender differences in the determination of union membership participation. *Work and Occupations, 17,* 131-151.

Cottle, T. J. (1992, July-August). Hard core: The wages of long-term unemployment. *North American Review,* pp. 43-48.

Coverman, S. (1988). Sociological explanations of the male-female wage gap: Individualist and structuralist theories. In A. H. Stromberg & S. Harkess (Eds.), *Women working: Theories and facts in perspective* (2nd ed.). Mountain View, CA: Mayfield.

Coverman, S. (1989). Role overload, role conflict, and stress: Addressing consequences of multiple roles. *Social Forces, 67,* 965-982.

Cramer, J. C. (1980). Fertility and female employment: Problems of causal direction. *American Sociological Review, 45,* 167-190.

Cullen, J. B. (1978). *The structure of professionalism: A quantitative examination.* New York: Petrocelli.

Cullen, J. B. (1985). Professional differentiation and occupational earnings. *Work and Occupations, 12,* 351-372.

Cullen, J. B., & Novick, S. M. (1979). The Davis-Moore theory of stratification: A further examination and extension. *American Journal of Sociology, 84,* 1424-1437.

Cutright, P. (1974). The civilian earnings of white and black draftees and nonveterans. *American Sociological Review, 39,* 317-322.

Dahl, R. (1957). The concept of power. *Behavioral Science, 2,* 201-215.

Dahrendorf, R. (1959). *Class and class conflict in industrial society.* Stanford, CA: Stanford University Press.

Dalton, G. W., Thompson, P. H., & Price, R. P. (1977). The four stages of professional careers: A new look at performance by professionals. *Organizational Dynamics, 12,* 19-42.

Dalton, M. (1950). Conflicts between staff and line managerial officers. *American Sociological Review, 15,* 342-351.

Dalton, M. (1959). *Men who manage.* New York: John Wiley.

D'Amico, R. (1982). Explaining the effects of capital sector for income determination. *Work and Occupations, 9,* 411-439.

D'Amico, R. (1984). Industrial feudalism reconsidered: The effects of unionization on labor mobility. *Work and Occupations, 11,* 407-437.

Daniels, A. K. (1969). The captive professional: Bureaucratic limitations in the practice of military psychiatry. *Journal of Health & Social Behavior, 10,* 255-265.

Davids, M. (1988, November). Labor shortage woes. *Public Relations Journal,* pp. 24-59.

Davis, F. (1959). The cabdriver and his fare: Facets of a fleeting relationship. *American Journal of Sociology, 65,* 158-165.

Davis, K. (1953). Reply. *American Sociological Review, 18,* 394-396.

Davis, K., & Moore, W. E. (1945). Some principles of stratification. *American Sociological Review, 10,* 242-249.

Daymont, T. N. (1980). Pay premiums for economic sector and race: A decomposition. *Social Science Research, 9,* 245-272.

DeFleur, L. B. (1985). Organizational and ideological barriers to sex integration in military groups. *Work and Occupations, 12,* 206-228.

Deitch, C., & Sanderson, S. W. (1987). Geographic constraints on married women's careers. *Work and Occupations, 14,* 616-634.

Dempster-McClain, D., & Moen, P. (1989). Moonlighting husbands: a life cycle perspective. *Work and Occupations, 16,* 43-64.

Deutsch, S. (1981). Work environment reform and industrial democracy. *Sociology of Work and Occupations, 8,* 180-194.

Deutschman, A. (1992, July 13). The upbeat generation. *Fortune*, pp. 42-54.

DeViney, S., & O'Rand, A. (1988). Gender-cohort succession and retirement among older men and women. *Sociological Quarterly, 29*, 525-540.

DiMaggio, P. J., & Powell, W. W. (1983). The iron cage revisited: Institutional isomorphism and collective rationality in organizational fields. *American Sociological Review, 48*, 147-160.

DiPrete, T. A. (1981). Unemployment over the life cycle: Racial differences and the effects of changing economic conditions. *American Journal of Sociology, 87*, 286-307.

DiPrete, T. A. (1987a). Horizontal and vertical mobility in organizations. *Administrative Science Quarterly, 32*, 422-444.

DiPrete, T. A. (1987b). The professionalization of administrative and equal employment opportunity in the U.S. federal government. *American Journal of Sociology, 93*, 119-140.

DiPrete, T. A. (1988). The upgrading and downgrading of occupations: Status redefinition vs. deskilling as alternative theories of change. *Social Forces, 66*, 725-746.

DiPrete, T. A., & Soule, W. T. (1986). The organization of career lines: Equal opportunity and status advancement in a federal bureaucracy. *American Sociological Review, 51*, 295-309.

DiPrete, T. A., & Soule, W. T. (1988). Gender and promotion in segmented job ladder systems. *American Sociological Review, 53*, 26-40.

Doerfler, M. C., & Kammer, P. P. (1986). Workaholism, sex, and sex role stereotyping among female professionals. *Sex Roles, 14*, 551-560.

Doeringer, P. B., & Piore, M. J. (1971). *Internal labor markets and manpower analysis.* Lexington, MA: D. C. Heath.

Domhoff, G. W. (1967). *Who rules America?* Englewood Cliffs, NJ: Prentice-Hall.

Domhoff, G. W. (1971). *The inner circles.* New York: Vintage.

Dore, R. (1973). *British factory-Japanese factory: The origins of diversity in industrial relations.* Berkeley: University of California Press.

Dornbusch, S., & Scott, W. R. (1975). *Evaluation and the exercise of authority*. San Francisco: Jossey-Bass.

Dubin, R. (1956). Industrial workers' worlds: A study of the central life interests of industrial workers. *Social Problems, 3*, 131-142.

Dubin, R. (1992). *Central life interests: Creative individualism in a complex world*. New Brunswick, NJ: Transaction Books.

Dubin, R., & Champoux, J. E. (1974). Workers' central life interests and job performance. *Sociology of Work and Occupations, 1*, 313-326.

Duncan, E. P., & Perrucci, C. (1976). Dual occupation families and migration. *American Sociological Review, 41*, 252-261.

Duncan, O. D., Featherman, D. L., & Duncan, B. (1972). *Socioeconomic background and achievement*. New York: Seminar Press.

Durkheim, E. (1933). *The division of labor in society* (G. Simpson, Trans.). New York: Free Press.

Durr, M. (1993). *Do cross-ethnic ties facilitate promotions?* Unpublished doctoral dissertation, State University of New York at Albany, NY.

Edwards, A. M. (1943). *Comparative occupational statistics for the United States, 1870-1940*. Washington, DC: Government Printing Office.

Edwards, R. (1979). *Contested terrain: The transformation of the work place in the twentieth century*. New York: Basic Books.

Eisenstein, J. (1978). *Counsel for the United States: U.S. attorneys in the political and legal systems*. Baltimore, MD: Johns Hopkins University Press.

Eisenstein, Z. R. (1982). The sexual politics of the new right: Understanding the "crisis of liberalism" for the 1980s. *Signs, 7*, 567-588.

Elder, G. H., Jr. (1974). Age differentiation and the life course. In A. Inkeles (Ed.), *Annual review of sociology, 1975*, Vol. 1. Palo Alto, CA: Annual Reviews.

Elder, G. H., Jr. (1978). Approaches to social change and the family. *American Journal of Sociology, 84,* S1-S38.

Elder, G. H., Jr. (1981). History and the life course. In D. Bertaux (Ed.), *Biography and society: The life history approach to the social sciences.* Beverly Hills, CA: Sage.

Emerson, R. M. (1962). Power-dependence relations. *American Sociological Review, 27,* 31-40.

England, P. (1982). The failure of human capital theory to explain occupational sex segregation. *Journal of Human Resources, 17,* 358-370.

England, P. (1984). Wage appreciation and depreciation: A test of neoclassical economic explanations of occupational sex segregation. *Social Forces, 62,* 726-749.

England, P., & McLaughlin, S. D. (1979). Sex segregation of jobs and income differentials. In R. Alvarez, K. G. Lutterman, & Associates (Eds.), *Discrimination in organizations.* San Francisco: Jossey-Bass.

Epstein, C. F. (1973). Positive effects of the multiple negative: Explaining the success of black professional women. *American Journal of Sociology, 78,* 912-935.

Epstein, C. F. (1980). The new women and the old establishment: Wall Street lawyers in the 1970's. *Sociology of Work and Occupations, 7,* 291-316.

Epstein, C. F. (1981a). *Women in law.* New York: Basic Books.

Epstein, C. F. (1981b). *The woman lawyer.* New York: Basic Books.

Eriksen, J. A. (1977). An analysis of the journey to work for women. *Social Problems, 24,* 428-435.

Eriksen, J. A., & Klein, G. (1981). Women's employment and changes in family structure. *Sociology of Work and Occupations, 8,* 5-23.

Erlanger, H. S. (1977). Social reform organizations and subsequent careers of participants: A follow-up study of early participants in the OEO legal services program. *American Sociological Review, 42,* 233-248.

Erlanger, H. S. (1980). The allocation of status within occupations: The case of the legal profession. *Social Forces, 58,* 882-903.

Etzioni, A. (1961). *A comparative analysis of complex organizations.* New York: Free Press.

Etzioni, A. (1965). Dual leadership in complex organizations. *American Sociological Review, 30,* 688-698.

Etzioni, A. (1969). *The semi-professions and their organization: Teachers, nurses, social workers.* New York: Free Press.

Etzioni, A., & Jargowsky, P. A. (1990). The false choice between high technology and basic industry. In K. Erikson & S. P. Vallas (Eds.), *The nature of work: Sociological perspectives* (pp. 304-318). New Haven, CT: Yale University Press.

Evans, M. D. R. (1989). Immigrant entrepreneurship: Effects of ethnic market size and isolated labor pool. *American Sociological Review, 54,* 950-962.

Evans, M. D., & Laumann, E. O. (1983). *Professional commitment: Myth or reality. Research in social stratification and mobility* (Vol. 2, pp. 3-40). Greenwich, CT: JAI.

Faia, M. A. (1981). Selection by certification: A neglected variable in stratification research. *American Journal of Sociology, 86,* 1091-1111.

Fantasia, R. (1988). *Cultures of solidarity: Consciousness, action, and contemporary American workers.* Berkeley: University of California Press.

Fantasia, R., Clawson, D., & Graham, G. (1988). A critical view of worker participation in American industry. *Work and Occupations, 15,* 468-488.

Farber, H. S., & Saks, D. H. (1980). Why workers want unions: The role of relative wages and job characteristics. *Journal of Political Economy, 88,* 349-369.

Farkas, G., Barton, M., & Kushner, K. (1988). White, black, and Hispanic female youths in central city labor markets. *Sociological Quarterly, 29,* 605-621.

Faunce, W. A. (1989). Occupational status-assignment systems: The effects of status on self-esteem. *American Journal of Sociology*, *95*, 378-400.

Featherman, D. L., & Hauser, R. M. (1976a). Sexual inequality and socioeconomic achievement in the United States, 1962-1973. *American Sociological Review*, *41*, 462-483.

Featherman, D. L., & Hauser, R. M. (1976b). Changes in the socioeconomic stratification of the races, 1962-73. *American Journal of Sociology*, *82*, 621-651.

Featherman, D. L., & Hauser, R. M. (1978). *Opportunity and change*. New York: Academic Press.

Fein, M. (1976). Motivation for work. In R. Dubin (Ed.), *Handbook of work, organization, and society*. Chicago: Rand McNally.

Feldman, D. C. (1976). A contingency theory of socialization. *Administrative Science Quarterly*, *21*, 433-452.

Feldman, D. C. (1981). The multiple socialization of organizational members. *Academy of Management Review*, *6*, 309-318.

Felmlee, D. H. (1982). Women's job mobility processes within and between employers. *American Sociological Review*, *47*, 142-151.

Felmlee, D. H. (1984). The dynamics of women's job mobility. *Work and Occupations*, *11*, 259-281.

Fennel, M. L., Rodin, M. B., & Kantor, G. K. (1981). Problems in the work setting, drinking, and reasons for drinking. *Social Forces*, *60*, 114-132.

Ferber, M., & Birnbaum, B. (1977). The "new home economics": Retrospects and prospects. *Journal of Consumer Research*, *4*, 19-28.

Ferber, M. A, Loeb, J. W., & Lowry, H. M. (1978). The economic status of women faculty: A reappraisal. *Journal of Human Resources*, *13*, 385-401.

Ferber, M., & McMahan, W. W. (1979). Women's expected earnings and their investment in higher education. *Journal of Human Resources*, *14*, 405-419.

Ferree, M. M. (1980). Working class feminism: A consideration of the consequences of employment. *Sociological Quarterly, 21,* 173-184.

Ferree, M. M. (1987). The struggles of superwoman. In C. Bose, R. Feldberg, & N. Sokoloff (Eds.), *Hidden aspects of women's work.* New York: Praeger.

Ferrence, T. P., Goldner, F. H., & Ritti, R. R. (1973). Priests and church: The professionalization of an organization. In E. Freidson (Ed.), *The professions and their prospects.* Beverly Hills, CA: Sage.

Fine, G. A. (1990). Organizational time: Temporal demands and the experience of work in restaurant kitchens. *Social Forces, 69,* 95-114.

Finlay, W. (1988). *Work on the waterfront: Worker power and technological change in a West Coast port.* Philadelphia: Temple University Press.

Fiorentine, R. (1987). Men, women, and the premed persistence gap: A normative alternative approach. *American Journal of Sociology, 92,* 1118-1139.

Fiske, E. B. (1989, September 25). Impending U.S. jobs "disaster": Work force unqualified to work. *New York Times,* pp. A1, B6.

Fitzpatrick, J. S. (1980). Adapting to danger: A participant observation study of an underground coal mine. *Sociology of Work and Occupations, 7,* 131-158.

Fligstein, N., & Fernandez, R. M. (1988). Worker power, firm power, and the structure of labor markets. *Sociological Quarterly, 29,* 5-28.

Fligstein, N., Hicks, A., & Morgan, S. P. (1983). Toward a theory of income determination. *Work and Occupations, 10,* 289-306.

Fligstein, N., & Wolf, W. (1978). Sex similarities in occupational status attainment: Are the results due to the restriction of the sample to employed women? *Social Science Research, 7,* 197-212.

Foner, N., & Napolic, R. (1978). Jamaican and black-American migrant farm workers: A comparative analysis. *Social Problems, 25,* 491-503.

Fontana, A., & Frey, J. H. (1990). Postretirement workers in the labor force. *Work and Occupations, 17*, 355-361.

Form, W. (1981). Resolving ideological issues on the division of labor. In H. M. Blalock, Jr. (Ed.), *Theory and research in sociology*. New York: Free Press.

Form, W. (1982). Self-employed manual workers: Petty bourgeois or working class? *Social Forces, 60*, 1050-1069.

Form, W., & Huber, J. (1976). Occupational power. In R. Dubin (Ed.), *Handbook of work, organization, and society*. Chicago: Rand McNally.

Form, W., & Huber, J. (1984). Occupational power. In R. Dubin (Ed.), *Handbook of work, organization, and society*. Chicago: Rand McNally.

Form, W., & McMillen, D. B. (1983). Women, men, and machines. *Work and Occupations, 10*, 147-178.

Fossett, M. A., Galle, O. R., & Burr, J. A. (1989). Racial occupational inequality, 1940-1980: A research note on the impact of the changing regional distribution. *Social Forces, 68*, 415-427.

Fox, M. F. (1981). Sex segregation and salary structure in academia. *Sociology of Work and Occupations, 8*, 39-60.

Fox, M. F. (1985). Location, sex typing, and salary among academics. *Work and Occupations, 12*, 186-205.

Fox, M. F., & Faver, C. A. (1981). Achievement and aspiration: Patterns among male and female academic career aspirants. *Sociology of Work and Occupations, 8*, 439-463.

Fox, M. F., & Hesse-Biber, S. (1984). *Women at work*. Palo Alto, CA: Mayfield.

Freidson, E. (1972). *The profession of medicine*. New York: Dodd, Mead.

Freidson, E. (1973). Professions and the occupational principle. In E. Freidson (Ed.), *The professions and their prospects*. Beverly Hills, CA: Sage.

Friedland, W. H. (1981). Seasonal farm labor and worker consciousness. In R. L. Simpson & I. H. Simpson (Eds.), *Research in the sociology of work* (Vol. 1, pp. 351-380). Greenwich, CT: JAI.

Gagnon, J. (1977). *Human sexualities*. Glenview, IL: Scott, Foresman.

Galbraith, J. K. (1971). *The new industrial state* (2nd ed.). New York: Mentor.

Ganster, D. C., & Schaubroeck, J. (1991). Work stress and employee health. *Journal of Management, 17*, 235-271.

Garson, B. (1975). *All the livelong day*. New York: Doubleday.

Gersuny, C. (1981). *Work hazards and industrial conflict*. Hanover, NH: University Press of New England.

Getman, J. G., Goldberg, S. B., & Herman, J. B. (1976). *Union representation elections: Law and reality*. New York: Russell Sage.

Giddens, A. (1973). *The class structure of advanced societies*. New York: Barnes & Noble.

Ginzberg, E. (1981). *The school/work nexus: Transition of youth from school to work*. New York: Phi Delta Kappa Educational Foundation.

Glaser, B. G. (1964). *Organizational scientists: Their professional careers*. Indianapolis: Bobbs-Merrill.

Glass, J. (1990). The impact of occupational segregation on working conditions. *Social Forces, 68*, 779-796.

Glenn, E., & Feldberg, R. (1977). Degraded and deskilled: The proletarianization of clerical work. *Social Problems, 25*, 52-64.

Glenn, E., & Feldberg, R. (1979). Clerical work: The female occupation. In J. Freeman (Ed.), *Women: A feminist perspective* (2nd ed.). Palo Alto, CA: Mayfield.

Glenn, N., & Weaver, C. N. (1982). Further evidence on education and job satisfaction. *Social Forces, 61*, 46-65.

Glisson, C., & Durick, M. (1988). Predictors of job satisfaction and organizational commitment in human service organizations. *Administrative Science Quarterly, 33*, 61-81.

Goldthorpe, J. H., Lockwood, D., Bechhofer, F., & Platt, J. (1969). *The affluent worker in the class structure*. Cambridge, UK: Cambridge University Press.

Goldthorpe, J. H., Lockwood, D., Bechhofer, F., & Platt, J. (1970). *The affluent worker: Industrial attitudes and behavior*. Cambridge, UK: Cambridge University Press.

Gone fishing. (1990, January 6). *The Economist*, pp. 61-62.

Goode, W. J. (1957). Community within a community: The professions. *American Sociological Review, 22*, 194-200.

Goode, W. J. (1960). Encroachment, charlatanism, and the emerging professions: Psychology, sociology, and medicine. *American Sociological Review, 25*, 902-914.

Gottfried, H. (1991). The transformation of micro-level control mechanisms in the temporary service industry. *Sociological Forum, 6*, 699-713.

Gove, W., & Geerken, M. R. (1977). The effect of children and employment on the mental health of married men and women. *Social Forces, 56*, 66-76.

Goyder, J. C., & Curtis, J. E. (1975). A three-generational approach to trends in occupational mobility. *American Journal of Sociology, 81*, 129-138.

Grandjean, B. (1975). An economic analysis of the Davis-Moore theory of stratification. *Social Forces, 53*, 543-552.

Grandjean, B. (1981). History and career in a bureaucratic labor market. *American Journal of Sociology, 86*, 1057-1092.

Grandjean, B., & Bernel, H. H. (1979). Sex and centralization in a semiprofession. *Sociology of Work and Occupations, 6*, 84-102.

Grandjean, B., & Taylor, P. A. (1980). Job satisfaction among clerical workers: "status panic" or the opportunity structure of office work. *Sociology of Work and Occupations, 7*, 33-53.

Granovetter, M. (1973). The strength of weak ties. *American Journal of Sociology, 78*, 1360-1380.

Granovetter, M. (1984). Small is bountiful: Labor markets and establishment size. *American Sociological Review, 49*, 323-334.

Greenberger, E., & Steinberg, L. D. (1983). Sex differences in early labor force experience: Harbinger of things to come. *Social Forces, 62*, 467-486.

Greenberger, E., Steinberg, L. D., & Ruggiero, M. (1982). A job is a job is a job. Or is it? *Work and Occupations, 9*, 79-96.

Greenwald, H. P. (1978). Politics and the new insecurity: ideological changes of professionals in a recession. *Social Forces, 57*, 103-118.

Greenwald, M. W. (1980). *Women, war, and work: The impact of World War I on women workers in the United States.* Westport, CT: Greenwood.

Greenwood, E. (1957). Attributes of a profession. *Social Work, 2,* 45-55.

Griffin, L. J., & Alexander, K. L. (1978). Schooling and socioeconomic attainment: High school and college influences. *American Journal of Sociology, 84,* 319-347.

Grimm, J. W., & Dunn, T. P. (1986). The contemporary foreman status: Evidence from an automobile assembly plant. *Work and Occupations, 13,* 359-376.

Grimm, J. W., & Kronus, C. L. (1973). Occupations and publics: A framework for analysis. *Sociological Quarterly, 14,* 68-87.

Grimm, J. W., & Stern, R. N. (1974). Sex roles and the internal labor market structures: The "female" semi-professions. *Social Problems, 2,* 690-705.

Gronn, P. C. (1983). Talk as the work: The accomplishment of school administration. *Administrative Science Quarterly, 28,* 1-21.

Gross, E. (1958). *Work and society.* New York: Thomas Y. Crowell.

Gross, E. (1989). Structural barriers and normative constraints in medical school: Comment on Cole and Fiorentine. *American Journal of Sociology, 94,* 856-869.

Gruber, J. E., & Bjorn, L. (1982). Blue-collar blues: The sexual harassment of women auto workers. *Work and Occupations, 9,* 271-298.

Gruenberg, B. (1980). The happy worker: An analysis of educational and occupational determinants of job satisfaction. *American Journal of Sociology, 86,* 247-271.

Grusky, D. B. (1983). Industrialization and the status attainment process: The thesis of industrialization reconsidered. *American Journal of Sociology, 88,* 494-506.

Grusky, D. B., & Van Rompaey, S. E. (1992). The vertical scaling of occupations. *American Journal of Sociology, 97,* 1712-1728.

Grusky, O. (1966). Career mobility and organizational commitment. *Administrative Science Quarterly*, *10*, 488-503.

Guest, R. (1992, June 18). Desperately seeking students. *Far Eastern Economic Review*, pp. 33-34.

Gurin, G., Veroff, J., & Feld, S. (1960). *Americans view their mental health*. New York: Basic Books.

Hackman, J. R., & Oldham, G. R. (1980). *Work redesign*. Reading, MA: Addison-Wesley.

Haga, W. J., Graen, G., & Dansereau, F. (1974). Professionalism and role making in a service organization: A longitudinal investigation. *American Sociological Review*, *39*, *122-133*.

Hage, J. (1989). The sociology of traditional economic problems: Product markets and labor markets. *Work and Occupations*, *16*, 416-445.

Halaby, C. N. (1979a). Sexual inequality in the workplace: An employer-specific analysis of pay differences. *Social Science Research*, *8*, 79-104.

Halaby, C. N. (1979b). Job-specific sex differences in organizational reward attainment: Wage discrimination versus rank segregation. *Social Forces*, *58*, 108-127.

Hall, D. T., & R. Mansfield (1975). Relationships of age and seniority with career variables of engineers and scientists. *Journal of Applied Psychology*, *60*, 201-210.

Hall, R. H. (1968). Professionalization and bureaucratization. *American Sociological Review*, *33*, 92-104.

Hall, R. H., (1975). *Occupations and the social structure* (2nd ed.). Englewood Cliffs, NJ: Prentice-Hall.

Hall, R. H. (1979). The social construction of the professions. *Sociology of Work and Occupations*, *6*, 124-126.

Hall, R. H. (1983). Theoretical trends in the sociology of occupations. *Sociological Quarterly*, *24*, 5-24.

Hall, R. H. (1988). Comment on the sociology of the professions. *Work and Occupations*, *15*, 273-275.

Hall, R. H. (1991). *Organizations: Structures, processes, and outcomes* (5th ed.). Englewood Cliffs, NJ: Prentice-Hall.

Haller, A. O., & Bills, D. (1979). Review of Treiman, *Occupational prestige in comparative perspective*. *Contemporary Sociology*, *8*, 721-734.

Haller, A. O., Otto, L. B., Meier, R. F., & Ohlendorf, G. W. (1974). Level of occupational aspiration: An empirical analysis. *American Sociological Review*, *39*, 113-121.

Halliday, T. C. (1987). *Beyond monopoly: Lawyers, state crises, and professional empowerment*. Chicago: University of Chicago Press.

Halpern, R. S. (1961). Employee unionization and foremen's attitudes. *Administrative Science Quarterly*, *6*, 73-88.

Hamilton, R. F., & Wright, J. (1981). The college educated blue collar worker. In R. L. Simpson & I. H. Simpson (Eds.), *Research in the sociology of work*, Vol. 1. Greenwich, CT: JAI.

Hannan, M. T., & Freeman, J. (1990). *Organizational ecology*. Cambridge, MA: Harvard University Press.

Hanson, S. L., Martin, J. K., & Tuck, S. A. (1987). Economic sector and job satisfaction. *Work and Occupations*, *14*, 286-305.

Hanushek, E. A. (1982). Sources of black-white earnings differences. *Social Science Research*, *11*, 103-126.

Hardy, M. A. (1982). Social policy and determinants of retirement: A longitudinal analysis of older white males, 1969-1975. *Social Forces*, *60*, 1103-1122.

Hareven, T. (1978). Introduction: The historical study of the life course. In T. Hareven (Ed.), *Transitions: The family and the life course in historical perspective*. New York: Academic Press.

Hartmann, H. I. (1981). The family as the locus of gender, class, and political struggle. *Signs*, *6*, 366-396.

Harvey, D. (1990). *The condition of postmodernity*. Cambridge, MA: Blackwell.

Hatt, P. K. (1950). Occupations and social stratification. *American Journal of Sociology*, *45*, 533-543.

Haug, M. R. (1977). Computer technology and the obsolescence of the concept of profession. In M. R. Haug & J. Dofny (Eds.), *Work and technology*. Beverly Hills, CA: Sage.

Haug, M. R., & M. Sussman (1969). Professional autonomy and the revolt of the client. *Social Problems, 17*, 153-161.

Hauser, R. M., & Featherman, D. L. (1977). *The process of stratification: Trends and analyses*. New York: Academic Press.

Hauser, R. M., & Logan, J. A. (1992). How not to measure intergenerational occupational persistence. *American Journal of Sociology, 97*, 1689-1711.

Hearn, H. L., & Stoll, P. (1975). Continuance commitment in low-status occupations: The cocktail waitress. *Sociological Quarterly, 16*, 105-114.

Hedley, R. A. (1984). Work-nonwork contexts and orientations to work: A crucial test. *Work and Occupations, 11*, 353-375.

Heilman, M. E., & Herlihy, J. M. (1984). Affirmative action, negative reaction? Some moderating conditions. *Organizational Behavior and Human Performance, 33*, 204-213.

Heilman, M. E., Lucas, J. A., & Kaplow, S. R. (1990). Self-derogating consequences of sex-based preferential selection: the moderating role of initial self-confidence. *Organizational Behavior and Human Decision Processes, 46*, 202-216.

Heilman, M. E., Simon, M. C., & Repper, D. P. (1987). Intentionally favored, unintentionally harmed? Impact of sex-based preferential selection on self-perceptions and self-evaluations. *Journal of Applied Psychology, 72*, 62-68.

Heinz, J. P., & Laumann, E. O. (1983). *Chicago lawyers: The social structure of the bar*. New York: Russell Sage.

Henretta, J. C., & Campbell, R. T. (1976). Status attainment and status maintenance: A study of stratification in old age. *American Sociological Review, 41*, 981-992.

Henry, K. (1972). *The large corporation public relations manager: Emerging professional in a bureaucracy?* New Haven, CT: College and University Press.

Herzberg, F. (1966). *Work and the nature of man*. Cleveland, OH: World.

Herzberg, F., Mausner, B., & Snyderman, B. B. (1959). *The motivation to work* (2nd ed.). New York: John Wiley.

Heydebrand, W. V. (1977). Organizational contradictions in public bureaucracies: Toward a Marxian theory of organizations. *Sociological Quarterly, 18*, 83-107.

Heydebrand, W. V. (1983). Technocratic corporatism: Toward a theory of occupational and organizational transformation. In R. H. Hall & R. E. Quinn (Eds.), *Organizational theory and public policy.* Beverley Hills, CA: Sage.

Heydebrand, W. V. (1989). New organizational forms. *Work and Occupations, 16*, 323-357.

Hill, S. (1981). *Competition and control at work: The new industrial sociology.* London: Heineman.

Hirschman, A. O. (1971). *Exit, voice, and loyalty.* Cambridge, MA: Harvard University Press.

Hirschman, C. (1991). What happened to the white ethnics? *Contemporary Sociology, 20*, 180-183.

Hirschman, C., & Wong, M. G. (1981). Trends in socioeconomic achievement among immigrant and native-born Asian-Americans. *Sociological Quarterly, 22*, 495-514.

Hochschild, A. R. (1969). The role of the ambassador's wife: An exploratory study. *Journal of Marriage and the Family, 31*, 73-87.

Hochschild, A. (1983). *The managed heart: Commercialization of human feeling.* Berkeley: University of California Press.

Hodge, R. W., Siegel, P. M., & Rossi, P. H. (1964). Occupational prestige in the United States: 1925-1963. *American Journal of Sociology, 70*, 286-302.

Hodge, R. W., Treiman, D. J., & Rossi, P. H. (1966). A comparative study of occupational prestige. In R. Bendix & S. M. Lipset (Eds.), *Class, status, and power: Social stratification in comparative perspective.* New York: Free Press.

Hodson, R. D. (1977). *Labor force participation and earnings in the core, periphery, and state sectors of production.* Unpublished master's thesis, University of Wisconsin, Madison, WI.

Hodson, R. (1984). Companies, industries, and the measurement of economic segmentation. *American Sociological Review, 49*, 335-348.

Hodson, R. (1988). Good jobs and bad management: How new problems evoke old solutions in high-tech settings. In P. England & G. Farkas (Eds.), *Industries, firms, and jobs: Sociological and economic approaches* (pp. 247-279). New York: Plenum.

Hodson, R. (1989). Gender differences in job satisfaction: Why aren't women more dissatisfied? *Sociological Quarterly, 30,* 385-399.

Hodson, R. (1991). Workplace behaviors: Good soldiers, smooth operators, and saboteurs. *Work and Occupations, 18,* 271-290.

Hodson, R., & Sullivan, T. A. (1990). *The social organization of work.* Belmont, CA: Wadsworth.

Hofferth, S. L., & Moore, K. A. (1979). Early childbearing & later economic well-being. *American Sociological Review, 44,* 784-815.

Hoffman, L. M. (1989). *The politics of knowledge: Activist movements in medicine & planning.* Albany: State University of New York Press.

Hogan, D. P. (1980). The transition to adulthood as a career contingency. *American Sociological Review, 45,* 261-276.

Hogan, D. P., & Pazul, M. (1982). The occupational and earnings returns to education among black men in the north. *American Journal of Sociology, 87,* 905-920.

Hollinger, R., & Clark, J. P. (1982). Employee deviance: A response to the perceived quality of the work experience. *Work and Occupations, 9,* 97-114.

Holmstrom, L. L. (1973). *The two-career family.* Cambridge, MA: Schenkman.

Hood, J. C. (1983). *Becoming a two-job family.* New York: Praeger.

Hope, K. (1982). A liberal theory of prestige. *American Journal of Sociology, 87,* 1011-1031.

Horan, P. M. (1978). Is status attainment research atheoretical? *American Sociological Review, 43,* 534-541.

Hout, M. (1984a). Occupational mobility of black men: 1962 to 1973. *American Sociological Review, 49,* 308-322.

Hout, M. (1984b). Status, autonomy, and training in occupational mobility. *American Journal of Sociology*, *89*, 1379-1409.

Hout, M. (1988). More universalism, less structural mobility: The American occupational structure in the 1980s. *American Journal of Sociology*, *93*, 1358-1400.

Huber, J., & Spitze, G. (1981). Wives' employment, household behavior, and sex-role attitudes. *Social Forces*, *60*, 150-169.

Huber, J., & Spitze, G. (1983). *Sex stratification: children, housework, and job*. New York: Academic Press.

Hughes, E. C. (1949). Dilemmas and contradictions of status. *American Journal of Sociology*, *50*, 353-359.

Hughes, E. C. (1958). *Men and their work*. Glencoe, IL: Free Press.

Hughes, E. C. (l965). The study of occupation. In R. K. Merton, L. Broom, & L. S. Cottrell (Eds.), *Sociology today*. New York: Harper & Row.

Hulin, C. L. (1966). Effects of community characteristics on measuring job satisfaction. *Journal of Applied Psychology*, *50*, 185-192.

Hull, F. M., Friedman, N. S., & Rogers, T. F. (1982). The effect of technology on alienation from work: Testing Blauner's inverted U-curve hypothesis for 110 industrial organizations and 245 retrained printers. *Work and Occupations*, *9*, 31-58.

Hunt, J. G., & Hunt, L. L. (1977). Dilemmas and contradictions of status: the case of dual-career families. *Social Problems*, *24*, 407-416.

Hunter, A. E. (1988). Formal education and initial employment: Unravelling the relationships. *American Sociological Review*, *53*, 653-765.

Hyman, R. (1988). Flexible specialization: Miracle or myth? In R. Hyman & W. Streeck (Eds.), *New technology and industrial relations* (pp. 48-60). New York: Blackwell.

Izraeli, D. N. (1979). Sex structure of occupations: The Israeli experience. *Sociology of Work and Occupations*, *6*, 404-429.

Jackall, R. (1988). *Moral mazes: The world of corporate managers*. New York: Oxford University Press.

Jackson, S. E., & Schuler, R. (1985). A meta-analysis and conceptual critique of research on role ambiguity and role conflict in work settings. *Organizational Behavior and Human Decision Processes*, *36*, 16-78.

Jacobs, D. (1981). Toward a theory of mobility and behavior in organizations. An inquiry into the consequences of some relationships between individual performance and organizational success. *American Journal of Sociology*, *87*, 684-707.

Jacobs, J. A. (1989). Long term trends in occupational segregation by sex. *American Journal of Sociology*, *95*, 160-173.

Jacobson, M. B., & Koch, W. (1977). Women as leaders: Performance evaluation as a function of method of leader selection. *Organizational Behavior and Human Performance*, *20,* 149-157.

Jaffee, D. (1989). Gender inequality in workplace autonomy and authority. *Social Science Quarterly*, *70*, 375-390.

James, D. R., & Soref, M. (1981). Profit constraints on managerial autonomy: Managerial theory and the unmaking of the corporation president. *American Sociological Review*, *46*, 1-18.

Janson, P., & Martin, J. K. (1982). Job satisfaction and age: A test of two views. *Social Forces*, *60*, 1089-1102.

Jencks, C., Bartlett, S., Corcoran, M., Crouse, J., Eaglesfield, D., Jackson, G., McClelland, K., Mueser, P., Olneck, M., Schwartz, J., Ward, S., & Williams, J. (1979). *Who gets ahead? The determinants of economic success in America*. New York: Basic Books.

Jencks, C., Smith, M., Acland, H., Bane, M. J., Cohen, D., Gintis, H., Heyns, B., & Michelson, S. (1972). *Inequality: A reassessment of the effect of family and schooling in America*. New York: Basic Books.

Jhabvala, F. (1977). The economic situation of black people. In D. M. Gordon (Ed.), *Problems in political economy* (2nd ed.) (pp. 153-160). Lexington, MA: D. C. Heath.

Johnson, T. (1972). *The professions and power*. New York: Macmillan.

Johnson, T. (1977). The professions in the class structure. In R. Scase (Ed.), *Industrial society: Class, cleavage, and control*. New York: St. Martin's.

Johnston, W. B., Packer, A. E. (Eds.). (1987). *Workforce 2000*. Indianapolis, IN: Hudson Institute.

Jolly, L. D., Grimm, J. W., & Wozniak, P. R. (1990). Patterns of sex desegregation in managerial and professional specialty fields. *Work and Occupations, 17*, 30-54.

Jones, F. L. (1983). Sources of gender inequality in income: What the Australian census says. *Social Forces, 62*, 134-152.

Jones, R. C. (1984). Changing patterns of undocumented Mexican migration to south Texas. *Social Science Quarterly, 65*, 465-481.

Kahn, R. L. (1972). The meaning of work: Interpretation and proposals for measurement. In A. Campbell & P. Converse (Eds.), *The human meaning of social change*. New York: Russell Sage.

Kahn, R. L. (1981). *Work and health*. New York: John Wiley.

Kahn, R., Wolfe, D., Quinn, R., Snoek, J., & Rosenthal, R. (1964). *Organizational stress: Studies in role conflict and ambiguity*. New York: John Wiley.

Kalleberg, A. L. (1977). Work values and job rewards: A theory of job satisfaction. *American Sociological Review, 42*, 124-143.

Kalleberg, A. L. (1983). Work and stratification: Structural perspectives. *Work and Occupations, 10*, 251-259.

Kalleberg, A. L. (1989). Linking macro and micro levels: Bringing the workers back into the sociology of work. *Social Forces, 67*, 582-592.

Kalleberg, A. L., & Griffin, L. J. (1977). Positional sources of inequality in job satisfaction. *Sociology of Work and Occupations, 5*, 371-401.

Kalleberg, A. L., & Griffin, L. J. (1978). Positional sources of inequality in job satisfaction. *Sociology of Work and Occupations, 5*, 371-401.

Kalleberg, A. L., & Griffin, L. J. (1980). Class, occupation, and inequality in job rewards. *American Journal of Sociology*, *85*, 731-768.

Kalleberg, A. L., & Lincoln, J. R. (1988). The structure of earnings inequality in the United States and Japan. *American Journal of Sociology*, *94* (supplement), S121-S153.

Kanter, R. M. (1977a). *Men and women of the corporation.* New York: Basic Books.

Kanter, R. M. (1977b). Some effects of proportions on group life: Skewed sex ratios and responses to token women. *American Journal of Sociology*, *82*, 965-990.

Kanter, R. M. (1979). Differential access to opportunity and power. In R. Alvarez & K. G. Lutterman (Eds.), *Discrimination in organizations* (pp. 52-68). San Francisco, CA: Jossey-Bass.

Kaplan, A. (1964). Power in perspective. In R. L. Kahn & E. Boulding (Eds.), *Power and conflict in organizations.* New York: Basic Books.

Kasarda, J. D. (1983). Entry-level jobs, mobility, and urban minority unemployment. *Urban Affairs Quarterly*, *19*, 21-40.

Kashefi, M. (1992). *Occupational transformation in the United States economy, 1970-1990: Is there any middle-range jobs reduction?* Unpublished paper, Eastern Illinois University.

Katz, D., & Kahn, R. L. (1978). *The social psychology of organizations* (2nd ed.). New York: John Wiley.

Kaufman, D., & Fetters, M. L. (1983). The executive suite: Are women perceived as ready for the managerial climb? *Journal of Business Ethics*, *2*, 203-212.

Kaufman, D. R., & Richardson, B. L. (1982). *Achievement and women: Challenging the assumptions.* New York: Free Press.

Kaufman, H. (1981). *The limits of organizational change.* Tuscaloosa: University of Alabama Press.

Kaufman, R. L. (1983). A structural decomposition of black-white earnings differentials. *American Journal of Sociology*, *89*, 585-611.

Kaufman, R. L., & Daymont, T. N. (1981). Racial discrimination and the social organization of industries. *Social Science Research, 10*, 225-255.

Kaufman, R. L., Hodson, R., & Fligstein, N. D. (1981). Defrocking dualism: A new approach to defining industrial sectors. *Social Science Research, 10*, 1-31.

Kaufman, R. L., & Spilerman, S. (1982). The age structure of occupations and jobs. *American Journal of Sociology, 87*, 827-851.

Kelley, M. R. (1990). New process technology, job design, and work organization: A contingency model. *American Sociological Review, 55*, 191-208.

Kemp, A. A., & Beck, E. M. (1986). Equal work, unequal pay: Gender discrimination within work-similar occupations. *Work and Occupations, 13*, 324-347.

Kerkhoff, A. C. (1976). The status attainment process: Socialization or allocation. *Social Forces, 55*, 368-381.

Kerkhoff, A. C., Campbell, R. T., & Trott, J. M. (1982). Dimensions of educational and occupational attainment in Great Britain. *American Sociological Review, 77*, 347-364.

Kessler, R. C., & McRae, J. A., Jr. (1982). The effect of wives' employment on the mental health of married men and women. *American Sociological Review, 47*, 216-227.

Kiechel, W., III. (1989, 14 August). Workaholics anonymous. *Fortune*, pp. 117-118.

Kilborn, P. T. (1990, June 3). Tales from the digital treadmill. *New York Times*, Sec. 4, pp. 1,3.

Kingston, P. W., & Nock, S. L. (1987). Time together among dual-earner couples. *American Sociological Review, 52*, 391-400.

Klegon, D. (1978). The sociology of the professions: An emerging perspective. *Sociology of Work and Occupations, 5*, 259-284.

Klein, K. J., & Hall, R. J. (1988). Innovations in human resource management: Strategies for the future. In J. Hage (Ed.), *Futures of organizations* (pp. 147-162). Lexington, MA: Lexington.

Kleiner, B. H., & Francis, G. (1987, January-March). Understanding workaholism. *Business*, pp. 52-54.

Kling, R., & Dunlop, C. (in press). Controversies about computerization and the character of white collar worklife. *The Information Society*.

Kochan, T. A. (1979). How Americans view labor unions. *Monthly Labor Review*, *102*, 23-41.

Kohn, M. L. (1969). *Class and conformity: A study in values.* Homewood, IL: Dorsey.

Kohn, M. L. (1971). Bureaucratic man: A portrait and interpretation. *American Sociological Review*, *36*, 461-474.

Kohn, M. L. (1976). Occupational structure and alienation. *American Journal of Sociology*, *82*, 111-130.

Kohn, M. L., & Schooler, C. (1973). Occupational experience and psychological functioning: An assessment of reciprocal effects. *American Sociological Review*, *38*, 97-118.

Kohn, M. L., & Schooler, C. (1978). The reciprocal effects of the substantive complexity of work and intellectual flexibility: A longitudinal assessment. *American Journal of Sociology*, *84*, 24-52.

Kohn, M. L., & Schooler, C. (1982). Job conditions and personality: A longitudinal assessment of their reciprocal effects. *American Journal of Sociology*, *87*, 1257-1286.

Kohn, M. L., & Schooler, C. (1983). *Work and personality: An inquiry into the impact of social stratification.* Norwood, NJ: Ablex.

Konrad, A. M., & Gutek, B. (1986). Impact of work experiences on attitudes toward sexual harassment. *Administrative Science Quarterly*, *31*, 422-438.

Kornhauser, W. (1965). *Scientists in industry.* Berkeley: University of California Press.

Kraft, P. (1979). The routinization of computer programming. *Sociology of Work and Occupations*, *6*, 139-155.

Kraut, A. I. (1975). Predicting turnover of employees from measured job attitudes. *Organizational Behavior and Human Performance*, *13*, 233-243.

Kraut, R. E., & Grambsch, P. (1987). Home-based white collar employment: Lessons from the 1980 census. *Social Forces, 66,* 410-426.

Kurke, L. B., & Aldrich, H. E. (1979). Mintzberg was right!: A replication and extension of "The nature of managerial work." Unpublished paper, Cornell University, Ithaca, NY.

Ladinsky, J. (1963). Careers of lawyers, law practice, and legal institutions. *American Sociological Review, 28,* 47-54.

Landon, D. D. (1990). *Country lawyers: The impact of context on professional practice.* New York: Praeger.

Landsberger, H. A. (1976). Labor movements, social movements, and social mobility. In R. Dubin (Ed.), *Handbook of work, organization, and society.* Chicago: Rand McNally.

Lane, A. (1968). Occupational mobility in six cities. *American Sociological Review, 33,* 740-749.

La Porte, T. R. (1965). Conditions of strain and accommodation in industrial research organizations. *Administrative Science Quarterly, 20,* 21-38.

Larson, M. S. (1977). *The rise of professionalism.* Berkeley: the University of California Press.

Laumann, E. O. (1983). Chicago lawyers: The social structure of the bar. *Work and Occupations, 12,* 500-503.

Lavin, D. E., Alba, R. D., & Silberstein, R. (1981). *Right versus privilege: The open admissions experiment at the City University of New York.* New York: Free Press.

Lawler, E. E., III (1973). *Motivation in work organizations.* Belmont, CA: Brooks/Cole.

Lawler, E. E., III, & Hall, D. T. (1970). Relationship of job characteristics to job involvement. *Journal of Applied Psychology, 54,* 305-312.

Lawler, E. E., III, & Porter, L. W. (1967). The effects of performance on job satisfaction. *Industrial Relations, 7,* 20-28.

Layder, D. (1984). Sources and levels of commitment in actors' careers. *Work and Occupations, 11,* 147-162.

Leicht, K. T. (1989a). On the estimation of union threat effects. *American Sociological Review, 54,* 1035-1047.

Leicht, K. T. (1989b). Unions, plants, jobs, and workers: An analysis of union satisfaction and participation. *Sociological Quarterly, 30*, 331-362.

Leigh, D. E. (1978). Racial discrimination and labor unions: Evidence from the NLS sample of middle-aged men. *Journal of Human Resources, 13*, 568-577.

Leigh, J. P. (1987). The effects of unemployment on the probability of suffering a disability. *Work and Occupations, 14*, 347-367.

Leiter, J. (1985). Work alienation in the textile industry: Reassessing Blauner. *Work and Occupations, 12*, 479-498.

Leitko, T. A., Greil, A. L., & Peterson, S. A. (1985). Lessons at the bottom: Worker nonparticipation in labor management committees as situational adjustment. *Work and Occupations, 12*, 285-306.

Lembright, M. F., & Reimer, J. W. (1982). Women truckers' problems and the impact of sponsorship. *Work and Occupations, 9*, 457-474.

Lenski, G. (1966). *Power and privilege.* New York: McGraw-Hill.

Leventman, P. G. (1981). *Professionals out of work.* New York: Free Press.

Lieberson, S. (1980). *A piece of the pie: Black and white immigrants since 1880.* Berkeley: University of California Press.

Lieberson, S., & O'Connor, J. F. (1972). Leadership and organizational performance: A study of large corporations. *American Sociological Review, 37*, 117-130.

Lin, N., Ensel, W. M., & Vaughn, J. C. (1981). Social resources and strength of ties: Structural factors in occupational status attainment. *American Sociological Review, 46*, 393-405.

Lin, N., Vaughn, J. C., & Ensel, W. M. (1981b). Social resources and occupational status attainment. *Social Forces, 59*, 1163-1181.

Lin, N., & Yauger, D. (1975). The process of occupational status attainment: A preliminary cross-national comparison. *American Journal of Sociology, 81*, 1163-1181.

Lincoln, J. R., & Kalleberg, A. L. (1985). Work organization and workforce commitment: A study of plants and employees in the U. S. and Japan. *American Sociological Review, 50,* 738-760.

Lincoln, J. R., & Kalleberg, A. L. (1990). *Culture, control, and commitment: A study of work organization and work attitudes in the United States and Japan.* New York: Cambridge University Press.

Lincoln, J. R., Kalleberg, A. L., Hanada, M., & McBride, K. (1990). *Culture, control and commitment: A study of work organizations and work attitudes in the United States and Japan.* Cambridge, UK: Cambridge University Press.

Linder, M. (1983). Self-employment as a cyclical escape from unemployment: A case study of the construction industry during the postwar period. In I. H. Simpson & R. L. Simpson (Eds.), *Research in the sociology of work: A research annual.* Greenwich, CT: JAI.

Linhart, R. (1981). *The assembly line* (M. Crosland, Trans.). Amherst: University of Massachusetts Press.

Lipsky, M. (1982). *Street level bureaucracy: Dilemmas of the individual in public service.* New York: Russell Sage.

Littek, W., & Heisig, U. (1991). Competence, control, and work design: Die Angstellten in the Federal Republic of Germany. *Work and Occupations, 18,* 4-28.

Locke, E. A. (1976). The nature and causes of job satisfaction. In M. D. Dunnette (Ed.), *Handbook of industrial and organizational psychology.* Chicago: Rand McNally.

Logan, J. R. (1976). Industrialization and the stratification of cities in suburban regions. *American Journal of Sociology, 82,* 333-348.

Logan, J. R. (1978). Growth, politics, and the stratification of places. *American Journal of Sociology, 84,* 404-416.

Logan, J. R. (1981). Class structure, the sexual division of labor, and working-class consciousness in Spain. In R. L. Simpson & I. H. Simpson (Eds.), *Research in the sociology of work: A research annual* (Vol. 1). Greenwich, CT: JAI.

Lohr, S. (1993, January 28). Big business in turmoil. *New York Times,* pp. A1, D8.

Lopata, H. Z. (1971). *Occupation: Housewife.* New York: Oxford University Press.

Lopata, H. Z., Norr, K. F., Barnewolt, D., & Miller, C. A. (1985). Job complexity as perceived by workers and experts. *Work and Occupations, 12*, 395-415.

Lorence, J. (1987a). Gender differences in occupational labor market structure. *Work and Occupations, 14*, 23-61.

Lorence, J. (1987b). A test of "gender" and "job" models of sex differences in job involvement. *Social Forces, 66*, 121-142.

Lorence, J. (1987c). Age differences in work involvement: Analysis of three explanations. *Work and Occupations, 14*, 533-557.

Lorence, J. (1987d). Subjective labor force commitment of U. S. men and women. *Social Science Quarterly, 68*, 745-760.

Lorence, J., & Mortimer, J. T. (1981). Work experience and work involvement. *Sociology of Work and Occupations, 8*, 297-326.

Lorence, J., & Mortimer, J. T. (1985). Job involvement through the life course: a panel study of three age groups. *American Sociological Review, 50*, 618-638.

Loscocco, K. A. (1989). The instrumentally oriented factory worker: Myth or reality. *Work and Occupations, 16*, 3-25.

Loscocco, K. A. (1990a). Reactions to blue collar work: A comparison of women and men. *Work and Occupations, 17*, 152-177.

Loscocco, K. A. (1990b). Career structure and employee commitment. *Social Science Quarterly, 71*, 53-68.

Loscocco, K. A., & Kalleberg, A. (1988). Age and the meaning of work in the United States and Japan. *Social Forces, 67*, 337-356.

Loscocco, K. A., & Rochelle, A. R. (1991). Influences on the quality of work and nonwork life: Two decades in review. *Journal of Vocational Behavior, 39*, 182-225.

Loscocco, K. A., & Spitze, G. (1991). The organizational context of women and men's pay satisfaction. *Social Science Quarterly, 72*, 3-19.

Lowe, G. S., & Northcott, H. C. (1988). The impact of working conditions, social roles, and personal characteristics in gender differences in distress. *Work and Occupations, 15,* 55-77.

Lyson, T. A. (1984). Sex differences in the choice of a male or female career line: An analysis of background characteristics and work values. *Work and Occupations, 11,* 131-146.

MacDonald, K., & Ritzer, G. (1988). The sociology of the professions: Dead or alive? *Work and Occupations, 15,* 251-272.

Machan, D. (1988, October 3). How Gus Blythe smelled opportunity. *Forbes,* pp. 104-113.

Machlowitz, M. (1981). *Workaholics.* Reading, MA: Addison-Wesley.

Macke, A. S. (1981). Token men and women: A note on the salience of sex and occupation among professionals and semiprofessionals. *Sociology of Work and Occupations, 8,* 25-38.

Macke, A. S., & Morgan, W. R. (1978). Maternal employment, race, and work orientation of high school girls. *Social Forces, 57,* 187-204.

Mackenzie, G. (1973). *The aristocracy of labor: The position of skilled craftsmen in the American class structure.* Cambridge, UK: Cambridge University Press.

Mandelbaum, D. R. (1978). Women in Medicine. *Signs, 4,* 136-145.

March, J. C., & March, J. G. (1977). Almost random careers: The Wisconsin school superintendency, 1940-1972. *Administrative Science Quarterly, 22,* 377-409.

March, J. C., & March, J. G. (1978). Performance sampling in social matches. *Administrative Science Quarterly, 23,* 434-453.

Marcson, S. (1966). *Scientists in government.* New Brunswick, NJ: Rutgers University Press.

Mare, R. D., & Winship, C. (1984). The paradox of lessening racial inequality and joblessness among black youth: Enrollment, enlistment, and employment, 1964-1981. *American Sociological Review, 49,* 39-55.

Mare, R. D., Winship, C., & Kubitschek, W. N. (1984). The transition from youth to adult: Understanding the age pattern of employment. *American Journal of Sociology, 90*, 326-358.

Marglin, S. A. (1974). What do bosses do? The origins and functions of hierarchy in capitalist production. *Review of Radical Political Economics, 6*, 60-112.

Marini, M. M. (1980). Sex differences in the process of occupational attainment. *Social Science Research, 9*, 307-361.

Marini, M. M. (1984). Women's educational attainment and the timing of entry into parenthood. *American Sociological Review, 49*, 491-511.

Markham, W. T., Macken, P. O., Bonjean, C. M., & Corder, J. (1983). A note on sex, geographic mobility, and career advancement. *Social Forces, 61*, 1138-1146.

Markham, W. T., & Pleck, J. H. (1986). Sex and willingness to move for occupational advancement: Some national sample results. *Sociological Quarterly, 27*, 121-143.

Marks, C. (1981). Split labor markets and black-white relations, 1865-1920. *Phylon Quarterly, 42*, 293-308.

Markson, E. W. (1986). Review of *The aging worker: Research and recommendations*. *Work and Occupations, 13*, 299-301.

Martin, J. K., & Hanson, S. L. (1985). Sex, family wage earning status, and satisfaction with work. *Work and Occupations, 12*, 91-109.

Martin, J. K., & Miller, G. A. (1986). Organizational, individual, and job-related correlates of job satisfaction and absenteeism. *Work and Occupations, 13*, 33-46.

Martin, J. K., & Sheehan, C. L. (1989). Education and job satisfaction: The influences of gender, wage-earning status, and job values. *Work and Occupations, 16*, 184-199.

Martindale, D. (1976). *The romance of a profession: A case history in the sociology of sociology*. St. Paul, MN: Windflower.

Marx, K. (1964). *Early writings* (T. B. Bottomore, Ed. & Trans.). New York: McGraw-Hill.

Marx, K. (1967). *Capital* (Vol. 1) (F. Engels, Ed.) (originally published 1867). New York: International Publishers.

Marx, K., & Engels, F. (1939). *The German ideology* (Translated Ed.). New York: International Publishers.

Maslow, A. (1954). *Motivation and personality*. New York: Harper & Row.

Mason, K. O., Czajka, J. L., & Arber, S. (1976). Change in U. S. women's sex-role attitudes, 1964-1974. *American Sociological Review, 41*, 573-596.

Mayer, S. S. (1979). Women in positions of authority: A case study of changing sex roles. *Signs, 4*, 556-568.

McClendon, M. J. (1976). The occupational status attainment process of males and females. *American Sociological Review, 41*, 52-64.

McGregor, D. (1960). *The human side of enterprise*. New York: McGraw-Hill.

McIlwee, J. S. (1982). Work satisfaction among women in nontraditional occupations. *Work and Occupations, 9*, 299-335.

McKelvey, B. (1982). *Organizational systematics: Taxonomy, evolution, classification*. Berkeley: University of California Press.

McLafferty, S., & Preston, V. (1991). Gender, race, and commuting among service sector workers. *Professional Geographer, 43*, 1-15.

McLaughlin, S. D. (1978). Occupational sex identification and the assessment of male and female earnings inequality. *American Sociological Review, 43*, 909-921.

McNamee, S. J., & Vanneman, R. (1983). The perception of class: Social and technical relations of production. *Work and Occupations, 10*, 437-469.

McNeil, K., & Miller, R. E. (1980). The profitability of consumer protection: Warranty policy in the auto industry, *Administrative Science Quarterly, 22*, 407-427.

McRoberts, H. A., & Selbee, K. (1981). Trends in occupational mobility in Canada and the United States: A comparison. *American Sociological Review, 46*, 406-421.

Mechanic, D. (1962). Sources of power of lower participants. *Administrative Science Quarterly, 7*, 349-364.

Meiksine, P. F., & Watson, J. M. (1989). Professional autonomy and organizational constraint: The case of engineers. *Sociological Quarterly, 30*, 561-585.

Merton, R. K., Reader, G. C., & Kendall, P. (Eds.). (1957). *The student physician: Introductory studies in the sociology of medical education*. Cambridge, MA: Harvard University Press.

Messner, S. F. (1980). Blau's theory of occupational differentiation: Problems in empirical examination. *Sociology of Work and Occupations, 7*, 395-424.

Meyer, J. (1977). The effects of education as an institution. *American Journal of Sociology, 89*, 55-77.

Meyer, J. W., Tuma, N. B., & Zagorski, K. (1979). Education and occupational mobility: A comparison of Polish and American men. *American Journal of Sociology, 84*, 978-986.

Miles, R. E. (1981). Governance of organizations: Leader-led roles. In G. W. England, A. R. Negandhi, & B. Wilpert (Eds.), *The functioning of complex organizations*. Cambridge, MA: Oelgeschlager, Gunn & Hain.

Milkovich, G. T., & Boudreau, J. W. (1991). *Human resource management* (6th ed.). Homewood, IL: Irwin.

Miller, A. R., Treiman, D. J., Cain, P. S., & Roos, P. A. (Eds.). (1980). *Work, jobs, and occupations: a critical review of the Dictionary of Occupational Titles*. Washington, DC: National Academy Press.

Miller, D. C., & Form, W. (1964). *Industrial sociology*. New York: Harper & Row.

Miller, G. (1978). *Odd jobs: The world of deviant work*. Englewood Cliffs, NJ: Prentice-Hall.

Miller, G. (1981). *It's a living: Work in modern society*. New York: St. Martin's.

Miller, G. (1991). *Enforcing the work ethic: Rhetoric and everyday life in a work incentive program*. Albany: State University of New York Press.

Miller, J. (1980). Individual and occupational determinants of job satisfaction: A focus on gender differences. *Sociology of Work and Occupations, 7*, 337-366.

Miller, J., Labovitz, S., & Fry, L. (1975). Inequities in the organizational experiences of women and men. *Social Forces, 54*, 365-381.

Miller, J., Schooler, C., Kohn, M. L., & Miller, K. A. (1979). Women and work: The psychological effects of occupational conditions. *American Journal of Sociology, 85,* 66-94.

Miller, S. J. (1964). The social bases of sales behavior. *Social Problems, 12,* 15-24.

Mills, C. W. (1956). *White collar.* New York: Oxford University Press.

Mills, C. W. (1957). *The power elite.* New York: Oxford University Press.

Mindiola, T., Jr. (1979). Age and income discrimination against Mexican Americans and blacks in Texas, 1960 and 1970. *Social Problems, 27,* 196-208.

Mintzberg, H. (1979). *The nature of managerial work.* New York: Harper & Row.

Mladenka, K. R. (1989). Barriers to Hispanic employment success in 1,200 cities. *Social Science Quarterly, 70,* 391-407.

Monk-Turner, E. (1983). Sex, educational differentiation and occupational status: Analyzing occupational differences for community and four-year college entrants. *Sociological Quarterly, 24,* 393-404.

Montagna, P. D. (1974). *Certified public accounting: A sociological view of a profession in change.* Houston, TX: Scholars.

Montagna, P. D. (1977). *Occupations and society: Toward a sociology of the labor market.* New York: John Wiley.

Moore, W. (1963a). But some are more equal than others. *American Sociological Review, 28,* 13-18.

Moore, W. (1963b). Rejoinder. *American Sociological Review, 28,* 26-28.

Morris, J., & Villemez, W. J. (1992). Mobility potential and job satisfaction: Mixing dispositional and situational explanations. *Work and Occupations, 19,* 35-58.

Morris, R. T., & Murphy, R. J. (1959). The situs dimension in occupational structure. *American Sociological Review, 24,* 231-239.

Morris, S., & Charney, N. (1983, June). Workaholism: Thank God it's Monday. *Psychology Today,* p. 88.

Mortimer, J. T. (1974). Intergenerational occupational movement. *American Journal of Sociology, 79,* 1278-1299.

Mortimer, J. T. (1978). Dual career families: A sociological perspective. In S. S. Petersen, J. M. Richardson, & G. V. Kreuter (Eds.), *The two-career family—Issues and alternatives.* Washington, DC: University Press.

Mortimer, J. T. (1979). *Changing attitudes toward work: Highlights of the literature.* Scarsdale, NY: Work in America Institute.

Mortimer, J. T. (1980). Occupation-family linkages as perceived by men in the early stages of professional and managerial careers. In H. Z. Lopata (Ed.), *Research in the interweave of social roles: Men and women,* Vol. 1. Greenwich, CT: JAI.

Mortimer, J. T., Hall, R. H., & Hill, R. (1978). Husbands' occupational attributes as constraints on wives' employment. *Sociology of Work and Occupations, 5,* 285-313.

Mortimer, J. T., & Kumka, D. (1982). A further examination of the "occupational linkage hypothesis." *Sociological Quarterly, 23,* 3-16.

Mortimer, J. T., & Lorence, J. (1979). Work experience and occupational value socialization: A longitudinal study. *American Journal of Sociology, 84,* 1361-1385.

Mortimer, J. T., & Lorence, J. (1981). Comment on Samuel and Lewin-Epstein. *American Journal of Sociology, 87,* 708-714.

Mortimer, J. T., Lorence, J., & Kumka, D. S. (1986). *Work, family, and personality: Transition to adulthood.* Norwood, NJ: Ablex.

Mortimer, J. T., & Simmons, R. (1978). Adult socialization. *Annual Review of Sociology* (Vol. 4, pp. 421-454). Palo Alto, CA: Annual Reviews.

Mottaz, C. J. (1981). Some determinants of work alienation. *Sociological Quarterly, 22,* 515-529.

Mottaz, C. J. (1987a). Age and work satisfaction. *Work and Occupations, 14,* 387-409.

Mottaz, C. J. (1987b). An analysis of the relationship between work satisfaction and organizational commitment. *Sociological Quarterly, 28,* 541-558.

MOW International Research Team (1987). *The meaning of working*. New York: Academic Press.

Mueller, C. W. (1974). City effects on socioeconomic achievement: The case of large cities. *American Sociological Review, 39*, 652-667.

Mueller, E., Hybels, J., Schmiedeskamp, J., Sonquist, J., & Staelin, C. (1969). *Technological advance in an expanding economy*. Ann Arbor, MI: Braun-Brumfield.

Mutran, E., & Reitzes, D. (1989). Labor force participation and health: A cohort comparison of older male workers. *Social Science Quarterly, 70*, 449-467.

Nasar, S. (1986, March 17). Jobs go begging at the bottom. *Fortune*, pp. 33-35.

Near, J. (1989). Organizational commitment among Japanese and U. S. workers. *Organization Studies, 10*, 281-300.

Nelkin, D., & Brown, M. S. (1984). *Workers at risk: Voices from the workplace*. Chicago: University of Chicago Press.

Nelson, J. I., & Lorence, J. (1988). Metropolitan earnings inequality and service sector employment. *Social Forces, 67*, 492-511.

Nelson, R. L. (1988). *Partners with power: Social transformation of the large law firm*. Berkeley: University of California Press.

Neugarten, B. L., Moore, J. W., & Lowe, J. C. (1965). Age norms, age constraints, and adult socialization. *American Journal of Sociology, 70*, 710-717.

Newman, K. S. (1988). *Fall from grace: The experience of downward mobility in the American middle class*. New York: Free Press.

News and comment. (1990, September). *Science, 249*, 1235-1237.

Nordlie, P. G. (1979). Proportion of black and white army officers in command positions. In R. Alvarez, K. G. Lutterman, & Associates (Eds.), *Discrimination in organizations*. San Francisco: Jossey-Bass.

Nuss, S., & Majka, L. (1983). The economic integration of women: A cross-national investigation. *Work and Occupations, 10*, 29-48.

Nystrom, P. C. (1981). Designing jobs and assigning employees. In P. C. Nystrom & W. H. Starbuck (Eds.), *Handbook of organizational design*, Vol. 2. New York: Oxford University Press.

Oakley, A. (1974). *The sociology of housework*. New York: Pantheon.

Oakley, A. (1980). Reflections on the study of household labor. In S. F. Berk (Ed.), *Women and household labor*. Beverly Hills, CA: Sage.

Oates, W. E. (1971). *Confessions of a workaholic*. Abingdon, MN: World.

Obradovic, J. (1972). Distribution of participation in the process of decision making on problems related to the economic activity of the company. In E. Pusic (Ed.), *Proceedings of the First International Conference on Participation and Self-Management*, Vol. 2. Zagreb, Yugoslavia: University of Zagreb.

O'Farrell, B., & Harlan, S. L. (1982). Craftworkers and clerks: The effect of male co-worker hostility on women's satisfaction with non-traditional jobs. *Social Problems, 29*, 252-265.

Oldham, G. R., & Hackman, J. R. (1981). Relationships between organizational structure and employee reactions: Comparing alternative frameworks. *Administrative Science Quarterly, 26*, 66-83.

Oldham, G. R., & Rotchford, N. L. (1983). Relationships between office characteristics and employee reactions: A study of the physical environment. *Administrative Science Quarterly, 28*, 542-556.

Oppenheimer, V. K. (1982). *Work and the family: A study in social demography*. New York: Academic Press.

O'Reilly, C. A., III, Caldwell, D., & Barnett, W. P. (1989). Work group demography, social integration and turnover. *Administrative Science Quarterly, 34*, 21-37

Osterman, P. (1988). *Employment futures: Reorganization, dislocation, and public policy*. New York: Oxford University Press.

O'Toole, J. (Ed.). (1973). *Work in America: Report of a special task force to the Secretary of Health, Education, and Welfare*. Cambridge: MIT Press.

O'Toole, J. (Ed.). (1984). *Work and the quality of life*. Cambridge: MIT Press.

Ouchi, W. (1981). *Theory Z*. Lexington, MA: Addison-Wesley.

Ouchi, W. G., & Wilkins, A. L. (1985). Organizational culture. In R. H. Turner & J. F. Short, Jr. (Eds.), *Annual Review of Sociology* (Vol. 11, pp. 457-483). Palo Alto, CA: Annual Reviews.

Padavic, I. (1991). Attractions of male blue-collar jobs for black and white women: Economic need, exposure, and attitudes. *Social Science Quarterly, 72*, 33-49.

Pampel, F. C., Land, K. C., & Felson, M. (1977). A social indicator model of changes in the occupational structure of the United States: 1947-74. *American Sociological Review, 42*, 951-964.

Pampel, F. C., & Weiss, J. A. (1983). Economic development, pension policies, and the labor force participation of aged males: A cross-national, longitudinal approach. *American Journal of Sociology, 89*, 350-372.

Papanek, H. (1973). Men, women, and work: Reflections on the two-person career. *American Journal of Sociology, 78*, 852-872.

Parcel, T. L., & Benefo, K. (1987). Temporal change in occupational differentiation. *Work and Occupations, 14*, 513-532.

Parcel, T. L., & Mueller, C. W. (1983). Occupational differentiation, prestige, and socioeconomic status. *Work and Occupations, 10*, 49-80.

Parelius, A. P., & Parelius, R. (1978). *The sociology of education*. Englewood Cliffs, NJ: Prentice-Hall.

Parker, S. (1982). *Work and retirement*. London: Allen & Unwin.

Parker, S. A., & Smith, M. A. (1976). Work and leisure. In R. Dubin (Ed.), *Handbook of work, organization, and society.* Chicago: Rand McNally.

Parnes, H. S. (Ed.). (1981). *Work and retirement: A longitudinal study of men.* Cambridge: MIT Press.

Parsons, T. (1940). An analytical approach to the theory of social stratification. *American Journal of Sociology, 45,* 841-862.

Parsons, T. (1959). Some problems confronting sociology as a profession. *American Sociological Review, 24,* 547-559.

Parsons, T. (1960). *Structure and process in modern society.* New York: Free Press.

Parsons, T. (1970). Equality and inequality in modern society or social stratification revisited. In E. Laumann (Ed.), *Social stratification: research and theory for the 1970's.* New York: Bobbs-Merrill.

Parsons, T. (1971). *The system of modern societies.* Englewood Cliffs, NJ: Prentice-Hall.

Parsons, T. (1974). The social structure of the family. In R. Anshen (Ed.), *The family: Its functions and destiny.* New York: Harper & Row.

Patchen, M. (1970). *Participation, achievement, and involvement on the job.* Englewood Cliffs, NJ: Prentice-Hall.

Peil, M. (1979). Urban women in the labor force. *Sociology of Work and Occupations, 6,* 482-501.

Penn, R. (1975). Occupational prestige hierarchies: A great empirical invariant? *Social Forces, 54 (2),* 352-364.

Pennings, J. M. (1980). *Interlocking directorates.* San Francisco: Jossey-Bass.

Perrow, C. (1979). *Complex organizations: A critical essay* (2nd ed.). Glenview, IL: Scott, Foresman.

Perrucci, C. C., Perrucci, R., Targ, D. B., & Targ, H. R. (1988). *Plant closings.* Hawthorne, NY: Aldine.

Perrucci, R. (1973). Engineering: Professional servant of power. In E. Freidson (Ed.), *The professions and their prospects.* Beverly Hills, CA: Sage.

Perrucci, R., & Gerstl, J. (1969). *Profession without community: Engineers in American society*. New York: Random House.

Persell, C. (1977). *Education and inequality: The roots of stratification in America's schools*. New York: Free Press.

Peters, T. J., & Waterman, R. H., Jr. (1982). *In search of excellence*. New York: Harper & Row.

Pfeffer, J. (1981). *Power in organizations*. Marshfield, MA: Pitman.

Pfeffer, J., & Baron, J. N. (1988). Taking the workers back out: Recent trends in the structuring of employment. In B. M. Staw & L. L. Cummings (Eds.), *Research in organizational behavior* (Vol. 10, pp. 257-303). Greenwhich, CT: JAI.

Pfeffer, J., & Davis-Blake, A. (1987). The effect of the proportion of women on salaries: The case of college administrators. *Administrative Science Quarterly, 32*, 1-24.

Pfeffer, J., & Davis-Blake, A. (1990). Unions and job satisfaction: An alternative view. *Work and Occupations, 17*, 259-283.

Pfeffer, J., & Langton, N. (1988). Wage inequality and the organization of work: The case of academic departments. *Administrative Science Quarterly, 33*, 588-606.

Pfeffer, J., & Ross, J. (1982). The effects of marriage and a working wife on occupational and wage attainment. *Administrative Science Quarterly, 27*, 66-80.

Pfeffer, J., & Ross, J. (1990). Gender-based wage differences: The effects of organizational context. *Work and Occupations, 17*, 55-78.

Pfeffer, J., & Salancik, G. R. (1978). *The external control of organizations: A resource dependence perspective*. New York: Harper & Row.

Phillips, R. L., Andrisani, P. J., Daymont, T. N., & Gilroy, C. L. (1992). The economic returns to military service: Race-ethnic differences. *Social Science Quarterly, 73*, 340-359.

Piore, M. B. (1972). *Notes for a theory of labor market stratification*. Working paper No. 95, Department of Economics. Cambridge: MIT.

Piven, F. F., & Cloward, R. A. (1989). *Why Americans don't vote*. New York: Pantheon.

Pleck, J. H. (1977). The work-family role system. *Social Problems, 24*, 417-427.

Plunkert, L. M. (1990, September). The 1980s: A decade of job growth and industry shifts. *Monthly Labor Review*, pp. 3-16.

Podmore, D., & Spencer, A. (1982). Women lawyers in England: The experience of inequality. *Work and Occupations, 9*, 337-361.

Pollan, S. M., & Levine, M. (1992, March 9). The graying yuppie: Reality zaps the baby-boomers. *New York Times*, pp. 28-37.

Porter, J. N. (1974). Race, socialization, and mobility in educational and early occupational attainment. *American Sociological Review, 39*, 303-316.

Porter, L. W., Lawler, E. E., III, & Hackman, J. R. (1975). *Behavior in organizations*. New York: McGraw-Hill.

Portes, A. (1984). The rise of ethnicity: Determinants of ethnic perceptions among cuban exiles in Miami. *American Sociological Review, 49*, 383-397.

Portes, A., & Jensen, L. (1989). The enclave and the entrants: Patterns of ethnic enterprise in Miami before and after Mariel. *American Sociological Review, 54*, 929-949.

Portes, A., & Manning, R. D. (1985). The immigrant enclave: Theory and empirical examples. In J. Nagel & S. Olzak (Eds.), *Ethnicity: Structure and process*. New York: Academic Press.

Portes, A., & Walton, J. (1981). *Labor, class, and the international system*. New York: Academic Press.

Portes, A., & Wilson, K. L. (1976). Black-white differences in educational attainment. *American Sociological Review, 41*, 414-431.

Powell, B., & Jacobs, J. A. (1984a). The prestige gap: Differential evaluations of male and female workers. *Work and Occupations, 11*, 283-308.

Powell, B., & Jacobs, J. A. (1984b). Gender differences in the evaluation of prestige. *Sociological Quarterly, 25*, 173-190.

Price, J. L. (1977). *The study of turnover*. Ames: Iowa State University Press.

Price, J. L. (1989). The impact of turnover on the organization. *Work and Occupations, 16*, 461-473.

Priest, T. B., & Rothman, R. A. (1985). Lawyers in corporate chief executive positions: A historical analysis of careers. *Work and Occupations, 12*, 131-146.

Putnam, G. W. (1990). Occupational sex segregation and economic inequality under socialism: Earnings achievement and earnings decomposition in Yugoslavia. *Sociological Quarterly, 31*, 59-75.

Quadagno, J. S. (1978). Career continuity and retirement plans of men and women physicians: The meaning of disorderly careers. *Sociology of Work and Occupations, 5*, 55-74.

Quick, P. (1977). The class nature of women's oppression. *Review of Radical Political Economics, 9*, 42-53.

Quinn, R. P., & Staines, G. L. (1979). *The 1977 quality of employment survey*. Ann Arbor: University of Michigan, Institute for Social Research.

Quinn, R. P., Staines, G. L., & McCullough, M. R. (1974). *Job satisfaction: Is there a trend?* Manpower Research Monograph No. 30, U.S. Department of Labor. Washington, DC: Government Printing Office.

Ragan, J. F., Jr., & Smith, S. (1981). The impact of differences in turnover rates on male/female pay differentials. *Journal of Human Resources, 16*, 343-365.

Rapoport, R., & Rapoport, R. (1971). *Dual career families*. New York: Penguin.

Regoli, R. M., Poole, E. O., & Schrink, J. L. (1979). Occupational socialization and career development: A look at cynicism among correctional institution workers. *Human Organization, 38*, 183-187.

Reich, M. (1971). The economics of racism. In D. M. Gordon (Ed.), *Problems in political economy*. Lexington, MA: D. C. Heath.

Reiss, A. J. (1961). *Occupations and social status*. New York: Free Press.

Report of Special Task Force to the Secretary of Health, Education, and Welfare. (1973). *Work in America*. Cambridge, MA: MIT Press.

Reskin, B. F., & Roos, P. A. (1990). *Job queues and gender queues: Explaining women's inroads into male occupations*. Philadelphia, PA: Temple University Press.

Rhee, J. M. (1974). The redistribution of the black work force in the South by industry. *Phylon Quarterly, 35*, 293-300.

Richman, L. S. (1988, April 11). Tomorrow's jobs: Plentiful, but . . . . *Fortune*, pp. 42-56.

Riley, M. (1971). Social gerontology and the age stratification of society. *Gerontologist, 11*, 79-87.

Riley, M., Johnson, M., & Foner, A. (Eds.). (1972). *Aging and society. Vol. 3: A sociology of age stratification*. New York: Russell Sage.

Ritzer, G. (1975). Professionalization, bureaucratization, and rationalization: The views of Max Weber. *Social Forces, 53*, 627-634.

Ritzer, G. (1989a). Sociology of work: A metatheoretical analysis. *Social Forces, 67*, 593-604.

Ritzer, G. (1989b). The permanently new economy: The case for reviving economic sociology. *Work and Occupations, 16*, 243-272.

Ritzer, G., & Trice, H. M. (1959). *An occupation in conflict: A study of the personnel manager*. Ithaca, NY: New York State School of Industrial and Labor Relations, Cornell University.

Ritzer, G., & Walczak, D. (1986). *Working: Conflict and change* (3rd ed.). Englewood Cliffs, NJ: Prentice-Hall.

Robinson, J. G., & McIlwee, J. S. (1989). Obstacles to unionization in high-tech industries. *Work and Occupations, 16*, 115-136.

Robinson, R. V. (1984). Structural change and class mobility in capitalist societies. *Social Forces, 63*, 51-71.

Roby, P. (1981). *Women in the workplace: Proposals for research and policy concerning the conditions of women in industrial and service jobs*. Cambridge, MA: Schenkman.

Roe, A. (1956). *The psychology of occupations*. New York: John Wiley.

Roethlisberger, F. J. (1945). The foreman: Master and victim of double talk. *Harvard Business Review*, *23*, 283-298.

Rogoff, N. (1953). *Recent trends in occupational mobility*. New York: Free Press.

Roos, P. A. (1981). Sex stratification in the workplace: Male-female differences in economic returns to occupation. *Social Science Research*, *10*, 195-223.

Roos, P. A. (1983). Marriage and women's occupational attainment in cross-cultural perspective. *American Sociological Review*, *48*, 852-864.

Rosen, B. C., & Aneshensel, C. S. (1978). Sex differences in the educational-occupational expectation process. *Social Forces*, *57*, 164-186.

Rosenbaum, J. A. (1981). Careers in a corporate hierarchy: A longitudinal analysis of earnings and level attainments. In D. J. Treiman & R. V. Robinson (Eds.), *Research in social stratification and mobility: A research annual*. Greenwich, CT: JAI.

Rosenbaum, J. A., & Kariya, T. (1989). From high school to work: Market and institutional mechanisms in Japan. *American Journal of Sociology*, *94*, 1334-1365.

Rosenbaum, J. E. (1975). The stratification of socialization processes. *American Sociological Review*, *40*, 48-54.

Rosenbaum, J. E. (1976). *Making inequality: The hidden curriculum of high school tracking*. New York: John Wiley.

Rosenbaum, J. E. (1979a). Organizational career mobility: Promotion chances in a corporation during periods of growth and contraction. *American Journal of Sociology*, *85*, 21-48.

Rosenbaum, J. E. (1979b). Tournament mobility: Career patterns in a corporation. *Administrative Science Quarterly*, *24*, 220-241.

Rosenfeld, R. (1978a). Women's intergenerational occupational mobility. *American Sociological Review*, *43*, 36-46.

Rosenfeld, R. (1978b). Women's employment patterns and occupational achievements. *Social Science Research*, *7*, 61-80.

Rosenfeld, R. (1979). Women's occupational careers: Individual and structural explanations. *Sociology of Work and Occupations, 6*, 283-311.

Rosenfeld, R. (1980). Race and sex differences in career dynamics. *American Sociological Review, 45*, 583-609.

Rosenfeld, R. (1981). Academic men and women's career mobility. *Social Science Research, 10*, 337-363.

Rosenfeld, R. (1986). U.S. farm women: Their part in farm work and decision making. *Work and Occupation, 13*, 179-202.

Rosenfeld, R., & Kalleberg, A. L. (1990). A cross-national comparison of the gender gap in income. *American Journal of Sociology, 96*, 69-106.

Rosenstein, J., & French, J. L. (1985). Attitudes toward unionization in an employee-owned firm in the Southwest. *Work and Occupations, 12*, 465-478.

Ross, C. E., Mirowsky, J., & Huber, J. (1983). Dividing work, sharing work, and in-between: Marriage patterns and depression. *American Sociological Review, 48*, 809-823.

Roth, J. A. (1972). Professionalism: The sociologist's decoy. *Sociology of Work and Occupations, 1*, 6-23.

Rothman, R. A. (1979). Occupational roles: Power and negotiation in the division of labor. *Sociological Quarterly, 20*, 495-515.

Rothman, R. A. (1984). Deprofessionalization: The case of law in America. *Work and Occupations, 11*, 183-206.

Rothman, R. A. (1987). *Working: Sociological perspectives*. Englewood Cliffs, NJ: Prentice Hall.

Rousseau, D. M. (1988). Human resource planning for the future. In J. Hage (Ed.), *Futures of organizations* (pp. 245-266). Lexington, MA: Lexington.

Roy, D. F. (1952). Quota restriction and goldbricking in a machine shop. *American Journal of Sociology, 9*, 427-442.

Roy, D. F. (1954). "Efficiency and the fix": Informal intergroup relations in a piecework machine shop. *American Journal of Sociology, 60*, 255-256.

Roy, D. F. (1959-60). "Banana time": Job satisfaction and informal interaction. *Human Organization, 18,* 158-168.

Rus, V. (1972). The limits of organized participation. In E. Pusic (Ed.), *Proceedings of the First International Conference on Participation and Self-Management* (Vol. 2). Zagreb, Yugoslavia: University of Zagreb.

Russell, R. (1983). Class formation in the workplace: The role of sources of income. *Work and Occupations, 10,* 349-372.

Russell, R. (1988). Form and extent of employee participation in the contemporary United States. *Work and Occupations, 15,* 374-395.

Rytina, S. (1992a). Scaling the intergenerational continuity of occupation: Is occupational inheritance ascriptive after all? *American Journal of Sociology, 97,* 1658-1688.

Rytina, S. (1992b). Response to Hauser and Logan and Grusky and Van Rompaey. *American Journal of Sociology, 97,* 1729-1748.

Safa, H. L. (1981). Runaway and female employment: The search for cheap labor. *Signs, 7,* 418-433.

Salz, A. (1944). *Occupations: Theory and history. Vol. 11, Encyclopedia of the social sciences.* New York: Macmillan.

Samuel, Y., & Levin-Epstein, N. (1979). The occupational situs as a predictor of work values. *American Journal of Sociology, 85,* 625-639.

Sandefur, G. D. (1981). Black/white differences in job shift behavior: A dynamic analysis. *Sociological Quarterly, 22,* 565-579.

Sandell, S. H. (1977). Attitudes toward market work and the effect of wage rates on the lifetime labor supply of married women. *Journal of Human Resources, 12,* 379-385.

Sayers, S. (1988). The need to work: A perspective from philosophy. In R. E. Pahl (Ed.), *On work: Historical, comparative, and theoretical approaches* (pp. 722-742). New York: Blackwell.

Schein, E. H. (1971). The individual, the organization, and the career: A conceptual scheme. *Journal of Applied Behavioral Science, 7,* 401-426.

Schein, E. H. (1985). *Organizational culture and leadership*. San Francisco: Jossey-Bass.

Schervish, P. G. (1983). *Vulnerability and power in market relations: The structural determinants of unemployment*. New York: Academic Press.

Schervish, P. G., & Herman, A. (1986). On the road: conceptualizing class structure in the transition to socialism. *Work and Occupations, 13*, 264-291.

Schneider, B. (1987). The people make the place. *Personnel Psychology, 40*, 437-453.

Schneider, B. E. (1986). Coming out at work: Bridging the private/public gap. *Work and Occupations, 13*, 463-487.

Schoenherr, R. A., & Greeley, A. M. (1974). Role commitment processes and the American Catholic priesthood. *American Sociological Review, 39*, 407-426.

Schooler, C., Miller, J. Miller, K. A., & Richtand, C. N. (1984). Work for the household: Its nature and consequences for husbands and wives. *American Journal of Sociology, 90*, 97-124.

Schor, J. B. (1992). *The overworked American: The unexpected decline of leisure*. New York: Basic Books.

Schreiber, C. T. (1979). *Changing places: Men and women in transitional occupations*. Cambridge: MIT Press.

Schriesheim, C. A. (1981). Job satisfaction, attitudes toward unions and voting in a union representation election. *Journal of Applied Psychology, 63*, 548-552.

Schroeder, S. J., & Finlay, W. (1986). Internal labor markets, professional domination, and gender: A comparison of laboratory employees in hospitals and chemical/oil firms. *Social Science Quarterly, 67*, 827-840.

Schwalbe, M. (1988). Sources of self-esteem in work: What's important for whom. *Work and Occupations, 15*, 24-35.

Scott, W. R. (1965). Reactions to supervision in a heteronomous professional organization. *Administrative Science Quarterly, 20*, 65-81.

Scully, J. (1992, December 15). Address. *New York Times*, p. B10.

Seashore, S. E., & Taber, T. D. (1975). Job satisfaction indicators and their correlates. *American Behavioral Scientist, 18*, 333-368.

Seeman, M. (1977). Some real and imaginary consequences of social mobility: A French-American comparison. *American Journal of Sociology, 82,* 757-782.

Seidman, A. (1978). *Working women: A study of women in paid jobs.* Boulder, CO: Westview.

Sell, R. R. (1982). A research note on the demography of occupational relocations. *Social Forces, 60,* 859-865.

Sell, R. R. (1983a). Transferred jobs: A neglected aspect of migration and occupational change. *Work and Occupations, 10,* 179-206.

Sell, R. R. (1983b). Market and direct allocation of labor through migration. *Sociological Quarterly, 24,* 93-105.

Sellers, P. (1990, June 4). What customers really want. *Fortune,* pp. 58-68.

Semyonov, M. (1981). Effects of community on status attainment. *Sociological Quarterly, 22,* 359-372.

Sewell, W. H., & Hauser, R. M. (1975). *Education, occupation, and earnings: Achievement in the early career.* New York: Academic Press.

Sewell, W. H., Hauser, R. M., & Featherman, D. L. (1976). *Schooling and achievement in American society.* New York: Academic Press.

Sewell, W. H., Hauser, R. M., & Wolf, W. C. (1980). Sex, schooling, and occupational status. *American Journal of Sociology, 86,* 551-583.

Seybolt, J. W. (1976). Work satisfaction as a function of the person-environment interaction. *Organizational Behavior and Human Performance, 17,* 66-75.

Shaiken, H. (1988). *Work transformed: Automation and labor in the computer age.* New York: Holt, Rinehart & Winston.

Shapiro, E. G. (1977). Racial differences in the value of job rewards. *Social Forces, 56,* 21-30.

Shaw, L. B. (Ed.). (1983). *Unplanned careers: The working lives of middle-aged women.* Lexington, MA: D. C. Heath.

Shaw, L. B. (1985). Determinants of the increasing work attachment of married women. *Work and Occupations, 12,* 41-57.

Sheldon, M. E. (1971). Investments and involvements as mechanisms producing commitment to the organization. *Administrative Science Quarterly, 16*, 143-150.

Shepard, J. M. (1971). *Automation and alienation: A study of office and factory workers*. Cambridge, MA: MIT Press.

Shepard, J. M. (1973). Specialization, autonomy, and job satisfaction. *Industrial Relations, 12*, 274-281.

Shepard, J. M., Kim, D. I., & Hougland, G. J., Jr. (1979). Effects of technology in industrialized and industrializing societies. *Sociology of Work and Occupations, 6*, 457-481.

Sheridan, J. E., & Slocum, J. W., Jr. (1975). The direction of the causal relationship between job satisfaction and work performance. *Organizational Behavior and Human Performance, 14*, 159-172.

Sheridan, J. H. (1988, January 18). Workin' too hard? *Industry Week*, pp. 31-36.

Shoemaker, D. J., Snizek, W. E., & Bryant, C. D. (1977). Toward a further clarification of Becker's side-bet hypothesis as applied to organizational and occupational commitment. *Social Forces, 56*, 598-603.

Siegel, P. M. (1971). *Prestige in the American occupational structure*. Unpublished doctoral dissertation, University of Chicago, Chicago, IL.

Simpson, I. H. (1989). The sociology of work: Where have the workers gone? *Social Forces, 67*, 563-581.

Simpson, I. H., & Simpson, R. L. (Eds.). (1983). *Research in the sociology of work: A research annual*. Greenwich, CT: JAI.

Simpson, I. H., Simpson, R. L., Evers, M., & Poss, S. S. (1982). Occupational recruitment, retention, and labor force cohort representation. *American Journal of Sociology, 87*, 1287-1313.

Simpson, R. L. (1981). Labor force integration and southern U.S. textile unions. In R. L. Simpson & I. H. Simpson (Eds.), *Research in the sociology of work: A research annual* (Vol. 1). Greenwich, CT: JAI.

Simpson, R. L., & Simpson, I. H. (1969). Women and bureaucracy in the semi-professions. In A. Etzioni (Ed.), *The semi-professions and their organization*. New York: Free Press.

Singelman, J., & Browning, H. L. (1980). Industrial transformation and occupational change in the U. S., 1960-1970. *Social Forces, 59,* 246-264.

Slomczynski, K. M., Miller, J., & Kohn, M. L. (1981). Stratification, work, and values: A Polish-United States comparison. *American Sociological Review, 46,* 720-744.

Smigel, E. O. (1954). Trends in occupational sociology: A survey of postwar research. *American Sociological Review, 19,* 398-404.

Smigel, E. O. (1964). *The Wall Street lawyer.* New York: Free Press.

Smigel, E. O., Monane, J., Wood, R. B., & Nye, B. R. (1963). Occupational sociology: A reexamination. *Sociology and Social Research, 47,* 472-477.

Smith, A. (1937). *The wealth of nations.* New York: Random House.

Smith, D. R. (1983). Mobility in professional occupational-internal labor markets: Stratification, segmentation, and vacancy chains. *American Sociological Review, 48,* 289-305.

Smith, M. R. (1979). Institutional setting and industrial conflict in Quebec. *American Journal of Sociology, 85,* 109-134.

Smith, M. R. (1988). *What is the effect of information technology on the organization of office work and why?* Working paper, Department of Sociology, McGill University, Montreal.

Smith-Lovin, L., & Tickameyer, A. R. (1978). Nonrecursive models of labor force participation, fertility behavior, and sex role attitudes. *American Sociological Review, 43,* 541-557.

Snyder, D., Hayward, M. D., & Hudis, P. M. (1978). The location of change in the sex structure of occupations, 1950-1970: Insights from labor market segmentation theory. *American Journal of Sociology, 84,* 706-717.

Snyder, D., & Hudis, P. M. (1976). Occupational income and the effects of minority competition and segregation: A reananlysis and some new evidence. *American Sociological Review, 41,* 209-234.

Sokoloff, N. J. (1980). *Between money and love: The dialectics of women's home and market work*. New York: Praeger.

Solo, S. (1990, March 12). Need help running your personal life? *Fortune*, p. 46.

Solomon, C. M. (1992, March). Managing the baby busters. *Personnel Journal*, pp. 52-59.

Sorensen, A. B. (1977). The structure of inequality and the process of attainment. *American Sociological Review, 42,* 965-978.

Sorensen, A. B. (1983). Sociological research on the labor market: Conceptual and methodological issues. *Work and Occupations, 10,* 261-287.

Sorge, A., & Streeck, W. (1988). Industrial relations and technical change: The case for an extended perspective. In R. Hyman & W. Streeck (Eds.), *New technology and industrial relations* (pp. 19-47). New York: Blackwell.

South, S. J., Bonjean, C. M., Corder, J., & Markham, W. T. (1982). Sex and power in the federal bureaucracy: A comparative analysis of male and female supervisors. *Work and Occupations, 9,* 233-254.

South, S. J., Bonjean, C. M., Markham, W. T., & Corder, J. (1983). Female labor force participation and the organizational experiences of male workers. *Sociological Quarterly, 24,* 367-380.

South, S. J., Markham, W. T., Bonjean, C. M., & Corder, J. (1987). Sex differences in support for organizational advancement. *Work and Occupations, 14,* 261-285.

Spaeth, J. L. (1979). Vertical differentiation among occupations. *American Sociological Review, 44,* 746-762.

Spangler, E., Gordon, M. A., & Pipkin, R. M. (1978). Token women: An empirical test of Kanter's hypothesis. *American Journal of Sociology, 84,* 160-170.

Spenner, K. I. (1979). Temporal change in work content. *American Sociological Review, 44,* 968-975.

Spenner, K. I. (1983). Deciphering Prometheus: Temporal change in the skill level of work. *American Sociological Review, 48,* 824-837.

Spenner, K. I. (1990). Skill: Meaning, methods, and measures. *Work and Occupations, 17,* 399-421.

Spilerman, S. (1977). Careers, labor market structure, and socioeconomic achievement. *American Journal of Sociology, 83,* 551-593.

Spitze, G. (1984). The effect of family migration on wives' employment: How long does it last? *Social Science Quarterly, 65,* 21-36.

Spitze, G. (1988a). The data on women's labor force participation. In A. H. Stromberg & S. Harkess (Eds.), *Women working: Theories and facts in perspective* (2nd ed.). Mountain View, CA: Mayfield.

Spitze, G. (1988b). Women's employment and family relations: A review. *Journal of Marriage and the Family, 50,* 595-618.

Spitze, G., & Huber, J. (1980). Changing attitudes toward women's nonfamily roles. *Sociology of Work and Occupations, 7,* 317-335.

Spitze, G., & Spaeth, J. L. (1979). Employment among married female college graduates. *Social Science Research, 8,* 184-199.

Spitze, G., & Waite, L. J. (1980). Labor force and work attitudes: Young women's early experiences. *Sociology of Work and Occupations, 7,* 3-32.

Starr, P. (1982). *The social transformation of American medicine.* New York: Basic Books.

Statham, A., Vaughan, S., & Houseknecht, S. K. (1987). The professional involvement of highly educated women: The impact of family. *Sociological Quarterly, 28,* 119-133.

Stearns, L. B., & Coleman, C. W. (1990). Industrial and local labor market structures and black male employment in the manufacturing sector. *Social Science Quarterly, 71,* 285-298.

Stein, N. W. (1981). *Occupational mandate: Mediated exchange and the science professions.* Unpublished doctoral dissertation, University of Minnesota, Minneapolis, MN.

Steinberg, R. (1982). *Wages and hours: Labor and reform in twentieth-century America*. New Brunswick, NJ: Rutgers University Press.

Steinberg, R. J. (1984). From laissez faire to a fair wage for women's work: A technical fix to the labor contract. *Contemporary Sociology, 13*, 15-16.

Steinberg, R. J., Haignere, L., & Chertos, C. H. (1990). Managerial promotions in the public sector: The impact of eligibility requirements on women and minorities. *Work and Occupations, 17*, 284-301.

Steinberg, S. (1983). Review of *A piece of the pie: Blacks and white immigrants since 1880* by Stanley Lieberson. *Contemporary Sociology, 12*, 93-94.

Steinmetz, G., & Wright, E. O. (1989). The fall and rise of the petty bourgeoisie: Changing patterns of self-employment in the postwar United States. *American Journal of Sociology, 94*, 973-1018.

Stern, R., & Whyte, W. F. (1981). Editors' introduction. *Sociology of Work and Occupations, 8*, 139-142.

Stevens, G., & Boyd, M. (1980). The importance of mother: Labor force participation and intergenerational mobility of women. *Social Forces, 59*, 186-199.

Stevenson, M. H. (1988). Some economic approaches to the persistence of wage differences between men and women. In A. H. Stromberg & S. Harkess (Eds.), *Women working: Theories and facts in perspective* (2nd ed.). Mountain View, CA: Mayfield.

Stewart, P. L., & Cantor, M. G. (Eds.). (1974). *Varieties of work experience*. Cambridge, MA: Schenkman.

Stewart, P. L., & Cantor, M. G. (Eds.). (1982). *Varieties of work*. Beverly Hills, CA: Sage.

Stewman, S. (1975). Two Warkov models of open system occupational mobility: Underlying conceptualizations and empirical tests. *American Sociological Review, 40*, 298-321.

Stewman, S. (1986). Demographic models of internal labor markets. *Administrative Science Quarterly, 31*, 212-247.

Stewman, S., & Konda, S. L. (1983). Careers and organizational labor markets: Demographic models of organizational behavior. *American Journal of Sociology, 88*, 637-685.

Stinchcombe, A. (1959). Bureaucratic and craft administration of production: A comparative study. *Administrative Science Quarterly, 4*, 168-187.

Stinchcombe, A. L. (1965). Organizations and social structure. In J. G. March (Ed.), *Handbook of organizations*. Chicago: Rand McNally.

Stolzenberg, R. M. (1975). Education, occupation and wage differences between white and black men. *American Journal of Sociology, 81*, 299-323.

Stolzenberg, R. M. (1990). Ethnicity, geography, and occupational achievement of Hispanic men in the United States. *American Sociological Review, 55*, 143-154.

Stolzenberg, R. M., & D'Amico, R. J. (1977). City differences and nondifferences in the effect of race and sex on occupational distribution. *American Sociological Review, 42*, 937-950.

Stone, E. F. (1976). The moderating effect of work-related values on the job scope/job satisfaction relationship. *Organizational Behavior and Human Performance, 15*, 147-167.

Strauss, G. (1974). Workers: Attitudes and adjustments. In J. M. Rosow (Ed.), *The worker and the job: Coping with change*. Englewood Cliffs, NJ: Prentice-Hall.

Styles, M. M. (1982). *Society and nursing: The new professionalism in professionalism and the empowerment of nursing*. Kansas City, MO: American Nurses' Association.

Sullivan, T. A. (1989). Women and minority workers in the new economy: Optimistic, pessimistic, and mixed scenarios. *Work and Occupations, 16*, 393-415.

Sutton, R. I. (1984). Job stress among primary and secondary schoolteachers: Its relationship to ill-being. *Work and Occupations, 11*, 7-28.

Szafran, R. (1984). Female and minority employment patterns in banks: A research note. *Work and Occupations, 11*, 55-76.

Szafran, R. F., Peterson, R. W., & Schoenherr, R. A. (1980). Ethnicity and status attainment: The case of the Roman Catholic clergy. *Sociological Quarterly, 21,* 41-51.

Szymanski, A. (1976). Racial discrimination and white gain. *American Sociological Review, 41,* 403-414.

Tannenbaum, A. S., Kavcic, B., Rosner, M., Vianello, M., & Wieser, G. (1974). *Hierarchy in organizations.* San Francisco: Jossey-Bass.

Tausky, C. (1984). *Work and society: An introduction to industrial sociology.* Itasca, IL: F. E. Peacock.

Tausky, C., & Chelte, A. F. (1983). Accountability and productivity: Some longitudinal data. *Work and Occupations, 10,* 207-220.

Tausky, C., & Chelte, A. F. (1988). Workers' participation. *Work and Occupations, 15,* 563-573.

Tausky, C., & Parke, E. L. (1976). Job enrichment, need theory, and reinforcement theory. In R. Dubin (Ed.), *Handbook of work, organization, and society.* Chicago: Rand McNally.

Taylor, F. W. (1911). *Principles of scientific management.* New York: Harper & Row.

Taylor, M. G., & Hartley, S. F. (1975). The two-person career: A classic example. *Sociology of Work and Occupations, 2,* 354-372.

Taylor, P. A., & Shields, S. W. (1984). Mexican Americans and employment inequality in the federal civil service. *Social Science Quarterly, 65,* 380-391.

Terkel, S. (1974). *Working.* New York: Pantheon.

Thomas, J. M. (1980). The impact of corporate tourism on Gullah blacks: Notes on issues of employment. *Phylon Quarterly, 41,* 1-11.

Thorsrud, E., Sorensen, B. A., & Gustavsen, B. (1976). Sociotechnical approach to industrial democracy in Norway. In R. Dubin (Ed.), *Handbook of work, organization, and society.* Chicago: Rand McNally.

Tinto, V. (1984). Patterns of educational sponsorship to work: A study of modes of early occupational attachment from college to professional work. *Work and Occupations, 11,* 309-330.

Toffler, A. (1990). *Powershift*. New York: Bantam.

Tolbert, C. M., II, Horan, P. M., & Beck, E. W. (1980). The structure of economic segmentation: A dual economy approach. *American Journal of Sociology, 85,* 1095-1116.

Topolnicki, D. (1989, July-August). Workaholics: Are you one? *Psychology Today*, p. 25.

Touraine, A. (1971). *The post-industrial society: Tomorrow's social history*. New York: Random House.

Treiman, D. J. (1977). *Occupational prestige in comparative perspective*. New York: Academic Press.

Treiman, D. J., & Hartman, H. I. (Eds.). (1981). *Women, work, and wages: Equal pay for jobs of equal value*. Washington, DC: National Academy Press.

Treiman, D. J., & Roos, P. A. (1983). Sex and earnings in industrial society: A nine-nation comparison. *American Journal of Sociology, 89,* 612-650.

Treiman, D. J., & Terrell, K. (1975a). Sex and the process of status attainment: A comparison of working women and men. *American Sociological Review, 40,* 174-200.

Treiman, D. J., & Terrell, K. (1975b). The process of status attainment in the United States and Great Britain. *American Journal of Sociology, 81,* 563-583.

Tsonc, P. Z. W. (1974). Changing patterns of labor force participation rates of nonwhites in the South. *Phylon Quarterly, 35,* 301-312.

Tuch, S. A., & Martin, J. K. (1991). Race in the workplace: Black/white differences in the sources of job satisfaction. *Sociological Quarterly, 32,* 103-116.

Tumin, M. (1953). Some principles of stratification: A critical analysis. *American Sociological Review, 18,* 387-394.

Tumin, M. (1963). On equality. *American Sociological Review, 28,* 19-26.

Turner, R. (1960). Models of social assent through education: Sponsored and contest mobility. *American Sociological Review, 25,* 855-867.

Tyree, A., & Hicks, R. (1988). Sex and the second movement of prestige distributions. *Social Forces, 66,* 1028-1037.

Tyree, A., & Smith, B. G. (1978). Occupational hierarchy in the United States: 1789-1969. *Social Forces, 65,* 881-899.

U.S. Department of Labor. (1939). *Dictionary of occupational titles.* Washington, DC: Government Printing Office.

U.S. Department of Labor. (1949a). *Dictionary of occupational titles. Vol. 1: Definitions of titles.* Washington, DC: Government Printing Office.

U.S. Department of Labor. (1949b). *Dictionary of occupational titles. Vol. 2: Occupational classification and industry index* (2nd ed.). Washington, DC: Government Printing Office.

U.S. Department of Labor. (1965a). *Dictionary of occupational titles* (Vol. 1) (3rd ed.). Washington, DC: Government Printing Office.

U.S. Department of Labor. (1965b). *Dictionary of occupational titles* (Vol. 2) (3rd ed.). Washington, DC: Government Printing Office.

U.S. Department of Labor. (1977, 1991). *Dictionary of occupational titles* (4th ed.). Washington, DC: Government Printing Office.

U.S. Department of Labor. (1980). *Perspectives on working women: A databook.* Bulletin 2080. Washington, DC: Government Printing Office.

U.S. Department of Labor. (1984). *Employment and earnings, 31.* Washington, DC: Government Printing Office.

U.S. Department of Labor. (1988). *Handbook of labor statistics.* Bulletin 2340. Washington, DC: Government Printing Office.

U.S. Department of Labor. (1990). *Employment and earnings, 37,* A-3. Washington, DC: Government Printing Office.

U.S. Department of Labor. (1991). *Employment and earnings, 38.* Washington, DC: Government Printing Office.

U.S. Department of Labor. (1993). *Compensation and working conditions.* Washington, DC: Government Printing Office.

Useem, M. (1979). The social organization of the American business elite and participation of corporate directors in the governance of american institutions. *American Sociological Review, 44,* 553-572.

Useem, M. (1982). Classwide rationality in the politics of managers and directors of large corporations in the United States and Great Britain. *Administrative Science Quarterly, 27*(2), 199-226.

Useem, M. (1984). *The inner circle.* New York: Oxford University Press.

Useem, M., & Karabel, J. (1986). Pathways to top corporate management. *American Sociological Review, 51,* 184-200.

Valadez, J. J., & Clignet, R. (1984). Household work as an ordeal: Culture of standards versus standardization of culture. *American Journal of Sociology, 89,* 812-835.

Vallas, S. P. (1987). White collar proletarians? The structure of clerical work and levels of class consciousness. *Sociological Quarterly, 28,* 523-540.

Vallas, S. P. (1988). New technology, job content, and worker alienation: A test of two rival perspectives. *Work and Occupations, 15,* 148-178.

Vallas, S. P. (1990). The concept of skill: A critical review. *Work and Occupations, 17,* 379-398.

Vallas, S. P., & Yarrow, M. (1987). Advanced technology and worker alienation: Comments on the Blauner/Marxism debate. *Work and Occupations, 14,* 126-142.

Van de Ven, A. H. (1979). Howard E. Aldrich: Organizations and environments. *Administrative Science Quarterly, 24,* 320-326.

Vanek, J. (1974). Time spent in housework. *Scientific American, 231,* 116-120.

Vaught, C., & Smith, D. L. (1980). Incorporations and mechanical solidarity in an underground coal mine. *Sociology of Work and Occupations, 7,* 159-187.

Vollmer, H. M., & Mills, D. L. (Eds.). (1966). *Professionalization.* Englewood Cliffs, NJ: Prentice-Hall.

Voydanoff, P. (1978). The relationship between perceived job characteristics and job satisfaction among occupational status groups. *Sociology of Work and Occupations, 5,* 179-192.

Vroom, V. (1964). *Work and motivation.* New York: John Wiley.

Wadley, J. K., & Lee, E. S. (1974). The disappearance of the black farmer. *Phylon Quarterly*, *35*, 276-283.

Waite, L. J. (1976). Working wives: 1940-1960. *American Sociological Review*, *41*, 65-80.

Waite, L. J., & Stolzenberg, R. M. (1976). Intended childbearing and labor force participation of young women: Insights from nonrecursive models. *American Sociological Review*, *41*, 235-252.

Walker, C., & Guest, R. (1962). The man on the assembly line. *Harvard Business Review*, *30*, 71-88.

Walker, C., Guest, R., & Turner, A. (1952). *The foreman on the assembly line*. Cambridge, MA: Harvard University Press.

Wallace, M. (1987). Dying for coal: The struggle for health and safety in American coal mining, 1930-82. *Social Forces*, *66*, 336-364.

Wallace, M. (1988). Labor market structure and salary determination among professional basketball players. *Work and Occupations*, *15*, 294-312.

Wallace, M. (1989). Brave new workplace: Technology and work in the new economy. *Work and Occupations*, *16*, 363-392.

Wallace, M., & Kalleberg, A. (1982). Industrial transformation and the decline of craft: The decomposition of skill in the printing industry. *American Sociological Review*, *47*, 307-324.

Wallace, M., & Rothschild, J. (Eds.). (1988). *Research in politics and society. Vol. 3: Deindustrialization and the restructuring of American industry*. Greenwich, CT: JAI.

Wallace, P. (1980). *Black women in the labor force*. Cambridge, MA: MIT Press.

Walsh, E. J. (1982). Prestige, work satisfaction, and alienation: Comparisons among garbagemen, professors, and other work groups. *Work and Occupations*, *9*, 475-496.

Walsh, J. P. (1989). Technological change and the division of labor: The case of retail meatcutters. *Work and Occupations*, *16*, 165-183.

Walton, R. E. (1980). Establishing and maintaining high commitment work systems. In J. R. Kimberly, R. H. Miles, &

Associates (Eds.), *The organizational life cycle*. San Francisco: Jossey-Bass.

Wanous, J. P. (1980). *Organizational entry: Recruitment, selection, and socialization of newcomers*. Reading, MA: Addison-Wesley.

Ward, R. A. (1984). *The aging experience: An introduction to social gerontology* (2nd ed.). New York: Harper & Row.

Warner, M. (1981). Organizational experiments and social innovations. In P. C. Nystrom & W. H. Starbuck (Eds.), *Handbook of organizational design* (Vol. l). New York: Oxford University Press.

Watanabe, T. (1992, January 14). When life on the job is literally killing you. *Los Angeles Times*, p. B8.

Weber, M. (1947). *The theory of social and economic organization* (A. M. Henderson & T. Parsons, Trans.). New York: Free Press.

Wendling, W. (1988, November). Responses to a changing work force. *Personnel Administrator*, pp. 50-54.

Wharton, A. (1989). Gender segregation in private-sector, public-sector, and self-employed occupations, 1950-1981. *Social Science Quarterly*, *70*, 923-940.

Whetten, D. (1980). Sources, responses, and effects of organizational decline. In J. Kimberly & R. Miles (Eds.), *Organizational life cycles*. San Francisco: Jossey-Bass.

White, H. C. (1971). *System models of mobility in organizations*. Cambridge, MA: Harvard University Press.

White, L., & Brinkerhoff, D. B. (1981). The sexual division of labor: Evidence from childhood. *Social Forces*, *60*, 170-181.

Wholey, D. R. (1990). The effects of formal and informal training on tenure and mobility in manufacturing firms. *Sociological Quarterly*, *31*, 37-57.

Whyte, W. F. (1946). When workers and customers meet. In W. F. Whyte (Ed.), *Industry and society*. New York: McGraw-Hill.

Wilensky, H. (1964). The professionalization of everyone? *American Journal of Sociology*, *70*, 137-158.

Wilkie, J. R. (1984). Social model-building. *Contemporary Sociology, 13,* 277-278.

Williams, C. L. (1989). *Gender differences at work: Women and men in nontraditional occupations.* Berkeley: University of California Press.

Wilson, K., & Martin, W. A. (1982). Ethnic enclaves: A comparison of the Cuban and black economies in Miami. *American Journal of Sociology, 88,* 135-160.

Wilson, K., & Portes, A. (1980). Immigrant enclaves: An analysis of the labor market experiences of Cubans in Miami. *American Journal of Sociology, 86,* 295-313.

Wilson, W. J. (1978). *The declining significance of race.* Chicago: University of Chicago Press.

Wimberly, R. C. (1983). The emergence of part-time farming as a social form of agriculture. In I. H. Simpson & R. L. Simpson (Eds.), *Research in the sociology of work: A research annual.* Greenwich, CT: JAI.

Winerip, M. (1990, March 30). Layoffs and age: Discrimination or prudence. *New York Times,* p. B 1.

Withey, M. J., & Cooper, W. H. (1989). Predicting exit, voice, loyalty, and neglect. *Administrative Science Quarterly, 34,* 521-539.

Wolf, W. G., & Fligstein, N. (1979a). Sex and authority in the workplace: causes of social inequality. *American Sociological Review, 44,* 235-252.

Wolf, W. G., & Fligstein, N. (1979b). Sexual stratification: Differences in power in the work setting. *Social Forces, 58,* 94-107.

Woodworth, W. (1981). Forms of employee ownership and workers' control. *Sociology of Work and Occupations, 8,* 195-200.

Wray, D. E. (1949). Marginal men of industry: The foremen. *American Journal of Sociology, 54,* 298-301.

Wright, E. O. (1978). *Class, crisis, and the state.* London: New Left.

Wright, E. O. (1979). *Class structure and income determination.* New York: Academic Press.

Wright, E. O., & Perrone, L. (1977). Marxist class categories and income inequalities. *American Sociological Review, 42,* 32-55.

Wright, J. D., & Hamilton, R. F. (1978). Work satisfaction and age: Some evidence for the "job change" hypothesis. *Social Forces, 56,* 1140-1158.

Wright, J. D., & Hamilton, R. F. (1979). Education and job attitudes among blue-collar workers. *Sociology of Work and Occupations, 6,* 59-83.

Wuthnow, R., & Shrumm, W. (1983). Knowledge workers as a "new class": Structural and ideological convergence among professional-technical workers and managers. *Work and Occupations, 10,* 471-487.

Yuchtman, E., & Samuel, Y. (1975). Determinants of career plans: Institutional versus interpersonal effects. *American Sociological Review, 40,* 521-532.

Zeitlin, M. (1974). Corporate ownership and control: The large corporations and the capitalist class. *American Journal of Sociology, 79,* 1073-1119.

Zeitz, G. (1984). Bureaucratic role characteristics and member affective response in organizations. *Sociological Quarterly, 25,* 301-318.

Zicklin, G. (1987). Numerical control machines and the issue of deskilling: An empirical view. *Work and Occupations, 14,* 452-466.

Zuboff, S. (1988). *In the age of the smart machine: The future of work and power.* New York: Basic Books.

Zucker, L. G. (Ed.). (1988). *Institutional patterns and organizations: Culture and environment.* Cambridge, MA: Ballinger.

Zucker, L. G., & Rosenstein, C. (1981). Taxonomies of institutional structure: Dual economy reconsidered. *American Sociological Review, 46,* 869-884.

Author Index

Cooper, W. H., 98
Corcoran, M., 153-154, 164
Corder, J., 66, 202, 205, 216, 227,
    309, 310
Cornfield, D. B., 20, 314, 317
Cottle, T. J., 31
Coverman, S., 118, 221, 223, 334
Cramer, J. C., 204, 328
Crouse, J., 153-154, 164
Cullen, J. B., 48, 141
Curtis, J. E., 153
Cushing, R. G., 140
Cutright, P., 265
Czajka, J. L., 206, 224

D
Dahl, R., 303, 321
Dahrendorf, R., 142
Dalton, G. W., 96
Dalton, M., 56
D'Amico, R. J., 197
Dansereau, F., 35
Davids, M., 251
Davis, F., 71
Davis, K., 138, 139
Davis-Blake, A., 148, 211, 276,
    280, 316
Daymont, T. N., 256, 257, 265
DeFleur, L. B., 226
Deitch, C., 339
Delacroix, J., 275
Dempster-McClain, D., 334
Deutsch, S., 318
Deutschman, S., 250
DeViney, S., 246
DiMaggio, P. J., 282
DiPrete, T. A., 28, 62, 148, 215,
    254, 265
Dobbin, F. R., 276, 282, 283
Doerfler, M. C., 345
Doeringer, P. B., 15
Domhoff, G. W., 146
Dore, R., 108

Dornbusch, S., 285, 303
Dubin, R., 106, 107, 355
Duncan, B., 130, 131
Duncan, E. P., 201, 339
Duncan, O. D., 125, 131, 150, 152,
    154, 164
Dunlop, C., 350, 366, 367
Dunn, T. P., 67
Dunnette, M. D., 54
Durick, M., 106
Durkheim, E., 166
Durr, M., 266

E
Eaglesfield, D., 153-154, 164
Edwards, A. M., 35, 130
Edwards, R., 25
Eisenstein, J., 52
Eisenstein, Z. R., 78
Elder, G. H., Jr., 236, 240
Emerson, R. M., 303
Engels, F., 71
England, P., 221, 222
Ensel, W. M., 154
Epstein, C. F., 204, 226, 267, 333
Eriksen, J. A., 200, 326
Erlanger, H. S., 49
Etzioni, A., 51, 67, 303, 349,
    368
Evans, M. D., 51
Evans, M. D. R., 264

F
Faia, M. A., 131
Fantasia, R., 294, 308, 312, 323
Farber, H. S., 312
Farkas, G., 239
Faunce, W. A., 105, 126
Faver, C. A., 206
Featherman, D. L., 131, 151, 153,
    164, 210, 258, 264
Fein, M., 89, 101, 295
Feld, S., 101

Subject Index

A

Administrators:
  as not-for-profit-sector term, 54
Adolescents, working:
  as disadvantaged in labor market, 238
  job types of, 238
  transition of to adult work, 239-241
Affirmative action hiring:
  and women and minorities in workplace, 310
Affirmative action plans:
  negative effects of, 231
  of U.S. Army, 261
Affirmative action regulations, 220
  government actions and, 268
  unintended consequences of, 229-232
Age, work:
  and gender, 245
  and unemployment, 243
  individual and, 234-236
  perspectives on, 235
  policy implications of, 244
  work satisfaction and, 235, 249
Age discrimination, 236, 246
Age Discrimination in Employment Act, 244
Age stratification, 235-236

horizontal dimension and, 236
Alienation, work, 111-117, 119
  environmental determinants of, 114-115
  forms of, 112-113
  inverted-U hypothesis of, 117
  meaninglessness, 113, 116
  objective, 112
  powerlessness, 112-113, 116, 117
  role of technology in, 115-117
  self-estrangement, 113, 116, 117
  social, 113, 116, 117
  sources of, 113-117
  structural, 112
  subjective, 112-113
American Association for the Advancement of Science, 248
American Psychological Association, 50
American Psychological Society, 50
Amway, 64
Arby's, 354
Asian-Americans:
  and income parity with whites, 263

B

"Baby bust" generation, 250, 252. *See also* Yiffies
Bell, D., xvii

Managerial hierarchy, 54
Managerial work. *See* Work, managerial
Manpower, 63
Mary Kay Cosmetics, 65
Maslow, A., 101
McDonald's, 58, 273, 354
  corporate culture of, 299

N
National Association for the Advancement of Colored People, 254
National Longitudinal Surveys (NLS), 247
New Deal era, 311
NORC scale of Occupational Prestige, 126, 128-130, 131
Norris-LaGuardia Act, 311
North-Hatt scale, 126
Norway:
  little labor-market segmentation in, 212

O
Occupation:
  as identity provider, 6
  definition of, 6-7
  social relationships and, 6
  status and, 124-164
  work and, 6
Occupational categories:
  shifts among by workers, 7
Occupational prestige:
  measures of, 126, 127.
  See also Occupational status
Occupational self-direction, 101
Occupational status, 124-164
  alternative measures of, 127, 130-131
  conflict model and, 137
  disappointments to, 163
  educational certification and, 131, 134

educational tracking and, 135-137
functional model and, 137, 138-142
measures of, 125-127
role of education in, 131, 134-137
structural model and, 137
Officials, 82
  as governmental agency term, 54
Organizational culture, 298-301
  sources of, 299-300
Organizational work experiences, 286-287
Organizations:
  and change, 288-297
  and the individual, 283-287
  and the vertical dimension, 276-282
  career ladders in, 276
  discriminatory hiring procedures of, 276
  employee behavior and, 274
  employee ownership in changing, 292-293
  employment in, 274-275
  formal hiring standards of, 277
  homosocial reproduction in, 284-285
  implications for human-resource policy in, 282-283
  individual mobility in, 283-285
  institutional model of, 282
  internal labor markets of, 276-282, 297
  Japanese approach to managing, 294-297
  job complexity in, 287
  job redesign in, 288-291, 292
  performance evaluations in, 285
  political arena and, 320
  population-ecology model of, 280-281

Sexual attraction:
in the workplace, 194
Sexual harassment:
definition of, 227-228
power and, 228
Situs:
as predictor of work values, 167
definition of, 167
parallel status ladders and, 167
Skilled workers, 68-69
Small business:
high failure rate of, 58
Social class:
top management and, 59
Socialization, 119
definition of, 92
Social mobility, 150-152
decrease in downward, 151
differences of between Great Britain and the United States, 151
differences of between Japan and the United States, 152
differences of between Poland and the United States, 152
downward, 161-164
increase in upward, 151
similarities of in Australia and the United States, 151
similarities of in Canada and the United States, 151
Social stratification, conflict model of, 137, 142-146, 149, 160
class consciousness and, 145, 146
class distribution of power and wealth and, 142-144
class locations and, 143
commodity consciousness and, 145
exploitation in, 142-143
supporting evidence for, 144-146

Social stratification, functional model of, 137, 138-142, 149, 160
differential rewards and, 138-140
supporting evidence for, 140-142
weaknesses of, 139-140
Social stratification, structural model of, 137, 146-150, 160
and differences among industries, 157-158, 161
and differences among organizations, 158-160, 161
basic argument of, 147
contest mobility and, 149
human capital factors and, 158
job ladders and, 148
merging of functional and conflict approaches in, 146-147
patterns of inequality and, 147-150
placement of individuals and, 157-160
"ports of entry" and, 148, 149, 158
promotions and, 159
sponsored mobility and, 149
tournament mobility and, 149
vacancy chain and, 147
Socioeconomic index (SEI), 130, 131, 152
Socioeconomic status, means of improving, 264-265
for blacks, 264
for Hispanics, 264-265
through military service, 265
Status attainment factors, 152-157, 161
college completion, 154
education, 153-154, 160
environmental, 156-157
ethnicity, 154
gender, 154
race, 154

uneven distribution of power of, 311

worker attitudes toward, 311-312

United Negro College Fund, 254

University of Minnesota Department of Industrial Relations, 348

Unskilled work. *See* Work, unskilled

Unskilled workers, 72-73

laborers as, 72

USX, 16

W

Wagner Act, 311

"White-collar woes," 111

White-collar work. *See* Work, white-collar

White-collar workers:

displacement of, 163

Women, working:

and the industrial sector and organizational practice, 215-216

as significant contributors to family income, 201

education of, 213-214, 216

factors associated with status of, 212-216

in nontraditional work, 224-228

job satisfaction of, 207-208

labor force experience of, 214-215

mothers' occupation and, 212-213, 216

orientations/attitudes of toward labor force participation, 205-206

reactions of toward work, 206-209

reasons of for working, 201

versus men in the vertical dimension, 210-212

work experience of, 205-206

Women's labor-force participation (WLFP), 195-200

and the vertical dimension, 209-212

demand for labor and, 204-205

discrimination and, 204, 216-224

education and, 328

factors affecting, 197-200

family finances and, 200-201

family roles and, 202-203, 206

fertility and, 203-204

geographic mobility and, 201-202

in Israel, 197

in World War I, 195

in World War II, 195

marriage and family and, 200-205

mental health and, 208-209

segregation and, 204, 216-224

sex-role socialization and, 197-200, 206, 218, 228

young children as inhibitor of, 203

Work:

abortion decisions and, 1

age and, 234-236

alienation from, 111-117

and children, 327-329

and family, 324, 325-339

and health, 339-342, 365

as necessity for good health, 32

as shaper of interpersonal relationships, 32

as socially constructed phenomenon, 5

as source of financial gain, 32

as source of self-esteem, 32

choosing, 122

decisions about having children and, 1

definitions of, 2-3, 4, 5, 347-349

futures of, 347-368

gender and, 194-232

geographic mobility and, 338-339